THE LAST BATTLE

PETER HART
THE LAST BATTLE

ENDGAME ON THE WESTERN FRONT, 1918

PROFILE BOOKS

First published in Great Britain in 2018 by
PROFILE BOOKS LTD
3 Holford Yard
Bevin Way
London WC1X 9HD
www.profilebooks.com

1 3 5 7 9 10 8 6 4 2

Typeset in Transitional by MacGuru Ltd
Printed and bound in Great Britain by Clays, St Ives plc

The moral right of the author has been asserted.

A CIP catalogue record for this book is available from the British Library.

ISBN 978 1 78125 482 0
eISBN 978 1 78283 176 1

CONTENTS

English Channel

HOLLAND

Dunkirk
Ostend
Blankenbergh
Bruges

BELGIAN–FRENCH

Ypres
Thielt
Lys
Ghent
Antwerp
Schelde

Courtrai
Armentères
Tourcoing
SECOND
BELGIUM

Bethune
Lille
Roubaix
Dendre
BRUSSELS

FIFTH
Tournai
Lessines
Hal

The front in
August 1918

Douai

Arras
FIRST

Valenciennes
Mons
The front in
November 1918

Amiens
Albert
Cambrai
Maubeuge
Sambre
Namur
THIRD
Charleroi
Meuse

Peronne
le Cateau
FOURTH
Froideville
Philippeville

Montdidier
St Quentin
Oise
Guise
la Chapelle
Chimay
Givet
FIRST
Serre
Hirson

THIRD
till 14.9
La Fère
A R D E N N E S

Compiègne
TENTH till 27.10 then THIRD
Laon
Sissonne
Mezières
Oise
Sedan
Soissons
FIFTH
Meuse
SIXTH
withdrawn 7.9
Aisne
FOURTH
Busancy
Stenay

PARIS
Reims
AM. FIRST from 22.9
(Replacing French
Second Army)
NINTH
withdrawn 24.7
Epernay
FRANCE

Verdun

Chalons
AM. SECOND
from 12.10
St Mihiel
N

The St Mihiel Salient
was recovered by the
American First Army
12–15 September

Moselle

ADVANCE TO VICTORY
August to November 1918

Nancy
TENTH
from 27.10
EIGHTH

British and Americans
French and Belgians
Front on 26 September

0   10   20   30   40   50 miles
0   20   40   60   80 kilometres

PREFACE

I remember someone saying before the war that he imagined that
when troops were in action under fire, each man thought to himself
that whoever else might be hit, he himself would be alright. Well
I don't think this is correct – at any rate not in this war. I think
men fully expect to be hit or killed, but carry on just the same.
Personally, I was always thinking I was going to get hit or killed and
was often surprised when I found I wasn't.[1]

Captain Henry Owens, 57th Field Ambulance, Royal Army Medical Corps,
57th Brigade, 19th Division

IMAGINE IT IF YOU CAN. You have been fighting for four long years.
Somehow you have survived, although many of your friends are dead.
Now, just when your ordeal seems to be coming to an end, you are
required to make one last effort, risking life and limb in the closing battles
to hammer home the defeat of the German Army. Not everyone can take
it easy on the final straight; not every soldier can 'shell hole drop', falling
back during attacks and leaving others to lead the way. The temptation
to shirk must have been enormous. Yet, for the most part, men dug deep
within themselves to summon up the resolve to fight on and 'finish the
job'. For many it would prove the greatest sacrifice. They were fatally
struck down just when a resumption of their civilian life was almost

within touching distance. The Allies may have been winning, but the casualty rates in the closing six weeks of the war were excruciating. Open warfare may have freed them from the grim tyranny of the trenches, but it left them exposed to even greater perils. The beckoning necessity of finishing the war, to avoid the spectre of a new harvest of death in 1919, meant that corners had to be cut, risks taken and lives lost. It may have been logical, but it was no less painful to the individuals caught up in their own personal Armageddon.

A great deal of attention is paid to the opening moves made in wars. This is particularly evident with the Great War. Much of the media interest during the recent centenary celebrations was taken up with an exhaustive coverage of the 1914 campaigns, with British attention focused almost entirely on the Battle of Mons. The treatment of the rest of the war has concentrated on the Allied defeat at Gallipoli, or the long drawn out tragedies of the Somme, Verdun and Passchendaele battles. There is also an obsession with the brilliance displayed by Germans in their tactical conduct of the Spring 1918 offensives. The result of such fixations is that the ultimate Allied victory a few months later must come as a real surprise as – 'suddenly' – the war is all over in November 1918. We need to explain what happened in the last few months of the war. From where exactly did the Allied victory emerge? Was the German Army really beaten? What haven't we been told in many of the conventional accounts of the war?

Certainly, one underlying truth of the Great War *must* be driven home: the war finished with the collective armies of France, Britain, America and Belgium achieving total domination over the German Army on the Western Front. It was in fact a rejection of this that formed the basis of the puerile Nazi voices of the inter-war years that told the Germans that they had been 'stabbed in the back'; that their army had never been defeated, that it had stood tall and strong, only to be over-whelmed by a combination of enemies within the state, in particular Communist agitators, their 'fellow travellers' in the Labour movement and – from their crazed perspective – the Jews.

In reality, the Allied victory arose from the accumulated strength and proven fighting prowess of the Allied armies, their underlying materiel supremacy and the gradual collapse of German discipline in the face of inevitable defeat, exemplified by the arrival in strength of the American Expeditionary Force in the summer of 1918. The defining sequence of events had begun with the French defeat of a last gasp German offensive at the Second Battle of the Marne in July 1918. It had continued with the stunning victory achieved by the British on 8 August at Amiens, which then premiered the 'Hundred Days' advance to victory. It is the later stages of that decisive series of battles that concern us here. The Germans had fallen back in disarray, taking shelter in the comforting fastness of the Hindenburg Line. This had served them well in the past – they had high hopes that it would serve them well again and were confident that they could prolong the war into 1919, if not beyond. Yet the Allied Supreme Commander, Maréchal Ferdinand Foch, coordinated a sequence of offensives that cracked open the Hindenburg Line with the result that German resistance began to crumble. The Fifth Battle of Ypres, the Battles of the Sambre, the Selle and the Meuse-Argonne – all victories for the Allies. Yet what do we remember of them? Scant details appear in general books on the war; indeed there is little of relevance in most works devoted solely to 1918. All that seems to matter is the death of the (then) relatively unknown poet Wilfred Owen during the crossing of the Sambre on 4 November 1918. This – though sad – should not be our focal point in considering these huge offensives. They were intended to smash through the German lines, allowing no time to rest, no chance to bring up reserves, no time for the German commanders to catch their breath and review the situation rationally. The German High Command was left helpless, scrambling to react to situations that were already in the past. Unable to second-guess where the Allies would strike next, and without the manpower or resources to be strong everywhere, they stumbled from disaster to disaster.

But it had not been easy.

For the Allies did not have a monopoly in courage. The German Army may have reached the end of its metaphorical rope in the summer of 1918, but, even after four years of carnage, there were still plenty of grim unbending soldiers willing to carry on fighting to the very end. Their spluttering machine guns and booming gun batteries took a heavy toll of the attacking Allies. Many German soldiers demonstrated an unbelievable resilience, contesting every yard of ground, despite the dawning realisation that their cause was hopeless. Their sacrificed lives bought time for their comrades to retreat, take up new defensive positions and continue the resistance. Heroism and tragedy were all around during the final days of that terrible war.

In order to secure victory in 1918, the Allied commanders had to take risks that would have seemed reprehensible a few months before – but they were desperate to keep up the momentum and prevent the Germans from settling into a new fortress line – where they could regain their strength, ready to renew the struggle. These risks maximised the advances the Allies achieved, but they meant troops were often caught isolated in open ground and casualties grew at a terrifying rate. When the German rearguards were overrun, there was little quarter given. This was fighting red in tooth and claw, with the additional frisson of men giving their all – yet still hoping against hope that they might yet stay alive and intact in a war that had killed and maimed so many of their friends. The all too frequent deaths so close to the Armistice gives a terrible poignancy to this last battle. This is not a dry military history recording the movements of every corps, division, brigade or battalion; the sheer scale of the fighting precludes any chance of that. The complexities of simultaneous campaigns occurring up and down the line has also required some juggling to maintain a coherent narrative. Nor have I dwelt overlong on the political machinations that ultimately would have delivered the Armistice on 11 November. My emphasis as a British historian is on the British Army, with an appreciative reflection of the massive contributions to victory made by the French, American and Belgian forces. I have tried to include some of the key German quotes to reflect what tough opponents the Allies faced on the other side of the trenches. This book reflects the essence of what happened in battle – and why. It is a tragic story told for the most part by those men who were lucky enough to survive. Many did not.

1

WHERE ARE WE?

I think after the war I shall write a book, and in it I shall put everything that is filthy and disgusting and revolting and degrading and terrifying about modern warfare – and hope thereby to do my bit towards preventing another.[1]

Lieutenant Burgon Bickersteth, Headquarters, 6th Cavalry Brigade, 3rd Cavalry Division

BY THE START OF 1918 it seemed as if all the participants were approaching exhaustion. Conflict between the great powers was not a matter of cunning plans and clever battlefield manoeuvres. It was total warfare, where armies of toiling millions smashed into each other repeatedly. An attritional nightmare, which would be determined by those with the greatest access to the raw numbers to feed the ranks, the productive capacity to manufacture the key weapons of war and unimaginable quantities of munitions, and the near unbounded economic resources required to pay for it all. As the original armies were eroded, new armies stepped forward into the trenches, year by year, to replace them. Conscription ensured enough men to feed the guns. The kind of war that exerted a tremendous strain on any nation, exposing and testing any flaws to destruction.

There is no doubt that, by 1918, France was in a parlous condition. Since 1914, a key industrial region of their country had been under German occupation, with the front lines creating a gigantic salient pushing towards Paris. As early as 22 August 1914, the French had lost 27,000 men dead in a single day, and had suffered over 2 million casualties (killed, wounded and imprisoned) by the end of the huge attritional battles of 1915. They then endured the long torture of Verdun which had scarred a generation of soldiers in 1916, before the failure of the over-ambitious Nivelle Offensive in April 1917 triggered a dreadful series of mutinies. The French Army was, however, a resilient force. After a period of careful 'husbandry' under their Commander in Chief, General Phillipe Pétain, the French had managed to recover some of their vigour and remained a formidable foe in 1918. The scale of the French sacrifice was immense: by the end of 1917 some 1,280,000 had died.

Even worse, the Russian Army had lost approximately 2 million dead during the campaigns against Germany and Austro-Hungary on the Eastern Front. Despite these horrendous losses, there always seemed to be more teeming millions of Russians to fling into battle and more ground into which they could retreat. Whatever disasters they suffered, there was no point at which the Germans could credibly have claimed that the Russian Army was beaten. Yet, behind that impervious façade, the war had hammered open the fault lines running right through the monolithic Tsarist state. By 1917, the country was teetering on the edge of revolution.

The third of the major Allies was Great Britain. The British had only played a peripheral role in the Battle of the Frontiers in 1914. Although the dominant world naval power, their initial military contribution, the British Expeditionary Force (BEF), was on a very small scale. There were some 400,000 regular soldiers, of which more than half were stationed at garrisons in various far-flung stations of the British Army. The BEF would grow steadily in size, but even so, their efforts at Neuve Chapelle, Second Ypres, Festubert and Loos in 1915 were mere adjuncts to the vast battles raging between the French and Germans in the Artois and Champagne regions. By 1916, the British had finally mobilised their true strength, attaining a maximum strength of around 2 million on the Western Front, but they would be tested to the limit during their first real experience of continental warfare during the long-drawn-out agony of the Battle of the Somme. In 1917, they had suffered more terrible casualties during the Battle of Arras, before being almost drained during the hell on earth that was the Third Battle of Ypres. By the end of 1917, the British Empire had recorded 494,800 dead, 1,425,184 wounded and 176,523 missing or prisoners – a total of 2,096,507 battle casualties on all fronts.[2]

Confronting the Allies was the Imperial German Army. The German High Command were always cognisant that, in a war with the two great powers, France and Russia, they would be hard pressed to win. The 'Schlieffen Plan' for 1914 had sought to concentrate the bulk of the German Army in a swift war of manoeuvre to beat France in the first months of the war. Russia was merely to be held back until France was out of the way, and only then would the German Army move east in strength. The British entry into the war had further exacerbated the underlying strategic conundrum for Germany, as the British Empire had an obvious latent power that could – in time – be mobilised against them. The German defeat by the French at the Battle of the Marne in September 1914 had doomed the Germans to fight on two fronts; a war they knew they were unlikely to win. In 1915, they had switched focus, attempting vainly to knock the Russians out of the war. Since the start of 1916, with the exception of the attack on the French at Verdun, the German Army had been on the defensive. Outnumbered and facing intense fighting on two fronts, they had fought with a desperate courage, skill and determination. As a major participant in most of the great battles of the war, it should be no surprise that they suffered accordingly. By the end of 1917, approximately 1,250,000 Germans had died.

Germany was allied to Austro-Hungary, Turkey and Bulgaria. These allies were involved in much serious fighting: the Austro-Hungarians fought bloody campaigns with the Russians on the Eastern Front and against the Italians; the Turks were engaged at Gallipoli, Mesopotamia and Palestine; while the Bulgarians engaged a French-British-Serbian force in Salonika. Yet the focus always remained on the main Central Power – Germany. The fighting against Germany would decide the war; anything else was a sideshow.

At sea, the German High Seas Fleet could not really hope to match the strength of the British Grand Fleet. The only real head-on clash at the Battle of Jutland in 1916 had merely confirmed that status quo. Thrashing about for other solutions and despite previous warnings from the Americans, the resumption of unrestricted German submarine warfare was a desperate attempt to starve out the British, who were not self-sufficient in food. The result, predictably, was the sinking of several neutral ships with American passengers aboard, which triggered the entry of the United States into the war on 6 April 1917. The immediate impact of this was to assist the British in solving the submarine problem through the introduction of the convoys, which collected merchantmen together under the protection of an escort. Even if the U-boats could locate a convoy in the vastness of the oceans, they would find them under the close protection of destroyers. The Americans provided not only extra shipping resources in merchantmen, but also numerous destroyer escorts that were so crucial to running the convoy system. With their help, it was soon evident that the British would not be starved out of the war. In 1917, the American Army was negligible, in a sense mirroring the British situation in 1914, but the vast American continent offered the promise of teeming millions of recruits to form new armies. As such, it was a potential threat hanging above the German High Command.

The main hope for the Germans was that, almost simultaneously with America's entry to the war, the mighty Russian juggernaut had finally been brought to its knees by its own internal problems. The rigidity of the despotic Tsarist regime meant that it was incapable of adapting, in any meaningful manner, to the plethora of economic, political and social problems that were exacerbated by the incredible stresses imposed by the war. Shortages of food in the cities led to riots, alongside industrial strikes and widespread political machinations. Normally the iron fist of the military would have been deployed to crush dissent, but the Tsar's armies were otherwise engaged with the German forces. In March 1917, Russia fell into chaos, afflicted by a variety of simultaneous revolts against a corrupt regime. Ultimately, Tsar Nicholas was forced to abdicate and a provisional government took over under Alexander Kerensky to try to control the situation. However, the underlying tensions remained, especially as fighting continued unabated on the Eastern Front throughout the summer of 1917. The result was a rise of the popularity of the Bolsheviks, culminating in the second Russian revolution, launched on 7 November 1917. The Allies refused to recognise the new Bolshevik government, well aware of its intention to make peace with the Germans. Naturally, the Germans were delighted – a provisional armistice was declared on 15 December and the mighty Russian Army soon melted away in nothingness. The formal peace would be signed on 3 March 1918. The war on two fronts was over for the Germans; but was it too late?

By February 1918, the war had reached a crucial stage. The removal of the 'Russian steamroller' from the war meant that many of the German divisions on the Eastern Front could be redeployed to the Western Front. The German Supreme Army Command (Oberste Heeresleitung or OHL) figureheaded by Field Marshal Paul von Hindenburg and his *eminence grise*, the Chief of Staff, Quartermaster General Erich Ludendorff, intended to use these additional forces to launch a series of spring offensives, meaning to finish the war before the Americans could arrive in any real strength in the summer. They resolved to target the BEF with the massive Operation Michael offensive in the Somme area. The intention was to break through and then role up the line, pushing to the north.

The British Army that the Germans faced in March 1918 was a very different body from the small professional force of 1914. The regulars then had been well-trained infantry, but collectively had little grasp of working together at any level above the battalion. The BEF also lacked many of the essential accoutrements of trench warfare, such as howitzers, high-explosive shells, mortars and hand grenades. The original Commander in Chief was Field Marshal Sir John French, who showed little sign of coping with the extremely challenging requirements of the post. Since December 1915, the BEF had been commanded by Field Marshal

Sir Douglas Haig. Born on 19 June 1861, his army career before the war had earned him the soubriquet, 'The Educated Soldier'. Originally a cavalry officer, Haig had demonstrated exceptional organisational skills during military service in both the Sudan and the Boer War. In the years leading up to the Great War he held a string of key staff appointments and was much involved in the creation of the Territorial Force. Haig was also responsible for the 1909 revision of the Field Service Regulations Part I, a simple manual that laid out general tactical principles for the British Army in action. On the outbreak of war in 1914, he had served as commander first of I Corps, then the First Army, before being promoted to command the BEF. Since then, Haig had played a crucial role in overseeing the conversion of the BEF into a massive continental army, while at the same time confronting the threat of the German Army in the field. However, as he faced up to the task of thwarting the imminent German offensive in March 1918, he was hampered by a great deal of political interference from home.

The British Prime Minister, David Lloyd George, had long coveted a greater influence on the military direction of the war. He belonged to a school of British politicians that sought an easier path to victory than the horrendous battles on the Western Front. These 'Easterners' sought to knock Germany's allies in the Central Powers out of the war. Back in 1915, the First Lord of the Admiralty, Winston Churchill, had played a significant role in launching the disastrous campaign against Gallipoli to force Turkey out of the war and thereby relieve the pressure on Russia. Now, Lloyd George was equally keen to push the merits of 'Easterner' offensives against the Turks in Palestine and Mesopotamia, against the Bulgarians in Salonika, or against the Austro-Hungarians in Italy. Indeed, he seemed willing to deploy Britain's forces almost anywhere but the Western Front, despite few of his senior British military advisors agreeing with him. They were 'Westerners' and their stance was exemplified by the views of the long-standing Chief of the Imperial General Staff, General Sir William Robertson, who was adamant that the war must be fought and won against the main enemy – Germany – on the Western Front. Germany was not propped up by her allies; if anything, the situation was reversed. The defeat of Turkey, Bulgaria or even Austro-Hungary would not decide the war. The German Army *had* to be defeated; it was the backbone of the Central Powers alliance. Here then, Robertson and Haig stood united against the siren voices of politicians, warning that the diversion of precious military resources to sideshow campaigns could leave the Allies weakened on the only front that really mattered.

Frustrated by the perceived intransigence of Robertson's opinions, Lloyd George sought to replace him as CIGS with the more mercurial talents of General Sir Henry Wilson. Although Wilson had brains, his judgement had often been questioned, as had his apparent willingness to acquiesce to many of the outré ideas promulgated by both British politicians and the French generals. In the first year of the war, in 1914, Wilson had a deeply divisive impact during his brief period as Deputy Chief of Staff to Haig's predecessor, Field Marshal Sir John French, but since then had gained renewed influence acting as an unofficial military advisor to Lloyd George. Ironically, Wilson himself was a 'Westerner', but he was a far more biddable figure, and hence more agreeable to Lloyd George than either the gruff figure of Robertson, or the taciturn Haig. Many of the British High Command, however, held grave doubts as to the competence and motives of Wilson, as exemplified by the remarks of General Sir Hubert Gough back in 1917.

> We soldiers ask with wonder what has he done to establish a reputation? There is only one answer. He talks – but he can't act. He has neither decision, capacity for organisation, or 'drive'. As to his private character, he is an active and thorough intriguer and that is well known. As to his influence with the French, it is due to his capacity for intrigue – for talk – and to the French incapacity to form a sound judgment on English soldiers. Such is my opinion of Henry Wilson, and it is shared by a great many soldiers. So you can see my reasons for considering him a danger in any position of power.[3]
>
> General Sir Hubert Gough, Headquarters, Fifth Army

Nevertheless, in December 1917 Lloyd George sent Wilson as Britain's military representative to the newly formed Supreme War Council designed to coordinate Allied strategic direction of the war. Robertson had no dispute with the formation of the council, but believed that as CIGS, in order to avoid a divided responsibility and an inevitable confusion in the overall direction of British military policy at the highest levels, he should have been Britain's military representative. After much adroit manoeuvring, Lloyd George, having calculated his options, finally took the plunge and, on 18 February 1918, replaced Robertson with Wilson as CIGS. Haig was not pleased, but, professional soldier that he was, he rejected the gesture politics of resignation and resolved to work to the best of his ability with Wilson.

Lloyd George was determined to restrict the number of men sent to the Western Front. The Prime Minister was convinced that Haig and his generals would merely waste any 'extra' manpower on yet more 'futile' attacks against the German lines. He saw no progression in BEF tactics; he saw only the butchers' bill of the Somme and Passchendaele. Political manpower committees restricted the reinforcements required to keep the British divisions up to strength. Hundreds of thousands of trained soldiers were retained in Britain, while the huge forces already committed to the campaigns in Italy, Salonika, Palestine and Mesopotamia helped further dissipate the strength of the Empire. The situation became so fraught that Haig had to reduce the size of his brigades from four to three battalions if he was to maintain his existing number of divisions. The ramifications of this difficult reorganisation had not yet been worked through when the German Army struck on 21 March 1918.

The German offensive tactics that day were based on a supremely effective barrage, which sought to eradicate any British artillery response while hammering the forward positions and targeting headquarters and communications to prevent any coherent response. Parties of storm troopers fed into the gaps, completing the chaos, and leaving the main body of troops following behind to overwhelm any remaining isolated pockets of resistance. The blow fell against General Sir Hubert Gough's Fifth Army in the Somme area, thereby hitting an army which was already seriously overstretched, and where the planned measures for a new system of 'defence in depth' had been neither carried out, nor the tactics properly assimilated. The Germans burst through the forward outpost zone, in places penetrating the intended battle zone, thereby triggering a headlong retreat by the Fifth Army back across the River Somme and over the old battlefields of 1916.

The initial apparent success of the German offensive provided a great test of the Anglo-French alliance. The cautious and uninspiring response of the French Commander in Chief, General Phillipe Pétain, proved a trigger to the appointment of General Ferdinand Foch as *de facto* Commander in Chief of the Allied Armies in France at an Allied conference in Doullens on 26 March. This had the positive approval of Haig, who recognised that they had to work together under tremendous German pressure, and who had already established a reasonable working relationship with Foch much earlier in the war. The particulars of the appointment were initially vague, but there is no doubt that ramifications were enormous. Despite the absence of an integrated Anglo-French staff, the strong personality of Foch, coupled with the acquiescence of Haig, Pétain and Pershing, meant that some unity of purpose was brought to the Allied operations on the Western Front.

Ferdinand Foch was born on 2 October 1851 and in his pre-war military career had been an influential theorist at the French Staff College. He believed that good morale and maintaining the offensive were the keys to success in battle. As a corps commander, he had performed well in the decisive Battle of the Marne in September 1914, and even better as Commander of the Northern Group of Armies, where he had worked closely with Haig in securing the line during the desperate First Battle of Ypres in October. Foch had mixed success in the huge French offensives launched throughout 1915 and 1916, but had been appointed the Chief of the General Staff in 1917. Foch remained a beacon of positive thinking and exuded a confidence that the Germans could – and would – be defeated.

Taken as a whole, the sequence of German spring offensives – in the Somme (Operation Michael: March–April 1918), in the River Lys sector (Operation Georgette: April 1918) and on the Chémin des Dames

(Operations Blücher and Gneisenau: May–June 1918) – had many features in common: initial stunning German breakthroughs, Allied reinforcements arriving just in time to stem the tide, after which the line was eventually stabilised with the Germans having achieved little, or rather nothing, of strategic importance. Both Foch and Pétain saw the resulting huge German salient (which stretched from the old lines on the Chémin des Dames as far forward as the River Marne) as nothing more than a trap, rendering the German units vulnerable to a devastating counter-attack.

It was evident that British and French hopes rested on the deployment of the millions of enthusiastic American soldiers that would be arriving on the Western Front during the summer of 1918. They would make all the difference to the situation, but how best to deploy them? The Americans had already overcome enormous difficulties just to get them out to the Western Front. In April 1917, they had joined the war with a miniscule regular army of only 25,000 men. As millions flocked to the colours, the problem came into sharp focus. Where were these men to be housed during training? Where would the uniforms come from? Just feeding them three times a day would require a stupendous organisational effort. Weapons and munitions were a serious problem, as American industry was not yet capable of supplying their needs. But in a world torn by war, who would have the spare capacity to supply them with the rifles, guns, howitzers and mortars, the millions of shells, the aircraft, the tanks, the gas masks and all the paraphernalia of modern warfare? The situation was complicated by the lack of experienced military personnel at every level of command. There were not enough corporals to instil basic drill into the teeming millions, far too few sergeants to lead the thousands of platoons under training, an endemic shortage of officers, a lack of the staff officers essential to bring an army into battle, and no-one with any experience of commanding such huge new armies in action.

The Allied High Command offered a pragmatic – or selfish – solution as they envisioned using the untrained multitudes of American recruits as a near bottomless well, from which they could draw manpower to replenish their own depleted ranks. The idea had a certain logic in that the

British and French already had the infrastructure firmly in place, ready to churn out countless fully trained and equipped soldiers, but the copious losses endured over the last three years of war meant that they now lacked the raw manpower necessary to service their needs. Yet the reality was that any American politician offering to subordinate the soldiers of the United States to foreign powers would be committing electoral suicide, no matter how worthy the cause. The existing American generals could hardly be expected to welcome the abrogation of everything they had worked for, to subordinate themselves under foreign generals at the very moment when their country faced war. As a compromise, the British offered to incorporate American battalions into British formations until they had amassed the experience in modern warfare to allow them to create, in turn, their own brigades, divisions and corps. This too was rejected. The American position was clear: although help from the British and French would be appreciated during various problematical aspects of the process, the Americans wanted to create their own army, fighting as an independent body in their own designated sector of the Western Front. Nothing else would do.

In May 1917, General John Pershing had been appointed to the command of the American Expeditionary Force (AEF). Born on 13 September 1860, Pershing attended the US Military Academy at West Point and graduated in 1886. His active service experience included colonial wars directed against the indigenous Apache and Sioux Indians, the Spanish American War of 1898, and the Philippine–American War of 1899–1902. His promotion accelerated following his advantageous marriage to the daughter of a senior Republican senator. Promoted to Brigadier General in 1906, in 1914 he was given command of the brigade stationed on the Mexican border and was thus involved in the expedition that chased the revolutionary forces of Francisco Villa around Mexico in 1916–17. These operations cannot be considered a success, but Pershing did enough under adverse conditions to impress President Woodrow Wilson.

Between 1914 and 1917, the American High Command – such as it was – had taken a professional interest in the war waging in Europe.

Nevertheless, they fell foul of the same mistakes that had dogged generals of all countries in this period. Lacking the personal experience of the power of massed artillery and machine guns, they tended to have an optimistic vision of the fighting capabilities and superior morale of the American soldier. Like so many before him, Pershing believed that 'his' men were special, able to rise above the mundane realities of the battlefield, using imaginative and bold tactics to secure a clean breakthrough and end the tyranny of trench warfare. The French, the British and the Italians could all have warned him of the danger of testing nationalistic myths on the battlefield, but Pershing was intransigent.

Pershing envisioned divisions of a much larger size than the accepted European norm in 1918. His aim was to combine crushing firepower with an inbuilt ability to withstand heavy casualties. Each American division would have nearly 28,000 men, organised into two brigades, each of two regiments composed of three battalions – some twelve battalions in all. On top of this were a further three machine-gun battalions and a full battalion of engineers. Before long, great camps had been set up across America, churning out semi-trained soldiers by the hundred thousand, but the task of creating full infantry divisions, complete with all the supporting formations that were truly 'ready for war' proved difficult. Although the 1st Division was sent across to the Western Front almost immediately in May 1917, it was by no means ready for any serious operational deployment. By the time of the German offensives in March 1918, only four American divisions were serving on the Western Front. Of necessity, Pershing had been forced to call on the experience of French and British personnel in order to complete the essential basic training in the techniques of trench warfare that his men required. Despite the occasional frictions, inevitable in any gathering of soldiers from different nationalities, there was also a sense of relief evident among the British tutors, worn down as they were by years of war.

> Our British instructor, said, 'I want to look your company over at close range as it marches by'. As the company passed he inspected them closely and tears filled his eyes. He said, 'My God! This is

Kitchener's army over again. We have nothing like this now; we have nothing left but boys.'[4]

Captain Henry Maslin, 1/105th Regiment, 53rd Brigade, 27th Division

In their turn, the Americans demonstrated a ready enthusiasm for the training they were being given in the weapons of war – new and old.

We received our Lewis guns. That same night First Sergeant Jesse Cavanaugh, Sergeants D. S. Scott, C. N. Nagle and several others sat up all night in the orderly room with the Sergeant instructor from the British and mastered the handling of that weapon. This was simply typical of the spirit that every man in L Company showed at every opportunity to fit himself for the actual work down front. We marched to a nearby town and received British steel helmets and gas masks; we turned in our American rifles and received British in return. At the end of one of our days of drill, the battalion was grouped on the field while Colonel Campbell of the training cadre gave a demonstration of bayonet work using as his 'pal' a British sergeant whom we recognised as the pugilist 'Bombardier' Wells.[5]

Captain Charles Scott, 3/105th Regiment, 53rd Brigade, 27th Division

The training of 27th Division seems to have proceeded relatively harmoniously. Yet other units developed a mutual incomprehension and dislike of their British instructors. It irritated many of the British veterans that the Americans lacked any grasp of the challenges of trench warfare.

The Americans were green – greener than the greenest grass. They knew this and they knew our men were old hands and they wanted to hear about the war from people who knew it from personal experience. But the stories they wanted to hear were stories out of *Boys' Own Paper*: gallant officers waving gleaming swords as they led their brave men in glorious charges; noble soldiers cradling their dying comrades in their arms as they listened to the last whispered message to mother – and so on. They had just no shadow of an idea what war was like. As for our men: they had struggled and lived in everlasting mud; they had been gassed, blown up and wounded; the war had been going on since the beginning of time and appeared to be going on for ever and ever; they had given up all hope of it ever ending and it was beyond their understanding that anyone should want to talk about it! The Americans couldn't understand this utter weariness about the war and the two sides never got on together – they just didn't speak the same language and the incomprehension was mutual.[6]

Lieutenant John Nettleton, 2nd Rifle Brigade, 25th Brigade, 8th Division

However, friction was not all the fault of the Americans. British accounts of the time are riddled with a patronising sense of superiority. That this was not unnoticed was evident in a post-war report from an American officer of their 30th Division. After saying that relationships were overall good, he introduced a note of caution.

Tommy considered himself a superior soldier to the American and took no pains to conceal it. In fact, he took every opportunity to impress on the mind of the American soldier that such was the case. Our soldiers resented any such attitude and denied that it was based on fact.[7]

Brigadier General Samson Faison, Headquarters, 60th Brigade, 30th Division

Overall, it is clear that British soldiers were often guilty of forgetting that they too had once been raw newcomers to battle, ignorant of the harsh truths of war. Elementary tact was often missing in the British approach and it is therefore unsurprising that many Americans judged the pompous messenger rather than the valid nature of the message they bore.

If the British were pleased to see the Americans arriving in numbers, then how much more hope did their advent bring to the French, who had been fighting for longer and had suffered far more casualties.

Swarms of Americans began to appear on the roads. They passed in interminable columns, closely packed in lorries, with their feet in the air in extraordinary attitudes, some perched on the tilt, almost all bare-headed and bare-chested, singing American airs at the top of their voices amid the enthusiasm of the inhabitants. The spectacle of these magnificent youths from overseas, these beardless children of twenty, radiating strength and health in their equipment, produced a great effect. They contrasted strikingly with our regiments in their faded uniforms, wasted by so many years of war, whose members, thin, their sunken eyes shining with a dull fire, were no more than bundles of nerves held together by a will to heroism and sacrifice. We all had the impression that we were about to see a wonderful operation of transfusion of blood. Life was coming in floods to reanimate the dying body of France, almost bled to death, since for four years that blood had flowed from countless wounds. Nobody thought that perhaps these soldiers were not trained, that perhaps they had nothing beyond this courage; these were foolish ideas that never entered our minds. In a sort of exalted vision of the future we looked upon them as an inexhaustible source of strength, carrying everything before it.[8]

Lieutenant Jean de Pierrefeu, Grand Quartier Général

The Americans were coming. But would they be in time?

ON 15 JULY, THE GERMANS TOOK A STEP FAR TOO FAR when they launched their *Friedensturm* (Peace offensive) with the objective of pushing east to secure the rail communications running through Rheims to Soissons to ease their difficult supply situation in the Marne salient. It was also to act as a diversion before the main effort of Operation Hagen, intended to obliterate the British in Flanders. Instead, they found themselves fighting a Second Battle of the Marne, one which would almost match the significance of the first. The Germans found the French waiting for them, not only armed with accurate intelligence from improved aerial reconnaissance, but now also experienced in countering German bombardment techniques. As one senior German general ruefully recalled:

The first position was a line of security outposts, which was weakly held. The artillery was positioned behind the main defensive position and echeloned in depth. Since the enemy knew that the attack would commence early on 15 July, during the night the entire French artillery conducted a massive counter-preparation fire against the German attack positions. The German infantry assault overran the resistance of the French outposts, which sacrificed themselves, but then had to advance three kilometres to the French main position, suffering heavy casualties from French infantry. Here the attack stalled.[9]

Generalleutnant Hermann von Kuhl, Headquarters, Army Group Rupprecht

On the front held by the French Fourth Army the German attack was a near total failure, as the French system of defence in depth worked perfectly: the outpost lines had been stripped of troops to avoid the crushing German barrage, while the French guns waited, ready to flay the German troops as they attacked the main French battle-zone positions. Staff officer Jean de Pierrefeu considered this a key moment.

July 15th was the culminating point of the 1918 campaign. On the evening of July 14th, after midnight, those of us who were walking upon the ramparts of Provins beneath the sky brilliant with stars, heard in the north-east the rumbling of the thunder of the French counter-preparation which, a good hour before the opening of the enemy preparation, was poured upon the German trenches filled with their storm troops. The last act of the great German tragedy of 1918 was beginning. Soon another drama was to commence, but this time it was Foch who was to stage it.[10]

Lieutenant Jean de Pierrefeu, Grand Quartier Général

The Germans were oblivious to the French preparations; it certainly proved a surprise to the German gunner, Leutnant Herbert Sulzbach.

At 1.10 am on the dot, on a broad front, the terrible brazen roar starts up again from the mouths of thousands and thousands of guns. In just the same way as the three and a half years of static warfare up to 21 March 1918 became commonplace, these offensives have lost all their novelty as far as I am concerned. You are so sure of your ground that you are convinced that everything is going to succeed – the barrage, and the infantry assault, and the victory! The barrage makes an incredible din, you can hear nothing, and can't see anything either because of the smoke; once again, the enemy do comparatively little firing, and don't bother us very much. At 4.50 the creeping barrage begins, and with it the infantry attack. My No. 5 Battery has unfortunately suffered heavy casualties. We ourselves have to keep our gas masks on for a long time, as the French are firing a mixture of gas and shrapnel. We can't get any clear picture of whether the infantry is advancing properly. And strangely enough, we have so far received no orders to move forward ourselves. The first thousand French who have been taken prisoner are just moving past in their light blue uniforms. As before, I talk to some of them and find it strange to hear that our plans for an offensive are supposed to have been accurately known for the last ten days. The attack is coming to a halt outside Prosnes: enemy resistance seems to be insurmountable. How is it going on our right and left flanks? 15 July passes without our being moved forward. We are very depressed indeed, because if a giant attack like this does not succeed straight off, it is all over.[11]

Leutnant Herbert Sulzbach, 5th Field Artillery Regiment, 9th Division

To the east of Rheims the Germans had more success against the French Fifth Army, pushing forward some 4 miles before the situation was stabilised. Pétain was deeply concerned and seemed on the point of abandoning any thoughts of a serious counter-offensive. Yet Foch stood firm, husbanding his reserves and refusing to allow the far more cautious Pétain to dissipate them in defensive actions to bolster the struggling Fifth Army. He also avoided returning four British divisions 'borrowed' from Haig and consigned them to the attack, a risk he felt was well worth taking, considering the much grander plan he had in mind.

For now, at last, the time was ripe for the great French riposte. The fierce figure of General Charles Mangin would lead the Tenth Army into the savage counter-offensive with the overall objective of pushing east into the German Marne salient, taking Soissons, and thereby threatening the security of all the German divisions south of the River Vesle. Alongside, also pressing eastwards, was the Sixth Army (General Jean-Joseph-Marie Degoutte) while the Ninth Army (General Antoine de Mitry) would attack north, flinging the Germans back across the Marne. Finally the Fifth Army (General Henri Berthelot) was to advance from the eastern face of the salient pushing north-westwards in an effort to close the trap on the German garrison within the salient. In all, some fifty infantry divisions and six cavalry divisions against fifty German divisions, many of which had already been hammered in the abortive Friedensturm offensive.

At 04.35 on 18 July the attack began with a massive bombardment rained down on the German positions as the French infantry burst from their trenches – it was soon evident that the Germans were not ready for this. Worse still, from their perspective, it was clear that the French Army under the leadership of Pétain had been successful in maximising the advantage from the seamless interaction of artillery, tanks and aircraft in support of the infantry. This was partially out of necessity – the French Army could not afford to suffer vast losses after the 1917 mutinies – but it also represented a tactical progression which had been long underway, reaching right back to the 1915 offensives. The French tanks, especially the new Renault FT tanks, were present in impressive numbers. The Renaults only had a crew of two, were relatively light and had an innovative rotating turret that could contain either a 37mm Puteaux gun or a Hotchkiss machine gun. Although they had a limited trench-crossing capability in comparison to the British lozenge-shaped tanks, they could – at a pinch – cross a 6-foot-wide trench. Their *raison d'être* was simple: in contrast to the heavier French St Chamond type and British Mark V designs which proffered large targets to the German gunners, the idea was to create a veritable swarm of the Renaults that could swamp the German artillery by sheer weight of numbers – aided and abetted by the judicious use of smoke shells. The Renault tank battalions contained some 75 tanks and were organised into Régiments d'Artillerie Spéciales of three battalions – some 225 tanks – at least in theory. The Renaults were a success, pushing forwards and leading the infantry as far as was possible. Although plagued by mechanical breakdowns, prone to ditching when crossing trenches and vulnerable to artillery shells, these were the problems that dogged most tank variants. The Renaults pointed to the future. This was a war of machines.

Yet at the heart of it was still the ordinary French infantryman, or *poilu*. Sweating and trembling perhaps, but nonetheless still pressing forward.

> Absolute peace reigns! No roar of guns, not even a rifle shot! We are silent and a bit cast down just waiting for the big moment. 04.35! A tremendous barrage roars out behind us with the sound of thunder; the creeping barrage that triggers our advance. The 75mm shells fly fast over our heads to explode in the valley at the edge of the forest. The heavier shells follow, flying far higher in the sky to explode on our distant objectives: gun batteries, German reserves, etc. Without losing a moment we go down to the river, each section behind its leader.[12]
>
> Sous Lieutenant Émile Morin, 42nd Régiment d'Infanterie, 41st Division

Another valuable part of the attacking force were the American 1st and 2nd Divisions, which had been temporarily assigned to assist the French, forming the bulk of the XX Corps, Tenth Army. Among their battalions going over the top that day were 2/5th Marines. They had a confusing start, receiving their movement orders far too late, and Lieutenant Elliott Cooke was seriously concerned as he tried to get a grip on the situation. If they lost their creeping barrage they surely would be shot to pieces.

> 'By the right flank!' I yelled at the long file of running men, 'By the right flank! Let's go!' They got it! Rifles swung to the right; bayonets glinted among the leaves. We crashed into a woven barrier of tree limbs. Barbed wire clawed at our pants and leggings. A grenade popped. Holy smoke! There were Germans right under our feet. I clawed out my automatic and fired twice without having much idea of what I was shooting at. A bullet clipped a brass ring from my belt and a rifle barrel was thrust between my legs. I tripped, caught myself and hurdled a line of fox holes. Our entire company

surged over, smothering the Germans' position. We had their front
line before either side knew what had happened. Several Heinies
jumped up, hands in the air. Putty-grey faces under coal-scuttle
helmets – a frightened half-starved looking gang of would-be prisoners. 'Take 'em back,' I directed a couple of old-timers. Without
any instructions, the prisoners started for the rear. They were in a
hurry to be gone. One of the men I had assigned as guard yelled
for them to halt. That scared the prisoners and they broke into a
trot. Whamp! The guard sent a shot over their heads. Squealing
with fright, the Germans fairly stampeded through the brush. The
guards hurried in pursuit, and all disappeared from sight through
the trees.[13]

First Lieutenant Elliott Cooke, 2/5th Marines, 4th Marine Brigade, 2nd
Division

One of Cooke's men spotted some Germans taking shelter in a log-cov-
ered dugout. He knew they had to 'mop them up', but they had no hand
grenades. Strangely, they found a case of German 'potato-masher'-style
grenades close by: now Cooke was in a real quandary – they had been told
to mop up, but also to beware of German booby traps on tempting items
just such as this. No one fancied entering the lions' den of the dugout, so
he decided to risk using the bombs.

We just had to use those grenades. 'Stand back,' I advised – and
took hold of one with the tips of my fingers. Gently, oh, very, very
gently, I raised the piece of ordnance from its bed of sawdust.
Behind me, I think Whitey said a prayer. I know I did. The thing
came up and nothing happened. I screwed the cap and took hold
of the cord that had to be pulled to ignite the fuse. Suppose the
grenade exploded when I pulled that string? Perspiration oozed
out all over me at the thought. I gave a jerk and the fuse came
to life. It buzzed like a bee in the hollow handle of the grenade. I
didn't waste any time getting rid of it through the dugout entrance.
We waited a moment and then heard it explode with a muffled
'Kker-boom!' As no Germans came out, we heaved grenades into
the bomb-proof until its log roof was askew and its revetments

dripping sand. If Becker had really seen some Bosche go into that hole, I'll bet what was left of them is still there. We sealed that dugout into a tomb.[14]

First Lieutenant Elliott Cooke, 2/5th Marines, 4th Marine Brigade, 2nd Division

Mangin's Tenth Army smashed through the German front lines, advancing over 5 miles, even attaining the nirvana of a Great War offensive by getting through to overrun the German gun batteries. Leutnant Herbert Sulzbach found his unit was rushed forward to try and staunch the breakthrough. On the night of 20/21 July, he was caught in a French bombardment.

The French begin to plaster the whole area with fire, and there is really no shelter at all in this shallow basement. We sit here like sardines in a tin, with all the orderlies round us, and get the telephone lines laid. I don't know the word indicating the difference in degree required to describe the wholly crazy artillery fire which the French turn on for the attack in the morning. The word 'hell' expresses something tender and peaceful compared with what is starting here and now. I have really had enough experience of barrage in offensives, both our own and the enemy's. It's as though all the barrages one had ever known had been combined to rattle down on us now. At 6 am I do observation for my batteries at the command post, but you can hardly keep going in this massed fire, you can hardly see anything because of the smoke, you have to keep throwing yourself flat on the ground, and you can't understand why you haven't been hit. I don't see how the French have managed this – first bringing our offensive of 15 July to an unsuccessful halt, and then, completely unobserved by us, preparing and carrying out an attack on a huge scale, with such quantities of troops and equipment.[15]

Leutnant Herbert Sulzbach, 5th Field Artillery Regiment, 9th Division

There seemed to be no respite. In the skies above them, French aircraft seemed to darken the sky, machine gunning and bombing targets of opportunity. Individual aircraft lacked a powerful weapons' capability, but numbers brought them strength, swarming down to harass the Germans and disrupting the arrival of reserves.

> French and British planes are coming over at us, thirty, forty and fifty planes at a time in waves close behind each other, flying in close formation but strung out in a line, and it's dreadful to know how beautifully they can see everything from up above; the bombers come over as well, chucking down their revolting cargo in the broad light of day; and in two ticks, of course, the French batteries have got our battery positions from the observation planes, and are plastering us with fire.[16]

Leutnant Herbert Sulzbach, 5th Field Artillery Regiment, 9th Division

Over the next few days, the bulging salient created by the German May 1918 offensives burst like a pricked balloon, but the French Fifth Army made only limited advances and was unable to 'close' the neck of the salient before most of the German forces within had managed to make good their escape. The Germans eventually stopped the Allies, establishing a new front stretching along the Vesle and Aisne rivers, but it meant they had fallen back almost to where they had started prior to their much-vaunted advances in the Blücher offensive some two months earlier. During the Second Battle of the Marne, the Germans suffered some 168,000 casualties, with around 29,000 prisoners lost, along with over 3,000 machine guns and 800 guns/mortars captured. The Allies suffered just over 95,000 casualties. Stunned, the Germans were forced to cancel Operation Hagen, their planned 'decisive' offensive in Flanders. The palliative respite afforded by the arrival of the German divisions freed from the Eastern Front by the fall of Russia was over. But worse still, the German Army was becoming drained as a military force. The practice of using elite Stormtrooper units had gradually removed the brightest, bravest and best of the German soldiers from the 'ordinary' German units. The elite were used as the spearhead right at the forefront of attacks, where they may have been effective, but the casualties suffered were excruciating. Those that remained were often war-weary, weakened by a restricted diet and becoming increasingly aware that the Allies were winning the logistical war.

The Second Battle of the Marne had demonstrated that the French Army was once again an effective force. This had been their moment, and it was a real turning point in the war. It unequivocally proved that the Germans could be beaten. But it was not just French troops that were hitting back: British, American and Italian divisions had also played their part, demonstrating the new strength of the Allied coalition operating under the overall direction of the inspirational Foch. There may still have been arguments and prickly clashes over national interests, but Foch deployed considerable powers of tact and persuasion to ensure that an outward unity of purpose was maintained. His reward was to be created a Maréchal de France: the door was ajar to an ultimate Allied victory. The arrival of the American divisions had switched the manpower equation in favour of the Allies. It was time to go on the offensive.

Foch called for a face-to-face conference with Haig, Pershing and Pétain, which was held on 24 July at his GHQ at Bombon. His Chief of Staff, General Maxime Weygand, prepared a memorandum, presented by Foch, which clearly portrayed the existing situation.

> We have already attained equality in the number of battalions at least, and, in a more general sense, in the number of combatants, though superiority in the total number of divisions is not yet on our side. The Germans have been compelled to throw so many divisions into action that, for the first time, we have a superiority in reserves; also, owing to the large number of exhausted Divisions they will be compelled to relieve from the battle-front, we shall likewise have a superiority in the number of fresh reserves. Moreover, all available information is in agreement as to the enemy being reduced to the state of being compelled to have two armies: an army for occupying the line, reduced in strength and condemned to be sacrificed; and a shock army, manoeuvring behind the flimsy protection of the other. This shock army, though trained with the utmost care by the German Supreme Command, has been already greatly weakened. In addition, the Allies have a material

superiority in aviation beyond dispute; also in tanks. In artillery our advantage is bound to be increased when and as the American artillery arrives. Finally, in the rear of the Allied armies, the powerful reserve of the American forces pours 250,000 men every month upon the soil of France. While on the enemy's side, we know the urgent measures which he has been forced to take in order to meet the crisis in the supply of men for the month of May; and it is apparent that, owing to the difficulty which the Germans find in keeping up the strength of their various units at the front, a new crisis is now asserting itself. In addition to all these indications that the factor of 'material force' is veering around in our favour, there can be added the moral ascendancy which has been maintained on our side from the beginning of the battle, owing to the fact that the enemy, despite his unprecedented efforts, has been unable to bring about the decisive result he needed to attain. And this moral ascendancy has been increased by the victory just won by the Allied armies. These armies, therefore, have arrived at the turning-point of the road. They have recovered in full tide of battle the initiative of operations; their numbers permit and the principles of war compel them to keep this initiative. The moment has come to abandon the general defensive attitude forced upon us until now by numerical inferiority and to pass to the offensive.[17]

Maréchal de France Ferdinand Foch

Foch then put forward plans for a series of limited offensives designed to improve the overall strategic situation on the Western Front. The reasoning was clear:

1. Operations having as their objective the clearing of the railway lines that are indispensable for the later operations of the Allied Armies, viz.:
(a) The freeing of the Paris–Avricourt railway line in the Marne region. This is the minimum result to be obtained from the offensive movement now going on.
(b) The freeing of the Paris–Amiens railway line by a concerted action of the British and French Armies.

(c) The clearing of the Paris–Avricourt railroad in the region around Commercy, by reducing the St Mihiel salient. This operation should be prepared without delay and executed by the American Army as soon as it has the necessary means.

2. Operations with a view to clearing the mining region of the North and to driving to the enemy once and for all from the vicinity of Dunkirk and Calais.

These operations pre-suppose two attacks, which may be carried out separately or conjointly. As previously stated, these actions must succeed each other at brief intervals, so as to embarrass the enemy in the utilisation of his reserves and not allow him sufficient time to fill up his units.

The attacks must be provided with everything necessary to make their success certain. Finally, and above all, surprise must be effected. Recent operations show that this is a condition indispensable to success.[18]

Maréchal de France Ferdinand Foch

But there was more. Foch allowed for the hope – not yet the belief – that the war might be ended in 1918.

It is impossible to foretell at present where the different operations outlined above will lead us, either in the matter of time or space. Nevertheless, if the objects they have in view are attained before the season is too far advanced, there is reason for assuming now that an important offensive movement, such as will increase our advantages and leave no respite to the enemy, will be launched toward the end of the summer or during the autumn. It is still too early to be more precise in regard to this offensive.[19]

Maréchal de France Ferdinand Foch

When faced with Foch's plans, Haig responded positively to the imperative placed upon the BEF to clear the German threat to the Paris–Amiens railway line and was rewarded by having the French First Army placed under his command to assist in the operations. Pershing was also keen to play his part in launching the first great American offensive by attacking at St Mihiel. Pétain – as ever – was cautious, feeling his armies had been drained by their efforts, but he eventually agreed to support the British in the Amiens offensive, and would also provide the required support to the American attempt to erase the St Mihiel salient.

As the tide turned on the Western Front, back in London Wilson, in his role as CIGS, had also been considering the shape of future operations. The result was *British Military Policy, 1918–1919* produced on 25 July. Ironically, in view of Foch's plans, Wilson, although agreeing for the need for limited offensives to 'clear the lines', was adamant that nothing much more could be done in 1918.

> The immediate preoccupation of the Allies must be to secure such a margin of safety for our line in France as will remove all anxiety as to our position. This will enable us to devote our efforts uninterruptedly during the ensuing period to preparation for the decisive phase and if necessary to detach troops to other theatres without misgiving. This will involve a series of operations with limited objectives designed to push the Germans back from in front of the vital strategical objectives, such as the Channel Ports, the Bruay coal mines, the Amiens centre of communication and Paris. The plans for those operations as well as the moment of their execution must be defined by the Allied Commander in Chief, but it is obvious that they should take place before the end of this campaigning season. It is also certain that they will require the active cooperation of every man and gun that we can keep in the field until late in the Autumn. There is therefore no possibility of sending any divisions to operate in other theatres until this aim is accomplished. Having removed all immediate anxiety as to the situation in France and obtained a sufficient margin of safety for our strategical position on the Western Front, a period of preparation should ensue during which all the Allied resources should be husbanded, organised and trained for the culminating military effort at the decisive moment. This will not be a period of passive defence, far from it, but it will be a period during which no final decision is attempted.[20]

> General Sir Henry Wilson, Imperial General Staff, War Office

After carefully analysing the relative strength of the forces available, Wilson concluded that the most advantageous time for an attack would be in 1919, not later than July. He cautioned sternly against waiting until 1920, as he feared the impact of Allied war weariness, coupled with the possibility of the German harvesting the potential of their gains in the east following the collapse of Russia. However, he looked to the Allied superiority of manpower he anticipated in 1919.

> That superiority, if properly supported by the fullest equipment of every mechanical auxiliary, and efficiently directed under one supreme command, will give us a fair chance of achieving substantial military success, while if the more favourable contingencies should arise our success should be decisive.[21]
>
> General Sir Henry Wilson, Imperial General Staff, War Office

Wilson's viewpoint was not so much wrong as mistimed. His views chimed in with those of Winston Churchill, who also believed that 1919 would be the climactic year of the war. On 22 June 1918, he had presented a review of war policy to the War Cabinet.

> Do the means of beating the German armies in the West in 1919 exist? Can the men be procured? If so, the mechanisms can be prepared. We still have the time. Have we the willpower and the command to look ahead and regulate action accordingly?[22]
>
> Minister of Munitions Winston Churchill

In the post-war years, much was made of another plan for future operations on the Western Front produced by Lieutenant Colonel John Fuller. This talented young staff officer had been responsible for the tactics employed by the Tank Corps in the Battle of Cambrai and he was convinced that he had divined the path to victory with his 'Plan 1919'.

> In order to render inoperative the Command of the German forces on any given front, what are the requirements? From the German front line the average distance to nine of their Army Headquarters is 18 miles; to three Army Group Headquarters 45 miles;

and the distance away of their Western General Headquarters is 100 miles. For purposes of illustration the 18-mile belt or zone containing Army, Corps and Divisional Headquarters will prove sufficient. Before reaching these Headquarters elaborate systems of trenches and wire entanglements, protected by every known type of missile-throwing weapon, have to be crossed. To penetrate or avoid this belt of resistance, which may be compared to a shield protecting the system of command, two types of weapons suggest themselves:

(i) The aeroplane.

(ii) The tank.

The first is able to surmount all obstacles; the second to traverse most. The difficulties in using the first are very great; for even if landing-grounds can be found close to the various Headquarters, once the men are landed, they are no better armed than the men they will meet; in fact, they may be compared to dismounted cavalry facing infantry. The difficulties of the second are merely relative. At present we do not possess a tank capable of carrying out the work satisfactorily, yet this is no reason why we should not have one nine months hence if all energies are devoted to design and production. The idea of such a tank exists, and it has already been considered by many good brains; it is known as the 'Medium D tank', and its specifications are as follows:

(i) To move at a maximum speed of 20 miles an hour.

(ii) To possess a circuit of action of 150 to 200 miles.

(iii) To be able to cross a 13- to 14-foot gap.

(iv) To be sufficiently light to cross ordinary road, river and canal bridges.

The tactics of the Medium D tank are based on the principles of movement and surprise, its tactical object being to accentuate surprise by movement, not so much through rapidity as by creating unexpected situations. We must never do what the enemy expects us to do; instead, we must mislead him, that is, control his brain by our own. We must suggest to him the probability of certain actions, and then, when action is demanded, we must develop it in a way diametrically opposite to the one we have suggested through our preparations.[23]

Lieutenant Colonel John Fuller, Headquarters, Tank Corps

There was much that was brilliant here, but this magnificent construct had its foundations resting on sand. There was one obvious flaw – the plan relied on the Medium D tank which was still stranded on the drawing board. There was no guarantee that it would be ready by the spring of 1919, or indeed whether the Medium D would ever be able to deliver the required level of performance. The plan was a fantasy.

Lacking any real command experience and carried away with a sense of their own ineffable brilliance, men like Wilson, Churchill and Fuller were unaware that the future was already upon them; they were oblivious to the terrible losses suffered by the German Army, coupled with the onset of a desperate war-weariness, which had at last rendered the Germans vulnerable.

While the visionaries pontificated, experienced British generals stood ready to grasp their chance. They knew – they had always known – that what was needed for victory was superior morale and firepower with the tactics to maximise their effect. But this had been at best an aspiration; one they had reached for at the battles of Neuve Chapelle, Loos, the Somme, Arras, Ypres and Cambrai. They had been thwarted by a lack of the right specialist weapons, enough munitions, the skilled soldiers, the difficulties of employing everything in the right tactical mix and – of course – by the constantly improving German defensive measures/tactics. Yet now the day had dawned with the advent of a new methodology to achieve the British aims: the 'All Arms Battle'. This was not the creation of any one man, but of a culture that sought to harmonise the use of weapons systems to maximum effect. For the past three years, the British Army had been studying itself, its French Allies and its opponents, desperate to secure the means of breaking not just into the German lines, but to achieve a breakthrough into the green fields beyond. Some have chosen to present this as the story of the development and use of the tank – but this was just one small part of the whole British arsenal.

Artillery remained at the epicentre of the British attack plans. But the thundering barrages had changed their focus. Early in the war they had attempted to destroy German trenches, kill the defenders and smash any resistance. Now the emphasis was on preventing the Germans from opening fire during the time that British troops were vulnerable while crossing No Man's Land. It was now recognised that it was of crucial importance to put out of action any German gun batteries able to range on the area. They had to be identified by a combination of careful aerial reconnaissance using high-quality glass negative photographs to allow the new methodology of photographic interpretation to reveal the hidden locations. This was combined with the new disciplines of flash spotting and sound ranging to enable almost every German battery to be revealed. Then they could either be blown out of existence by high-explosive shells, or, more efficiently, drenched in poison gas to render the operation of the guns almost impossible. Meanwhile a complex system of creeping barrages could suppress the fire of German machine guns, mortars and rifles. Originally this was just a single line of shells proceeding across No Man's Land just in front of the advancing infantry, obscuring the defenders' view and forcing them to keep their heads down until it was too late. By 1918, it had developed into a complex series of moving barrages, some even tracking backwards and forwards, but always ahead of the British soldiers. Then the artillery had long ago developed the ability to 'box off' an area, dropping standing barrages to prevent German reinforcements, or counter-attacks, from reaching the crucial battle zones.

One function of the guns had been to some extent overtaken by the advent of the tank. Tests in 1915 had shown that firing air-burst shrapnel was the most effective method of cutting wire then available. Unfortunately, this required considerable practical skills and was extremely time-consuming. The advent of No. 106 graze fuses, which detonated at the slightest touch, had allowed the use of high-explosive shells to clear wire since the spring of 1917, yet the ultimate answer came with the ability of the tanks to clear a physical path as they trundled through the barbed wire ahead of the infantry. This, coupled with the advent of 'shooting off the map' and the accurate calibration of the guns, meant that surprise was once again a factor in the British assault. The painful process of remapping the entire Western Front to the required standard of accuracy had been completed. Long preliminary bombardments were no longer necessary to clear the wire and blast the trenches. The tanks could create a path through while the creeping barrage prevented German front-line troops from opening fire without unduly exposing themselves.

The origin of the tank lay in the perceived requirement for an armoured vehicle capable of crossing a cratered No Man's Land layered with barbed wire, to cross over the wide German trenches and carry an armament capable of destroying their strongpoints. The first Mark I tanks were tracked vehicles with a distinct lozenge shape, requiring an eight-man crew and coming in two varieties: the 'Male' armed with two 6-pounder guns and three machine guns and the 'Female' with five machine guns. No-one knew their capabilities or had any idea how to deploy them to best advantage in battle. A process of painful trial and error began with their first employment at the Battle of Flers-Courcelette on 15 September 1916. Early results were disappointing: it was soon apparent that they were extremely unreliable mechanically, very slow, the crews lacked sufficient training, the heat and polluted atmosphere inside the tank severely restricted the time a crew could hope to operate effectively, neither the tank personnel nor the infantry had any experience of cooperating or communicating on the battlefield and they were vulnerable to shellfire.

However, Haig and others recognised the potential of tanks as a useful adjunct to the infantry. Over the next two years much progress had been made. New models had pushed the boundaries back, culminating in the deployment of the Mark V and Mark V* in 1918. These were slightly faster and far more reliable, but still identifiable as the progeny of the Mark I. Many of the problems remained, but the hard work of Tank Corps officers like Fuller had built up an effective *modus operandi*. The tanks would train with the infantry behind the lines and in an attack could use their fascines (huge rolls of brushwood carried on the roof of the tank) to cross the widest trenches, whereupon they would work in conjunction with the infantry to attack pillboxes or machine-gun posts holding up the troops. Problems persisted as they remained more prone to breakdown or crew exhaustion than would have been wished; communication in battle was still difficult and they offered a large target to concealed guns. But they offered a valuable service and certainly had an impact on the morale of German defenders who often attributed many of their woes to the tanks.

An additional variant of tank was the specially adapted supply tanks that could carry forward in relative safety the huge quantities of ammunition required. One other type of tank had been developed, the Medium Mark A, or Whippet, as it was better known. As the name might indicate, these were intended to be fast-moving machines with a three-man crew armed with four machine guns, and it was hoped that they would be capable of taking on the cavalry role of penetrating behind the German lines to attack gun lines and headquarters, sever communications and disrupt the arrival of reinforcements. This was largely an aspiration, as fast was a relative word; the Whippet could only reach a speed of around 8 miles per hour. Few of them ever had the chance to show what they could do.

The cavalry had a severely diminished role within the scheme of things, but was still the only truly fast-moving force available in the event of a breakthrough, although armoured cars had started to erode even that proud boast. Cavalry could not operate over shell-torn ground, barbed wire was anathema to them and they were very vulnerable to machine guns and artillery. Yet they were all there was and had in the past proved effective in operating against troops whose morale had been shattered or against troops in headlong retreat. They may have been vulnerable, but they still contributed to the whole picture.

Gas had become a crucial part of the deadly mix of weaponry directed at the Germans. The initial chlorine cloud gas attacks of 1915 had been replaced by a complex array of chemical weapons, such as the deadly phosgene gas, which could be delivered through several means including cloud releases from cylinders, gas shell or canister. Another pernicious chemical weapon was mustard gas, which was a potent vesicant agent that could create a mass of painful blisters, particularly around the lymphatic glands, with the ability to seep through a man's uniform to attack the skin beneath. The eyes were often badly affected, causing temporary blindness, but it also damaged the bronchial tubes and lungs. In extreme cases it could kill, but its main impact was the way in which it degraded the fighting ability of soldiers. As a 'persistent' gas it could remain a menace for up to two days, impregnating the soil and surface water. In contrast, the far deadlier phosgene would dissipate in under an hour. This made mustard gas ideal for use against artillery batteries, which could not easily move within the timetable of an imminent attack.

The original intention of killing the victims of gas attacks had been tempered by the universal issue of efficient gas masks. By 1918, gas was used to make life difficult for the soldier. Once forced to don his mask he would have difficulty in seeing through the misted-up lens, he would be unable to hear commands, and his breathing capacity would be restricted, rendering any physical task difficult or impossible. It was realised that gas could be used to 'drench' an area and deny it to the Germans during the crucial period of an attack, so it was particularly useful when attempting to suppress the fire of identified German gun batteries. Gas masks could also be overloaded by extreme concentrations of gas as delivered by Livens projectors. Much of this was not new, or indeed unique to the British. The Germans, blessed with a far larger and more responsive chemical industry, led the way for much of the war. The British had a lot of ground to make up, lacking the requisite plant manufacturing capacity, or indeed the specialist knowledge and workforce. These obstacles had been overcome and a whole new chemical industry created to service the requirements of gas warfare. The varied means of deploying gas had been mastered and tactical difficulties in deploying the weapons had been largely mastered. Gas shells had gained an increased importance, for their ubiquity wore down the spirit of the German infantry, while their ability to silence supporting gun batteries helped gain the fire supremacy which played a huge part in restoring the potency of Allied offensive operations.

Aircraft were another vital ingredient in the all-arms cocktail of death. Ground strafing was widely accepted as a vital means of disrupting the German ground operations. The aircraft could not drop very many, or very heavy, bombs; the machine guns could fire only in bursts of a few seconds – but there were an awful lot of aircraft in the skies by the summer of 1918. The Royal Air Force also played a vital part in maintaining secrecy before the barrage started and the troops went over the top. Scout aircraft (fighters in modern parlance), had to prevent German aircraft flying photographic reconnaissance missions over the British rear areas, in an effort to conceal for as late as possible the build-up of artillery and infantry. At the same time, reconnaissance aircraft had to carry out a detailed photographic survey to reveal every detail of the German defences; artillery observation still had to be continued – all this without making it obvious that an offensive was imminent. It was a big responsibility but the Germans were badly outnumbered in the skies – sometimes by up to five to one.

Every type of aircraft had its role in a major attack: the night before, the huge Handley Page bombers would fly up and down over the area, concealing the engine roar of the hundreds of tanks; the scouts, such as the Sopwith Camel, the SE5 A, the Sopwith Dolphin and the Spad XIII would clear the skies of any German aircraft, but also attack targets of opportunity on the ground, harassing any German troop movements. DH4 and DH9 bombers would attack airfields to stifle any German aerial response at source, while others would launch interdiction raids on roads and bridges, railheads, railway stations and rail junctions, all to try and prevent the arrival of reinforcements – or if things went well – harass any German retreat. Meanwhile, the RE8 photographic reconnaissance and artillery observation aircraft would carry out contact patrols, plotting the progress of the advance and carrying out the routine, but vitally important, task of bringing down artillery fire where required to dissipate German pockets of resistance on the ground. Finally, a squadron of Armstrong Whitworths was assigned to liaise with the tanks providing reports of their progress and – importantly – how many had broken down or been knocked out, diving down where necessary to assist with bombs and machine guns.

Whatever other arms were added to the mix, the infantry remained the very bedrock of modern combat. Somebody always had to occupy – and hold – the ground. That job fell to the infantry. The infantrymen of 1918 were very different beasts from the men who had gone to war four years before. The BEF regular soldiers of 1914 were professional soldiers with a strong grip on the basics of their trade. They could fire around fifteen aimed shots a minute with high standards of marksmanship; they were competent with the bayonet and could carry out simple fire and movement tactics in attack. Yet they had many physically unfit reservists among their ranks, men who had experienced years of a civilian existence before suddenly being recalled to 'the colours' on the outbreak of war. These men lacked physical conditioning and were soon exposed by the physical demands of warfare, especially by the 'Great Retreat' that followed the Battle of Mons on 23 August 1914. Although within their ranks they had many who had served in the Boer War, or small-scale colonial conflicts, they had no experience of continental warfare against European standards of firepower. During the war, as a collective, the BEF lost some of its core skills of marksmanship and rapidity of fire, but gained a raft of new talents more suited to the exigencies of modern warfare. New weapons were mastered and assimilated into tactical operations. Hand grenades transformed the business of trench and dugout clearance, while the Stokes mortar and rifle grenades gave the infantry platoon their own 'artillery'. The introduction of the Lewis light machine gun meant that the firepower of a section could exceed anything the old regulars could achieve. Tactics had developed throughout the war from the original rushes of fire and movement in 1914, through to the concept in 1916 of successive waves of men intended to build up pressure and break down any German strongpoints. By 1918, things had completely changed, with the widespread introduction of small section strings of six to eight soldiers who would advance carefully behind a screen of scouts, feeling their way forward and always trying where possible to take the path of least resistance.

The nature of BEF officers had also mutated over the four years of intense warfare. Many of the regular officers in 1914 had certain prized core merits, including a commendable commitment to the welfare of their men, personal courage and determination. But it was also clear that the majority lacked a wider tactical perspective beyond the narrow horizons of the company or battalion action, while they failed to grasp the necessity of maintaining a local tactical reserve in both offence and defence. Beyond a reliance on the trusty Lee Enfield .303 rifle, there was also little appreciation of the intricacies of effective deployment of the auxiliary firepower of their machine guns, while they had no concept of working in proper harmony with the guns of the Royal Artillery. Many lieutenant colonels and majors were also lacking in personal stamina, either through their age, or a simple lack of physical fitness. This rendered them vulnerable to the grinding fatigue, stress and physical privations endemic on active service. Such men were soon found wanting, often cracking under the strain. As the British Army grew, casualties eroded the original officer corps, which was forced to expand beyond the original base of public-school-educated officers and to bring in the grammar-school-educated, the commercial clerks, industrial foremen and – most importantly of all – former NCOs who had already demonstrated their leadership qualities and soldierly skills in action. Once the initial requirement to fill all the officer positions in the New Armies had been met, a more performance-based regime appeared. Officers who did well, or had clear potential, were identified and sent on courses to learn their trade.

As the war progressed, many officers were granted accelerated promotion, and the average age of senior ranks dropped as younger, fitter and more mentally responsive men began to push their way into the reckoning at battalion and brigade command levels. The obverse was that men found wanting, through physical frailty, indecisiveness, lack of leadership skills or tactical ineptness in action, were gradually removed from positions of command. It was at times a ruthless process, and although some incompetents still escaped the cull, the overall standard of officers had much improved by 1918. It was still not a proper meritocracy, as there was no competitive promotion system, and in some units both favouritism and prejudice still had an influence. Yet this does not negate a very real advance towards an awareness of the pragmatic military qualities required during a war.

The officers of 1918 had less command experience as measured in time, but they had far more battle experience than their predecessors. Collectively they were well suited to the very different challenges of the combination of formal trench-to-trench attacks and exploitation following success in a variety of circumstances, ranging from assaulting – or enfolding – German rearguard strongholds to an open pursuit. There was recognition of the necessity of allowing the smooth delegation of command to junior officers, as speed of reaction to a developing situation was often of prime importance. Opportunities could be lost, or threats not dealt with, if officers sought to defer to higher authorities and did not exercise their own judgement. Boldness could bring great rewards, but rash mistakes would cost even more lives. Not all officers were capable of this difficult balancing act, although many tried to square the circle with considerable success.

Yet it was perhaps just as important that collectively the British NCOs had gained a mastery of their role in the new tactics. The corporal was now a crucial figure. Advancing as they did in sections as short strings of men, the lance corporal or corporal had a crucial role to play. There was often no officer or senior NCO nearby, yet the men still needed effective leadership. Without it, 'shell-hole dropping' could become rife if men were tempted to seek safety rather than push home an attack. Junior NCOs needed to understand the tactics and make quick decisions in the press of battle. In their role of supervising the performance of ingrained drills in deploying firepower, or in bombing up trenches, or in ensuring dugouts were clear of Germans, they had to understand their section's role within the overall plan, even deciding at times during an assault whether to push on, or to prepare positions for defence against German counter-attacks.

The role of staff officers had also developed apace since 1914. Then many officers had considered staff work as a chore, something mundane, and there was an unseemly rush to secure regimental service. Yet the role of staff officers is paramount to the efficient operation of any army at war. Collectively they combine all the mundane functions of logistics and then meld them with all the detailed planning required for any kind of effective military operation. A whole new generation of properly trained staff officers had arisen over the four years of war. The complexities had been mastered. It was now realised that time was of an essence in initiating any action. The commander needed to think ahead, issuing warning orders at the earliest possible moment of planned offensive actions – before the existing fighting had finished. In chess terms they needed to think two moves ahead. This allows requisite logistical measures to be commenced, such as the moving up of ammunition supplies for the artillery and getting troops into the right 'starting' positions ready to fall into the line as required. While these preparatory actions were being initiated, the commander and his operational staff would be engaged in reconnaissance, detailed planning and production of battle orders delineating what was planned to happen. These orders would cascade down to the subordinate formations, whose staff would fill in the relevant details to achieve the objectives required from them, before passing them on down the chain of command. There were meant to be checks and balances within the system to avoid unrealistic assumptions from higher up the chain being incorporated into the plans. When the machine ran smoothly – which as a human system was not always – then, when the final orders were produced, the troops ready in their assembly trenches, the supporting tanks and machine guns in place, the RAF up in the skies, the guns ready with barrage plans and ammunition and everyone prepared for action, there would be a seamless progression into battle with no delay. Meanwhile the process for the next step is already under way – in other words staff were responsible for a continuous process of reconnaissance and advance planning for a variety of contingencies. It was realised that exploitation operations to capitalise on a successful attack had to be pre-planned and preferably not rely on pure extemporisation. If possible, officers and NCOs had to know what was intended within the overall plan, what the current battle situation was likely to be, and the likely position of both support troops and German counter-attacking reserves. This, of course, was an aspiration and the confusion of battle often rendered it impossible.

The much-maligned staff officers were also responsible for the systematic analysis of operations seeking to glean valuable lessons and determine the most effective solutions to the multifarious problems of warfare. The results would form the constant stream of training pamphlets in the SS series that were disseminated throughout the BEF. To the modern eye the process is reminiscent of a system of 'best practice'

– looking at what worked best in the recent past and what might work again in the future. In the summer of 1918, Lieutenant Colonel Cuthbert Headlam was busy working on the latest version of SS 135 which had already been through two editions: *Instructions for the Training of Divisions for Offensive Action, December 1916* and *The Training and Employment of Divisions, January 1918*. The 'learning curve' was made flesh by men like Headlam, who were part of the continuous process of analysis and interpretation throughout the army.

> I have been in the office all day – very busy, muddling away in the production of 'doctrine'. I am beginning to write off all the military jargon very quickly, but it is not easy to remember all the details and even more difficult to avoid constant repetition. The factor that makes any writing upon military things rather difficult is that war is not a science. One cannot lay down definite rules which are applicable on all occasions and yet one must state clearly general principles. You observe that the distinction is a fine one and therefore one has to weigh very carefully anything one writes in a manual or pamphlet which is to be a textbook in the Army. One can avoid pitfalls if one puts a thing absolutely generally – but if one does that, the work is not likely to be of much practical value. One has to come down from one's pedestal and to try and give practical advice and accurate information that will be of real value.[24]
>
> Lieutenant Colonel Cuthbert Headlam, Training Branch, General Headquarters, BEF

His version would appear in November 1918: SS 135 *The Division in Attack*. Their efforts were jocularly summed up in verse:

> The Colonel Commanding the Bollockyboos
> Has strictly revised all his previous views …
> He keeps his battalion, untiring, approving,
> All moving and firing and firing and moving;
> They know about guns, they know about tanks,
> They'll take any risk that you like with their flanks;
> They're perfectly sound on the use of the ground,

They all are at one that training is fun
And there's nought they don't know about killing the Hun.[25]

Major Robert Barrington-Ward, Training Branch, General Headquarters, BEF

Even when all the latest methodology was applied, plenty of things still went wrong: individuals made mistakes, units failed to carry out orders, battlefield communications failed, there were lapses in cooperation with neighbouring units and predictions as to the course of events were erroneous. Then of course, sometimes things simply went wrong, because they went right for the Germans. Yet the overall results were a qualitative improvement on the staff ineptitude of earlier years.

There had been an informal trial of the new 'All Arms Battle' tactics on 4 July at the Battle of Hamel, conducted by the Australian Corps, under the command of Lieutenant General Sir John Monash. This was an ideal choice, for Monash was a superb organiser who had grasped the essence of the new tactics and was able to develop a coherent plan in close association with Brigadier General Anthony Courage of the Tank Corps. Monash envisioned an attack by six Australian battalions on a front of 6,000 yards supported by over 600 guns – although there was to be no preliminary bombardment. To maintain the surprise, the pre-calibrated guns would stay silent until the moment of the assault. The sixty tanks were a crucial ingredient in the plans. They were to approach the lines covered by the sound of low-flying aircraft and general artillery fire. Then the barrage would crash out, targeted on the German batteries located by a combination of aerial reconnaissance, flash spotting and sound ranging. Shells would also lash down on all identified strongpoints, machine-gun posts and headquarters. The creeping barrage which began to unfurl across No Man's Land was made up of a carefully chosen mixture of 60 per cent shrapnel, 30 per cent high explosive and 10 per cent smoke shells designed to obscure events. The tanks attacked alongside the infantry, keeping as close as possible to the creeping barrage and crushing the German barbed wire defences and creating lanes for the following infantry. In an effort to reduce casualties, all German strongpoints would be tackled where possible by the tanks as directed by the infantry, who would attract their attention by the use of rifle grenades. A smaller second wave of tanks would replace losses and help maintain the momentum. Aircraft would watch out for anti-tank guns and engage in ground attacks on all promising targets. Supply tanks would replenish ammunition, trench mortar shells, hand grenades, barbed wire and the many other military stores required to consolidate the captured positions. When the battle commenced at 03.10 everything went smoothly, and Hamel was captured in an advance of up to 2,000 yards. A successful template had been established. Monash was not the innovator, but rather a disciple of the new methodology. But nevertheless, the Battle of Hamel was important: for here everything came together in a perfect demonstration of the new 'mechanical' battle. Finally, the British Army had achieved the ability to suppress the German defensive fire for the crucial period while the assault troops were crossing No Man's Land.

The next stage was the full-scale attack in the Amiens area by the British Fourth Army (General Sir Henry Rawlinson), alongside the French First Army (General Marie-Eugène Debeney), launched on 8 August in accordance with the wishes of Foch, under the overall command of Haig. The barrages opened at 04.20, as the British infantry made their attack, with the French attacking forty minutes later. The Fourth Army had a successful day, for although the III Corps struggled in difficult terrain north of the Somme, both the Canadian Corps and Australian Corps surged forwards to great effect south of the river, making an advance of up to 10 miles. The German artillery was either destroyed or 'neutralised', and most batteries were soon overrun by the advancing tanks and infantry. Without support from the guns the German infantry were left naked before their enemies. The arrival of tanks, coupled with the increased firepower of infantry able to deploy Stokes mortars, rife grenades and Lewis guns, overwhelmed any pockets of resistance. The French First Army also did well, advancing some 6 miles and threatening the capture of the town of Montdidier. The Germans suffered some 27,700 casualties of which over 15,000 were prisoners of war. They had lost over 400 guns and many mortars and machine guns. Ludendorff memorably summed it up: 'August 8 was the black day of the German

Army in the history of this war.'[26] This was Hamel writ very large: the 'All Arms Battle' in its entirety.

Foch charged Rawlinson with pushing on towards Ham, while Debeney advanced towards Chaulnes and Roye, with additional help from the French Third Army (General Georges Humbert) on his right flank. Debeney needed considerable prodding from behind the scenes from Foch, who was concerned that his First Army was not keeping up with its Canadian neighbours. Perhaps in response to this, the French improved their performance on 10 August, matching the British progress and advancing an impressive 5 miles along a 15-mile front. Yet the cost was still painful for individuals who lost their friends.

> Sad news: Trillat, 'old man Trillat', has been killed. He and I were the only captains still alive after the battle of Mount Kemmel. Will it be my turn next? Poor old Trillat: in every attack he led his men fearlessly onwards, we saw him at the Chemin des Dames not even ducking when the machine guns opened fire, at the Kemmel, urging his company on. And now, a shell has fallen right on him as he was having a bite to eat by the roadside! One of his officers has had an arm blown off. All his men are shocked and have tears in their eyes at such a senseless end to a life. There he is, stretched out at our feet, with a gaping hole in his neck and half of his head missing. One can scarcely recognize him; what remains of his face is covered with blood, and blackened by powder.[27]

Major Henri Desagneaux, 359 Régiment d'Infanterie, 129th Division

It was during the next phase that one of the great lessons of the Great War was fully assimilated first by Haig, and then by Foch. As the Germans fell back, their reinforcements moved up, the Allied numerical superiority waned, the British units began to tire and the German resistance began to stiffen, especially when they could occupy the trenches that littered the old 1916 battlegrounds. By 10 August, just forty of the original 415 tanks were still in action. The attack began to run out of steam, little ground was gained on 11 August and the Germans were showing signs of stabilising the front. Further attacks would generate significant casualties without commensurate success. This was apparent to Rawlinson, well briefed by Lieutenant General Sir Arthur Currie (Canadian Corps) and Lieutenant General Sir John Monash (Australian Corps). Both these commanders firmly believed that their operations should be suspended until they had been able to reorganise, amass their forces and prepare properly for a renewed assault – in particular to allow time for the location of new German batteries. Foch was still intent on driving them forward, and at first Haig seemed prepared to consider only a short pause of a couple of days before a remarkable intervention by his subordinates finally changed his mind.

> At 10 am Sir Henry Rawlinson came to see me and brought photographs showing the state of the enemy's defences on the front Roye-Chaulnes. He also showed me a letter which he had received from General Currie commanding the Canadian Corps stating that to capture the position in question would be a very costly matter. He (Currie) was opposed to attempting it. I accordingly ordered the date of this attack to be postponed, but preparations to be continued with vigour combined with wire cutting and counter-battery work.[28]
>
> Field Marshal Sir Douglas Haig, General Headquarters, BEF

On the afternoon of 15 August, Haig had a face-to-face meeting with Foch to secure approval for the suspension of attacks by the Fourth Army and French First Army. He was wisely armed with a positive alternative in that he proposed to transfer his remaining reserves to the Third Army (General Sir Julian Byng) for an attack north of the River Somme.

> Foch now wanted to know what orders I had issued for attack: when I proposed to attack? Where? And with what troops? I think he really wanted a written statement to this effect from me for his records! I told Foch of my instructions to Byng and Horne; and that Rawlinson would also cooperate with his left between the Somme and the Ancre when Third Army had advanced and withdrawn some of the pressure which was still strong in that sector. I spoke to Foch quite straightly, and let him understand that I was

responsible for the handling of the British forces. Foch's attitude at once changed and he said all he wanted was early information of my intentions, so that he might coordinate the operations of the other armies, and that he thought I was quite correct in my decision not to attack the enemy in his prepared position.[29]

Field Marshal Sir Douglas Haig, General Headquarters, BEF

As might be imagined, Foch's version of this crucial meeting with Haig is far less dramatic. Perception is, after all, is in the eye of the beholder.

He repeated his reasons for believing that the attack south of the Somme would be hard and success doubtful, even at the price of considerable losses. He thought that the result sought might be obtained through means which, though indirect, were more sure, that is by having the British Third Army attack north of the Ancre, on the front Miraumont-Monchy le Preux, in a south-easterly direction, thus turning the line of the Somme south of Péronne. I definitely came around to the opinion of Field Marshal Sir Douglas Haig, and I modified my orders of August 12th for the Somme operations. But I made it a condition that the impetus given to the attack of the British Third Army should be such as to ensure the resumption of the drive south of the river with a view to attaining the objectives previously assigned to it.[30]

Maréchal de France Ferdinand Foch

For all his somewhat blustering tone, Haig was, after all, still conforming to the agenda set by Foch: the requirement to keep up the pressure on the Germans allowing them no time for rest, to reorganise, to think. But the conversation marked another stage in the acceptance, at the highest level, of the concept that persevering with any offensive beyond a few days would result in diminishing returns. From this point on they would strike hard at the point of their choosing, reap the benefits of the unleashed whirlwind, but then move on to the next offensive somewhere else. In effect they would be inside the command loop of the German generals: by the time they had observed what was happening, decided how to respond and begun to act, the focal point of the Allied offensive would have shifted, leaving the process to repeat. Thus, the Battle of Amiens ended. An advance of 12 miles had been made, but more important were the crippling losses and damage to morale suffered by the German Army. Allied casualties totalled 46,000, but the Germans lost up to 75,000 casualties, of whom nearly 30,000 were taken prisoner.

On 21 August, the Battle of Albert began as the British Third Army (General Sir Julian Byng) launched a vigorous offensive north of the Somme. In 1917 they would have had to undergo the laborious task of moving the artillery on to the front, but now each army had enough guns to allow a self-sufficient barrage. Meanwhile Mangin and his French Tenth Army were pressing hard north from Soissons, advancing 2–3 miles, taking over 8,000 prisoners and 100 guns. The French Sixth and Fifth Armies were also attacking across the River Vesle. In Flanders, the Germans did not wait to be attacked, but hastily withdrew from the bulbous Lys salient they had captured at such cost in April. In the south, plans were afoot for the Americans to pinch out the St Mihiel salient. Foch had an overall underpinning strategy to squeeze the Germans between the jaws of two converging attacks: the British and the left of the French armies would drive towards Cambrai; while the right of the French armies and the Americans would push towards Mézières. This was the hub at the centre of the German rail communications in northern France. Several of the major train lines between the occupied territory and the homeland ran through the town, and if these could be severed then the German logistics would be fatally disrupted. Meanwhile, the French armies in the centre would try and push the Germans back from the Aisne river line.

Amid the successes and the planning for the future, one very real problem facing the British was becoming evident – the declining strength of the Tank Corps. Their role in the attack, often at the 'sharp end' of battle, meant that losses in tanks and their crews were intolerable in the long term. In addition, the tanks still broke down with depressing regularity, but it was also apparent that the crews were operating in intolerable conditions. The air pollution inside a tank was a shocking cocktail of harmful chemicals that, along with the heat, drained the very life from the crews. The tank battalions had been withdrawn for two weeks in early September for rest, repairs and reorganisation, but the situation had not really been improved by this short-term remedial measure. It was far too late to bring forward a building programme for tanks to be used in the late 1918 campaign and there was a continuing crisis in the supply of trained crews for what they had, never mind any new tank battalions. If the war was to be won in 1918, then the tank contribution would be provided from the resources already possessed.

Intelligence sources revealed a severe German manpower shortage resulting in the frequent disbandment of units. Conscripts had been called up a full two years ahead of what would have been normal and the cupboard was almost bare. Under these circumstances, the German Army would be unable to maintain its front-line strength for much longer. Interviews with prisoners of war and captured documents revealed that overall German morale was friable, with some doubt as to whether the infantry would engage their enemies with the rifle, or would rather leave the real defensive work to their machine gunners. They were known to have severe supply problems with a general shortage of key materials. The German logistical situation was exacerbated by a dearth of lorries, petrol, draught horses and horse fodder, which made movement away from the railheads difficult. Taken as a whole, the German divisions were therefore increasingly lacking both the fresh drafts and the supplies needed to allow them to regenerate before returning to the line; which meant that their fighting efficiency was being badly degraded. Given time, they would be able to bring in and train another year of conscripts and rebuild their shattered formations. Both Foch and Haig were determined to deny them any such period of grace.

On 22 August, Haig sent a telegram to his army commanders to delineate the changed circumstances they now faced if they were to press home their advantage.

> To turn the present situation to account, the most resolute offen-
> sive is everywhere desirable. Risks, which a month ago would have
> been criminal to incur, ought now to be incurred as a duty. It is no
> longer necessary to advance in regular lines and step by step. On the

contrary, each division should be given a distant objective which must be reached independently of its neighbour, and even if one's flank is thereby exposed for the time being. Reinforcements must be directed on the points where our troops are gaining ground, not where they are checked. A vigorous offensive against the sectors where the enemy is weak will cause hostile strongpoints to fall, and in due course our whole army will be able to continue its advance. The situation is most favourable; let each one of us act energetically and without hesitation push forward to our objective.[31]

Field Marshal Sir Douglas Haig, General Headquarters, BEF

This was logical, but the consequences would be felt in thousands of British homes. Risks taken in pushing forward with open flanks meant that troops would often be exposed to higher casualties than might have been suffered with a more cautious approach. It was a price that Haig was willing to pay.

It was increasingly evident that many of the German soldiers had lost all hope of victory. Any optimism triggered by the spring advances had been dissipated. By September 1918, they found themselves almost back where they had started. The German effort to win the war before the arrival of significant American troops had clearly been stymied and the initiative had passed to the Allies. Leutnant Herbert Sulzbach was a loyalist and a devoted soldier – but even he could see which way the wind was blowing.

Our opponents, however, cannot be said to have achieved their main objective in any way at all: that is, to break through our line or to turn our flank and roll up our front. It was, however, a defeat in so far as the enemy deprived us of the initiative. But Ludendorff will find a way out! It is clear to us, in any event, that we miscalculated, and we have no idea what is going to happen to our offensive now. However, now and then we do have the feeling that it will be barely possible for us to get the better of this giant army of Frenchmen, Englishmen and Americans and their swarms of auxiliary nations, their incalculable quantities of equipment, raw materials and food supplies. But we just have to do it! And so we have moved into the fifth year of war, and no end is in sight yet.[32]

Leutnant Herbert Sulzbach, 5th Field Artillery Regiment, 9th Division

Perhaps indeed all was not lost? As the Germans retreated, the British found themselves once again facing what the Allies knew as the Hindenburg Line. First constructed as a fall-back position during the Somme fighting of 1916, it consisted of multiple trench lines, augmented by fortified villages, concrete machine-gun posts, reinforced deep dugouts and lashings of barbed wire, barring progress or channelling advancing troops into killing grounds dominated by flanking machine guns. By 1918, it had become a series of fortifications that stretched along the whole front and to which the Germans had given rather magnificent names. The Wotan Line ran from the English Channel to Arras, where it segued into the Siegfried Stellung – the original Hindenburg Line – running down to Soissons, where it became the Alberich Line, stretching to Lâon, from where the Hagen Line extended to the Swiss frontier. Behind this intimidating fortress line was the Herman Stellung, which continued into the Hundung-Brunhilde and Kriemhilde Stellungs, with, behind them, the Freya Stellung, a third series of positions still under construction. Finally, there was a plan to fall back to the much shorter Antwerp-Meuse Line, but this entailed the abandonment of all their gains of 1914. Yet the sacrifice would allow them the chance to concentrate resources, defend their borders and prolong the war deep into 1919, or even 1920. This last possibility was a constant anxiety to both Foch and Haig. They knew they had to keep up the momentum; they knew the mastery of defensive skills the Germans had demonstrated in the past – they must not be given a moment longer than necessary before the Hindenburg Line was assaulted by the Allies.

The Hindenburg Line had been adapted to incorporate many of the concepts of defence in depth introduced by the Germans in 1917. A Forward Battle Zone was succeeded by the Main Battle Zone and the Greater Battle Zone, followed by the Rearward Position and Rearward Battle Zone. The garrison of the forward zones was meant to disrupt an Allied attack, forcing the deployment of the supporting formations and

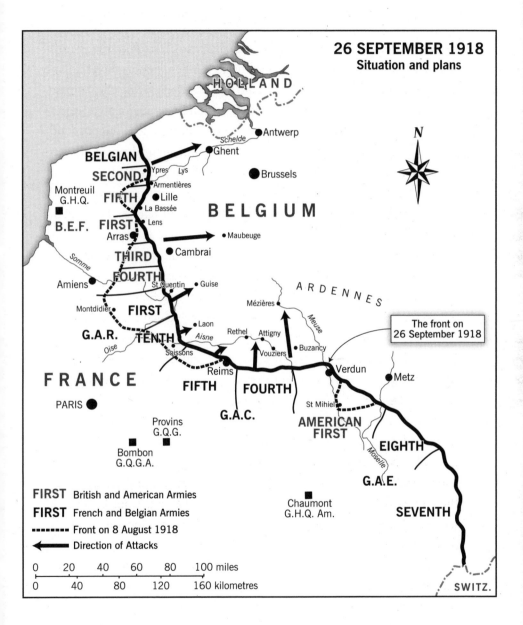

26 SEPTEMBER 1918
Situation and plans

HOLLAND

N

Schelde
Antwerp
Ghent

BELGIAN
SECOND
Ypres Lys
Armentières
Brussels

Montreuil
G.H.Q.
FIFTH
Lille
La Bassée

BELGIUM

B.E.F.
FIRST
Arras
Lens

Maubeuge

THIRD
Cambrai

Somme
FOURTH

ARDENNES

Amiens
St Quentin
Guise

Mézières
Meuse

Montdidier
FIRST
Laon
Rethel Attigny

The front on
26 September 1918

G.A.R.
TENTH
Oise
Aisne
Soissons
Vouziers
Buzancy

FRANCE
Reims
Verdun
Metz

PARIS
FIFTH
FOURTH
G.A.C.
St Mihiel

AMERICAN
FIRST

Provins
G.Q.G.

EIGHTH
Moselle

Bombon
G.Q.G.A.

G.A.E.

FIRST British and American Armies
FIRST French and Belgian Armies
------- Front on 8 August 1918
◄── Direction of Attacks

Chaumont
G.H.Q. Am.

SEVENTH

0	20	40	60	80	100 miles
0	40	80	120	160 kilometres	

SWITZ.

thereby disorganising the overall plan of assault. In the Forward Battle Zone troops were deployed sparingly, amid strongpoint posts with a heavy dependence on machine guns and single field guns firing from enfilading positions. The forward edge of the Greater Battle Zone was the 'front line' that covered the artillery gun positions. It was envisioned that this would be where the main battle was fought as the reinforcing *Eingreif* Divisions arrived to boost the garrison from their positions some 10–12,000 yards behind the front line. The *Eingreif* divisions were intended to interlock with the existing forward units to allow a decisive intervention either by an immediate impromptu counter-attack to prevent the Allies consolidating a captured position, or by a more considered prepared assault if the lost ground had such tactical significance that its loss threatened the overall integrity of the defences. The Hindenburg Line had been considerably modified to allow a defence in depth to be achieved with an Outpost Line thrust forward from the main line, utilising many of the former British defences that had been overrun in the March 1918 offensive.

The question was, what were the Allies going to do now? The choice was stark. It was the view of Wilson and the ever-cautious Pétain that they should hang on, consolidating their lines, garnering all their resources for what they considered would be the decisive battle in 1919. Cometh the hour and cometh the man. Foch was determined to seize the moment; the situation was sufficiently promising for him to envision a final series of lunges to try and finish off the Germans at the earliest possible moment, now that they had at last shown weakness. Although he still believed the war would probably only be won in 1919, Foch recognised the opportunity to finish the Germans in 1918. Earlier, Lloyd George had been an amused observer of Foch's physical demonstration of his tactical approach in front of the somewhat bemused figure of the British Foreign Secretary, Arthur Balfour.

> We then saw the General standing in front of the statesman indulging in violent pugilistic gestures first with his fists and then with his feet. We discovered afterwards that he was illustrating the great plan of his counter-offensive. When it began, he would hit here and hit there – he would use not only his two arms but both

his feet, hitting and kicking without cease so to give the enemy no time to recover. It turned out to be a dramatic forecast of the method which the great soldier was soon to employ.[33]

Prime Minister David Lloyd George

Now Foch was intent on making this a reality. He envisioned a series of assaults stretching along much of the Western Front. This was only rendered possible because the Allies had at last reached a position where they could plan a major offensive without laboriously moving the guns and stockpiling the millions of shells that would be required. This meant no long delays and the flexibility to launch a crushing assault without the lengthy warning periods that had preceded attacks during most of 1916 and 1917. The geographical separation between multiple attacks would stretch the German ability to concentrate their own reserves where they were needed. On 26 September, the Americans and French were to land the first blow, striking deep into the Meuse-Argonne area. Next day, 27 September, the British First and Third Armies would attempt to breach the Hindenburg Line pushing towards Cambrai. On 28 September, the French, Belgians and the British Second Army would launch forward in the Ypres area. Lastly, on 29 September, Fourth Army would assault the Hindenburg Line in the St Quentin Canal area.

These plans were bold – and, given the direction established by Wilson in his paper *British Military Policy, 1918–1919*, the intent of Foch and Haig to assault the Hindenburg Line caused consternation. Wilson had sanctioned attacks to clear the danger to Paris and the Channel Ports, to push the Germans back from the strategic rail junctions such as Amiens. Yet what Foch required of Haig and the BEF was a very different matter: this was a major assault against the most vaunted German fortifications on the Western Front – a fortress that had stood inviolate against previous attempts to secure a significant breach. On 1 September, Haig was mortified to receive a somewhat pusillanimous warning from Wilson.

The following telegram from Wilson reached me this morning. It is marked 'H.W. Personal' and was sent off yesterday:

Just a word of caution in regard to incurring heavy losses in attacks on the Hindenburg Line as opposed to losses when driving the enemy back to that line. I do not mean to say that you have incurred such losses, but I know the War Cabinet would become anxious if we received heavy punishment in attacking the Hindenburg Line WITHOUT SUCCESS. Wilson

It is impossible for a Chief of Imperial General Staff to send a telegram of this nature to a C-in-C in the field as a 'personal' one. The Cabinet are ready to meddle and interfere in my plans in an underhand way, but do not dare openly to say that they do not mean to take the responsibility for any failure though ready to take credit for every success! The object of this telegram is, no doubt, to save the Prime Minister in case of any failure. So I read it to mean that I can attack the Hindenburg Line if I think it right to do so. The CIGS and the Cabinet already know that my arrangements are being made to that end. If my attack is successful I will remain on as C-in-C. If we fail, or our losses are excessive, I can hope for no mercy. What a wretched lot of weaklings we have in high places at the present time.[34]

Field Marshal Sir Douglas Haig, General Headquarters, BEF

Haig's response was acerbic and took advantage of the 'personal' nature of the correspondence initiated by Wilson.

With reference to your wire *re* casualties in attacking the Hindenburg Line. What a wretched lot! And how well they mean to support me!! What confidence![35]

Field Marshal Sir Douglas Haig, General Headquarters, BEF

Wilson's faltering explanation that the Cabinet feared heavy losses cut no ice at all with the furious Haig, who was explicit in his contempt.

For many of these men the last battle still lay ahead. How ignorant these people are of war! In my opinion it is much less costly in lives to press the enemy after a victorious battle than to give him time to recover and organise afresh his defence of a position! The later must then be attacked in the face of hostile artillery and machine guns, all carefully sited.[36]

Field Marshal Sir Douglas Haig, General Headquarters, BEF

Haig was keen and ready for war. His men were less enthusiastic. That was understandable. The frenetic pace of the fighting over the last six months had exhausted many; yet although the men may have moaned among themselves – and to anyone who would listen – their underlying resolve to 'stick it out' remained intact.

Yes, the battalion has had a pretty sticky time, and there are many good fellows gone, though, all considered, our luck as regards offi-cers' casualties holds good. The battalion has gone up this morning, having been out only two days. They are in reserve for a stunt once more which means they'll drop into it once again, I suppose. I wish to God we could get out for a decent spell. The men are wonderful, but they're very, very tired.[37]

Lieutenant Alan Philbrick, 9th London Regiment (Queen Victoria's Rifles), 175th Brigade, 58th Division

2

BATTLE OF MEUSE-ARGONNE

We had been thinking ourselves veterans, but when one considers the matter we had not been under heavy fire before, and the experience was something we could have got along very well without.[1]

Lieutenant Robert Casey, A Battery, 124th Field Artillery 33rd Division

THE AMERICANS WERE COMING and they would have the honour of striking the first blow in Foch's interlinked series of gigantic offensives. The AEF had continued to build up its strength on the Western Front throughout 1918. Mirroring the British deployment at the start of the war, at first they had little impact on the shape of the war on the ground, other than participating in a few minor skirmishes. But slowly the pace of operations began to pick up: they made a significant contribution to the defensive battles fought by the French at Chateau-Thierry in late May; then they demonstrated both their courage and tactical naivety in the battle for Belleau Wood in June. It was a learning experience, right enough, but still only a minority of American soldiers had experienced the interminable shelling, the stench of gas, the raking machine guns

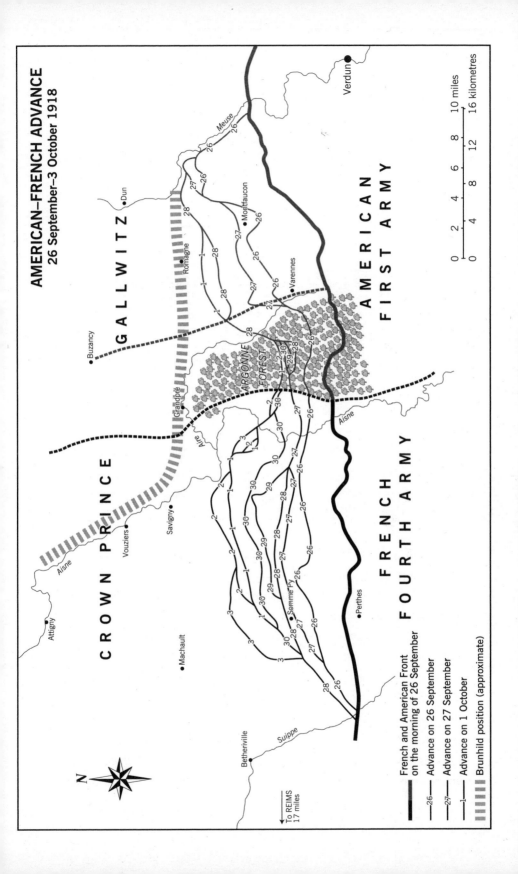

AMERICAN–FRENCH ADVANCE
26 September–3 October 1918

GALLWITZ

CROWN PRINCE

AMERICAN FIRST ARMY

FRENCH FOURTH ARMY

ARGONNE FOREST

Verdun

• Dun

Romagne •

• Montfaucon

Varennes •

• Buzancy

Grandpré

Aire

• Vouziers

• Savigny

Aisne

Aisne

Meuse

• Attigny

• Machault

Betheriville

Suippe

• Perthes

Somme Py •

To REIMS
17 miles

N

French and American Front
on the morning of 26 September
—26— Advance on 26 September
—27— Advance on 27 September
—1— Advance on 1 October
Brunhild position (approximate)

0   2   4   6   8   10 miles
0   4   8   12   16 kilometres

and the reality of fighting German soldiers who begged to differ that they were inferior to the 'Doughboys'. In July, the Americans had demonstrated further promise fighting alongside the French during the Second Battle of the Marne. As the weeks went by, more and more American divisions completed their training and were fed into the line, in addition to divisions recalled from 'loan' to the British and French, until finally the American First Army became a reality, with Pershing assuming command in addition to his AEF responsibilities.

On 12 September 1918, the First Army made its debut as a fighting formation in the Battle of St Mihiel. This was a considerable success, assisted by the coincidence that the Germans were already in the process of withdrawing from the St Mihiel salient when the assault commenced. Nevertheless, it was an invaluable 'dry run' through the basic requirements for a major offensive. The French provided the experienced II Colonial Corps and considerable artillery, aircraft, tank and logistical support, but such cooperation was the everyday lynchpin of Allied operations in 1918. Detailed plans had been produced by the American staff, the required logistical preparations carried out and a heavy barrage crashed down on the German lines. The American troops went over the top in fine style and soon brushed aside the German rearguards to achieve their objectives and pinch out the whole of the salient. It seemed that perhaps the more sanguine American soldiers were right; maybe war on the Western Front was easy? Sadly, any such optimists would soon be disabused of such views.

The next challenge was of a far greater order of difficulty. On 26 September, Foch had ordered the American First Army to attack alongside the French Fourth Army (General Henri Gouraud) in the Meuse-Argonne area. This was a real challenge and might be seen as Foch exacting a high price for allowing the Americans to fight together in an army. Their battlefield was a shallow valley some 20 miles wide, an area of rolling ridges dotted with woods, crossed by small streams, all bounded by the deep River Meuse to their right. This in turn was backed by the Heights of the Meuse, which provided an invaluable vantage point for flanking fire from the east. On the left, also standing above the valley, were the tangled hills and ravines of the Argonne Forest, flanked by the River Aire to the east and the River Aisne to the west. This time the Germans were not withdrawing – far from it. Having occupied the area since 1914, they had plenty of time to prepare, and had created a series of barbed wire traps, carefully sited trenches, concrete bunkers and machine-gun posts, with plentiful artillery positions lurking out of sight. Their efficient railway system also promised rapid reinforcements in the event of a serious Allied assault – up to six divisions could be rushed up in within 48 hours. Three main systems of defences barred the way: the Giselher Stellung Line stretched on either side of the Montfaucon Hill in the centre of the valley; 10 miles behind that there was the Kriemhilde Stellung, stretching from Grandpré through Romagne to Brieulle sur Meuse; and, finally, a further 5 miles back, the Freya Stellung. These heavy-duty fortifications were intended to cover the Sedan-Mézières railway, the capture of which would break the German front asunder, isolating their armies to the north. Foch required Pershing to complete the capture of the Kriemhilde Stellung within two days. They were then to push on to the town of Stonne, thereby assisting the advance of Gouraud's Fourth Army, which was to push through the Champagne district towards Rheims.

There were enormous logistical difficulties in transporting the bulk of the First Army, some 600,000 men, the 50 to 60 miles from the St Mihiel Salient area to relieve the 200,000 men of the French Second Army in the Meuse-Argonne area. All this across an area that was ill served with roads and railways, and had to be shared with French units. Just moving the artillery would be a labour of Hercules, involving the movement of thousands of guns and hundreds of thousands of tons of ammunition. As an added complication, this all had to be carried out at night in an effort to preserve an element of surprise. Unsurprisingly, staff movement plans faltered in the face of the realities – and to make matters worse it had begun to pour with rain. Once the troops were in position – so easily written yet so difficult to achieve – the Americans were ready to attack.

The First Army would attack on a 24-mile front, stretching from the west side of the Argonne Forest to the River Meuse. Next to the French Fourth Army, which would be advancing on their left, were I

Corps (28th, 35th, 77th, and 92nd Divisions); V Corps (32nd, 37th, 79th
and 91st Divisions) in the centre; and III Corps (3rd, 4th, 33rd and 80th
Divisions) on the right. The assault divisions would advance supported
by a barrage fired by nearly 2,711 guns. Pershing was aware of the danger
of rapid German reinforcements, so he planned for an advance of 10
miles to overwhelm the Kriemhilde Stellung within the first day; this was
ambitious in the extreme and demanded the near-immediate capture of
the imposing Montfaucon Hill position, which rose over 250 feet above
the surrounding terrain. One further problem facing Pershing was that
several of his most practised divisions – the 1st, 2nd, 42nd and 89th –
had been employed in an effort to guarantee success in the St Mihiel
offensive. This meant that the initial Meuse-Argonne assault would have
to be made by far less experienced troops. Pershing was conscious of the
inexperience of his divisions, and saw his role as driving them on, while
monitoring the command performance of his generals to ensure that they
demonstrated sufficient vigour. Of sophisticated tactics he knew little; all
his divisions would advance forward at the same Zero Hour – 05.30 on 26
September – charged with overcoming whatever got in their way. There
was no subtlety – just the vigorous application of brute force.

The Argonne Forest was an obvious problem as it was a terrifying
prospect for any troops. A wild, almost mountainous terrain, some 6
miles wide and 22 miles long, impenetrable by tanks and tailor-made for
defence, with a jumble of high jagged ridges, deep ravines and swamp-
lands, shrouded by forest and tangled undergrowth. The obstacles of
nature were trumped by a lethal concoction of concealed trenches, concrete machine-gun posts and masses of barbed wire. It was decided that
the French and Americans were to push forward on either side of the
forest, looking to pinch out the resulting salient, with the 77th Division, commanded by Major General Robert Alexander, moving straight
through the forest itself. His divisional artillery had been generously supplemented by six French batteries of 75mm guns, one battery of 155mm
guns and some 190 trench mortars, but Alexander was disarmingly frank
in his post-war admission as to the difficulties his men faced.

I endeavoured to determine upon some outstanding tactical feature of the terrain of the Bosche organizations, which would indicate an appropriate manoeuvre for the purpose of overcoming opposition. I was unable to discover in the Forest proper any such position. Consequently, at the inception of the operations, all that I could contemplate was a straight push forward of the whole line; and I was obliged to depend upon the initiative of the subordinate commanders, specifically the platoon and company commanders, for the proper manoeuvre of their units when the necessity for such manoeuvre became apparent. Therefore, no effort was made by me in my orders to specify anything more than a straight push to the front.[2]

Major General Robert Alexander, Headquarters, 77th Division

His artillery batteries also had problems as they were moved into position. Although the trees had been thinned out around the front-line trenches, further back, where the gun lines would be, the ridges were still heavily wooded. Tracks had to be hacked out to manhandle the guns into position and this was just the start of the hard labour.

Ammunition was the chief difficulty. The firing would be intense. Consequently, vast quantities of shells would be required at the emplacements. Time was short. Word to commence firing might come at any minute. Yet a point on the road about 400 metres from the guns was the nearest place to which projectiles could be transported on wheels. The G.S. carts dropped them there, and the battery men carried them one by one through the tangled underbrush.[3]

Second Lieutenant Charles Camp, Headquarters, 305th Field Artillery, 77th Division

Then there was the need to clear a field of fire for the guns themselves, which proved to be no easy matter.

For two days, the sound of saws and axes rang through the woods. Every tree which in any way obstructed the passage of shells was cut through so far that a few more strokes would bring it down. All along the ridge where the artillery was massed the splendid beeches which furnished such perfect concealment before the battle were to be demolished. They were like a drop curtain on a stage: the audience looks at the forest scene; then the stage is darkened for a moment, and when the lights are turned on the forest had disappeared, and the guns that have been hidden are revealed. About 10 o'clock in the evening the order was given to fell the trees doomed to sacrifice. Details of men went out with axes to give the final blows. There was a grating, crunching sound, then a terrific crash, and the first great monarch of the forest plunged head foremost down the hill. From that moment on, the woods re-echoed with the swishing and crashing of falling trees, until the roar was so great it seemed as if the enemy must hear it. Toward midnight the work was all but finished and the sound died down; and then for some time, save for the hit-or-miss shelling by the Germans, the quiet was unbroken.[4]

Captain James Howard, Headquarters, 304th Field Artillery, 77th Division

As the 77th Division moved into the line on the night of the 25 September, many of the infantry were issued with totally unfamiliar grenades and pyrotechnics. The American soldiers were still unaware of many of the new weapons and techniques of trench warfare; things that had become second nature to the experienced units of the British and French armies.

An officer stood at the roadside explaining their various purposes and methods of functioning, and expounding, like a patent-medicine artist at a fair, their many sterling qualities. 'This one will call down a friendly barrage in your front; you better take a couple. This one will indicate your position to a passing aeroplane, works equally well by day or night, every soldier should have one (wait till the plane circles about and drops six white stars). This will burn through flesh and bone and provide a high quality of illumination for night attacks – may be thrown by hand or from the rifle. And here is one – with apologies for the fact that it weighs 10 pounds – that will destroy man and beast within a radius of 40 yards' – pressing it into the arms of some bewildered soldier! And so on till his voice was lost in the darkness.[5]

Captain Walter Rainsford, 3/307th Regiment, 154th Brigade, 77th Division

The gunners were understandably tense as they waited to begin the barrage all along the line. There was always the fear that the Germans might divine their intentions, might open fire first with a massive counter-battery bombardment to sweep the guns away. Curiously, the regimental secretary of 304th Field Artillery had been invited to accompany the men to the front.

I looked at my watch. It was 20 minutes past 12. 'Crack! Crack! Crack!' Seemingly just outside our door three shells broke. Then a number more distant. I reached for my mask, but neither the Captain nor his Lieutenant glanced up from their work. The Bosche was sending them over in quantities now. Their crashing explosions sounded like a bombardment, and I was certain that our surprise plans had become known to the enemy and that he was anticipating our attack by a couple of hours. I expected a show of excitement, hurried orders brought and given, a certain tenseness of dramatic crisis, but Captain Lyman went on reading, 'Target No. 3: base deflection left fifteen, range two seven hundred, twelve rounds sweeping', and McVaugh would reply, 'Check!' Again, the klaxon sounded and we held our breaths while we adjusted masks. On the tail of its mournful sound an orderly burst into the room, 'A shell in the gun pit, Sir, and a man badly wounded!' he reported. In a few moments, the stretcher-bearers brought in the form of Private Clarence Manthe, wounded so seriously that one glance told me the only issue. Captain Lyman knelt beside him and soothed him by words of well-earned praise, while the surgeon worked to make the last hour of the lad less painful. I sat beside Manthe to ease his passing, pressing my canteen to his lips when the fever burned. 'You are going over, boy', I said softly. 'Is there a message I can take?' 'My mother, tell her I died like a soldier,' he whispered. I voiced a prayer, the captain kneeling alongside and

Manthe[6] closed his eyes for the last sleep. A few minutes later I nodded to the surgeon. He felt for pulse and heart, then placed a tag with pencilled date and hour upon the breast and drew a blanket over the dead.[7]

Regimental Secretary Perry Newberry, Headquarters, 304th Field Artillery, 77th Division

In the front line, Captain Walter Rainsford was waiting with the men of L Company.

The upper air grew alive with whistling sounds; on the high ground in front the shock of explosions merged into one deep concussion that rocked the walls of the dugouts. The night was thick with mist and bitterly cold – a pale thread of moon gliding and disappearing amidst the moving vapour, the lurid glare flickering up and down along the front. As the night dragged on the mist thickened, wrapping the world in its blind, cold blanket, and blotting out the last stark tree-stump ahead.[8]

Captain Walter Rainsford, 3/307th Regiment, 154th Brigade, 77th Division

At 05.50 they went over the top. This then was their moment. Almost at once they were lost.

I climbed out with the nearest platoon into darkness and impenetrable fog mixed with powder-smoke, started them forward by compass, and went to look, or feel, for the others. I didn't find them again until afternoon. Our artillery was supposed to have blown a passage through the heaviest wire between some craters marked on the map near the head of the Ravin Sec, but there didn't seem much chance of finding it by sense of touch. The heavy fog had kept the powder-smoke down, and as morning began to lighten I found myself adrift in a blind world of whiteness and noise, groping over something like the surface of the moon. One literally could not see 2 yards, and everywhere the ground rose into bare pinnacles and ridges, or descended into bottomless chasms, half filled with rusted tangles of wire. Deep, half-ruined trenches appeared without system or sequence, usually impossible of crossing, bare splintered trees, occasional derelict skeletons of men, thickets of gorse, and everywhere the piles of rusted wire. It looked as though it had taken root there among the iron *chevaux de frise* and had grown; and it was so heavy that only the longest-handled cutters would bite through it. There seemed to be very little rifle-fire going on and the shelling was still almost all in front and growing more distant.[9]

Captain Walter Rainsford, 3/307th Regiment, 154th Brigade, 77th Division

Having lost touch with the other companies of his battalion, Rainsford was stumbling blindly forward, trying to collect what men he could. At this stage in the attack, the visibility and undergrowth were more of a problem than the Germans.

I figured that we had gone nearly a mile forward without meeting any Germans save two or three killed by shells; the fog was as blind as ever, and we hadn't an idea of what was happening on the ridges to either flank; I knew we were too far to eastward but didn't want to leave the high ground until we could see something. We had got beyond the bare moon-country into a dense forest of undergrowth, and were working out the very recently occupied trenches and boyaus when, about noon, the mist suddenly rolled up. There appeared first a deep valley to the west, then a farther slope of brush with scattering pine trees, the sun shining on their wet tops, and finally the wooded ridge to southward from which we had come.[10]

Captain Walter Rainsford, 3/307th Regiment, 154th Brigade, 77th Division

Pushing forward with more confidence, now they could actually see where they were going, they encountered their first German opposition. They tried to deploy their new rifle grenades, but their lack of experience was soon sadly obvious.

We slipped and slid down to the valley bottom and were met with automatic rifle fire from the farther crest. We were able to outflank them on both sides, though, and they didn't make much of a stand. I told Lieutenant Rogers to try out our new model thermite rifle grenades on them, but nothing occurred, and I didn't discover till long afterward that the detonators came in separate boxes.[11]

Captain Walter Rainsford, 3/307th Regiment, 154th Brigade, 77th Division

Among the second wave of advancing troops was machine gunner Corporal Thomas Grady, who was moving forward in support of the 2/306th Regiment.

Reached his second line trench and was showered with shrapnel and machine-gun fire. Mounted our guns and fired a few bursts of harassing fire into the thickets, and the 'Doughboys' went over. Before we could dismount and catch up, they plunged ahead regardless. We finally caught up to them in the third line where they captured five machine guns and about fifty prisoners. *Beaucoup* dead and wounded lying around. Plugged on slowly and it was a tough grind for us. Snipers were active and we lost a couple of scouts. Pulled up a terrible hill and noticed two Jerry observation balloons about 2 miles ahead. For the next hour we were shelled pretty heavy. We cleared out a couple of machine-gun nests in short order. Up and down hills, thru swamps and mire, and constantly climbing over fallen trees, and tangled wire.[12]

Corporal Thomas Grady, 2/305th Machine Gun Battalion, 153rd Brigade, 77th Division

They made some progress, but that night the whole forest was full of confused and separated elements of the assault units. Rainsford summed it up perfectly as he tried to find his way back to his battalion headquarters.

It was black night, and my guide confided the news that, though he knew where Battalion headquarters was, he didn't know how to get there. It reminded me of the lost Indian who said, 'Indian not lost. Indian here. Wigwam lost!' Only now it seemed probable that both the wigwam and the Indian were lost, together with most of the tribe. My conversation with the guide did not assist me to any idea of 'where it was', though he still had confidence in his knowledge of it; and by one o'clock, in a 15-foot trench, with unscalable walls of mud and a stream along its bottom, I knew where nothing was except the guide, my company headquarters, and half a platoon. It rained all night and we slept in the stream.[13]

Captain Walter Rainsford, 3/307th Regiment, 154th Brigade, 77th Division

These almost insuperable problems would only intensify as the fighting continued. Far behind them, plagued by the dreadful communications and minimal visibility, the divisional headquarters and gunners were effectively blind to what was going on in the depths of the forest that lay in front of them.

As we advanced, however, north of the Bosche first line, the opposition encountered became at each step more determined in character and our losses began to mount up rather rapidly. It seemed that the enemy garrison of the forest was very deeply echeloned in depth, and that consequently, as the leading enemy elements fell back, they received more and more support from the organisations in rear. The opposition encountered was not sufficient to stop the line, but it was sufficient to inflict considerable losses upon our advancing infantry. It is to be noted here that after the initial push at 5.30 am, which had been preceded by the fire of preparation, practically no assistance whatever could be rendered to the infantry by the artillery against the enemy front line. The reason for this lack of assistance was in no sense the fault of the artillery, but was entirely due to conditions of terrain. The Forest was so thick that no observation of fire was possible. In addition to this, the opposing lines during practically all of the time that we were within the Forest proper were within 50 to 100 metres of each other. Consequently, fire from our friendly artillery would have been as dangerous to my line as to the enemy.[14]

Major General Robert Alexander, Headquarters, 77th Division

His infantry would bitterly endorse this viewpoint. As neither the French on their left, nor the Americans on their right had made much progress in enveloping the forest, the men of 77th Division were on their own in the woods.

On the rest of the I Corps front, the 28th Division had made progress before grinding to a halt in front of a rocky outcrop extruding from the flank of the Argonne Forest. Alongside them, the 35th Division operations were noteworthy for a concentrated attack by some 142 Renault tanks and a few of the heavier Schneider tanks. They were under the charge of a charismatic officer, Lieutenant Colonel George Patton of the 1st Tank Brigade. He planned to attack in force on either side of the fordable River Aire running down alongside the east side of the Argonne Forest. The tanks went forward and the impatient Patton had soon left the headquarters and pursued them on foot. The chaos he encountered might have disturbed him, but it was not surprising as the American tanks and infantry had had no chance to train together. Neither arm really understood what the other was doing.

> At 9.30 we came to a town called Cheppy. I went past the infantry as we were supposed to have taken the place. But all at once we got shot at from all sides. Pretty soon some of our infantry came running back. So, as none of my men had any rifles, I went back with the infantry, but stopped before they did. Also I stopped in a better place just back of a crest. When we got here it began to clear up and we were shot at to beat hell with shells and machine guns. Twice the infantry started to run, but we hollered at them and called them all sorts of names so they stayed. But they were scared some and acted badly, some put on gas masks, some covered their face with their hands but none did a damned thing to kill Bosches.[15]
>
> Lieutenant Colonel George Patton, Headquarters, 1st Tank Brigade, Tank Corps

Patton was clearly losing control of his temper – a trait that would be a hallmark of his rumbustious career. His behaviour was utterly unacceptable and should have been considered as murder.

Some of my reserve tanks were stuck by some trenches. So I went back and made some Americans hiding in the trenches dig a passage. I think I killed one man here. He would not work so I hit him over the head with a shovel. It was exciting for they shot at us all the time, but I got mad and walked on the parapet. At last we got five tanks across and I started them forward and yelled and cussed and waved my stick and said come on. About 150 'Dough-boys' started but when we got to the crest of the hill the fire got fierce right along the ground. We all lay down. I saw that we must go forward or back and I could not go back so I yelled, 'Who comes with me?' A lot of 'Doughboys' yelled, but only six of us started. My striker, me and four 'Doughs'. I hoped the rest would follow but they would not. Soon there were only three but we could see the machine guns right ahead so we yelled to keep up our courage and went on. Then the third man went down and I felt a blow in the leg but at first I could walk so I went about 40 feet when my leg gave way. My striker, the only man left, yelled, 'Oh God, the Colo-nel's hit and there ain't no one left!' He helped me over to a shell hole and we lay down and the Bosches shot over the top as fast as he could. He was very close. The tanks began getting him and in about an hour it was fairly clear. Some of my men carried me out under fire which was not at all pleasant.[16]

Lieutenant Colonel George Patton, Headquarters, 1st Tank Brigade, Tank Corps

Patton's orderly (or 'striker' as he calls him), Private Joseph Angelo, was the only one of the six volunteers to survive Patton's headstrong initia-tive. Massed tanks or not, the men of the 35th Division were caught in terrible shellfire as they struggled forward, and although they eventually captured Varennes late in the day, it was at a terrible cost.

Elsewhere, there were mixed results for the First Army. On the right, next to the Meuse, the III Corps made excellent progress, breaking through the Gishelher Stellung with an advance that stretched up to 4 miles. However, the crucial attack in the centre of the line on the Mont-faucon Hill, made by V Corps, under the command of General George

Cameron, soon stumbled to an embarrassing halt despite early gains. Unwisely, the raw 79th Division had been assigned the task of capturing the stronghold, despite the fact it had only been in France since early August 1918. During its short history, it had already been plundered for replacements for other divisions, and many of the men had only been in the army a matter of five months. The divisional commander was Major General Joseph Kuhn, an engineer with minimal pre-war involvement with the infantry and, like so many of the American generals, he lacked any experience in commanding a formation on the scale of a division. His men faced a determined German garrison, deploying the full gamut of deadly machine-gun fire, crunching bombardments and deadly counter-attacks. The 313th and 314th Regiments of the 157th Brigade made the initial assault, attacking on a 2-mile front, followed up by the 158th Brigade. The 313th Regiment had to pass through the Bois de Melancourt, then across a gap to the Bois de Cuisy; while in contrast the 314th Regiment on their right faced open ground across to the town of Melancourt and then up to the heights of Montfaucon – all to be negotiated under heavy fire. Each approach posed different military problems and their commanders proved unable to coordinate the attacks, while back at headquarters Kuhn had no idea what was going on. The approach of the 314th was benefited by fog, but when it lifted they were exposed to a devastating fire and could get no further than Melancourt. Meanwhile, 313th captured the Bois de Melancourt, then struggled across the gap between the woods, took the Bois de Cuisy and even penetrated the town of Montfaucon itself. But it was all to no avail as they were then thrown back by strong German counter-attacks.

Kuhn was considered to have performed poorly on the first day. Captain Charles Donnelly, serving with the artillery of the neighbouring 32nd Division, was contemptuous of the 'old school' attributes of Kuhn and his like. One brief encounter crystallised his opinion.

> The General and his aide were afoot, dressed in well-pressed spotless uniforms, shining boots and wearing stocks. Stocks were made of stiff white linen and were worn inside the stand-up collars of blouses on social or formal occasions, but on a battlefield during

combat? This was the commanding General of the 79th Division! He stopped about 50 feet away from us and sent his aide to ask what the situation was like with the 199th. I had an immediate dislike of the General. Why send his aide to get information which we could have given him directly? It seemed as though he did not want to get too close to us for fear of getting contaminated in some way. The aide, a young Lieutenant, was burdened with his own trench coat and the general's, a pair of field glasses, map case, his own and the general's gas masks and attached to his Sam Browne belt were a pistol, ammunition clips, first aid kit, canteen and a compass. I thought to myself, 'You old bastard. You treat your aide as though he were a servant. And the way your troops are behaving reflects the kind of leadership they have been getting!'[17]

Captain Charles Donnelly, 1/119th Field Artillery, 32nd Division

Afterwards a controversy arose as to whether elements of the neighbouring 4th Division (Major General John Hines), could, or indeed should, have helped 79th Division capture Montfaucon Hill that day. His 7th Brigade had strayed across the notational divisional/corps border shared with 79th Division, forcing the retreat of some of the German garrison on the eastern slopes of Montfaucon. As his troops had attained their objectives by 12.00, Hines, prompted by his brigadiers, suggested that 4th Division should attack the Montfaucon Hill from the east flank, while the 79th Division continued to push ahead from below. This intriguing suggestion fell on deaf ears. Brigadier General Alfred Bjornstad, the Chief of Staff of III Corps, would have none of it, ordering the 4th Division to keep out of 79th Division ground and to push forward, aiming for the Kriemhilde Stellung while ignoring the gaping opportunity to his left flank. Bjornstad would later claim that he was afraid that if he let his III Corps troops 'trespass' into the 79th Division sector, they might be shelled by V Corps artillery with terrible consequences. This, though, may well be dissembling; the III Corps Commander Major General Robert Bullard had issued strict instructions before the battle – his divisions were to press on, ignoring the trials and tribulations of their neighbours.

Before the attack, I had called together my division commanders
and told them that in every fight in which I had thus far taken
part I had heard division, brigade and regimental commanders
excuse their failures to continue the advance by blaming the units
on their right, or left, for a failing to come forward with them. 'I
shall take no such excuse on this occasion,' I added. 'Each of your
divisions maintains its reserve for the very purpose of protecting
your flanks.'[18]

Major General Robert Bullard, Headquarters, III Corps

The controversy over the alleged missed opportunity would rage on for
decades. What is certain is that the 4th Division did not help with a flank
attack on Montfaucon.

On 27 September, Kuhn threw his men forward again. And this time
an assault by his 157th Brigade actually took Montfaucon Hill. In a sense,
this was an achievement, but it was far too late. The 48-hour 'grace' was
up and German divisions had rushed to reinforce the locality – indeed
four had already arrived by nightfall on 26 September. Many more were
on the way. Dreams of breaching the Kriemhilde Stellung were exposed as
just that – dreams. For the next few days the American First Army would
be advancing, but they were advancing with ever greater difficulty towards
a metaphorical brick wall.

To modern eyes, a far greater scandal than the failure to capture
Montfaucon Hill was the American treatment of their African-American
soldiers. This is typified by the fate of the 369th Regiment (originally the
15th New York Regiment), the first African-American recruited regiment
to serve on the Western Front. Racial discrimination, indeed outright
segregation, was endemic in American society, but thousands of African-
American citizens had volunteered or been called up, many full of the
hope that when they returned their efforts would be recognised and
rewarded by a reduction in that prejudice. Although senior officers were
mostly white, African-Americans were also commissioned, which seemed
a small step forward. However, the omens remained bleak, given the backdrop of vicious race riots in the summer of 1917. The New Yorkers were
the recipients of overt racism from within the army and from the local

community during their training at Camp Wadsworth in South Carolina. When sent out to France they were initially consigned to a non-combat role as a labour battalion, amid claims that 'white' American soldiers would not serve with them. However, the French Army, desperate for more men and with its successful experience of using African colonial infantry, had a far greater appreciation of the potential military merits of 369th Regiment. In May 1918, they were transferred to serve first in the French 16th Division, with which they had active service in the Second Battle of the Marne, and then the 161st Division. Their colonel was proud of his men, but his remarks reveal his own racism.

> The French officers say they are entirely different from their own African troops and the Indian troops of the British, who are so excitable under shellfire. Of course, I have explained that my boys are public school boys, no caste prejudice, accustomed to the terrible noises of the subway, elevated and street traffic of New York City (which would drive any desert man or Himalaya mountaineer mad) and are all Christians. Also, that while the more ignorant ones might not like to have a black cat hanging around for fear it would turn into a fish or something, they have no delusions about the Bosche shells coming from any 'Heathen Gods'. They know the damn child-killing Germans are firing at them with pyro-cellulose and they know how the breech mechanism works. I've learned more about the military game, at least the fighting of this war, since I have been here with the French than I learned in all the years as drummer boy, Private, Sergeant, Captain, Major and Colonel Second Nebraska Infantry, Spanish War, manoeuvres, Officers' School, etc., etc. And another thing, I believe I know more about Negro soldiers and how to handle them, especially the problem of Negro and white officers, than any other man living today. Of course, the other regiment I commanded for three years was a white regiment, so I had a lot to learn, but I've learned it and I wouldn't trade back now.[19]

Colonel William Hayward, Headquarters, 369th Regiment, 161st Division

On 26 September, as part of Gouraud's Fourth Army, the 369th were attacking across the River Dormoise, a tributary of the River Aisne that ran down the west side of the Argonne Forest, so near yet so far from Pershing's First Army. Pershing did, however, show enough interest to remove all the remaining African-American officers; the 369th was to be an all-white officered unit. The 2nd and 3rd Battalions were used in the initial assault and they had considerable success, as the German opposition seems to have evaporated in the face of the phenomenal French barrage that preceded them. It was not surprising.

> Where there had been a trench 7 feet or more deep, there now existed hardly an impression in the earth; where there had been an impassable barrier of barbed wire, snarled as only the Germans and the devil know how to arrange it, there was now only a few occasional strands of wire protruding or laying on the ground here and there; where there had been a grove of trees, now only a few gaunt, seared spars pointed heavenward.[20]
>
> Sergeant Hannibal Davis, 1/369th Regiment, 161st Division

At first all went well, but as they approached the Dormoise, the 3/369th found a swamp defended by several German machine guns. Captain Hamilton Fish, the commander of K Company, sent a message back to the colonel, selecting Private Elmer McCowan for this dangerous mission.

> The Captain asked me to carry despatches. The Germans pumped machine-gun bullets at me all the way. But I made the trip and back safely. Then I was sent out again. As I started with the message the Captain yelled to bring him back a can of coffee. He was joking, but I didn't know it at the time. Being a foot messenger, I had some time ducking those German bullets. Those bullets seemed very sociable, but I didn't care to meet up with them, so I kept right on travelling on high gear. None touched my skin, though some skinned pretty close. On the way back, it seemed the whole war was turned on me. One bullet passed through my trousers and it made me hop, step, and jump pretty lively. I saw a shell hole 6 feet deep. Take it from me, I dented another 6 feet when I plunged into it hard. In my fist I held the Captain's can of coffee! When I climbed out of the shell hole and started running again, a bullet

clipped a hole in the can and the coffee started spill. But I turned around, stopped a second, looked the Kaiser in the face, and held up the can of coffee with my finger plugging up the hole to show the Germans they were fooled. Just then another bullet hit the can and another finger had to act as a stopgap. It must have been good luck that saved my life, because bullets were picking at my clothes and so many hit the can that at the end all my fingers were hugging it to keep the coffee in. I jumped into shell holes, wriggled along the ground, and got back safely. And what do you think? When I got back into our own trenches I stumbled – and spilled the coffee![21]

Private Elmer McCowan, 3/369th Regiment, 161st Division

Unlikely though this story may appear, it was confirmed by the battalion adjutant, who added something rather more significant about Private McCowan's conduct that day.

When that soldier came back with the coffee his clothes were riddled with bullets. Yet half an hour later he went back into No-Man's Land and brought back a number of wounded until he was badly gassed. Even then he refused to go to the rear and went out again for a wounded soldier. All this under fire. That's the reason he got the Distinguished Service Cross.[22]

Lieutenant George Miller, 3/369th Regiment, 161st Division

Much hard fighting followed, with the 369th giving a good account of itself in the drive towards the town of Séchault. It is difficult not to look at the story of Private Elmer McCowan as a parable illustrating the treatment of the willing soldiers of the 369th Regiment and all of the other African-American regiments by the American military establishment.

All told, the first few days of the Meuse-Argonne offensive had been a painful experience for the Americans, as the casualties ratcheted above 45,000. The move to the Meuse-Argonne had been overly rushed, far too soon after the St Mihiel attack, but also the wrong units had been assigned to tackle the most challenging objectives. Logistics were a complete nightmare, as the inadequate infrastructure of the area was combined with the relative inexperience of the American staff officers. Preparations had been too hurried, completed in days rather than the weeks or even months required to ensure real success. As ever, the battlefield communications had failed, with commanders in the field often left unaware of what was happening to their men. The absence of heavy tanks was regrettable but sadly unavoidable, for the British had none spare due to their own shortages and the near continuous programme of attacks scheduled in the north. The initial allocation of light Renault tanks had been rapidly eroded and within days reduced to almost nothing. Worst of all, the Germans had moved some sixteen divisions to the front. On 29 September, Pershing temporarily suspended offensive operations except for the continuing battle in the Argonne Forest itself. He would reshuffle his divisions, replacing those found wanting or too battered to continue; bringing in his more experienced divisions.

From afar, calculating eyes were assessing the performance of the American First Army: indeed, Foch, Haig and Pétain were all still hopeful of persuading Pershing to let them employ his divisions within their armies. On 30 September, Foch visited Haig and the two old comrades discussed the American effort.

> As regards the American operations west of Meuse, he says Americans have employed too many troops on that front, and have blocked one another's advance. In fact, they have not been able to feed so many divisions in that area. But they are going on attacking and are 'learning all the time'. Pétain is now using some American troops to push on towards Machault (southeast of Rethel). I asked Foch to send three American Divisions to Plumer. Foch said it was not possible at present as 'Their *amour propre* made the Americans determined to press on to Mézières!' But later on, 'He would see what could be done when Pershing has learnt the difficulty of creating an army.'[23]

Field Marshal Sir Douglas Haig, General Headquarters, BEF

An earlier visit by the French Prime Minister Georges Clemenceau on 29

September had triggered considerable unpleasantness, as he was caught up in the awful logistical mess and consequent enormous traffic jams behind the American lines, and thus had to abandon his planned visit to Montfaucon. This unfortunate experience led Clemenceau to believe the chaos was caused by the administrative incompetence of the American staff and ultimately attributed it to Pershing, whom he saw as incompetent. This escalated as he demanded Foch do something about it and 'take the situation in hand'. When Pétain joined in, claiming that American lack of progress was costing French lives on the neighbouring Fourth Army front, the situation began to drift out of control. But Foch was equal to the challenge, in effect, protecting Pershing from Clemenceau's wrath, at some cost to their own relationship, and, instead of attempting to 'order' or 'command' Pershing, which would have been futile, instead successfully pressed Pershing to launch a second wave of attacks as soon as possible in October.

BACK IN THE COLD DARK CONFINES of the Argonne forest, the 77th Division was struggling on. By now it was apparent what torments lay ahead of inexperienced troops in trying to wrest such ideal defensive ground from the Germans.

> A more difficult country for an infantry advance, or one better suited to delaying rearguard action, it would be hardly possible to find. The ridges were cloaked in a dense growth of small trees and the bottoms choked with underbrush; it was seldom possible to see over 20 yards, often not five; the keeping of direction and of contact was a problem new with every moment, and each opening through the leafy wall was a death trap. There was rifle fire from across the narrow valleys – it needed but a few men to do it, well hidden in chosen spots, and looking for a glimpse of khaki among the green, or the shaking of bushes; there were bursts of automatic fire down the narrow lanes – if the gun had been sighted already, the sound of crashing progress was target enough; there was the slow steady drain of casualties, with never a blow to be struck in

return, and oh, the long weary way those wounded had to travel back.[24]

Captain Walter Rainsford, 3/307th Regiment, 154th Brigade, 77th Division

Captain Thornton Thayer of 305th Field Artillery was meant to be acting as a forward observation officer, advancing alongside the 307th, but he found the heavy woodland nullified all his best efforts to assist the infantry.

Observation of fire was practically impossible, and although I went forward to the infantry front line, and even beyond it, in an effort to obtain information that would enable us to fire more effectively, it proved almost useless. On one occasion, we worked well out in advance of our own line in hopes of being able to observe the effectiveness of a rolling barrage which they were to follow up. Sniping fire from enemy machine guns stopped us and, for a quarter of an hour during which time we had to work back across a 20 foot band of barbed wire and dodge across a wood road that he had covered with a machine gun, it was a toss-up as to whether or not we wouldn't be picked off by our own people as they came up. Although I extended my search over all of the high ground in the vicinity and did manage to find a couple of places from which some view could be had, observation of fire in the Argonne Forest proved a failure.[25]

Captain Thornton Thayer, B, Battery 305th Field Artillery, 77th Division

Far too many shells were dropping short, smashing down on to the American-held positions to cause bitterly resented casualties. The difficulties faced by the gunner in coordinating artillery fire with the troops on the ground were grudgingly appreciated by Captain Rainsford when they tried to advance on 30 September.

Two battalions were deployed in double line for a concerted assault behind half an hour's artillery preparation. This artillery preparation had frankly become a thing to dread. There was no direct observation of their fire, due to the blind character of the country and the still apparent lack of aeroplanes; nor was there any direct communication from the infantry units to the batteries. If a platoon or company were suffering from the fire of their own guns, they could send a runner with a message to that effect to Battalion headquarters, perhaps half a mile or more distant through the woods; and Battalion headquarters, if their wires had not been blown out, would communicate with regimental headquarters, who in turn would take it up with the artillery; and the artillery would quite likely reply that the infantry were mistaking enemy fire for their own. Of course, a more reasonable course for the infantry unit was to move out, provided that this could be done. But what was also probably a fruitful cause of trouble was an almost criminal inexactness on the part of very many infantry officers in map reading. The terrain was undoubtedly difficult for the attainment of this exactness and of certainty; but that alone would not sufficiently account for the mistakes made. It was the one salient point on which the training of infantry officers was found to be deficient. Many a company commander or liaison officer was entirely capable of waving a vague finger over a valley marked on the map, while stating that the troops in question were, 'On that hill!' and, if pressed to be more precise, he would give as their coordinates figures which represented a point neither in the valley to which he was pointing nor on the hill on which they were.[26]

Captain Walter Rainsford, 3/307th Regiment, 154th Brigade, 77th Division

The casualties suffered from their own guns during the barrage seemed even more pointless with the discovery that the Germans had already evacuated their positions. Then, on 1 October, as Rainsford and his men pushed forwards, they encountered a further line of German trenches with thick barbed wire and a large number of machine guns. The weather was not helping and his men were suffering in the pouring rain and bitter cold. The German wire was left untouched by the American artillery, but the German machine gunners and snipers were making their presence felt. Next day, Rainsford got the orders to attack again.

I sent back a runner, a red-headed Irishman named Patrick Gilligan, to hurry forward my rear platoons, and had just gotten word to the others to be ready for an instant advance in open order, when the shelling started. I wondered whether my men realized what they were up against. The barrage was stunning to watch for those 20 minutes, there within 50 yards of it – the thick smoke among the leaves, the black fountains of earth, and the great yellow trees crashing down in front. Then it ceased, and at once the whole forest began to echo with a sound like a hundred pneumatic riveters at work. We moved forward into a close wall of foliage, combed and re-combed by the traversing bullets, and we fired blindly into the leaves as we went. The noise was deafening, and I could hear H and E [Companies] going into action on our right rear, but nothing from the left. Then Gilligan came up with the other two platoons and saluted with a grin. I told him that I had thought he was lost or headed home, though in reality I didn't see how they had come so quickly nor found me so directly. 'Never fear, Captain,' he answered, 'and praise God it's here that we are and in time for it all, and yourself so safe!' And even as he spoke he was down with a bullet through the brain. I think he was the first to be killed.[27]

Captain Walter Rainsford, 3/307th Regiment, 154th Brigade, 77th Division

Despite the odds, they managed to break through the German line and found themselves on the broad top of a ridge, totally isolated, with their left flank and rear both wide open to attack. They were soon ordered to withdraw – it had all been for nothing.

During that afternoon and evening of 2 October, Major Charles Whittlesey with six companies of 308th Regiment, a stray company of 307th Regiment and two companies of 306th Machine Gun Battalion, a total of about 670 men, found themselves isolated after an attack on the Mont d'Charlevaux in the Argonne Forest. Soon they were completely surrounded and the miscellaneous body would be christened the 'Lost Battalion' as they dug in close to a road within the Ravine d'Charlevaux.

Later in the day it became apparent we were cut off and completely surrounded with machine guns set up on all sides. It was understood by all the men to keep quiet and be alert for any possible attack. We were told we had to hold our position until the rear troops could move up. Scouts were sent out to find open way back for communication to our regimental headquarters, but no way could be found and many of the scouts never returned. Those who did return reported they could only go a short distance before they were blocked by the enemy. Many efforts were made on the first day, but to no avail.[28]

Private John Nell, 2/308th Regiment, 154th Brigade, 77th Division

Their shallow trenches were afflicted with a torrent of hand grenades, mortar bombs and machine-gun fire, all of which sometimes prefigured sudden violent attacks that had to be beaten back. Most frustrating of all were shells crashing down from their own artillery. Even when it was 'quiet' there was still the occasional deadly crack of the German sniper's rifle to fear – particularly near the spring water supply. These men were really suffering.

Our little plot of ground was not a pretty sight. Graves everywhere, but necessarily so shallow that limbs of our comrades would show through the bit of soil we had been able to scoop over them. And wounded in almost every funk hole. Hunger was gnawing and thirst parching us all, especially those of us who had been gassed during the strenuous drive preceding our present adventure.[29]

Private Arthur Looker, 1/308th Regiment, 154th Brigade, 77th Division

As the days went by, the cold and wet conditions began to drag down the physical condition of the survivors. Relief operations had been commenced, but the 77th Division lacked the strength to break through after their own week of hard fighting. The 'Lost Battalion' would have to fend for themselves for five long days. The denouement of their story must wait.

It was evident throughout the Meuse-Argonne fighting that the Americans were still facing terrible logistical challenges. Their huge

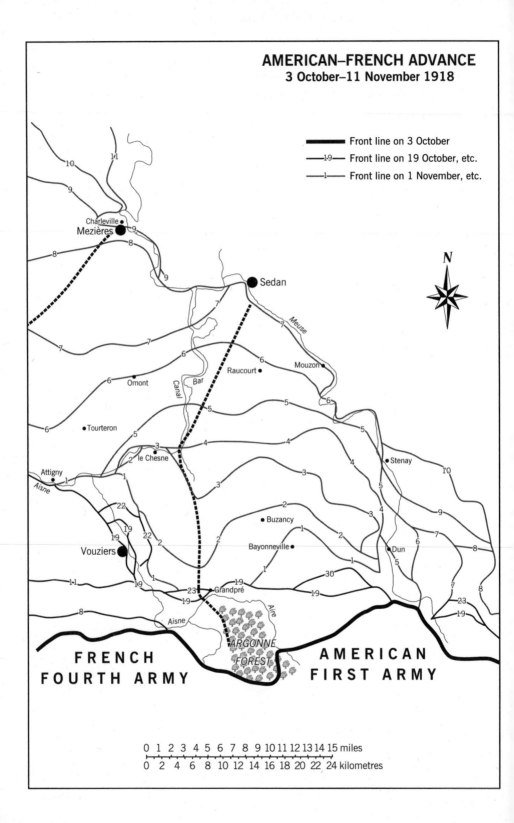

AMERICAN–FRENCH ADVANCE
3 October–11 November 1918

Front line on 3 October
Front line on 19 October, etc. — 1·9
Front line on 1 November, etc. — 1

N

Charleville
Mezières

Sedan

Meuse

Mouzon

Raucourt

Omont

Bar

Canal

Tourteron

le Chesne

Stenay

Attigny

Aisne

Buzancy

Vouziers

Bayonneville

Dun

Grandpré

Aisne

Aire

ARGONNE
FOREST

FRENCH
FOURTH ARMY

AMERICAN
FIRST ARMY

0 1 2 3 4 5 6 7 8 9 10 11 12 13 14 15 miles
0   2   4   6   8 10 12 14 16 18 20 22 24 kilometres

divisions demanded a torrent of stores and munitions had to be funnelled to them. But here at least the copious amount of American manpower proved invaluable.

> A road of pre-war days was shown on the map. As we passed over this distance in the first day's attack there was no sign of this road except stones scattered in two or three years' ploughing by the enemy's grout guns. It had been shell cratered over and over. As our infantry line advanced, it was followed along this old road by a great force of engineers and pioneers who, by sheer numbers, with tooth and nail, scratched and levelled and macadamized a road over which ambulances, food, ammunition and artillery followed almost as rapidly as the troops advanced. The workmen formed practically a continuous line on both sides of the road and swarmed back of the side lines like ants, gathering gravel and broken stone to be thrown upon the roadbed. They worked night and day without cessation, with a devotion not surpassed by the men who were risking their lives in the very front lines. They could use only the lightest implements, because their trains with heavier tools could not be brought for some time upon the ground. The men gathered stones by hand and brought them to the road bed where they sank in the mud of late shell craters almost as if they had been dropped into a bottomless sea, so soft was the ground and so destructive the passage of vehicles. It was an exhausting, heart-breaking, discouraging, ever-continuous operation, but the road worked, and gradually solidified and hardened.[30]

> Major General Robert Bullard, Headquarters, III Corps

With the construction of several such roads, the logistical mess was gradually alleviated.

On 4 October, the main American Meuse-Argonne offensive burst back into full life as a massive creeping barrage signified a major attack intended to overrun the rest of the Argonne Forest, to capture the Kriemhilde Stellung position at Romagne, and to take the Cunel Heights on the eastern side of the Meuse. The attacks were largely a failure, with severe casualties and minimal progress. One 23-year-old officer tried to describe the daunting nature of the German shelling they encountered during their attack.

> Everything happened that never happens in the storybooks of war. We literally lost each other. There were no bugles, no flags, no drums, and as far as we knew, no heroes. The great noise was like great stillness, everything seemed blotted out. We hardly knew where the Germans were. We were simply in a big black spot with streaks of screaming red and yellow, with roaring giants in the sky tearing and whirling and roaring. I have never read in any military history a description of the high explosives that break overhead. There is a great swishing scream, a smash-bang, and it seems to tear everything loose from you. The intensity of it simply enters your heart and brain and tears every nerve to pieces. Although so many men had been killed, there was nothing to do but keep on going.[31]
>
> Lieutenant Maury Maverick, 28th Regiment, 2nd Brigade, 1st Division

As he stumbled forward, the moment he had been dreading happened in another sudden deafening explosion.

> A shell burst above my head. It tore out a piece of my shoulder blade and collar bone and knocked me down. It was a terrific blow, but I was not unconscious. I think it was the bursting of the shell, the air concussion, which knocked me down, and not the shell itself. It was not five seconds, it seemed, before a Medical Corps man was dressing my wounds. He cut my coat away from the wound and wrapped up my shoulder in such a way that it would not bleed too much. As he lifted me from the ground, I looked at my four runners, and I saw that the two in the middle had been cut down to a pile of horrid red guts and blood and meat, while the two men on the outside had been cut up somewhat less badly, but no less fatally. It reminded me of nothing I had ever seen before, except a Christmas hog-butchering back on the Texas farm.[32]
>
> Lieutenant Maury Maverick, 28th Regiment, 2nd Brigade, 1st Division

Maverick's experience was repeated thousands of times. Little was achieved after hard fighting with advances that barely scratched the surface of the German defences.

To the left of the Argonne Forest, the French Fourth Army was also struggling in its push through the Champagne region and had requested American assistance. Having been assigned the American 2nd and 36th Divisions, the French planned a renewed assault on the dominant feature of the Blanc Mont Ridge overlooking the village of Somme-Py. This was defended by strong trenches along the top of the ridge, coupled with the usual concealed machine-gun posts able to sweep the slopes with a deadly fire.

Despite the odds, here at least the Americans would have morale-boosting success. At 05.50 on 3 October, the relatively experienced 2nd Division would be launched into the attack, backed up by a strong bombardment and the assistance of some forty-eight French tanks, while French divisions attacked on either flank. Under the plans, the 4th Marine Brigade was to be responsible for storming the left face of Blanc Mont, while another brigade ascended to the right. It was a fearsome proposition and Private Carl Brannen decided to take every precaution he could.

> I knew that my time would come sooner or later. The Marine song had the words in it:
> *If the Army and the Navy ever look on Heaven's scenes*
> *They will find the streets are guarded by the United States Marines*
> After looking at that ridge ahead, I decided that my next duty might be helping guard the heavenly streets. As it turned out, that was almost the case. Two or three hours before daylight, the word was passed along to get ready for the attack. Everyone checked his bayonet to see that it was fastened on good with the latch. Ammunition was inspected, and the flaps of the belt unhooked so that a fresh clip could be gotten into the rifle quickly. Each man had two extra bandoleers of ammunition around his shoulders. I made sure the bandoleers of ammunition were in front of my chest. The issued razor was in the right-hand pocket of my blouse and the

YMCA-issued Bible was in the left-hand pocket. I was using all of the protection that I could think of.[33]

Private Carl Brannen, 2/6th Marines, 4th Marine Brigade, 2nd Division

As dawn broke the marines attacked, climbing up the long slopes of Blanc Mont under heavy fire.

We came out of our trench and began the ascent in combat formation. The rows of men moved forward unhesitatingly but fell like ten pins before the deadly machine-gun fire. I was a runner to carry messages from flank to flank of my Company and the one adjoining, trying to keep the units in contact with each other as the now thin lines swept over the crest. I was with a Lieutenant of the 78th Company when we entered the forest of small pines which were along the crest and down its slopes on the other side. We were firing on the retreating enemy as we advanced, sometimes dropping to a knee for better aim. A bullet hit my bayonet about an inch from the muzzle of the rifle while I was carrying it at port arms position, shattering the bayonet and leaving me only a stub. A Marine near me rushed at three Germans who were also near. I speeded up and rushed at them, too, with my rifle lowered to use my bayonet. They surrendered, and then I noticed them looking at my bayonet. I tried to read their minds. They must have thought that I had broken off my bayonet in a man. Later a man in my Company saw me with my stub of a bayonet and said, 'Old Brannen stuck his bayonet in one – and broke it off!'[34]

Private Carl Brannen, 2/6th Marines, 4th Marine Brigade, 2nd Division

Hidden machine guns were a terrible menace, but still, with the right kind of luck, they could be overwhelmed.

We were in open country, following the barrage. Before us, all up the hill, were German dugouts with machine-gun emplacements manned by eight or ten men each. At 6.20 am, Johnny Kelly ran ahead as soon as he spotted a Bosche gun sputtering away at us, disappearing in the smoke of our own barrage. The barrage was not impenetrable; with luck one could get through it without being hit. Johnny charged up to a machine-gun emplacement holding about ten Germans. He put the gunner out of action with a grenade. Another square-head came out, and Johnny shot him through the heart with his pistol, which runners were entitled to carry. I was amazed that he hit the German, because our .44 Colts were difficult to shoot very accurately even under ideal conditions. The remaining eight Germans surrendered, and Johnny proudly marched them back, waving to the boys and shouting, 'I told you I was going to get the first one!'[35]

First Lieutenant James Sellers, 2/6th Marines, 4th Marine Brigade, 2nd Division

Private John Kelly would be awarded the Medal of Honour for his actions. After mopping up German dugouts with grenades, the 6th Marines were further harassed by more German machine guns.

The Lieutenant asked for some men to go around each flank. Three of us went to the left. When we were in close proximity to the nest, we were a little too exposed, and the fellow on my right fell, killed. As I jumped for protection into a ditch nearby, a fusillade of bullets caught me below the heart on the left side, through one lens of the field glasses, and against my bandoleer of ammunition. The best I remember, ten bullets in my own belt exploded, but they had deflected the enemy bullets, saving my life. My own bullets ripped my coat to shreds as they exploded and went out over my left shoulder by the side of my face. My cloth bandoleer and the field glasses caught on fire. I got them off me and then replaced the field glasses around my neck again as they quit burning. I collected myself together and, with the other companion in the ditch, looked for our machine gunner but saw that Americans were now in possession. I suppose we had helped by drawing fire while the others rushed, for on going up there I found three dead Germans stretched by two guns.[36]

Private Carl Brannen, 2/6th Marines, 4th Marine Brigade, 2nd Division

Brannen had used all his nine lives, but had not escaped entirely unscathed, suffering a series of minor wounds which forced his evacuation to a base hospital. As the marines struggled forwards, machine guns were not the only danger, as German shells began to crash down among them.

> Scarcely more than an arm's length from me another shell fell into the middle of the huddled group. An unforgettable 'My God' came from one of the men and he was dead. The shell had passed through the man's body to strike the ground without exploding. So heavy was the impact on the hard, rocky ground that rocks thrown up injured another man nearby. Falling on the hard surface, had it detonated, the explosion would have made mincemeat out of all of us.[37]

> Corporal Warren Jackson, 1/6th Marines, 4th Marine Brigade, 2nd Division

The Americans had taken the ridge. But the battle was by no means resolved as the Germans began to counter-attack trying to encircle the marines up on Blanc Mont.

> We advanced too far, the French did not keep up with us, so that we were being fired upon from the front, each side and nearly from the rear. We were afraid that the Germans were going to close in together in the rear and cut us off from our lines. We fought desperately to keep the Germans from carrying out their plans. We were on a prairie with machine-gun bullets hitting all round. They were hitting only inches from me on each side, and knocking dirt into my face.[38]

> Private William Francis, 5th Marines, 4th Marine Brigade, 2nd Division

Hard fighting would drag on for days, but eventually the American grip on the vital Blanc Mont ridge was consolidated.

Despite these valiant efforts in support of the French Fourth Army the Americans still could not win the respect of Foch or Haig. The British and French Armies were making tremendous progress in the north, and they could not help but look covetously at the teeming masses of American soldiers. But the Americans' inexperience was frittering away their manpower advantage.

> Brigadier General Charlie Grand arrived from Foch's HQ and stayed the night. He states that Foch's Staff are terribly disappointed with results of American attack west of the Meuse. The Enemy is in no strength in their front, but the Americans cannot advance because their supply arrangements have broken down. The divisions in the front line are really starving, and have had to be relieved in order to be fed! There are many fine divisions there and cannot be used owing to incapacity of American HQ Staff. General Weygand (Foch's Chief of Staff) spent five hours with Pershing recently explaining the situation, but Pershing won't allow any of his divisions to be transferred to another sector, where they might produce decisive results.[39]
>
> Field Marshal Sir Douglas Haig, General Headquarters, BEF

Pershing would stand firm, rightly confident that he was supported by the American government.

By 6 October, in the Argonne Forest, the situation of Major Charles Whittlesey's 'Lost Battalion' was getting desperate. Air supply drops, attempted by American DH4 bombers, understandably failed to succeed in landing stores within such a minute area, which only measured some 350 yards long by 50 yards deep. The trapped men were fast running out of food, water and medical supplies.

> The number of dead was rapidly increasing, as was the count of the wounded. It was a deplorable and dismal sight to witness the poor fellows who were suffering with immense pain and bleeding terribly. The wounded knew their time was limited. Every once in a while, you could see a wounded man pass out and then see another get shot and wounded, as if to take his place. I well remember one poor fellow lay on top of the ground close to the hole I was in. He had a large shrapnel about 6 inches long buried in upper leg and a bullet in his stomach. He lay there two days before he passed out.

Another man not far from him had shrapnel in his head. Both
men suffered tremendously before the reprieve of death overtook
them.[40]

Private John Nell, 2/308th Regiment, 154th Brigade, 77th Division

With no medical supplies and very little accessible fresh water, there was
nothing the men could do to keep their wounds clean. The result was a
plethora of medical complications as the wounds began to putrefy.

> We could do nothing for the wounded. What little supplies each of
> us carried had long since been used. Even shirts, socks and under-
> wear had been torn into bandages. Many wounded men would
> almost rot before they died – the stink was almost unbearable.
> They surely were brave though, knowing that we didn't have any
> food or water to give them, they didn't ask for much and didn't
> complain much either for the intense pain they must have been
> in. At night, sometimes we would be able to bury a few of them in
> shallow graves, or just throw dirt over them in their dugout.[41]

Private Ralph John, 1/308th Regiment, 154th Brigade, 77th Division

Still they endured, rejecting a courteously worded invitation to surrender from the Germans in such a robust manner that it triggered a final
furious attack by Germans, some armed with flame-throwers. Somehow,
Whittlesey and his men still held out. But as they began to run short of
ammunition it seemed to be getting hopeless. Then, suddenly, it was all
over. At around 19.00, on the evening of 7 October, they were finally
relieved when an attack broke through from the 307th Regiment. By this
time, it has been estimated that they had suffered 118 dead and 252
wounded in a total casualty list for all reasons of 444.[42] Whatever their
suffering, Major General Robert Alexander, the gruff commander of the
77th Division, refused to accede to the already burgeoning myth of the
'Lost Battalion'.

> This command was neither 'lost' nor 'rescued'. It suffered heavy
> losses; it was subjected to fire from both enemy, and supposedly
> friendly artillery – the French – in spite of my determined protest

– placed artillery fire on this ravine the morning of the 7th of October, being quite convinced that the command must have surrendered. Notwithstanding all of this, Major Whittlesey and his command held the position to which they had proceeded under my order and were found by me, when I visited them on the very early morning of October 8th, an organised command, in good order, and in excellent spirits.[43]

Major General Robert Alexander, Headquarters, 77th Division

No sooner had one myth been generated than another one was created on the right of the Argonne woodlands. On 8 October, the 82nd Division had been ordered into the attack to the right of the 77th Division. As the 328th Regiment moved forward, they were threatened by several German machine-gun positions stationed along a woody ridge. In the confusion, Sergeant Bernard Early and a party managed to infiltrate behind the German lines, but when Early was wounded in a burst of machine-gun fire, his subordinate, Corporal Alvin York took over command of the survivors.

As soon as the machine guns opened fire on me, I began to exchange shots with them. I had no time to do nothing but watch their German machine gunners and give them the best I had. Every time I saw a German I just 'teched'[44] him off. At first I was shooting from a prone position; that is lying down; just like we often shoot at the targets in the shooting matches in the mountains of Tennessee; and it was just about the same distance. But the targets here were bigger. I just couldn't miss a German's head or body at that distance.[45]

Corporal Alvin York, 2/328th Regiment, 164th Brigade, 82nd Division

When the German officer and five soldiers suddenly charged him with their bayonets, York was equal to the occasion.

They had about 25 yards to come and they were coming right smart. I only had about half a clip left in my rifle; but I had my pistol ready. I done flipped it out fast and 'teched' them off, too. I 'teched' off the sixth man first; then the fifth; then the fourth; then the third; and so on. That's the way we shoot wild turkeys at home. You see we don't want the front ones to know that we're getting the back ones, and then they keep on coming until we get them all.[46]

Corporal Alvin York, 2/328th Regiment, 164th Brigade, 82nd Division

It was later claimed that York had fired twenty-eight shots to kill twenty-eight Germans. It was perhaps this lethality that would ultimately trigger the surrender of some 132 prisoners and several machine guns to York and his small party. The details of this feat have been vigorously disputed, but it made a hero of Alvin York, who would be awarded the Congressional Medal of Honour and much feted in his later life. As part of the larger picture, the advance of the 82nd Division would ultimately trigger a German withdrawal, and by 10 October the Argonne had at last been cleared.

On that very day there would be a demonstration of a different kind of heroism in the skies above them. The American aviators were as inexperienced as their counterparts on the ground and tended to a certain rigidity of tactics, but their overall commander, Brigadier General William Mitchell, was a great believer in the influence of air power in ground warfare and espoused a relentless aggressive approach. At 15.30, Captain Eddie Rickenbacker (94th Aero Squadron) led a mission to shoot down a German observation balloon floating high in the sky above Dun sur Meuse. With him were elements of 94th, 147th and 27th Aero Squadrons, all flying Spad scouts. As Lieutenant William Brotherton dived down to attack the balloon, he was being covered by Lieutenant Wilbert White (147th Pursuit Squadron), accompanied by Lieutenant James Meissner and a recently joined young pilot, Lieutenant Charles Cox. Having completed his tour of duty, this was to be White's last flight before he returned home to the States. Rickenbacker was about a mile away when he noticed eleven Fokker DVIIs diving past him.

Evidently the Fokker leader scorned to take notice of me, as his scouts passed under me and plunged ahead towards White's formation. I let them pass, dipped over sharply and with accumulated speed bore down upon the tail of the last man in the Fokker formation. It was an easy shot and I could not have missed. I was agreeably surprised, however, to see that my first shots had set fire to the Hun's fuel tank and that the machine was doomed. I was almost equally gratified the next second to see the German pilot level off his blazing machine and with a sudden leap overboard into space let the Fokker slide safely away without him. Attached to his back and sides was a rope which immediately pulled a dainty parachute from the bottom of his seat. The umbrella opened within a 50 foot drop and settled him gradually to earth within his own lines.[47]

Captain Edward Rickenbacker, 94th Aero Squadron, 2nd Pursuit Group

The surviving Germans continued to dive down on what looked like a far easier prey – and unerringly picked on the hapless ingénue to the complex disciplines of air fighting – Lieutenant Charles Cox.

Their leader dove on a new pilot in our formation of three. 'Whitey' leading, instantly turned in his tracks to drive the Hun off and save the new pilot – naturally excited and apt to lose his head when he heard bullets crack around.[48]

Lieutenant James Meissner, 147th Aero Squadron, 2nd Pursuit Group

Cox was almost helpless as his inexperience was combined with an engine that had been misbehaving throughout the flight. Lieutenant Wilbert White was his flight commander and clearly took his responsibilities to protect his charge seriously.

He knew I had a bad motor and was inexperienced at the front and all the way to the lines he kept close and waved his arm occasionally to cheer me. Brotherton went down and was hit from the grounds as he dived. White turned to the left back towards our lines when a Hun came down directly behind me and about 400 yards back. White turned back and as he passed opposite me I turned. The float in my carburettor flipped up and my motor cut out an instant slowing me up. I saw White and the Hun going directly at each other, the former climbing a little.[49]

Lieutenant Charles Cox, 147th Aero Squadron, 2nd Pursuit Group

Meissner was following White, but it all happened far too quickly for him to have any chance of intervening as the tragedy unfolded.

> I turned back too, but was further away and could just watch what was happening. The Fokker kept diving on Cox as White raced back, head on at it, firing without effect. He must have realised that Cox would be shot down unless he put the Bosche out of the fight, so he never swerved. I watched them come together, thought for a moment they would just pass side by side, but the next instant off came a wing of each plane amid a cloud of splinters and shreds of fabric and down they went spinning like tops.[50]
>
> Lieutenant James Meissner, 147 Aero Squadron, 2nd Pursuit Group

Meissner was not the only witness, as Rickenbacker also had a clear view of what happened.

> White rammed the Fokker head on while the two machines were approaching each other at the rate of 250 miles per hour! It was a horrible yet thrilling sight. The two machines actually telescoped each other, so violent was the impact. Wings went through wings and at first glance both the Fokker and Spad seemed to disintegrate. Fragments filled the air for a moment, then the two broken fuselages, bound together by the terrific collision, fell swiftly down and landed in one heap on the bank of the Meuse![51]
>
> Captain Edward Rickenbacker, 94th Aero Squadron, 2nd Pursuit Group

All the witnesses were convinced that Wilbert White[52] had sacrificed his own life to save the young man who was in his charge.

> It was sickening to fly then to the spot where they had collided and think what their thoughts must have been the last instant before they met – Spartans both. White was married, had two children, was to have received orders returning him to the States in a few days and he knew it. But he never hesitated when he saw his duty cut out, which makes his act all the more heroic.[53]
>
> Lieutenant James Meissner, 147th Aero Squadron, 2nd Pursuit Group

The American forces were creating a fresh military tradition with new heroes, new myths and legends in the bitter fighting of the Meuse-Argonne offensive.

From 7 to 12 October, the American First Army slowly battered its way through to reach the Kriemhilde Stellung that barred the way to Stomme and Mézières. They moved forward in a series of small painful baby steps, never breaking through, never achieving their real objectives. After a metaphorical girding of loins, and much more behind-the-scenes prodding from the ever-impatient Foch, another major assault was launched on 14 October. In this, the 32nd Division, commanded by Major General William Haan, was given the challenge of taking the key strongpoints of Côte Dame Marie and Romagne in the Kriemhilde Stellung. It is fair to surmise that Private Horace Baker, attacking with the 3/128th Regiment, was not confident of their chances that day. When his Sergeant told them there was just eight minutes to go before they went over the top, it triggered a period of melancholy introspection.

The time had come that I had dreaded so long. The order was received in silence. I reflected, 'I may have only eight minutes to live'. Perhaps you will wonder what one thought of at such a critical time. Well, there were many things, some flippant, some serious. It seemed a long eight minutes. I thought of home and loved ones, of my buddies on that battlefield, of my soul's condition, of the future, of food, of bullets, of victory, of death, of heaven. And with a smile I tried to see if I was any worse scared than I had been. My nerves had been strung at high tension for days, and especially that morning the shelling had put them at their highest, so I can't say the news scared me at all. When one has been looking over a dreary, bloody battlefield for days and expecting any minute for the scene to change and the 'Pearly Gate' to be standing there, his nerves can't bear much more. The only effect of the terse announcement during the next few minutes was that I became a little bit chilly, that was all. I noted all the fellows near me and poor Shirey[54] in particular. He had aged much since the drive began, and I felt that he too realized that he would be a battle casualty. It was the last time I ever saw him. The moments ticked slowly away, and when the Zero Hour came, we went over the top.[55]

Private Horace Baker, 3/128th Regiment, 64th Brigade, 32nd Division

He advanced amid the second wave towards the village of Romagne, Baker's inexperience betrayed by his hapless efforts to fire the French Chauchat light machine gun with which he had recently been equipped. He had been shown how to load the gun, but nothing else. Now he tried to fire it for the first time.

> I turned my attention to my Chauchat. I had not yet been taught how to shoot it, but evidently it would shoot, so, loading it, I set it down as it should have been and began trying to work the thing. I tried this thing and then that and finally I accidentally let loose a contraption and the thing went 'Bam!' I looked to see if it was pointed toward the Germans and it was, so I had not hit any of our men. It was set on single shot, and though I have since wished it had been on automatic, perhaps it was lucky that it wasn't. Then I began firing at the Germans, aiming as best I could with the old blunderbuss. Soon it jammed, but I had it working again in a jiffy. This happened again and again and finally, when I had shot about thirty rounds, was losing some of my fear, and beginning to enjoy it, Cameron stuck his head over the embankment and yelled, 'Quit shooting with that Chauchat!' So here I was in the midst of a battle with orders not to shoot![56]

Private Horace Baker, 3/128th Regiment, 64th Brigade, 32nd Division

As the reinforcements arrived the Germans began to surrender in droves. The 32nd Division had taken Romagne, and had managed to break through the Kriemhilde Stellung at last. They had made their divisional general a very happy man – especially as his 126th Regiment had also captured the neighbouring dominant feature of the Côte Dame Marie. Here an intrepid eight-man patrol had resourcefully used dead ground to get right up onto the summit, triggering panic, before calling up reinforcements who swiftly ejected the German garrison.

My Division is in fine spirits though tired as hell. This has been by far the fiercest fight we have ever been in. Yesterday morning we went through a trench system (the Kriemhilde Stellung), protected in front by three bands of wire. It seemed almost prohibitive, and we would not have gotten through had it not been for perfect artillery fire, so well in hand that where the infantry got through the barrage went on, and where it didn't get through the fire was dropped back on the trenches. We got through with two battalions, but were held up with the other two; but the artillery, from good observation points which had been found, was recalled to the points where the infantry didn't get through and supported the infantry there until they did get through. Someday I want you to come out and look at the positions my Division took yesterday morning. It is a veritable Gibraltar.[57]

Major General William Haan, Headquarters, 32nd Division

The conditions in the front line, however, meant that it was inevitable that few of his men shared Haan's rejoicing. The survivors faced dreadful torments that tested them to their limits.

Several men were killed by direct hits of gas shells, but the adjusting of gas masks before the gas had time to concentrate saved us from having casualties by gas. The rain continued to come down in torrents and the shelter holes occupied by the men filled up with water, leaving us with only one alternative, viz: getting out of the water and exposing ourselves to the enemy shell fire and possible death, or to remain in the holes with our bodies submerged in the cold water. Between the two, we decided to remain in the shelter holes. It was a discouraging situation. Dysentery aggravated the already bad condition and the men began to speculate on what would happen to them were they compelled to remain in this position all night. To add to the horror of the situation, our own artillery shot several shells into our lines about 3 o'clock in the afternoon, and while the shells fell short, they helped to make our condition still worse.[58]

Captain Paul Schmidt, 1/127 Regiment, 64th Brigade, 32nd Division

With the fall of the Kriemhilde Stellung on 16 October and its curse therefore broken, the Americans had finally achieved the objectives set for the first day of the offensive – way back on 26 September – and could hope to move forward.

Viewed from the German perspective, the situation was looking increasingly bleak for the soldiers attempting to hold back the hordes of Americans. This was not their first battle, many were veterans that had mastered their warlike trades, but their numbers were being eroded away by the relentless fighting, as was apparent to Leutnant Otto Lais.

> Weak, decimated infantry companies, machine-gun companies that were so small that the weight of the ammunition, without which a machine gun has no value, utterly exhausted the spiritually spent, starving gunners, fought against freshly introduced American battalions and regiments right up to war establishment. Tens fought against hundreds or more; our few hundreds against thousands from over there. Most of the infantry close support batteries, now reduced to two guns, had no horses left. Sweating and straining, the gunners hauled on ropes to drag their guns through the swampy crater field of the wooded valley to positions where they could engage oncoming tanks.[59]
>
> Leutnant Otto Lais, Baden Infantry Regiment 3/169, 84th Brigade, 29th Division

And yet the American strength kept growing. Even as Lais bemoaned his fate, Pershing planned a major reorganisation of his forces that came into force on 16 October. The Second American Army came into existence, to be commanded by Lieutenant General Robert Bullard, while Lieutenant General Hunter Liggett took command of First Army, with Pershing now commanding the resulting American Army Group. Bullard was dismayed with the state of the notational Second Army, which was holding the line achieved by the St Mihiel offensive.

> In trying to supply deficiencies in the Second Army I find the usual defect, to wit: too much talk, no great deal of expectation, and too little realization. This has been the great American failing in the

war. We have talked at long range. We have filled the air with loud words about things we are going to do. Is it a characteristic of us Americans to make a 'blow' about everything that we do? Before we did anything toward getting into the war, we were crying out over the world that we were going to have more and bigger guns and more men and more munitions and more ships and more and swifter airplanes, submarines, and chasers, and more and deadlier gas, and more and bigger and deadlier everything than any or all the other belligerents. It is not much of an exaggeration to say that we made good only on the men: the gas came too late, and the airplanes and many of the other things did not come at all.[60]

Lieutenant General Robert Bullard, Headquarters, Second Army

Bullard was being a little harsh here on the American effort. Despite it all, the Second Army was already taking shape and was intended to be ready to launch an offensive driving towards Metz in November.

A LOGICAL ANALYSIS OF the Battle of Meuse-Argonne is not always complimentary to the American performance. It has been claimed that they deployed too many of their giant divisions, that they clogged up the narrow front, creating chaos in the movement of troops, supplies, munitions and the wounded. The German soldiers were fighting a battle based on the minimum deployment of troops nestling in well-sited machine-gun posts, defended by barbed wire and the natural terrain, with artillery in support. The consequences of attacking these with massed infantry soon became evident. There was a widespread perception that the Americans advanced in fine style until they were hit by heavy fire, when they tended to flounder. Junior officers and NCOs needed experience to grow into their role. In the noise and shock of battle, their training to date was not good enough to allow them to perform even simple tactical drills when terrified and confused as to what was happening around them. Many soldiers lacked the technical skills required to employ machine guns, grenades, rifle grenades and mortars to maximum effect in eradicating the strongpoints that blocked their way.

It has also been asserted that numerous egregious errors were made by their generals, but these blunders were almost inevitable given their negligible experience at that level of command. It is true that some generals missed fleeting chances for greater success, but with dreadful communications and the situation wreathed in chaos, they surely cannot be blamed for erring on the side of caution. Those senior commanders not dismissed out of hand for their failures were surely learning, but were they learning the 'right' lessons? It was almost perverse how otherwise intelligent officers could get the wrong end of the stick. A typical example is the over-robust defence by Major General Robert Alexander of the merits of the good old-fashioned Springfield rifle.

> I thought I noticed that there was a disinclination to utilize to its full potential power the infantry rifle. Whether this disinclination came from lack of proper training, I am not prepared to say, but dependence seemed to be made upon machine guns, grenades and the other auxiliaries to the partial exclusion of rifle fire. I am quite convinced that we cannot too strongly insist upon our desire to bring about the full utilisation of this fire. The other auxiliaries, machine guns, hand grenades, 37mm, are useful in their way, but they are merely auxiliaries, and intelligent use of the infantry rifle wins battles when no other instrumentality will suffice.[61]
>
> Major General Robert Alexander, Headquarters, 77th Division

Such traditionalist thinking, harking back to old virtues, reflects similar misconceptions uttered by British and French generals earlier in the war. They too had had to assimilate knowledge the hard way – and it had often taken more than one brutal lesson inflicted on their men before they understood. Of course, the rifle still had its place in modern warfare, but the massed firepower generated by the proper coordinated use of machine guns, mortars and grenades was an essential part of the 'All Arms Battle'. Even more so was the absolute necessity for proper artillery support: the destruction of strongpoints, clearance of wire, creeping barrages, the gas-shell suppression of German batteries, the smoke shells obscuring defenders' vision and the standing barrages to defend gains from counter-attacks. An understanding of these complexities was of far more importance than fussing about the rifle prowess of individual soldiers. Then again, staff officers needed a mastery of logistics to ensure that the guns could be got to the front and supplied with the ammunition they needed. Modern warfare was just so damned complicated at every level. Above all, the Americans needed time to learn, but their battle experience was all compressed within a couple of months. Yet when all the analysis is done, perhaps the dominant emotion we are left with is a heartfelt admiration for the sheer spirit of these relatively untrained troops. Whatever their tactical shortcomings, the Americans were willing fighters, putting their lives on the line in the Allied cause. Whatever the cost, they were slowly forcing the Germans back. Their time would come.

3

BATTLE OF CANAL DU NORD

I made me will out – because we knew we were in for a bad 'do' next morning. You had to fill it in in the back of your pay book, the form was there. I never bothered until that night. I could see the writing was on the wall. I was only eighteen years of age, so I made it out to my mother, didn't I?[1]

Private John Grainger, 1/7th Bn Lancashire Fusiliers, 125th Brigade, 42nd Division

THE SECOND INSTALMENT of the Allied offensives ordered by Foch was to be launched on 27 September by the British First and Third Armies on the German Hindenburg Line positions along the Canal du Nord. This would be a significant test of the new 'All Arms Battle' tactics. The German defences were strong and there would be scant margin for error. However, the seemingly endless supplies of British munitions pouring into the Western Front were beginning to make a very real difference, as all the elements required for the attack could now be amassed with relative ease. Each individual British army now had sufficient resources to allow a major attack to be launched without the necessity for a prolonged

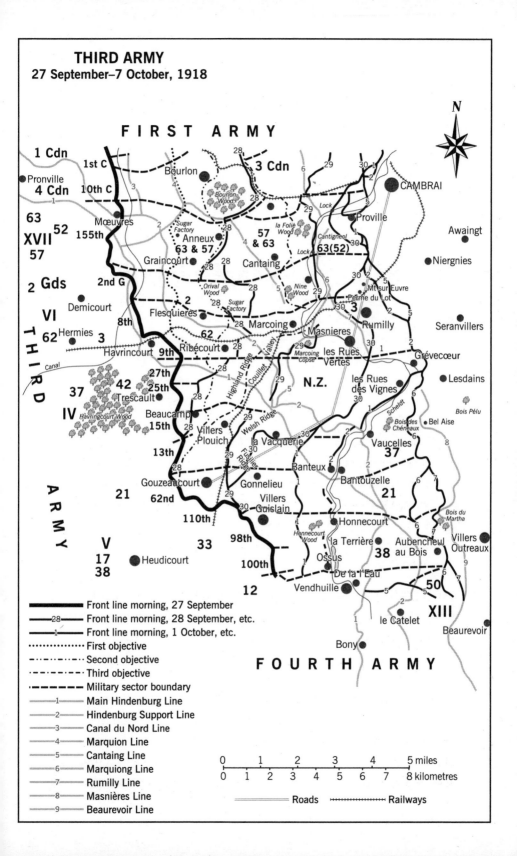

THIRD ARMY
27 September–7 October, 1918

FIRST ARMY

1 Cdn
1st C
10th C
4 Cdn
Pronville
63
52
XVII
155th
57
2 Gds
2nd G
VI
62
Demicourt
3
8th
Hermies
IV
37
42
27th
25th
Trescault
15th
13th
21
62nd
V
17
33
98th
38
110th
100th
12

Bourlon
Bourlon Wood
Mœuvres
Sugar Factory
Anneux
63 & 57
Graincourt
Orival Wood
Flesquières
Sugar Factory
Ribécourt
Havrincourt
9th
Havrincourt Wood
Beaucamp
Villers Plouich
Gouzeaucourt
Gonnelieu
Villers Guislain
Heudicourt
Honnecourt Wood

3 Cdn
Bourlon
28
la Folie Wood
57 & 63
Cantaing
28
Nine Wood
5
Marcoing
28
Highland Ridge
Couillet Valley
Welsh Ridge
Fusilier Ridge
29
30
la Vacquerie
30
Banteux
29
30
Honnecourt
la Terrière
Ossus
De la l'Eau
Vendhuille

CAMBRAI
Proville
Cantigneol
Lock
63(52)
30
Mt sur Euvre
Ferme du Lot
30
3
Rumilly
30
Masnières
les Rues Vertes
Marcoing Copse
N.Z.
les Rues des Vignes
30
Scheldt
Bois des Chéneaux
Vaucelles
37
Bantouzelle
21
Honnecourt
Aubencheul au Bois
38
50

Awaingt
Niergnies
Seranvillers
Grévecœur
Lesdains
Bois Pélu
Bel Aise
Bois du Martha
Villers Outreaux
XIII
le Catelet
Beaurevoir

Bony

FOURTH ARMY

N

Legend:

—— Front line morning, 27 September
—28— Front line morning, 28 September, etc.
—1— Front line morning, 1 October, etc.
.... First objective
-·-·-·-· Second objective
–·–·–·– Third objective
– – – – Military sector boundary
——1—— Main Hindenburg Line
——2—— Hindenburg Support Line
——3—— Canal du Nord Line
——4—— Marquion Line
——5—— Cantaing Line
——6—— Marquiong Line
——7—— Rumilly Line
——8—— Masnières Line
——9—— Beaurevoir Line

0 1 2 3 4 5 miles
0 1 2 3 4 5 6 7 8 kilometres

═══ Roads   ++++++ Railways

gestation period as munitions and guns were laboriously moved in from other fronts. In the northern sector of the intended attack, the First Army (General Sir Henry Horne) was required to seize the Bourlon Ridge, before pushing on to secure its left flank along the River Sensée. Meanwhile, the main attack would be conducted by the Third Army (General Sir Julian Byng), which would drive forward to attain a line stretching from Le Cateau to Solesmes along the River Selle.

It was apparent that the Canadian Corps of the First Army would be required to force a crossing of the Canal du Nord. The canal was dry in sections, as the outbreak of war had forestalled its completion, yet, even when dry, it still represented a serious physical obstacle, being up to 60 feet deep in places, some 120 feet wide and with 12-foot-high revetted banks. The Germans had filled much of the bed of the canal with barbed wire, and numerous machine-gun posts adorned the eastern bank. The Canal du Nord Line itself was not hugely strong and there was a well-grounded belief that the trenches would not provide much shelter if hit by a heavy bombardment. But about 2,000 yards behind was the Marquion Line, while a further 5–6,000 yards further back lay the Marcoing Line, which lay directly across the path to Cambrai.

The Canadian Corps commander, Lieutenant General Sir Arthur Currie, was a confident soul, but even he could not help but record his misgivings in a diary entry for 8 September, when he first had an inkling of what lay ahead of his men.

> It is my opinion that a frontal attack on the German positions east of the canal would be unwise for the following reasons:
> 1. The canal itself is a serious obstacle,
> 2. The marshes on the eastern side make difficult going,
> 3. It is strongly defended by machine guns from the trench system running parallel to the canal,
> 4. The high ground to the east gives a perfect command of the approaches,
> 5. The more we advance to the eastward the more violent becomes the enfilade fire.[2]
>
> Lieutenant General Sir Arthur Currie, Headquarters, Canadian Corps

Not only would they have to overwhelm the Canal du Nord Line itself, but also successively the Marquion and Marcoing lines. Yet his orders gave him no option and Currie began to formulate his plans.

Currie decided that in the northern sector occupied by the Canadian Corps, the canal was impassable, as it was both flooded and surrounded by marshlands, so the whole corps had to cross in the southern 2,600 yards of their frontage and then would have to expand like a fan, in a north-easterly direction, ultimately covering a front of 9,500 yards. The initial assault would be launched by the Canadian 1st and 4th Divisions who were charged with taking Bourlon Wood – the dominating position that had slowed down and thwarted the Battle of Cambrai attack on 20 November 1917. For the second stage, the 3rd Canadian and British 11th Divisions would join them as they pushed on over the high ground to secure a line stretching from the Canal de L'Escaut just to the north-east of Cambrai, right across to the Sensée Canal in the north. The first steps of this scheme were undoubtedly risky. The Canadian Corps would be unnaturally compressed into a small area, vulnerable to a German barrage in the hours leading up to the attack. Both Horne and Byng had their doubts, but Currie had Haig's confidence and the plan stood – there was, after all, little obvious alternative.

With a great deal of potential for things to go wrong, Currie rose to the challenge by adopting a rigorous process of detailed planning. The role of the artillery was paramount, but he envisioned no preliminary bombardment; instead the attack would be launched under the cover of a hugely powerful creeping barrage, composed of a mixture of 50 per cent shrapnel, 40 per cent high explosive and 10 per cent smoke shells, but which would also incorporate the fire of the heavy guns as well as the more usual field batteries. Into this potent mixture would be poured streams of long-range machine-gun bullets fired by the collected Vickers guns of the Machine Gun Corps, further supplemented by massed mortar fire. The very narrow front posed spatial difficulties for the artillery and Currie divided his field brigades in two, with part of his force limbered up ready to move forward in order to provide continuous artillery support in successive stages of the advance as the infantry moved out of range of the original supporting fire. But to do this the guns and limbers would have to get across the canal – and Currie had the foresight to make sure his Canadian Engineers were ready to immediately construct numerous bridges.

The difficulties facing General Sir Julian Byng's Third Army should not be ignored. The XVII Corps and the Guards Division of the VI Corps also faced an attack across the Canal du Nord, after which they were to advance in conformity with the Canadian Corps. The VI Corps also had the dubious pleasure of assaulting the Flesquières Ridge, with the additional arduous requirement to clear the Hindenburg Support Line existing on the reverse slope.

It is sometimes forgotten that improvements in British planning and assault tactics were not the unique preserve of the Canadian and Australian Corps. Considerable progress had been made right across the BEF so everyone knew their role during the attack.

> The army organisation in these days has certainly been brought to a fine art, particularly the cooperation between infantry, artillery, air force and tanks. For the coming battle, each Company commander has a barrage schedule, which when referred to in conjunction with a map, will show the exact position of the barrage at any given time. Every Battery has, of course, a similar schedule with ranges and times shown. I am also to have a special 'contact' plane for the benefit of my own company. The duty of the observer is to fly over the ground where I am expected to be and to sound his klaxon horn. I shall then light red flares. He will mark my position on a map tracing, fly back to divisional headquarters and drop it by parachute; and then return to observe me once more.[3]
>
> Lieutenant Frank Hawkings, Anson Battalion, 188th Brigade, 63rd Division

Security was tight, but there were sufficient controlled briefings to ensure that most subordinate commanders knew what they were meant to do and what was meant to be happening all around them.

Whenever anything is doing, the last three days are called X, Y and Z days. For about ten days we have been preparing for a big battle, though it only began to be known five days ago. I believe it is a big show, probably the biggest in the war and it is of absorbing interest. All plans are laid up to a point, and then they cease, as that point means success, and then comes a new catch word – 'exploiting success'. My map is of all colours of the rainbow, each meaning a different thing – and the preliminary movement is most complicated. I have painted one for each company commander, and for once I think every officer knows what is being attempted on his flanks to a distance of a corps frontage on either side. I am not quite clear though how many corps will really attack, but rumour has it that four armies are going. At any rate one feels there is a plan, and that is very encouraging.[4]

Major Charles Dudley Ward, 1st Welsh Guards, 3rd Guards Brigade, Guards Division

The Guards Division had been given a particularly difficult task, breasting not only the Canal du Nord, but also the Hindenburg Line itself. This was something to make even the most experienced troops hesitate. The thorough briefing they received, however, had improved their spirits to some extent – even in the leading assault battalion.

A relief map had been constructed on a shelving bank by the roadside, and we gathered round it, a Company at a time, while an officer explained the plan of attack. The canal was indicated by a white tape, and the various roads, trenches and other features were marked out with coloured stones. It was considered that the canal, though dry in this area (it had been in course of construction at the beginning of the war), was too formidable a barrier along most of its length to be crossed in face of the enemy, so we were to storm it on a narrow front of only about 150 yards, from the 'Lock' to just north of 'Mouse Post', a broken-down bridge on the road leading to Graincourt.[5]

Private Frederick Noakes, 1st Coldstream Guards, 2nd Guards Brigade, Guards Division

Put thus, this sounded simple enough, but these men were veterans and they realised that for all the planning this would still be a desperate enterprise which they would be lucky to survive.

> Next day was devoted to preparing our kit, drawing extra ammunition, rations, etc., and to writing letters in which we could say little of real significance. The mail came up during the afternoon and many of us received the satisfaction of a last message from home. For some it was, in the most literal and tragic sense, the 'Last Post'.[6]
>
> Private Frederick Noakes, 1st Coldstream Guards, 2nd Guards Brigade, Guards Division

The night before battle was a miserable business. The cramped area designated for the Canadian assembly trenches meant they were even more crowded than usual. It was perishing cold, it was wet and the Zero Hour of 05.20 could not come quickly enough.

> Just after we got lined up there, it started to rain. We had quite a little rain and I can remember trying to cover up the Lewis gun with my groundsheet. A fellow by the name of McTavish was my Number Two – him and I were trying to hide under the other groundsheet to keep out the rain. It quit raining just shortly before Zero Hour. It was very dark and misty. We were always told when Zero Hour was – but they don't need to tell you – because Zero Hour's when that barrage opens up![7]
>
> Private Bob Stevenson, 46th (South Saskatchewan) Battalion, 10th Brigade, 4th Canadian Division

When the barrage began, it was devastating all along the attack frontage of First and Third Armies. The sheer power of the bombardment gave the attackers some hope that they could survive; that this time the Germans would be crushed by the sheer weight of shells crashing down on their defences and gun batteries.

> Shells in hundreds, in thousands, of every size and calibre, shrieked down close over our heads and burst in front of the trench, at first

close to the parapet, then gradually creeping towards the German lines, a flail of death-dealing eruptions which must surely sweep everything living from its path. Great gouts and fountains of flame, scarlet and green and gold – thousands of flashes stabbing the night incessantly – an indescribable hell of noise that numbed the senses and stupefied the brain.[8]

Private Frederick Noakes, 1st Coldstream Guards, 2nd Guards Brigade, Guards Division

Then the moment came as the Canadian infantry jumped off into the unknown in the northern sector. For all the briefings, these men often had little idea of what really lay ahead of them.

I was worried, really worried about it. The canal was ahead of us and we didn't know if there was water in it or not. Each section was given a rope. If there was water in there, somebody in the section had to get out and he had to pull the rest out, but I don't know how it was going to be done. I hadn't gone 10 feet before I got hit. Seven pieces in my right arm and a bad bruise across the back of my head. I don't remember hitting the ground.[9]

Sergeant Don McKerchar, 46th (South Saskatchewan) Battalion, 10th Brigade, 4th Canadian Division

Although there was plenty of machine-gun fire, there was only a minimal German counter-barrage. Some of the Canadians strayed a little too close to their own creeping barrage and paid the penalty. Speed was of the essence; was it better to get as close as possible to the back of the barrage, risking casualties from their own shrapnel, or hold back and possibly give the Germans time to ready their machine guns? The Canadians were desperate to get across the bed of the canal as quickly as possible – they must have felt like rats in a trap.

When we ran up the other side we run into their barbed wire. We had this really terrific barrage on it that tore it up pretty bad. We partly ran into our own barrage. Once or twice before, I noticed them make mistakes like that – get going too fast and run into your own barrage. So we had to wait until it lifted, which was of course only a few minutes.[10]

Private Bob Stevenson, 46th (South Saskatchewan) Battalion, 10th Brigade, 4th Canadian Division

A few minutes could seem like hours in these circumstances, and Private Stan Colbeck was lucky to have an experienced NCO close at hand. Men like this could make all the difference to their survival chances.

Sergeant Major Rogers kept a lot of us young fellows from getting killed by our own barrage. He wouldn't let us advance until our barrage lifted. We had to carry scaling ladders as the canal was very deep where we crossed over. Myself and a pal named Brown, we carried the ladder so we were the first up and we had gone a little way when a shell exploded right behind us. It hit us like a giant fist in the small of the back. I thought I was blown in two: I was all numb. I asked Brown if he was okay. He said he thought so! The screams behind us I will never forget. Brown and I were fine, but that shell wiped out our whole section.[11]

Private Stan Colbeck, 46th (South Saskatchewan) Battalion, 10th Brigade, 4th Canadian Division

However, once they were out of the canal bed the worst was over, as the German resistance began to collapse in front of the relieved Canadians as they pushed onwards.

Not so very far above them, Lieutenant Ronald Sykes of the RAF was flying his single-seater Sopwith Camel scout and engaging in numerous ground-strafing patrols in support of the advancing troops.

Bombing airfields, firing into ammunition dumps, attacking German troops on the move, especially troops that were retreating. They often retreated in confusion if they were attacked by aircraft. We had four little bombs carried under the fuselage on the rack. We didn't think the bombs did much good, in fact they told us the effect on the morale was far greater than any material damage they did. So, we usually dropped them in one go and made a bigger bang! The German riflemen had straight sights for shooting at our infantry, they didn't have any deflection sights for shooting at aircraft. We felt fairly safe with those: we thought they aimed straight at the aircraft and the bullets went astern because they hadn't aimed off to allow for speed. But if you came to a German machine-gun post, they'd usually got deflection sights and that was very different – they were likely to hit you.[12]

Lieutenant Ronald Sykes, 201 Sqdn, RAF

He set off flying at around 1,000 feet over the battlefield. It was an amazing sight as the bombardment crashed down.

A shell burst below me – and within a second the whole of the ground seemed to be turning over, boiling up in brown earth that had been thrown up and smoke from the bursting shells. I thought, 'Well nobody can live down there and I don't think I'm going to live long if I stay over the top of it!' So, I went straight on to the clear air over the German support areas. There I found the sunken roads were full of German troops – within seconds they'd all vanished into the grass verges – so I strafed the verges. I got rid of three of my four little bombs. Then four Fokkers came down from above, but I saw them coming and I'd had quite a lot of practice at taking evasive action, so I went down to ground level round the trees and zig-zagged back kept out of their way. We'd been told to attack troops and not go in for aerial combat, as other squadrons were up above to do that. As I got back into the battle smoke they broke away to the east and left me. I went back to the German infantry, just finished up my little strafe there, got rid of my last bomb. Then the smoke over the battle area was clearing and I could see the trenches. I spotted one advance trench with some Germans. I dived on it, fired, pulled up and did what I call a cartwheel over the far end of it and down again. I didn't shoot because they were running down the trench and seemed to have their hands up as I got close to them. I pulled up again and as I came back some British troops were just arriving and the Germans started to climb over the parapet going off to the west in single file as prisoners.[13]

Lieutenant Ronald Sykes, 201 Sqdn, RAF

The Canadians surged forward and successfully enveloped the German positions in Bourlon Wood. They had taken their initial objectives, but the second phase objectives of the Marcoing Line, the heights above Cambrai, and the de L'Escaut Canal all remained just out of reach, as the Germans managed to stem the advance by utilising these naturally strong defence works. The 4th Canadian Division was also hampered by the perceived failure of the XVII Corps on their right to keep pace with their advance, exposing the Canadians to considerable enfilade fire, which meant they made little further progress. To the left of the Canadians, the 11th and 56th Divisions made excellent progress, driving forward as far as Épinoy before nightfall.

To the south of the Canadian Corps, the 63rd (Royal Naval) Division was compressed on a narrow front just south of Moeuvres on the left flank of XVII Corps, where they were to support the advance of the 52nd Division. The 188th Brigade experienced considerable stiff fighting.

> We were met by a murderous hail of machine-gun bullets which bowled over a number of men. The line halted and the men sought cover in shell holes from whence they peered through the smoke looking for a sight of the enemy. A Petty Officer, an Able Seaman and myself took cover in a shell-hole and I pulled out my map and endeavoured to take stock of the situation. The Able Seaman gave a groan and dropped with a bullet through his side. He lay dying in the bottom of the shell-hole, and the Petty Officer was hit in the foot shortly afterwards. As the fire was heaviest on the right, I decided to move forward on the left flank. But the stream of bullets which were whizzing past us had put the wind up the troops and though I ran forward and ordered the advance, it was some time before I could get them to move swiftly. However, after a little urging from the Petty Officers, we moved forward over the ridge and down the opposite slope. I ordered a Leading Seaman to fetch up two Lewis guns to keep by me, but as he turned to obey a 5.9" burst between us blowing me over and severely wounding him in the throat and leg. Our appearance must have alarmed the Bosche, as the fire perceptibly slackened and we moved rapidly forward to

a position several hundred yards ahead, about 300 yards from a sugar factory. Then the machine-gun fire swelled out again and there were so many casualties that I called a halt and we arranged ourselves in a semi-circle of shell-holes and old Bosche artillery dugouts.[14]

Lieutenant Frank Hawkings, Anson Battalion, 188th Brigade, 63rd Division

A period of consolidation followed during which they sent out patrols probing towards the sugar factory that lay just beyond the Hindenburg Support Line. Having recognised the strength of the German position, they made an urgent request for extra artillery fire support. Hawking was then ordered to resume the attack at 14.15.

As soon as the 18-pounders were in action on the factory, I jumped up and ordered the advance, and this time the men, having become restive with the long halt, were not long in moving forward. We proceeded down the hillside to the left of the factory towards the Bapaume-Cambrai road. Here there was a short delay while we cleared some dugouts of Bosche artillery men. The bag included a Colonel. The Bosches had an awful wind-up, and hastened to barter for their lives with watches and cigars. I hurriedly collected the men and we made a rush across the road to the open country beyond, which sloped up towards the village of Graincourt about a mile away. Here we found detachments of the enemy in full retreat with their machine-guns, and these made good targets for my Lewis-gunners. They also made fruitless efforts to get their guns away. One gun – a 5.9" – was firing at us point-blank range, but fortunately my casualties were few. It was about 400 yards away when we first spotted it, but before we got any nearer, a gun team came galloping down from the village with spare horses for the gunners. The gun was swiftly limbered up and the whole caval-cade turned and made for the village at full gallop, with the officer leading. I hastily got a Lewis-gun in position, and then opened a strong fire with rifles as well. My Lewis gunner very wisely directed his fire on the leading horses and as soon as they fell, the remainder were quickly scuppered. When we reached the gun, not a man was alive. I must say that they showed grit in attempting to get it away.[15]

Lieutenant Frank Hawkings, Anson Battalion, 188th Brigade, 63rd Division

The 63rd Division completed the mopping up of the Hindenburg Support Line. But overall the XVII Corps fell short of its final objectives, lagging some 3,000 yards behind the right flank of the Canadian Corps.

South of XVII Corps was the Guards Division of VI Corps. Having reached their jumping-off trenches they settled down to await their fate. A small tot of rum did little or nothing to cheer them up.

We waited in silence, each man occupied with his own thoughts and no doubt wrestling with his own secret fears. I think that half-hour was probably the worst I have ever spent. Slowly and inexorably the minutes passed, second by second, and the time approached which might be the end of everything for me. The suppressed quivering in my limbs was not entirely due to the cold, and I had to clench my teeth hard to prevent them from chattering. All my efforts to screw up my courage, all my fatalistic self-assurances that 'what is to be, will be', became more and more useless, and hope seemed to ooze away with every second. At last the order was passed along in a whisper to fix bayonets, and we knew that the time had come. It was almost a relief to do something.[16]

Private Frederick Noakes, 1st Coldstream Guards, 2nd Guards Brigade, Guards Division

Soon the moment came, Zero Hour; the cacophony of the creeping barrage burst out all around them and they went over the top.

Then, all together, we were scrambling up the short ladders which had been placed against the side of the trench. Our chief thought was to get on our feet as quickly as possible, for the bullets were sweeping low and one stood in greater danger of a fatal wound while crawling over the parapet than when standing upright.

Several men in the Platoon were hit during those first few seconds, but I was untouched.[17]

Private Frederick Noakes, 1st Coldstream Guards, 2nd Guards Brigade, Guards Division

Some of the German guns had survived the counter-battery fire and they opened fire, trying to stem the attack as the Guards were crossing No Man's Land.

It seemed impossible that anyone could come alive through that cyclone of destruction. The sensation of standing up and crossing open ground under heavy fire is one which I find difficult, almost impossible, to describe in any ordinary terms. On first scrambling to my feet, I had a feeling of being stark naked, without a vestige of protection; and this was coupled with an extraordinary sensation – curiously like relief – that I was no longer personally responsible for my own safety. The issue was entirely out of my hands, I had nothing to do with it, and it mattered not at all whether I kept my head down or walked erect. The terrific uproar around made conscious thought and feeling impossible, and I stumbled forward with the others over the churned-up ground, heedless of the bullets which constantly cracked past, and watching, as if they did not concern me, the showers of sparks which shot up from the ground on all sides as shells exploded; in the general din, they seemed to be almost noiseless. It was like walking in a nightmare of Hell.[18]

Private Frederick Noakes, 1st Coldstream Guards, 2nd Guards Brigade, Guards Division

The Coldstream Guards also suffered a delay caused by a couple of German machine guns in the 'Mouse Post' strongpoint tucked away under the ruined bridge. Captain Cyril Frisby and Lance Corporal Thomas Jackson[19] together led a party forward under intense fire and rooted the Germans out from their reinforced concrete defences. Both would be awarded the Victoria Cross. Then the advance resumed, with Frisby leading the way, although by then he was suffering from the effects of a slight leg wound.

The steeply sloping sides, originally faced with brickwork, were badly broken by shellfire in many places, so that descent was comparatively easy; we climbed and slithered to the bottom, crossed piles of rubble and pools of mud and water, and scrambled up the farther bank. Here, Captain Frisby was waiting, just below the summit, and despite the hail of bullets which was still sweeping the ground, he gave a helping hand to each of us who needed it and had a cheerful word for everyone as we passed him. By the time we were across the canal it was getting quite light and I could see my immediate surroundings plainly, so that it must have been nearly half-past six. The German counter-barrage was by now much less vigorous, though their machine guns were still very active from the summit of the ridge.[20]

Private Frederick Noakes, 1st Coldstream Guards, 2nd Guards Brigade, Guards Division

Despite all their fears, the attack had been a success. Soon the second wave were leap-frogging them, pressing on to the next objectives.

Lord Gort, leading the front platoons into position for assault, was slightly wounded in the left eye. His head bandaged by his soldier servant, Guardsman Ransome, he carried on and, inspired by his example, we swept over the canal and on towards Flesquières, from which came heavy fire from guns planted in houses. A shell burst close to Gort, wounding him badly in the left arm. Bleeding profusely from a cut artery, he refused to go to a dressing station, and ordered Ransome to apply a tourniquet. But his energy drained away, and Captain Simpson, commanding our Company, took command of the Battalion. As we plodded on, to our amazement Gort reappeared. He leapt from his stretcher and rushed to join in again. The sight of this dauntless man, with his square figure, clipped moustache, fair windswept hair, cap tilted over his left ear and blood-soaked bandages, leaping into action, stirred our hearts and impelled us to efforts we thought were beyond our powers. We cleared a trench held by a crowd of Germans, and seized the next one, rounded up dozens of prisoners and took over two batteries of field guns. The goal achieved, Gort gave in at the point of collapse. The Germans spotted two men on the horizon and opened fire. They were Gort, staggering along, helped by Ransome. A shell severed one of Ransome's arms, and Gort hobbled on, found a medical officer and returned with him. They did their best for Ransome[21] but it was too late. Deeply distressed, Gort spoke of him as, 'One of the finest men who ever lived.'[22]

Private Norman Cliff, 1st Grenadier Guards, 3rd Brigade, Guards Division

Gort himself would survive the war and went on to command the BEF in 1940.

Further south was the IV Corps, who formed the right flank of the advancing Third Army. As they had to wait for the neighbouring division to achieve its objectives, the start time was some three hours later than their neighbours. They were required to attack the Hindenburg Line running obliquely across their front, pushing towards Beaucamp and Villers Plouich. Private John Grainger remembered waiting to go over the top in front of Havrincourt Wood.

We got our rum ration. You were just standing waiting; you couldn't be playing bloody football! Just waiting and hoping to God it would soon be over! You had to control yourself! There was no use getting a flap on because you'd upset some of the other lads. You knew you'd got to do it and you couldn't do anything about it! You'd got to blank your mind out about it! See how it goes on![23]

Private John Grainger, 1/7th Bn Lancashire Fusiliers, 125th Brigade, 42nd Division

When Grainger and the 1/7th Lancashire Fusiliers went over the top, the attack soon broke down as they came under heavy machine-gun fire.

We were off. Of course, when we got so far there was thick barbed wire about 4 foot high. We couldn't do much about that! We had to get through it, we'd got wire cutters and all that, but the trouble was your bloody rifle was in the road. I got tangled up it – it tore your trousers to bits! It would make a right ruddy gash – it was nasty stuff! Bloody shells dropping hither and thither! All of a sudden, this left arm dropped. My bloody arm was hanging like it was in two pieces! Do you know I never felt a thing – and the bottom of my trousers from my knees down was soaking wet in blood. I thought, 'My God!' I didn't know what the hell had happened to me! I just says to the Corporal, 'I think I've been hit!' He says, 'Well you know what to do – bugger off and get back as fast as you can! Dump everything you've got here!' I dumped everything except my tin hat, took my pack off and everything! As I was walking back there were crowds of Jerry prisoners coming in – they joined up with me! One of them saw this arm, so he took my braces off, put them round my neck and made a sling for the bottom part of my arm. All I wanted to do was get in the wood and get to a first aid post.[24]

Private John Grainger, 1/7th Bn Lancashire Fusiliers, 125th Brigade, 42nd Division

Grainger was evacuated back to safety. Despite enduring some terrible operations on his arm he would remain partially disabled for life.

There was much heavy fighting in the nearby Beaucamp sector. Leutnant Baldamus and the German Infantry Regiment 1/66 counter-attacked to achieve considerable initial successes.

We could hear hand grenades exploding, so the trench fight must have already begun. At the 2/66th sector headquarters east of Beau-camp, Captain Rieger ordered the Company to take the position west of Beaucamp, which was now in enemy hands. Even before the company began the attack, a British tank, which had bypassed the 1/66th position, inflicting heavy casualties, was knocked out by a 1/66th anti-tank rifle. In order to roll-up the communications trench which led to the 1/66th position from the north, a hand grenade squad was immediately formed: it had recently conducted attack practise at the training area. The attack was conducted aggressively and succeeded completely. Initially the British fought back, but after a few waves of hand grenades they climbed out of the trench in groups and ran over the open field to the rear, pursued by enthusiastic fire from us, some of it delivered standing.

The company succeeded, with light loss, in retaking the whole 1/66 position west of Beaucamp and re-establishing contact with 27th Regiment. The company's situation was nevertheless anything but rosy. The British lay in the large shell craters in front of the 1/66 position and half-left behind the company was the village of Beaucamp, occupied by the British, from where they tried to roll-up the 1/66 trench: after some small initial success, they were thrown back again. As security against Beaucamp, a platoon occupied a communications trench leading to the rear. The British in Beaucamp continually fired into the company rear, killing the brave Senior Sergeants Kilz and Schmidt with bullets to the head.[25]

Leutnant Baldamus, Infantry Regiment 1/66, 13th Brigade, 7th Division

The advance of the British to their left meant that it was all in vain and Baldamus and his regiment were forced to retire to a line from Marcoing-Villers Plouich. This was fairly typical, as localised German successes were undermined by the overall success of the British advance.

On 28 September, the First and Third Armies pushed on further, gaining between 2,000 and 5,000 yards and overrunning the Marcoing Line, while a firm northern boundary to the salient was created along the Sensée Canal. Yet there was a still a heavy price to pay. When the 1st Coldstream Guards marched back to their billets, there was no disguising that they had been through a traumatic ordeal. Their diminished numbers alone would make it evident. There was little joy in their victory.

We were all tired to the point of exhaustion, and limp from lack of food; our mouths and throats were dry as lime-kilns. Nerves were on edge and tempers frayed, as always after the intense strain of going over the top and any small disagreement was liable to flare into a quarrel. We trudged wearily along in the darkness, with little of the Guards' traditional smartness. True, one or two incurable optimists tried to start a song, but we lacked the energy, or inclination to keep it going, and it died a natural death after a few bars.[26]

Private Frederick Noakes, 1st Coldstream Guards, 2nd Guards Brigade, Guards Division

Yet collectively the First and Third Armies had achieved great things. They had advanced on a front 12 miles wide, punching up to 5 miles into the German defences. They may not have achieved all their objectives, but given the strength of the defensive system they had demonstrated that the Germans could no longer withstand a major assault. The attacks would continue for the next couple of days, securing a crossing over the Schelde Canal on the right and leaving the First Army troops facing the last defences around Cambrai. That would be the next step forwards.

4

FIFTH BATTLE OF YPRES AND BATTLE OF COURTRAI

The dismal belt of land devastated by four years of war lies behind. In front, and slightly below us, is spread a flat, unshelled plain, intersected by winding 'beeks', and dotted with undamaged farms, hamlets, and a few trees. The ground, neglected agriculturally, is covered with long ripe grass.[1]

Brigadier General James Jack, Headquarters, 28th Brigade, 9th Division

ANOTHER DAY: ANOTHER ATTACK. Politics played no small part in the genesis of the Flanders operations launched on 28 September as the third in the great series of offensives organised by Foch in late September. King Albert I of Belgium was keen that his divisions should play a real part in the offensive designed to finally liberate his people from German occupation. Foch had acquiesced and, with British agreement, created a Flanders Army Group, which consisted of twelve Belgian infantry divisions, the ten divisions of the British Second Army and six French divisions all under the nominal command of Albert, although operations were to be directed

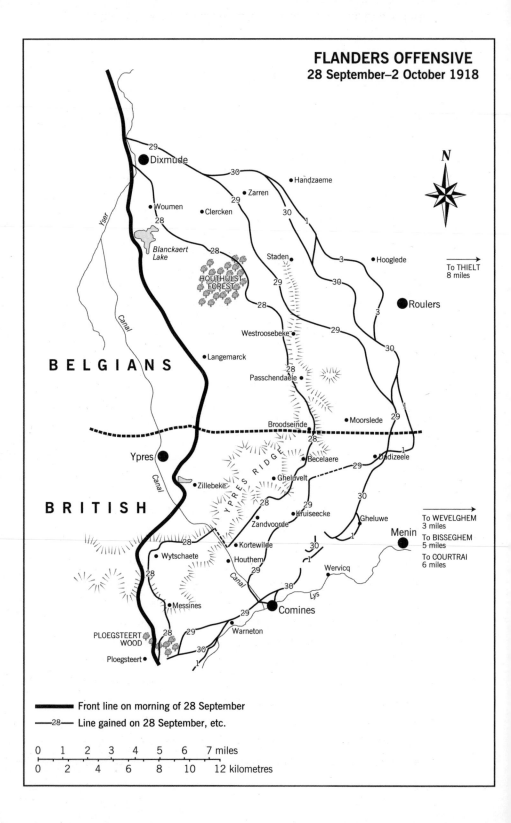

FLANDERS OFFENSIVE
28 September–2 October 1918

N

Dixmude
Handzaeme
Zarren
Woumen
Clercken
Blanckaert Lake
HOUTHULST FOREST
Staden
Hooglede
Roulers
Westroosebeke
Langemarck
Passchendaele
Moorslede
Broodseinde
Ypres
Becelaere
Zillebeke
Gheluvelt
Dadizeele
Y P R E S R I D G E
Zandvoorde
Kruiseecke
Gheluwe
Kortewilde
Menin
Wytschaete
Houthem
Wervicq
Messines
Comines
Lys
PLOEGSTEERT WOOD
Warneton
Ploegsteert

Yser
Canal
Canal
Canal

BELGIANS

BRITISH

To THIELT
8 miles

To WEVELGHEM
3 miles
To BISSEGHEM
5 miles
To COURTRAI
6 miles

━━━ Front line on morning of 28 September
──28── Line gained on 28 September, etc.

| 0 | 1 | 2 | 3 | 4 | 5 | 6 | 7 miles |
| 0 | 2 | 4 | 6 | 8 | 10 | 12 kilometres |

by his Chief of Staff, General Jean Degoutte, who was 'double-hatted' as the commander of the French Sixth Army. It was decided to ignore the German possession of the Messines Ridge, but the Second Army was to gain the Gheluvelt Plateau before pushing forward to Zandvoorde and Kruiseecke. Meanwhile, to the north, the Belgian Army would secure a line stretching from Clercken through to Broodseinde, thereby recapturing the Passchendaele Ridge of evil memory.

The planning process swung into action, with a minor problem being the differences in bombardment tactics between the British and Belgians. These wrinkles were soon smoothed away, although the Belgians clung to a preliminary three-hour bombardment, in contrast to the now established British practice of a sudden crushing bombardment and creeping barrage beginning at the appointed Zero Hour of 05.30. Arrangements were made for gun positions to be pre-prepared for a mixture of field, medium and heavy guns close up to the existing front lines, so that when the infantry attacked, these guns could be immediately moved forward to allow a much deeper penetration of the German lines while still covered by barrage fire. Individual guns were sent forward independently to operate in close support to the infantry so that they could bring down fire as required to eradicate pockets of German resistance.

One 'old stager', Captain Francis Hitchcock, was much taken by the briefing that he and other officers of 88th Brigade received from Lieutenant General Claude Jacob, the commander of II Corps on 23 September.

> He had a great personality, and I was very impressed with his charming manner. He informed us of the following facts: the impending attack at Ypres by the Second Army, the approximate date, etc. He showed us the divisional boundaries and objectives, all marked in coloured pencil on the familiar map, 'Sheet 28'. The Belgian Army would cooperate on our left and the right flank of the attacking troops would pivot on St Eloi. He impressed on us the need for the use of the rifle and bayonet, and recalled the awful phase which our Army had passed through in '16 and '17, owing to the troops being so frightfully weak in musketry. Many divisions, through excessive use of hand grenades, had lost confidence in the

rifle as the infantryman's weapon. He said in the coming attack it was proposed to almost completely eliminate bombs. The General said that as practically all the landmarks had disappeared in the Salient, we would have to pin great faith on our compasses. Owing to the sodden state of the country, and the few lines of communication, he stated that he had arranged for our ammunition to be dropped near the advancing troops by aeroplanes when signalled for by ground flares, by the infantry. Turning to Brigadier General Freyberg, VC, he asked, 'How did that experiment work in your brigade the other day?' 'Oh,' replied the Brigadier, 'A box of S.A.A. fell on top of an advancing platoon, and one man was killed!'[2]

Captain Francis Hitchcock, 2nd Leinster Regiment, 88th Brigade, 29th Division

When Hitchcock moved forward to carry out a reconnaissance of the sector in which they were to attack, he discovered that his memories of previous service in the Ypres Salient some three years before would be of little value. Shellfire had recast the landscape, erasing woods, churches and villages to leave a brownscape of featureless shell holes, with a criss-crossing mesh of trenches, barbed wire, derelict tanks, splintered tree stumps and patches of pinkish brick dust. The German positions were not strongly held, but there was still a network of concrete pillboxes with masses of barbed wire scattered about the mud.

Considerable thought had been given to the problems of fighting in open warfare beyond the established trenches.

Fortunately, we got the chance to train in September and we took full advantage of it. We found that widely extended lines of infantry could be replaced largely by tiny columns in single file, the smallest command, which again is the only possible number which can be handled by one man, the section. But we found that we wanted something more than this. What of the people who were nearest to the enemy during an advance? Were small columns, however small, entirely suitable in a close country, for example, where there is a possibility of a machine gun lying for you in ambush? From time immemorial, columns, of whatever size, have always been covered by skirmishers. Now one was, and is, convinced that the art of skir-mishing was lost to us after the Peninsular War, and that we have no idea what really good skirmishing is; and giving one's mind to this all-absorbing subject one began to work out a system based on the following: in the first place, a line of men extended at very wide intervals is simply asking for trouble. They are no protection, for they always get lost; they are no menace to an enemy, who merely has to cut them off; and they have no confidence in themselves, since man, especially if he is town-bred as most of our people are, is a gregarious animal, and is consequently completely out of his element when by himself in close country. And if we are agreed that we must have these wide extensions, and that we must have men together, it follows that we must work those men in pairs – mates – they used to call themselves; men who always work together, but who do not keep together like a pair of plough-horses, for while one man goes forward he is always covered by the other fellow's rifle.[3]

Lieutenant Colonel William Croft, Headquarters, 27th Brigade, 9th Division

At Plumer's Second Army headquarters there was a large-scale model which allowed key officers from each division to be shown the general layout of the battlefield and give them the opportunity to visualise their role within the greater scheme of things. It is evident that the prepara-tions were taken extremely seriously, as many of these men had been witness to disasters caused by slapdash planning or cutting corners in the preparations for previous offensives.

Failure may follow the best laid plans, carried out by the finest troops, because after all, one can only guess the enemy's strength and what he will do, the weather and other factors. But the risks of failure, or even of unduly long casualty lists, are tremendously increased by unsound or incomplete plans; by troops not thoroughly knowing their role, or being insufficiently rested before action; by slack disci-pline, shortage of training and poor leading. Having had ample time to prepare, time fully used, we must make no avoidable mistakes. For the many instant decisions required in action one has to rely on the courage and training of junior leaders. The general plan can be little altered once battle is joined, except by the use of reserves.[4]

Brigadier General James Jack, Headquarters, 28th Brigade, 9th Division

As ever, the British plan was based on the primacy of their artillery. That superiority had been painstakingly accumulated through the industrial strength that allowed the manufacture of thousands of guns and millions of shells. The gun detachments had all been trained; the gunnery specialists had mastered the science of gunnery. Now the guns would be unleashed to blast the way forward across the low ridges beyond Ypres.

All evening after dark, tractors and caterpillars, ammunition lorries and siege trains had been clanking and lurching up the roads in one long stream. About midnight the preliminaries seemed to be complete; silence settled over the ridge, only disturbed by an occasional dull boom or sharp crash as one of our own heavies behind us spoke forth his message, or a Bosche harassing shell burst over one of the now silent tracks or crossroads, or near the bridges. Even such sounds as these died out about 1 o'clock. Here and there in the darkness around us a little twinkling light would peep out for a moment as some gun crew tested their night lines and carefully laid their steel baby on her line, laid her with the utmost accuracy, the outcome of hours of work by the battery officers in the command posts. In the low dugouts beside the guns, fuse-numbers were fixing and setting their fuses; limber gunners in the blackness were giving a last affectionate touch up with their oil-rags to yawning breeches.[5]

Lieutenant Harold Nelson, 140th Heavy Battery, 36th Brigade, Royal Garrison Artillery

For an hour or so, the gunners were ordered to turn in and try and get some sleep to leave them fresher for the battle to come. Then the last meteorological corrections were made to allow for variations in wind, barometric pressure and temperature. The guns were loaded and ready to open fire. The three-hour Belgian bombardment would begin at 02.30, supported by the British heavy guns firing at all the German gun batteries on their front that were capable of firing into the Belgian sector.

At last the order to 'Fire' comes, and the barrage unfurls all along the line. In a flash night becomes day. Nelson attempts to create an ono-matopoeic soundscape.

There is a faint cry away on our right – somebody yells 'FIRE!' And the blackness is rent in twain – almost you think the ground is lifting under your feet. The whole world trembles – buildings, ruins, dugouts, doors, tables, your map-board are rattling and full of tremors. Then a moment's silence, and then Spit! Flash! Boom! Boom! BOOM! Bang! Bang! Grrh-humph! Flash! Boom! Boom! Crash! Crash! BER-BOOM! (the big men in the rear) and, away in front, thud – rattle – thud – thud – thud – thousands of thuds – rattle thud – CRASH! Ripples of crashes. BOOM! The 18-pounders are rattling old Fritz to some pretty tune. Can you see the sweating figures? BOOM! Grrh-humph! Grr-humph! That is the 6-inch Mark XIXs waking Jerry from his slumbers 25,000 yards away. Go-brumph! Go-brumph! Go-brumph! there go the 60-pounders, the 'silent devils' that Jerry hates the worst of all. BER-BOOM! That is a 12-inch railway mounting, BER-BOOM! Two of them – splen-did! What a hell over there beyond the black line of that ridge. Spit! Crash! CRASH! Thud! Thud! Thud! Boom! Flash! Crash! BOOM! You don't know what 'Life' spelt with a big 'L' is till you lived through such moments as these. Look at Fritz now – in his trenches, his pill-boxes, his dugouts and shanties; he is running about afraid – horribly AFRAID; his morale is now low, and soon be lower still; he can't man his guns; he can't get near them and live; his biggest group of batter-ies practically has not fired a round, as we were told at daybreak our shooting had been magnificent. Look into his trench and outposts – Crash! Blast! Smash! Whistling shrapnel – whirring, torn and cruelly jagged H.E. – look at him waiting for us, crouching in his corners, the cold sweat fearful on his face. When are they coming! Why don't they come? Fear and a still bigger fear behind those two questions. Do we feel pity for him? No![6]

Lieutenant Harold Nelson, 140th Heavy Battery, 36th Brigade, Royal Garrison Artillery

As the artillery raged on the men prepared to go over the top.

> The men were in the best of spirits making their tea and were
> much amused at the attempts of the pipers to 'tune up' in the roar
> of the barrage. The cursed rain was now coming down as it always
> did for all the British operations in the Ypres Salient. Having had
> a short spell of fine weather, we were all in hopes of a fine day for
> the attack, as rain had such a terrible effect on the sodden and
> churned-up Ypres terrain. However, it was not to be.[7]
>
> Captain Francis Hitchcock, 2nd Leinster Regiment, 88th Brigade, 29th
> Division

Strangely, the weather turned out to be the worst of their worries. From
the moment of Zero Hour at 05.30, the British heavy guns commenced
a heavy bombardment of all identified German batteries, deluging them
with gas shells to neutralise them at the critical moment. Other heavy
batteries joined in with the creeping barrage, adding their weight to the
wall of shells. The Royal Artillery also provided a thick smoke barrage and
counter-battery fire to neutralise any possible interference from German
batteries along the Messines Ridge, which flanked the intended line of
advance from the Ypres Salient.

In the event, the German retaliation was feeble. Thanks to the collective work of the RAF photo-reconnaissance squadrons, the flash spotters
and the sound rangers, most of the German gun batteries had been successfully identified and silenced. The creeping barrage was almost perfect,
sweeping away most of the German opposition. The surviving pillbox
garrisons were picked off by employing the efficient tactics that had been
so painfully mastered in the 1917 fighting on these self-same ridges:
pinning fire on the front to mask the approach of flanking parties intent
on assaulting the rear entrance or lobbing grenades through the slit. The
Leinsters reached Hooge with few casualties. Nevertheless, it was hardly
a pleasant experience.

> A torrential rain was now driving in our faces, and we got soaked
> to the skin as we moved off from Hooge, C Company leading, with
> platoons on a wide frontage, in snake formation, on the north side

and parallel with the Menin Road. The going was very heavy over the bleached rank grass. There were numerous shell craters and disused telephone lines mixed up with the rusty strands of old wire entanglements. The whole area was intersected with trenches of every description, which had to be negotiated – consequently the advance was tedious. The Lewis gunners had a hard task carrying the weighty Lewis guns. Here and there we passed an old derelict field gun, or a recently abandoned one in its muddy pit. Where the edge of Inverness Copse had been, we passed British graves of 1914, and I particularly noted 2nd Worcestershire Regiment and 2nd Connaught Rangers printed on the wooden crosses. They were all dated October and November 1914. Along the Menin Road on our right flank we could see our Brigadier riding with his staff. We now got orders to close on the road, as no enemy were in sight. We formed up and moved off in fours towards Gheluvelt. As we marched we heard that the Messines Ridge had been captured by our troops. We passed a few Bosche transport waggons complete with horses; these were quickly annexed by our people for rations. Abandoned guns, also left at the last moment with smashed sights, were ditched along the roadside. Several shells burst over us without doing any damage, and the column of fours was not broken. On the western outskirts of the Gheluvelt shambles at exactly 11.30 the Battalion halted and fell out. Immediately out came the mess tins, and 'drumming up the char' commenced.[8]

Captain Francis Hitchcock, 2nd Leinster Regiment, 88th Brigade, 29th Division

Near Stirling Castle, Brigadier General George Jackson had a dark – but to him – amusing encounter with a British soldier in the Jackdaw Tunnels, as Jackson's 89th Brigade came up in support behind the advance brigades of 29th Division.

It was raining hard, but we were all at the top of our form because the fight was going so well. A sentry presented arms to me at the mouth of one of the tunnels. Even the 29th did not, as a rule, pay compliments during a battle, so I asked him what he was playing at, and why he did not watch the mouth of the tunnel in case any Bosche came up from the dugouts, which had not yet been searched. He stood aside to let me see, at the same time saying, 'The tunnel is all right!' I saw a German, whom he had bayoneted and pushed into the narrow opening, doubled up like a Jack-in-the-box, to stop any one coming up.[9]

Brigadier General George Jackson, Headquarters, 89th Brigade, 29th Division

Still further they went, reaching the line of the Kruiseecke Spur, where, at the end of October 1914, the British line had been overwhelmed by the German onslaught.

In all a strip of devastated ground some 5 miles deep was gained on 28 September. The entire Third Ypres battleground had been overrun in a single day. Alongside the left flank of II Corps, the Belgian Army had advanced with an equal effectiveness. The Belgian contribution is often forgotten, but nine Belgian divisions were involved, with seven of them in the front line as they attacked on a frontage of 15,000 yards. They overcame any pockets of serious resistance they encountered, pushing forward, with their right wing securing Passchendaele; the centre overran the hitherto impenetrable dark fastness of Houthulst Forest, while to the north they angled back their line of advance to connect with the original Belgian trenches just to the south of Dixmude. The French VII Corps and three cavalry divisions were still back in reserve.

The aviators of the RAF had also played their part that day despite the poor flying conditions caused by the rain and low cloud. The RE8 artillery cooperation aircraft were forced to fly low and suffered several losses to German ground fire. The SE5a, Sopwith Camel, Sopwith Dolphin and Bristol Fighters were engaged in patrols to fend off and destroy any German scouts, while seizing every chance to engage in low-level ground strafing to harass German troops wherever they were sighted on the battlefield. Although bomb loads and bomb aimers were both still inadequate, there was also a concentrated effort to disrupt possible German reinforcements by attacking nearby the railheads and rail junctions. In one such case at 17.00, the DH9 two-seater bombers of 206 Squadron were ordered to bomb a German counter-attack division that had been reported detraining the Menin station.

> It would have been suicidal to fly in formation with cloud down to ground level in places; so it was decided we should take off independently at short intervals, and fly at a set speed and height on a compass course and after a calculated time come down low, until we could locate Ypres. Atkinson and I took off first, followed by the others in turn; all our available aircraft – fifteen – had been laid on. Atkinson and I found Ypres on schedule and flew low along the Menin Road just above the clouds. As we neared Menin we suddenly ran into a clear area, like a dome over the target with the ceiling about 3,000 feet or so. We climbed to about 1,500 feet for our bombing run, dropped our 12 x 25lb bombs and machine gunned the station area, which was full of rolling stock with German troops all over the place unloading and forming up. As we turned away we saw the next one of our machines arrive and repeat the act, followed at regular intervals by all the others in turn; bombing from about 3,000 feet. Atkinson and I achieved complete surprise and were not fired at during our attack, but by now every 'Archie' gun and machine gun in the Menin area seemed to be pooping off at our machines; we could see clearly the gunners in their emplacements. However, 1,500 to 3,000 feet was reckoned a pretty safe height in those days, too high for effective machine gun fire and too low for the guns, they just could not swing their guns fast enough to follow their target, and all their shells were bursting 400 yards astern. None of us were hit and after our last machine had bombed and shot up the station I fired the signal to break off combat and return home.[10]

Second Lieutenant John Blanford, 206 Squadron

It was subsequently reported that they had disrupted the detrainment of the German division to such an extent that an expected counter-attack never materialised.

All told, it was evident that the first day of the fighting had been a stunning achievement by the British and Belgian Armies. It was even

more impressive in contrast to the awful butchery during the Third Battle
of Ypres, peaking at the fighting in Passchendaele, which had occurred
here just a year before.

> The day's success has been astonishing: an advance of over 5
> miles – more than in four months' bloody fighting last year. No
> doubt the hostile shelling has been less severe than formerly, and
> his infantry, behind ample defences, have not put up their wonted
> resistance. Nevertheless, allowing for every mercy (including our
> smoke screens), the good leading and drive of all ranks from sunrise
> to sundown, through this bullet-swept wilderness, has been admi-
> rable, hustling the enemy off his feet.[11]
>
> Brigadier General James Jack, Headquarters, 28th Brigade, 9th Division

The long siege of Ypres was over at last. The Germans were well aware of
the scale of the defeat suffered by their Fourth Army, with Crown Prince
Rupprecht, commanding Army Group Rupprecht (Second, Fourth, Sixth
and Seventeenth Armies) ruefully commenting that, 'The worst is that
according to a report from Fourth Army, the troops will no longer stand
up to a serious attack.'[12]

On 29 September, General Degoutte decided to continue to push
his men forwards. He instructed the Belgian divisions to advance on
Morslede, while Plumer's Second Army was to take up a line along the
River Lys. The 1st Royal Inniskilling Fusiliers had been in reserve, but
were now following up the advancing troops over the Gheluvelt plateau
and moving towards the small village of Terhand. The rain was still
pouring down. Although the advance was successful, there was soon work
for the toiling stretcher-bearers, such as Private Wilfred Heavens.

> A shell dropped at the head of one of the platoons and wounded
> the Platoon officer. As he fell, the pack on his back caught alight.
> Inside his pack he was carrying flares used for signalling our posi-
> tion to aeroplanes, which started to burn and would have caught
> his tunic alight had not a sergeant and two privates near him
> rushed up and dragged the pack off. They had no sooner done this
> than another shell came over and dropped at the same spot, killing

outright the officer and Sergeant, and wounding the two Privates. By this time, we had reached them with the stretcher and, laying it down, were just going to attend the wounded, when another shell dropped a couple of yards away. I fell flat down on my face and, rising after the explosion had finished, found that the other two bearers had vanished. The Company had advanced on, and I was left alone with the two wounded men. One was now unconscious and the other had a broken leg. He was thoroughly scared with shock, and cried piteously for me to take him away before another shell came and killed him. I did not stop to bandage or splint his leg but, grasping him under the arms, dragged him away from the place as fast as I could. His broken leg trailed over the ground, causing him great pain and making him yell. I had only got a few yards away when another shell came over and burst right alongside the dead officer and Sergeant.[13]

Private Wilfred Heavens, 1st Royal Inniskilling Fusiliers, 109th Brigade, 36th Division

Heavens eventually caught up with the rest of the Inniskillings, but found them in a poor state of morale. The rain pelting down on them was doing nothing to improve their mood.

The men were lying about everywhere fast asleep. Some were in shell holes, trying to get cover from the rain, then woke up and found themselves half covered with water which had collected in the hole during the night. Others were lying in the grass under a waterproof sheet. Several men were missing, and we were asked if we had taken them down wounded to the dressing station. We had not, but later we found that they had been seen in the dressing station with light bullet wounds in their hands and arms, which were probably self-inflicted as we had not yet had any rifle fire to contend with, although the troops in front had.[14]

Private Wilfred Heavens, 1st Royal Inniskilling Fusiliers, 109th Brigade, 36th Division

The operational front had widened as the XIX Corps took Zandvoorde and Holebeke in reaching the line of the River Lys, while to the south, the X Corps advanced to seize Wytschaete and the Messines Ridge, which had been abandoned. The Germans planned a retreat to a series of defensive positions covering Menin and Roulers: Flanders I stretching north from Bousbecque on the River Lys to Morselede; the Gheluwe Switch running from Wervicq to Gheluwe; and Flanders II running north from just west of Menin up to De Ruiter, just 2 miles from the major railhead of Roulers.

By 1 October, the German resistance had begun to stiffen as their reinforcements were rushed up to bolster the defence. Part of Flanders I had been overrun, but Flanders II and the Gheluwe Switch stood firm. Private Wilfred Heavens and the 1st Royal Inniskilling Fusiliers played a part in the II Corps advance, overwhelming a German rearguard that was occupying an isolated farmhouse to the east of Dadizeele. They knew that even in retreat the Germans could pose a deadly threat.

> After a scuffle or two, we drove him helter-skelter across an open ploughed field into a wood beyond. The farmyard was converted into an advance dressing station. We were soon busy bandaging up and sending away the wounded. The village of just behind us was being shelled so badly that it was almost suicide to enter it. Shells were dropping frequently round the village church on the main road, and all troops, with the exception of traffic, crossed the fields avoiding the village. As we ventured from the farmyard into the ploughed field we were met with machine-gun fire from the wood beyond, which was so effective that we were forced to retire back to the farmyard, leaving many wounded behind on the field.[15]

Private Wilfred Heavens, 1st Royal Inniskilling Fusiliers, 109th Brigade, 36th Division

Afterwards, Heavens went out to collect the casualties and in among the men who had been genuinely wounded, he also found a case that aroused his deepest suspicions.

> We were met by a man wounded in the wrist. The wound seemed to be self-inflicted, as the flesh surrounding the bullet hole was

burnt almost black, proving that the muzzle of the rifle had been almost touching his wrist when the trigger had been pulled. He was in a terrible state, groaning and pleading that he had not done it deliberately, but that his rifle had gone off as he fixed his bayonet.[16]

Private Wilfred Heavens, 1st Royal Inniskilling Fusiliers, 109th Brigade, 36th Division

As the troops advanced across the recent battlefield they saw many strange sights. Corpses were littered about the landscape and every so often they would find a macabre tableau, reflecting the moment of death.

The whole of the front of the house had fallen into the road. The inside was visible and there were German soldiers sitting at a table, others apparently waiting on them, doing various things – it was just like a waxwork. They didn't seem injured, they seemed as if they had just been suddenly struck dead.[17]

Private Victor Polhill, No. 1 Observation Group, Royal Engineers

Battlefield clearance began as soon as feasible. During the process, groups of corpses were often discovered, revealing the sheer savagery of the fighting. In many cases, it was evident that no quarter had been given – or sought.

We were on fatigue collecting equipment which had been dumped by the wounded and taken off the dead. Reaching the main railway line between Roulers and Menin, we found any amount of dead lying across the lines, both British and German. We removed their equipment and stacked it in a heap. Further along, we came to a German blockhouse on the side of the line. Going to the back, we found steps leading to the top, where we found a destroyed German machine gun and a dead gunner by the side of it. He had commanded a splendid position, and this no doubt accounted for the numerous British casualties lying on the lines in front. Once our chaps had reached him, he had gone through it, for his body was terribly battered about.[18]

Private Wilfred Heavens, 1st Royal Inniskilling Fusiliers, 109th Brigade, 36th Division

As the divisions poured forward, the supply situation for both the Second Army and the Belgian Army became somewhat desperate. The wasteland behind them acted like a wall across their supply lines, slowing everything down to a crawl. As presaged in Lieutenant General Claude Jacob's briefing a few days before, the situation grew so desperate that the RAF found themselves given a vital role, the DH9s of 218 Squadron being ordered to drop food rations to the advanced troops.

> We were given a map reference of where they were and told to go and drop bags of bully beef. The observer had three sandbags filled with about fifty tins of bully beef to one sandbag. When we came to the destination, I saw the Belgian soldiers in their blue uniforms who seemed to expect me. I came down to about 100 feet and did a series of figure of eights. When we were over the troops my observer dropped the sandbags – the ground was all muddy so he just lifted them out and dropped them – there was no parachute attached to them. All those figure of eights fooled my sense of direction and I just flew on the direction I thought was the way home – I would have got to the North Sea and then all I had to do was turn left until we got to Dunkirk. But I was flying and flying and no North Sea appeared. Then I remembered the compass and I looked at it and saw I had been flying south-east – taking me further and further into enemy territory! So I flew on a course north-west.[19]
>
> Second Lieutenant Frank Burslem, 218 Squadron, RAF

In all, the RAF dropped some 15,000 individual rations totalling some 13 tons in weight. Yet this was little more than a fig leaf to cover up a massive problem.

Over the next couple of days, further prospects of British and Belgian progress were stymied by the Flanders II line. It was clear that nothing less than a proper artillery barrage would suffice to eject the Germans. Between 28 September and 3 October, the Flanders Army Group had been responsible for capturing 10,000 German prisoners, 300 guns and 600 machine guns. The German front was crumbling; surely all that was required was one more thrust. Yet a delay of nearly two weeks ensued.

The Allies wanted to attack, they had the men, they had the guns, but they were not ready.

THE LOGISTICAL CHAOS EXPERIENCED during the offensive in Flanders was a warning that such factors were likely to increase during the later stages of the offensives. The problem of getting munitions and supplies forward could not be solved by the 'sticking plaster' of air supply drops. Typical was the situation of the II Corps, whose sole source of supply was what was left of the old pavé Menin and Zonnebeke roads. Even when basic repairs had been carried out, these roads remained in a dreadful condition. The result was a traffic jam of biblical proportions.

> I had never previously realized the number and variety of vehicles which move in support of three Divisions; indeed, I think this road fed only the 9th and 36th Divisions. There were limbers by scores with rations; there were G.S. wagons with forage for the battalion transports forward; there were Royal Engineer wagons, mess-carts, guns and ammunition; there were lorries stuck in shell-holes in the road, and the cause of most of the trouble. On every odd bit of ground bordering the road were French cavalrymen. The surface and the language were equally bad, and there was mud everywhere. I had to wind my way through these troubles for several miles. During my journey, there was practically no movement of the traffic. It had taken C Company's transport 14 hours to do the 6 miles from Ypres to the Ridge, and the Company bivouacked on the road for a night. A Gotha flew down that road at midnight, dropping bombs at regular intervals. I'm glad I missed that. There must have been many casualties, for that road was a mass of animals and men. Why only one Gotha was out that night beats me.[20]

Captain Densmore Walker, 109th Machine Gun Company, 36th Division

Even when they were across the old Salient battlegrounds, things did not improve much, as the German demolitions had created gaping craters in the roadway to further impede progress. Improvised mines were a terrible threat, as the Germans buried artillery shells, leaving just enough clearance for a wooden plank carefully positioned above the nose of the shell, before being buried in debris. If a vehicle ran over the plank it would set off the shell, causing further chaos. There were many variants on these themes.

> The common booby traps took the form of a tin filled with explosive, a spring-loaded lid with a plunger and detonator fitted inside. They were planted in shallow holes in the road surface and covered over. The mule's feet would not explode them, but immediately the wheels and the 'piece' came on to the lid, up they all went. It was particularly dangerous to remove these traps when corroded, as any movement might explode them. The traps were always dealt with by the Royal Engineer officer. I had another tricky problem concerning the removal of some 10 cwt of liquid perdite in jars placed in a culvert on the only main road leading to the front, over which the division would have to move in their advance. The detonators were much rusted and I was relieved when they were disconnected and the explosive dumped in nearby shell holes by my sappers. Immediately I reported all clear, the guns and wagons began to roar up the road towards the enemy positions.[21]
>
> Lieutenant Godefroy Skelton, 205th Field Company, Royal Engineers, 35th Division

The railways were also treated to a systematic demolition programme, with shells buried and then exploded about every 80 yards, while gun-slabs were detonated at every rail joint. The repairs required a massive engineering infrastructure programme. They could be rushed, but manpower and skill shortages meant that it all still took time.

Foch was anxious to secure the earliest possible restart for offensive operations in Flanders, at the latest by 10 October, but the logistical imperatives could not be denied. In the meantime, this did not mean that the Second Army did nothing. Everything possible was done to pin German forces on this front, while the British First, Third and Fourth Armies attacked to the south. A programme of harassing bombardments, energetic patrolling and raids left the Germans fearful that any day the 'real' attack might come, and the resulting tension – not knowing when the attack might be launched, but knowing it would be soon – had an enervating impact on the German troops huddled in their trenches and dugouts.

At 21.00 on 10 October, one typical harassing raid was launched when Lieutenant Richard Read led a raid on the German positions clustered round the eastern outskirts of Gheluwe. A box barrage would be fired to cut off the target sector before Reed, accompanied by another officer, two NCOs and twelve men, crept forward towards the village.

> The guns started and a shell seemed to drop about every twenty seconds, as we judged, beyond the target, although clods of earth and iron smacked against the trucks behind us, and we were glad of the small cover the ditch afforded. Then an SOS rocket rose from our front. Tension rose, as I hoped fervently that the shelling would stop, I remember a machine gun spitting out as from the ground – firing, mercifully, at an angle – as we stumbled forward. As I ran I emptied my revolver at the flashes. It stopped, and almost as it did so I saw two upraised arms and a German steel helmet, but was too late to avoid falling into the pit on top of the owner. Scrambling to our feet, the German raised his arms again shouting, 'Kamerad!' and something about 'Muder und kinder'. He was thoroughly frightened, as half a dozen bayonets were now pointed at him. Suddenly I thought of the gun, and scrambled out of the pit to see a running figure carrying something heavy in the greenish light of an ascending rocket. I yelled to the men, who fired as hard as they could, but the quarry escaped into the darkness beyond. We were disappointed at this, but soon recovered our good spirits when eyeing our prisoners.[22]
>
> Lieutenant Richard Read, 4th Royal Sussex Regiment, 101st Brigade, 34th Division

They made it safely back and sent their prisoner off back to their brigade headquarters for interrogation.

Overall, such raids, and photographic reconnaissance by the RAF, revealed no signs of any desperate German efforts to create new defence lines in Flanders. It was therefore suspected that the Germans were preparing to retire, not just to Lille, but all the way back to the River Schelde. Still, nothing was certain, and consequently plans were prepared to launch an assault on the Flanders II on 14 October. This time the main assault was to be made by the French, while the Belgians protected the left flank and Plumer's Second Army continued to cover the right flank by advancing to, and holding, the line of the River Lys. Plumer warned his corps commanders that, as the evacuation of Lille might well be triggered at any time during by the next attack, they should be ready to launch attacks across the Lys at Wervicq, Lauwe and Marcke.

Before the attack, Brigadier General Bernard Freyberg made an inspection tour of his jumping-off lines in the Ledeghem area. Here he found the men in sombre mood as they prepared for yet another attack.

> It was a fine starlight night when I went round the assembly area. The men were all sitting with their legs dangling into the newly dug trenches ready to disappear into them should the shelling become dangerous. I told the men all the latest news, and said that in my opinion the war would be over with another few attacks. I was very much struck by the nonchalance of the men, who seemed to have become automatons in the last few weeks; there was no life in them; their pulses were slower than usual. An attack had ceased long since to act as a stimulant; only the feeling that it had to be gone through with kept the men going.[23]

Brigadier General Bernard Freyberg, Headquarters, 88th Brigade, 29th Division

However, as Freyberg left, there was incident that might well have considerably cheered his men – as he had the misfortune to fall head first into a farmyard pond in the dark and was covered with a reeking black slime. Shortly afterwards, Freyberg encountered Lieutenant Colonel Henry Weldon of the 2nd Leinsters, who rapidly made his excuse and departed, subsequently remarking that, 'Anything rather than a continuation of that dreadful stink!'[24] Fryberg wryly wrote, 'It was bad enough to fall into the mess, but worse to have everyone avoiding me!'[25]

At 05.35 on 14 October, the creeping barrage for the Battle of Courtrai commenced. It proved to be deadly: a mixture of smoke, shrapnel and high explosive with lashings of machine-gun bullets and a dose of thermite for good measure.

> The signal was one shot fired from a 15" naval gun many miles behind the line, and it broke an utter silence with the great crack of it speeding overhead, followed by the queer echoing roar of its passage growing less and less, till, just as it had about ceased to be audible, the barrage burst with one tremendous crash. It was like some stupendous orchestra, grand, inspiring, exhilarating, beyond imagination. I remember standing up with my back to the barrage and Sergeant Major Cross beside me, and making exactly the same gesture to the troops that Hugh Allen used to make to the chorus of the Bach Choir when it was time for it to stand up. Of course, no word of command could possibly have been heard. The barrage was marked at every 100 yards or so by phosphorous shells, burst in the air, pouring out a golden rain like fireworks, and it was by the guidance of these that we followed.[26]
>
> Lieutenant Philip Ledward, 15th Hampshire Regiment, 122nd Brigade, 41st Division

The German response was weak, but a few shells still crashed down amongst the advancing infantry. As ever it was all a matter of blind luck as to who lived – and who died.

> They got a big one right in amongst us before we had gone 100 yards; about a dozen men went down. I was walking at the time with one of my subalterns and he got a lot of it and died of his wounds soon after. A tiny piece went through my hand, and if it hadn't been for feeling the warm blood, I shouldn't have known I had been hit.[27]
>
> Lieutenant Philip Ledward, 15th Hampshire Regiment, 122nd Brigade, 41st Division

As Ledward and his men got near their objectives, without having seen a single German soldier alive or dead, they began to suffer one of the most hated afflictions of the infantry, a British gun firing short due either to the wrong range corrections being made by the gunners, or, more likely, the effects of worn-out gun barrels.

We were harassed by one of our own field guns firing short: two or three shots skimming just over my head and I saw one of these pitch between two soldiers walking about 25 yards in front of me. It killed them both instantly but it didn't blow them to bits. The effect was very strange. The instantaneous absolute stillness of both bodies – even as they were falling – made it look as if they were liquid being poured into a mould, into the positions in which they lay after falling, where they instantly became as still as marble.[28]

Lieutenant Philip Ledward, 15th Hampshire Regiment, 122nd Brigade, 41st Division

As the 15th London Regiment charged forwards they found that the German infantry seemed to be beaten down and cowed by the sheer brute power of the barrage.

We were very excited and there was a lot of noise. Kept expecting to be knocked out by a shell but wasn't. We went across ditches and through wire, getting more wetted and torn. Occasionally we stopped by a pillbox to collect prisoners but there was no resistance. Feeling 'don't care' we lighted cigarettes as we went forward. Mash threw a bomb in a place in which we thought were Germans, but instantly a big firework display started – it was a Very light store. The place, made of thin timber, caught fire. The prisoners were quite meek and mild. In one dugout Palmer found a Jerry parcel containing a very nice cake so we devoured this going forward. It was good. Very heavy mist this morning and we lost direction a bit and went far past our objective so had to sort ourselves out.[29]

Private Henry Pope, 2/15th (Civil Service Rifles), London Regiment, 90th Brigade, 30th Division

When things went well, there were moments of humour, but it was viscerally terrifying for the Germans attempting to 'negotiate' a surrender, well aware that a momentary misunderstanding would condemn them to a bloody end at the end of a bayonet.

Prisoners kept emerging in a state of sheer terror, some crying bitterly, others cursing the Kaiser. Our chief difficulty was that they imagined – not without reason – that it was safer to stay with us. We had to drive them towards the rear with threats and even kicks. We arrived at our objective without difficulty and my officer and myself took a stroll to find the next battalion.[30]

Sergeant Charles Jones, 2/15th (Civil Service Rifles) London Regiment, 90th Brigade, 30th Division

It wasn't that easy everywhere. The 8th Scottish Rifles had already conducted a series of reconnaissance patrols towards Gheluwe and established that the German defences were based on a series of pillboxes. The maturity of the planning process was admirable: they conceived a twin-flanking attack in conjunction with the neighbouring 5th King's Own Scottish Borderers to eradicate these threatening strongpoints with minimal casualties.

Gheluwe was to be treated to an intense bombardment of shell, smoke-shells and thermite by our friends the gunners and Royal Engineers, and the barrage was to advance at the rate of 100 yards every two minutes. True to time, the battalion at 14.30 (Y Company leading) was on the jumping-off position, which had been taped out to help to maintain direction. The Bosche, sensing what was in store for him, was pushing over shrapnel and gas in an angry manner. A heavy mist hung around, and a dense smoke cloud added to the murkiness. Occasional flares pierced the darkness, followed by the rat-tat-tat of machine guns, and the dull thud of a bomb. The men were in great form. The leading company's small advance groups were keeping up a steady nagging. Shortly before Zero hell arose around us. Thermite shells burst over Gheluwe and sent tongues of flame leaping into the air. The advance began, and despite many difficulties direction was maintained. East of Gheluwe, touch was established with the KOSB, and some 100 prisoners fell into our hands, together with machine guns and stores. The poor old Bosches were terror-stricken, and clamoured piteously for mercy. On continuing the advance from the first objective we encountered most deadly machine-gun fire issuing from a pillbox which covered a flat area of ground immediately in the line of our advance. Many fell victims to its deadly accuracy. Messages issued direct along the firing line and through battalion headquarters resulted in outflanking this stronghold, and, with a further advance, a half-battery of field guns fell into our hands.[31]

Captain William Ferguson, 8th Scottish Rifles, 103rd Brigade, 34th Division

This demonstration of advanced infantry skills took place at one of the early defensive positions occupied by the 7th Division as they began the defence of Ypres in October 1914. The BEF had come on a long way; veterans of a different sort, but still hardbitten soldiers who were now supported by unimagined firepower.

All along the line the Allies advanced: the pace varied, but nevertheless progress was made. The Belgians advanced some 3 miles, accompanied by the left of the British Second Army. On 15 October, the advance was to resume at 09.00, but as reports from the previous day seemed to indicate that one of the likely Lys crossing points at Comines had been abandoned, the XV, X and XIX Corps of the Second Army, which were all by this time lined up behind the Lys in their role as a flank guard, were given permission to try and get across the river – but only if it could be achieved without heavy losses. Patrols duly crossed the Lys, which was covered by strong barrages, and found they encountered only patchy resistance. Soon feasible bridgeheads had been established and were ripe for exploitation. Elsewhere good progress continued.

Even amid successful operations, tragedy could still strike at any moment. That night Private Wilfred Heavens watched as a moment's stupidity by a single irresponsible individual triggered fatal consequences.

As it got dark, it became cold, and we crouched in the bottom of our funk holes and tried to go to sleep. Finding this almost impossible, some of the chaps chanced it and lit a cigarette, placing a waterproof sheet over their heads when they struck a match to prevent the flame from showing above the funk holes and hedge. We were warned not to strike any more matches and to keep our cigarette ends well down in the holes. Some time elapsed, and one of the chaps, thinking he would like a smoke put a sheet over his head and struck a match – and for a fraction of a second the flame showed above the funk holes. We shouted as loudly as we dared, 'Put that light out!' but the damage had been done. Five minutes later a shell screamed over the hedge and dropped in a funk hole next to the one the light had come from, and three away from the one I was in. It was followed by piercing screams, and the two occupants were killed outright and two men in the next hole were badly wounded. We jumped out of the hole and ran towards the wounded. One was in a terrible condition, so bad that it was impossible to do anything for him in the dark. Two of the bearers put him on a stretcher and carried him away as fast as they could. The other man was also badly wounded, his elbow had been completely blown away, the bone was broken and the lower part of his arm was hanging by a piece of skin. The severed artery was bleeding terribly, and the loss of blood completely unnerved the man. I fixed a tourniquet just above the wound and then made a rough splint. Some of the blood had gathered in the remains of the sleeve of his tunic and was dripping from his elbow and, realising this, the man began to rave and accused me of not putting the tourniquet on properly. To try and appease him I tightened the tourniquet more still and assured him that he was losing no more blood, but he still raved on, exclaiming that he did not want to leave his wife and children. We got him to the dressing station and the Medical Officer cut off his tunic, cut the skin joining his forearm and then released the tourniquet, remarking that under the circumstances it had been put on very well. Returning to the funk holes, we found that the other two bearers had returned. When they had arrived at the dressing station they found that their wounded man had died, which was not surprising. The man who had struck the light had escaped without a scratch.[32]

Private Wilfred Heavens, 1st Royal Inniskilling Fusiliers, 109th Brigade, 36th Division

However, Heavens was also a witness to a very different side of human nature.

As dawn approached we were ordered to attack the village again. Our Sergeant Major expostulated with the Company officer, who sent back word to Battalion headquarters that his company was not strong enough, totally unfit to attack again and that it would be suicide. The reply was that the village must be taken at all costs. The sergeant major decided that he and five volunteers would creep towards the village first, and see how things were before the company should be sacrificed to the slaughter of the German machine guns. They started out and advanced stealthily towards a house they felt certain contained a machine gun – in the hope of surprising the gunners and capturing it. Unfortunately, they were spotted and the gun opened up and the five men dropped one after the other. The Sergeant Major, a little in advance of the men, seeing his men fall, rushed the position by himself and gained it. We saw no more of him, and he was either killed or taken prisoner, the general belief being the latter, for later when we gained the same spot there was no sign of his corpse or of blood. We grabbed the stretcher as soon as we saw the men fall and crept out to them, but the five of them were dead.[33]

Private Wilfred Heavens, 1st Royal Inniskilling Fusiliers, 109th Brigade, 36th Division

Not all acts of supreme courage are rewarded with medals and plaudits.

The German line was crumbling all along the Western Front as the advances by the British First, Third and Fourth Armies, coupled with the renewed offensive by the Second Army and Flanders Army Group, left the German Sixth Army facing the British Fifth Army exposed to threats on both flanks. They were joined in the retreat by Crown Prince Rupprecht's struggling Fourth Army, which was forced to fall back to the Bruges-Thielt area. In response, the right of the Second Army, hand in hand with the Fifth Army, surged forwards. On 19 October, Foch ordered the whole Flanders Army Group to march on Brussels. That day, the Second Army took Courtrai, and by 20 October was across the Lys.

It's a shame to see these Belgium people, some with their homes wrecked and living in cellars. We were billeted in one place where all the town had collected in a cellar of a 'Brasserie'. It is another life to them to see a 'Tommie' – the kiddies clambered round, old men wished to shake hands, also the women, and if we had let the mademoiselles they would have kissed us, and it was terrible when Fritz put over some shells – they would all go on their knees and pray; some crying and others screaming.[34]

Private Wal Law, 4th Royal Sussex Regiment, 101st Brigade, 34th Division

The Fifth Army advanced towards Lille as their first objective, before pushing on to the line of the River Schelde. The artillery had avoided firing into this major city, but the population seemed quiescent as some of the first battalions arrived on 17 October, at least at first:

Shortly before midday, the battalion found itself marching along the tramlines in the suburbs of Lille. As the men tramped down the empty road to Pont de Canteleu, two children appeared, timid and round-eyed. 'Where is everybody?' asked the Commanding Officer, in his best French. Apparently, our noble opponents had spread it abroad that we should kill everyone we saw, and all had been warned to remain in their cellars. The children retired, and shortly after one or two women and one or two old men appeared. Finding us friendly, their relations were summoned in shrill tones, and before long the street was thronged with people. Never was such a scene! Everyone cheered and sang, laughed and wept. Flags of the Allies, sold to the French by the Germans ere their departure, soon adorned every window. 'Vivent les Anglais!' went up from hundreds of throats. Everyone embraced everyone else; officers and men alike were kissed and kissed again by the enthusiastic people, while horses and equipment were soon half smothered in flags and flowers. Progress became very difficult, so dense was the crowd and so anxious to express their joy and gratitude. Of all the sights of the war there were few, if any, half so moving as the picture of this almost miraculous awakening of these unhappy folk from their long and cruel nightmare. How they laughed and cried! With what intense feeling they sang the 'Marseillaise'! Not a man

was there who did not feel that here at last was a reward worth all
the misery and dangers of our campaigning.[35]

Captain Charles Wurtzburg, 2/6th King's Liverpool Regiment, 171st
Brigade, 57th Division

Later Lieutenant Philip Dodgson would be a proud participant in a
formal parade by the men of 4th Division to mark the 'formal' entry into
the city of Lille. This was the chance for the French civilians to show
their gratitude.

Thank goodness it was fine as we had to get up horribly early. It
really has been rather a wonderful experience. For about 2 miles the
streets were packed with people on either side and it was good to
see them all so happy. In addition to the fact that I was at the head
of the leading Battery, I was made extra conspicuous by my horse
getting thoroughly excited by the crowds of people and the noise
they made as they did a certain amount of clapping and cheering,
and the more they did the worse she got. Fortunately, at the critical moment in the Grande Place she behaved rather better. They
made us march at attention the whole way, which made it rather
impressive but a bit boring. One rather longed to do something in
return when we saw these French people taking off their hats and
shouting, 'Vive L'Angleterre!' and all that sort of thing. I wonder
how long it will last? I don't think they'll ever treat us in the same
way as the other French people do: four years with the Huns will
take a lot of forgetting![36]

Lieutenant Philip Dodgson, A Battery, 235 Brigade, Royal Field Artillery,
47th Division

Lieutenant Colonel Rowland Feilding and his men were billeted in civilian homes in the outskirts of the city. He was horrified at the evidence of
squalor left behind by the Germans as they abandoned their billets.

He did not dare flatten Lille as he has so many other cities; but, in
leaving, presumably as an emblem of his hatred, he has used the
upstairs rooms of many of the houses as latrines. In a bedroom of
a great house of this suburb of great houses where we are billeted,

where the Brigadier has his Headquarters, and where I dined tonight, a certain article was found in a bedside cupboard. It had been used for a purpose for which it was not designed, and on the cupboard door was chalked a notice in German which, translated, read something as follows: 'Here is a breakfast for an Englishman, made by a good German!' What do you think of that for Kultur? Can you conceive of the most reckless *enfant terrible* of our race descending to so depraved and childish a revenge as this?[37]

Lieutenant Colonel Rowland Feilding, 1/15th London Regiment (Civil Service Rifles), 140th Brigade, 47th Division

The Fifth Army pushed forwards, advancing through the towns of Tourcoing and Roubaix as they approached the Schelde, which marked the next feasible German defensive line.

The country between us and the River Scheldt was flat in the main, dotted with houses and small woods, and rising slightly towards Froyennes, whence it fell away to an open stretch of grassland up to the near bank of the river. It was an excellent position for a rearguard to hold; and in addition, on the Tournai-Courtrai road, about 1 mile north of Froyennes, the enemy enjoyed magnificent observation from the Convent, and also for his guns from Mont St Aubers, a conspicuous eminence on the far side of the river. He had a considerable number of guns and evidently an ample supply of ammunition. We, on the other hand, suffered the usual disadvantages of an attacking force in open warfare. We had no knowledge of the strength or location of the enemy, while our own movements could not be concealed. Moreover, the hasty advance and the interruption of communications due to the complete demolition of all bridges, the damage to roads by mines, and the absolute destruction of all railways – every single metal on the lines having had a piece blown out – had effectually prevented the advance of any heavy artillery, and the 18-pounders which we had were but scantily provided with ammunition.[38]

Captain Charles Wurtzburg, 2/6th King's Liverpool Regiment, 171st Brigade, 57th Division

Captain Francis Jourdain was a very junior staff officer serving with the headquarters of 16th Division in 1918, and when he was called on to take up greater responsibility during the fast-paced advance – it did not go at all well.

> The division had been advancing every other day with very little opposition. Everybody was out one day: the GS02 and GS01 were going round the line or somewhere. For some reason, it became imperative to tell the division to move forward tomorrow. As likely as not the divisional clerks told me. 'You'd better get something out!' So, I issued the order, but forgot to make arrangements for the rations. Of course, they got their rations, but from the formal point of view the arrangements had not been made to deliver their rations further on. Which was pointed out to me when various people came back – and no doubt would have been pointed to me in no uncertain way if I'd gone any way near the line at that time![39]

Captain Francis Jourdain, Headquarters, 16th Division

In that assumption Jourdain was almost certainly right!

With success adorning the efforts of the Flanders Group of Armies it was unfortunate that a row would flare up between Haig and Foch over the question of when Plumer's Second Army would return to Haig's direct command. Haig felt it should be done at once, but Foch refused, as he wanted King Albert to be able to enter Brussels at the head of an Allied Army. The resulting spat reflects the tensions inevitable in joint allied operations at the end of a supremely stressful period. They may have been winning, but both Haig and Foch were overworked, stressed by numerous hitches, and – in the background – beginning to wrangle over the nature of possible Armistice terms to be offered to the Germans. The impasse was ultimately resolved when Foch agreed to hand back Second Army to Haig on 4 November. There may have been upsets, but the underlying relationship between Foch and Haig remained sound.

On all fronts, there was a considerable problem with the German booby traps left promiscuously scattered behind them. The advancing British infantry had been warned to be careful, not to touch 'attractive'-looking possible souvenirs and where possible to stay out of dugouts or houses until the specialist sappers of the Royal Engineers had the chance to identify and defuse any booby traps – the improvised explosive devices (IEDs) of their day. However, on 24 October, Lieutenant Joseph Platnauer, a gas specialist of the Special Brigade, Royal Engineers, had a terrible experience while engaged in clearing out a series of underground dugouts in the Hénin-Liétard sector[40] that had been reported as being mined, booby-trapped and filled with gas. It was clearly a very dangerous mission.

> I realised that it was useless and dangerous to take 150 men down dugout steps into the unknown though my rough plan, made from vague intelligence reports, showed at least four entrances and sleeping quarters underground for about 1,000 men. Leaving the Company in the open, I took two senior sergeants and began to reconnoitre. We trod warily on the way down – cutting anything that looked like trip wires – and there were quite a number. Then the three of us worked our way slowly to the lower level, and by torchlight made our way gingerly along the corridors, noting with astonishment the strength and thickness of the concrete, and the tiers of well-constructed bunks – a veritable palace compared with our familiar infantry hovels.[41]
>
> Lieutenant Joseph Platnauer, O Company, 4th Battalion, Special Brigade, Royal Engineer

All was going well, or at least it was until disaster struck. Perhaps they were a little complacent in the way they carried out their inspection of the dugout system, but gas had been their specialism.

> One of the sergeants called back from a bend, 'Some exploded shells in this corner! Maybe gas shells!' They were 6" and 8" howitzer projectiles, split open with some small explosive charge, the whitish-yellow powder of freshly exposed mustard gas in heaps beside them!!! Previously, I had been working in my gas mask with mouthpiece and nose-clip in position, but with eyes exposed at times because of the difficulty of seeing in unfamiliar surroundings.

The smell of pungent 'garlic' made it essential to don the whole
face-piece before going further. Rounding the bend, to my consternation, I saw the two sergeants, Jo Cross and Don Britton, bending
over the big shells and examining the stuff without their gas-masks
on. I yelled to them in no uncertain terms to put their gas masks
on immediately. Both were old regulars, both wore Mons Stars –
they should have known better. I realised afterwards that, having
worked so much with our own gas, they had a contempt for gas
in general. Though we had all been through German mustard gas
bombardments and knew the smell of it and that, normally, it was
not particularly lethal, this was their first experience of it in high
concentration and at close quarters; alas, it was their last. A small
party brought down drums of paraffin and petrol, saturated the
wooden props and other combustible material and set the place
alight. I understand that the damn place underground burned by
slow combustion for days. I was not there to witness it; neither were
the two sergeants. Cross[42] died in his billet the next morning and
Britton[43] was taken to hospital *in extremis*. And I, having inhaled
comparatively little of the foul stuff, woke up the same morning,
temporarily blinded, sores on the forehead and under the arms and
with no voice.[44]

Lieutenant Joseph Platnauer, O Company, 4th Battalion, Special
Brigade, Royal Engineers[45]

Platnauer was evacuated to England and over time made a full recovery.

As the Second and Fifth Armies advanced, the unusual became
normal: trench warfare was suddenly in the past and it was back to the
future in the sense that they were advancing through unspoilt countryside, villages and towns all unafflicted by bombardments.

It was open warfare at last – the kind of warfare preached at
courses and always laughed at. The day of those who had known
open warfare in South Africa had come. The normal formation
of advance was one battalion of the brigade as advanced guard,
with two 18-pounders attached to them, the remainder marching in column of route. The daily trek was about 7 to 10 miles,

according to the amount of opposition encountered, which at first was not great. On crossing the Belgian frontier near Howardries, on our way to the river L'Escaut, the battalion was spotted by the enemy from Fort Maulde and was forced to make a hurried move to the village of Rongy, where it was shelled intermittently with gas throughout the night to the terror of the inhabitants.[46]

Captain Horace Samuelson, 9th London (Queen Victoria's Rifles), 175th Brigade, 58th Division

German artillery firing gas shells could be a terrifying prospect, especially if they caught troops asleep at night. Private James Garrett had a close escape when taking shelter in a barn at Rongy.

Two platoons managed to get in and remained for about twenty minutes listening to the dropping shells and ducking our heads every time one whizzed over the barn. We finally all got settled down in billets, where we felt more or less safe. Somehow it seems to be a natural instinct with soldiers that if they have a cover of any description for their heads, a waterproof sheet even, they are quite safe and no shell will harm them. After a meal and the necessary sentries had been posted we all made ourselves as comfortable as we could. We were all rudely awakened by a loud crash and a shower of tiles and plaster from the roof. There was a scramble for a few seconds and all with one accord put on their gas masks, for the crash turned out to be a gas shell falling through the roof. The room was thick with fumes of mustard gas, so we all retired into the street where we found the air clearer, but still tainted. Several more shells were dropped in a close area and many other troops were in the same plight as ourselves.[47]

Private James Garrett, 9th (Queen Victoria's Rifles) London Regiment, 175th Brigade, 58th Division

Of course, the civilians were almost helpless; lacking gas masks they were terribly vulnerable to the noxious gases. Indeed, dealing with civilian gas casualties was one of the worst experiences of a pacifist Quaker, Lloyd Fox, who had volunteered for service as a driver with the Friends Ambulance Unit. He was based at Courtrai Convent in late October 1918.

I found four or five members of the unit with a doctor installing themselves in a very large convent. Huge rooms. No lighting, no heating! Quite a respectable billet. The Germans were using a large amount of mustard and phosgene gas. The second day there I was sent to a village close to what was believed to be the line then held by the British, although everything was very fluid then – nobody quite knew where the lines were getting to because the Germans were dropping back. In the afternoon, army lorries started arriving full of gassed women and children. The German had soaked the place with mustard gas to hold up the British advance and the unfortunate civilians had gone down into their cellars, which was the worst place, because it was an inert gas. Over a period of two or three hours we had something like twenty lorry loads of women and children – about a thousand altogether. We all did our stint looking after them in the wards. Some beds, some stretchers, most of them just lay in blankets on the floor. We spent a good deal of our time dealing with those that had died – particularly the children, taking them down to the convent mortuary at the bottom of their garden. Then, just to make things a little worse for everybody, the Germans staged an air raid on the bridge at the bottom of the convent garden which ran down to the river. Fortunately, our convent wasn't hit, but those casualties who were well enough to take any notice of what was going on were pretty miserable to hear the bombs coming down and wondering what was going to happen to them.[48]

Lloyd Fox, Friends Ambulance Unit

The next day Lloyd Fox had the dreadful duty of selecting civilians for treatment at the convent from among a mass of civilian gas casualties.

I was taken by a young army doctor to a large hall in Courtrai where we found over a hundred gassed women and children. All the men of course had been driven back by the Germans behind the lines – it was only women and children. There they were with one old lady trying to give them drinks. Terribly affected by the mustard and phosgene, which had practically destroyed the sight of many of them. Their eyes were all swollen, they couldn't see. We washed their eyes out with bicarbonate of soda. Their breathing was starting to get very bad, because the phosgene particularly affected the lungs. The army captain took me round the ward and we got to the end and he said, 'I can do nothing – it's up to you! You pick out twenty of the gassed people that you think may have some chance of living and take them up to the convent!' There was I, a youngster, given what seemed to be the opportunity of saving the life of twenty people. All I could do was pick twenty of the toughest-looking children – I thought they might have some chance of survival – and I took them to the convent. I felt it was a great responsibility to leave about eighty women and children to die with nobody to look after them. The following day I saw one of the gas orderlies come out of the ward in tears. He said, 'I can't stand it in there any longer – they're just choking to death! Mostly the children you brought in two days ago – go and see for yourself what it's like!' I went in and the unfortunate children were black in the face, practically nothing could be done for them. I think in all there were something like 800 killed by the gas at that time. It passed more or less unnoticed. The war news was more concerned with the falling back of the Germans, but it was one of the worst episodes of civilian gassing in the war.[49]

Lloyd Fox, Friends Ambulance Unit

Lloyd Fox never forgot these scarring experiences.

One terrible menace that could not be attributed to the Germans was the influenza epidemic that began raging through all the armies on the Western Front in 1918. This pestilence had begun with little warning, initially presenting itself as little more than the usual annual mutation of the influenza virus, but this time it had a vastly increased level of lethality. At first it was barely noticed amidst the mass killing of the war, but slowly it became apparent that something unusual was occurring. No-one knew where this new threat had arisen, but as Spain was where one of the first observed mass outbreaks had occurred, it was called 'Spanish Flu'. Subsequent medical investigators have blamed a genetic shift of the influenza virus originating somewhere in China. The 'new' virus was sufficiently different to its predecessors in that there was a complete loss of the 'herd' immunity. Deadly outbreaks in the American training camps meant that, as the Americans were shipped to Europe, they helped spread the disease far and wide on the Western Front, jumping No Man's Land to afflict both sides in the trenches. A virus did not take sides in mankind's petty wars.

People began dying in great numbers, sometimes overnight and often within a couple of days of infection. Around 25 per cent of the population seemed to catch it, but this was far higher where people lived cheek by jowl – as in the army.

> Our worst enemy at present, however, is influenza. The villages we have been passing through were rampant with it, and we now have a hundred severe cases down with it, all fixed up in a big barn, one corner of which we are using as orderly room. The Medical Officer and his old factotum, Bob Cawley, are worked to death, and trying to attend to civilians as well. No chance of moving any to hospital. Late tonight an urgent message came from Bob Cawley's billet for the M.O. Before the M.O. reached there, Bob was dead. He had been busy in the barn a couple of hours before, making his patients comfortable for the night. Wherever he has gone, Bob won't be happy unless he has someone to patch up and make comfortable. He could be gentle enough to mend angels' wings, or strong enough to hold the devil himself still, while he straightened a crumpled horn for him. Medical Officers have come and gone, medical services have been reorganised, reduced, increased and changes of all kinds have occurred in his department, but Bob Cawley[50] has gone on for ever (at least since 1914, before which nothing seems to have happened). He is buried in a nice little field at the back of the little estaminet in Petit Turcoing, and the husband of the lady who kept the estaminet carved very special cross for the grave, for did not Bob save Madame's little girl from *La Grippe*?[51]

> Lance Corporal Walter Williamson, 6th Cheshire Regiment, 21st Brigade, 30th Division

The epidemic seemed to be particularly deadly to young adults aged from approximately 15 to 40, a most unusual pattern of morbidity. The death rate among soldiers could also be much higher as they were often already debilitated by their gruelling experiences in the trenches.

Doctors were almost helpless before this new 'plague' and the medical profession as a whole was already overstretched trying to deal with the millions of wounded. Air Mechanic Leonard Gordon-Davies was one of those afflicted and he remembered the extreme treatment resorted to by his doctor.

> We had a period of flu. A lot of people caught it and it got more and more severe until practically everybody seemed to have got this flu. The Doctor was treating these people with aspirins and he ran out of supplies. We got very high temperatures and had to stay in bed. The Doctors said, 'We've got no means of bringing your temperature down, we've got to take some drastic action!' Those of us who had a very high temperature we had to sit in our beds and he came along with buckets of cold water and chucked them over us! That brought the temperature down and our spirits as well. We hadn't got the strength to get out of the bed. We certainly felt much better for our temperatures being back – below normal I should think. We slept in a wet bed! We couldn't dry our things until next morning. As soon as we began to feel a bit better we were forced out of bed, told to get out, which we did and felt better so doing. It was a very near thing and a lot of people must have died. We all seemed to get over it![52]
>
> Air Mechanic Leonard Gordon Davies, 5th Brigade, RAF

Units were devastated by the virus, and manpower was short enough before this further burden. Tens of millions would die around the globe before the virus burnt itself out; indeed the death toll dwarfed that of the Great War itself.

5

BATTLE OF ST QUENTIN CANAL AND BEAUREVOIR

I am not, nor am I likely to be, a *'famous* general'. For that must we not have pandered to Repington[1] and the gutter press? But we have a surprisingly large number of *very capable* generals. Thanks to these gentlemen, and to their 'sound military knowledge built up of study and practice until it has become an instinct'; and to a steady adherence to the principle of our Field Service Regulations Part 1 are our successes to be chiefly attributed.[2]

Field Marshal Sir Douglas Haig, General Headquarters, BEF

THE FOURTH OF FOCH'S CAREFULLY SEQUENCED SERIES of attacks was scheduled to be launched on 29 September, this time by the Fourth Army commanded by General Sir Henry Rawlinson. He was confronted by one of the very strongest sections of the Hindenburg Line, which posed two very different problems: the St Quentin Canal ran for some 6,250 yards underground in a tunnel from near Vendhuille to Bellicourt, before running on the surface in front of the main Hindenburg Line right down

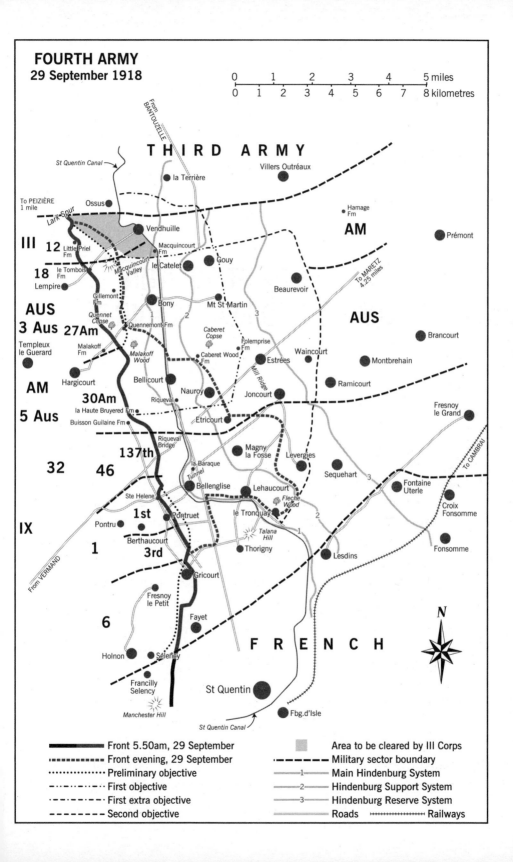

FOURTH ARMY
29 September 1918

0   1   2   3   4   5 miles
0   1   2   3   4   5   6   7   8 kilometres

T H I R D   A R M Y

St Quentin Canal

From BANTOUZELLE

la Terrière

Villers Outréaux

To PEIZIÈRE 1 mile

Ossus

Lark Spur

AM

Prémont

III   **12**   Little Priel Fm

Vendhuille

Macquincourt Fm

le Catelet

Gouy

18   le Tombois Fm

Macquincourt Valley

Beaurevoir

To MARETZ 4.25 miles

Lempire

Gillemont Fm

Bony

Mt St Martin

AUS

AUS

3 Aus   **27Am**

Quennet Copse

Quennemont Fm

Caberet Copse

Folemprise Fm

Brancourt

Templeux le Guerard

Malakoff Fm

Malakoff Wood

Caberet Wood Fm

Estrées

Waincourt

Montbrehain

AM

Hargicourt

Bellicourt

Nauroy

Joncourt

Ramicourt

5 Aus   **30Am**

la Haute Bruyered Fm

Riqueval

Etricourt

Mill Ridge

Fresnoy le Grand

Buisson Guilaine Fm

To CAMBRAI

Riqueval Bridge

137th

Magny la Fosse

Levergies

Sequehart

32   **46**

la Baraque Tunnel

Bellenglise

Lehaucourt

Fleche Wood

Fontaine Uterle

Ste Helene

le Tronquay

Croix Fonsomme

IX   **1st**   Pontruet

Pontru

Talana Hill

Fonsomme

1   Berthaucourt

3rd

Thorigny

Lesdins

From VERMAND

Gricourt

Fresnoy le Petit

6   Fayet

F R E N C H

N

Holnon

Sélency

Francilly Selency

St Quentin

Manchester Hill

St Quentin Canal

Fbg.d'Isle

━━━━━ Front 5.50am, 29 September
■■■■■ Front evening, 29 September
••••••• Preliminary objective
–•–•–• First objective
–••–••– First extra objective
– – – – Second objective

▨ Area to be cleared by III Corps
– – – Military sector boundary
──1── Main Hindenburg System
──2── Hindenburg Support System
──3── Hindenburg Reserve System
═══ Roads   ++++++ Railways

to Lesdins, a couple of miles from the town of St Quentin, which lay in the French sector. The underground sector may have had no open canal to act as an obstruction, but the ground above it was covered by exceptionally strong trench lines, each with several deep belts of barbed wire. There was also an elongated spoil mound stretching along above the course of the canal, some 30 feet wide and dotted with both machine-gun posts and anti-tank gunpits. Further underground workings led down to a complex series of galleries and chambers, which stretched from the canal tunnel right back to the villages of Bellicourt and Bony. Behind the main Hindenburg Line systems lay first the Le Catelet-Nauroy Line and then the Beaurevoir Line.

One advantage held by the Fourth Army staff during the planning phase was that a set of memoranda and maps had been captured during the Battle of Amiens on 8 August, which revealed the intimate details of the Hindenburg Line defences. It described not only the layout of trenches, dugouts, machine-gun posts, headquarters and barbed wire, but also the exact location and calibre of every artillery and mortar battery and their observation posts, and detailed all the pre-planned defensive barrage lines. It further revealed the rear elements including ammunition and supply dumps, the railheads, infantry camps, signal arrangements, electrical power stations and airfields.

Yet before Rawlinson's divisions could storm the Hindenburg Line proper, they would have to take the former British defences, which on 21 March 1918 had been overrun by the Germans. Then they had to overcome the German Outpost Line which ran along the high ground overlooking the Hindenburg Line from the west. This was essential, for if the Germans retained control of these positions then British field artillery would not have the range to fire directly onto the main defences. The capture of the Outpost Line would in itself be a major operation, to be carried out in the face of almost matching numbers of German troops. This would have been impossible in earlier years, but the staff officers responsible for the planning were confident that German morale had degenerated to a point whereby they would fragment under a deluge of artillery fire.

On 18 September, the attack began, powered forward by a barrage from the 1,488 guns allotted to support the operations. One small cog in that mighty wheel was Major Joseph Rice, who was responsible for the accuracy and time-keeping of the 18-pounders of his battery as they poured shells into the German positions. It was to prove a difficult task, as their battery was targeted in relentless fashion by German howitzers.

The barrage began at 5.20 am and almost as soon as it started the Bosche turned on to us with a 10.5 cm howitzer battery. It also rained heavily the whole time. As far as officers were concerned I always had one only on the position during barrages, and I always took my portion first to make sure that the show was going punctually and accurately. I got Sergeant Sykes, who was acting Battery Sergeant Major at the gun position, to check the laying of the right half-battery while I signalled all the 'lifts' and checked the left half-battery. This haphazard distribution of duties between Sykes and myself decided, as it turned out, which one of us was to survive. We were shelled steadily and accurately till a quarter to seven, Sergeant Sykes and I dodging about between the various slit trenches and the guns. It was a jolly good show by the Battery, as of course there is no question of allowing enemy fire to interfere with the firing of a barrage as long as men and guns are available, and everyone carried on his own job quite coolly. The culminating tragedy happened near the end of the shelling. I was near No. 5 gun and Sergeant Sykes was near No. 3 when a shell arrived between No. 2 and No. 3, killing him, and knocking out practically the whole of both detachments. I got to his side just before he died, but only by about five seconds. Both guns were knocked out of action, but we kept the barrage going with the remainder. When Lieutenant Lamb came out to relieve me at about 7 o'clock the shelling had ceased, but we had had six killed and four wounded.[3]

Major Joseph Rice, C Battery, 82 Brigade, Royal Field Artillery, 18th Division

Sergeant Francis Sykes[4] was buried in the cemetery at Moislains, where he had recently attended the burial of a popular officer, Second Lieutenant Archibald Irving,[5] little knowing that he too would be buried there a couple of days later.

The Australian Corps was at the very forefront of the attack. It had developed assault tactics to a fine art, but the battalions were being gradually eroded by the heavy casualties unavoidable in their role as an elite assault force. Still they braced themselves once more, and smashed into the German defences, pushing them back and penetrating deep into the Outpost Line. Because these veterans had gained such a reliable proficiency they were often picked out for the most dangerous attacks. Lieutenant Edgar Rule and his men of the 14th Australian Battalion had been fighting all day, when Rule was ordered to lead his company into the attack against a strong German position at 23.00. Having already been lightly wounded in the back by a hand grenade, he was both physically and mentally exhausted.

> In despair, I turned to Tom Griffith, an officer of A Company, and told him that it was madness to attempt it. To my surprise, he yelled out as he started bombing up the sap, 'Have a bloody go at them!' This pulled me together and out on the top the bombing section and I clambered. We must have gone about 100 yards, with 40 still to go, when these guns opened again. I looked around and my heart sank. Here was the whole company bunched in a heap. On account of the lead that was flying, we all got down flat on the ground. Bullets were licking up the dirt all around us. I heard a man yell just behind me and then he lay quiet. What to do was past me; I was just on the point of ordering a bolt, when one of the boys with a Lewis gun crawled up alongside me, and in a second opened fire along their trench – and to our surprise silenced the Huns. A little farther along another of the lads took his cue and opened fire. After each burst these gunners would yell, 'Now's your time; rush them!' We all upped and ran for dear life towards those Huns, yelling like lunatics.[6]

> Lieutenant Edgar Rule, 14th Battalion, 4th Brigade, 4th Australian Division

As they burst into the open, the three German machine guns opened up again. But the covering fire from the Lewis guns had the desired effect.

> The Huns must have had their heads down below the parapet; for the balls of fire seemed to be going round in a circle just level with our heads, and the most of them going over. When we were within 30 yards, some of the Huns heaved some bombs, and then they bolted for their lives. We could see them climbing out of their trenches and vanishing in the darkness. Just as we got near where the bombs had fallen, the things went off and scuttled a few more of the lads, but the worst of the job was done, and we were very thankful.[7]
>
> Lieutenant Edgar Rule, 14th Battalion, 4th Brigade, 4th Australian Division

Having gained the trench, they then had to bomb along it to eradicate any pockets of German resistance. There was a rough code of conduct about the means of surrendering and its acceptance – or otherwise. Machine gunners were particularly at risk, and Rule was tempted to take his vengeance when he later discovered some Germans cowering in a dugout. He believed these had been the machine gunners that had so plagued them during the attack.

> I've yet to see a man shot down in cold blood after his hands have gone up, though the temptation is great sometimes. We came on the Huns who had caused all our trouble. Four of them were in a dugout, and from the top of it you could look right down this trench. Here were all the empty cartridge cases, but they had planted their machine gun somewhere and we could not find it. The way they cringed and whined filled me with disgust, and if I could have squared my conscience to keep quiet for the rest of my life I'd have laid the lot out. Every time you catch a Hun now, you have the same music; I can never imagine Aussies cringing like they do. I always feel I'd like to put my boot in their faces.[8]
>
> Lieutenant Edgar Rule, 14th Battalion, 4th Brigade, 4th Australian Division

On the other hand, if there was any hesitation in the Germans surrendering, then the response would be a swift – mopping up was a cruel business.

> The men who were bombing were picked men and nothing short of death could stop them. They were led by the gamest man I'd seen for many a day – Sergeant Bauchop.[9] We had 800 yards of trench to clear in order to obtain contact with the 46th, and in doing this we captured nine enemy machine guns, two field guns and a tank gun; no mean achievement for fifty men. As Company commander, I came along with the rear of the Company, and as I walked along the top of the trench I could see the Huns flying in all directions to escape from Lofty and his bombers. Several in a dugout refused to come out; there was no time to argue, and they were quite harmless when the bombers left them.[10]

> Lieutenant Edgar Rule, 14th Battalion, 4th Brigade, 4th Australian Division

The men around him were approaching the end of their tether, but still they had fought with incredible determination.

> By now most of us had reached that state in which you can do without sleep; it is much the same as with hunger, after the first hunger has passed – you do not care if you never get anything to eat again. Eyes were the worst trouble, they were becoming bloodshot.[11]

> Lieutenant Edgar Rule, 14th Battalion, 4th Brigade, 4th Australian Division

Although battle-hardened warriors, they were still human. However tough they might be, they could not go on like this for much longer. But the Australian accomplishments that day had been prodigious. From the captured ridge positions of the German Outpost Line they could now look straight down on the Hindenburg Line proper, while they had taken over 4,000 prisoners, 76 guns and 300 machine guns.

The British III Corps to the north, and the IX Corps to the south of the Australian Corps had far more trouble in their advance, as the Germans put up a determined defence at strongpoints such as the fortified village of Épehy. The Australians were excellent troops, but at times honest pride in their impressive achievements could lead them to denigrate the performance of British troops at times like this.

> The best troops of the United Kingdom have long ago been used up and we now have a class of man who is without initiative or individuality. They are brave enough, but are simply unskilful. They would be all right if properly led, but their officers, particularly the junior officers, are poor; young men from the professions and from office stools in the English cities, who have had no experience whatever of independent responsibility or leadership. Very few English divisions can today be classed as first-class fighting troops, relied upon to carry out the tasks set. On the other hand, the Canadians and Australians have never failed to achieve all their objectives strictly according to plan.[12]
>
> Lieutenant General Sir John Monash, Headquarters, Australian Corps

This was an unfair assessment. The Australian and Canadian Corps had retained the four battalion brigades when the rest of the British Army had been reduced to three battalions earlier in 1918. They were also homogenous forces that had built up harmonious working practices across the years, relationships that had not been disrupted by constant changes of divisions between corps that were common among their British equivalents. They also leaned heavily on support from the British batteries of the Royal Artillery. In addition, Haig had reserved the Australians and Canadians specifically as assault divisions, so they had been spared some of the more routine fighting that was the lot of British divisions. When it came to the point, the British Army was still mainly British, and there were several British divisions that approached, and even matched, the benchmarks set by the Australians and Canadians. Collectively these British soldiers would prove well able to carry out their role within the 'All Arms Battle', and although they may have faltered at times, and may not always have been as quick to advance as their colonial comrades, they got there in the end.

The fighting around Épehy gives a good example of the strengths and weaknesses of the British troops. Within the village itself was the Fisher's Keep, a German defensive position blessed with commanding views over the approaches, while behind the village was a network of strongly fortified trenches taking full advantage of a confusing mixture of low ridges and valleys leading back to the St Quentin Canal. The 12th Division as a whole was charged with capturing Épehy and pushing forward a further 2 miles. The 7th Royal Sussex were to attack to the right of Épehy itself. Under the battalion plans, A Company would be in the lead, commanded by Captain Stephen Andrews, and they were to advance to the branch line railway just in front of the complex of defences that had grown around the Malassise Farm. Zero Hour was set for 05.20.

> We were guided to our assembly positions and waited in the rain and mist for the 'off', while the officers and NCOs checked up the various details of the advance. With the Company were two splendid fellows, Lieutenant J. A. Wright (whose brother had just joined the battalion) and Second Lieutenant S. G. Huggett, and I believe that there was a third subaltern, but of this I am not certain. We started off at Zero with Wright in charge of the left leading platoon, and soon afterwards they ran into a German post. I was told by the NCO who brought the platoon on that some of the enemy held up their hands and Wright took his men towards them without firing. Suddenly a number of shots were fired from the post at very close range, killing Wright[13] and killing or wounding several of his men, but the remainder dealt with all the occupants there before the arrival of our supports. Beyond this, very little resistance was encountered, and in due course the company found itself at the railway crossing and squatted down to await the arrival of the rest of the battalion. At this time, it was still rather misty and visibility was restricted to a fairly short distance, but Huggett and I realised that something had gone wrong, as heavy machine-gun fire could be heard on our left and slightly to the rear, while as Zero +90 minutes approached there was no sign of the rest of the battalion.[14]

> Captain Stephen Andrews, 7th Royal Sussex Regiment, 36th Brigade, 12th Division

Almost everything had gone wrong for the main body of the battalion as they moved up behind Andrews and A Company. With them was Lieutenant Harding Farrow.

> We were shelled heavily while taking up our positions, which must have been nearly 800 yards behind our own front line. During this period, we had about six casualties, including my Sergeant Major; we also had to put up with a very heavy downpour of rain throughout the night. We started off at Zero and were supposed to leave Épehy on our left, but unfortunately, owing to our smoke barrage and also to the mist, we made over rather too much to our left, and it was then that the enemy in Épehy spotted us. We were then easing over slowly to the right, so as to leave Épehy on our left, when suddenly a German tank (as we imagined) came along and for a few seconds gave us hell. I am afraid we scattered. However, almost immediately, those on the tank gave us the signal, 'All OK' but the damage had already been done, and Reading, who was commanding D Company, and myself did our best to collect our men together again; it was just then I got a machine-gun bullet through my leg, and when reporting at Battalion headquarters I remember Reading being carried in on a stretcher with a similar wound in his knee. I consider that it was a mistake for our assembly positions to have been so far behind our own front line. The misty morning and our own smoke barrage were our first enemies, and then being strafed for those few seconds by our own tank fairly put the lid on things. The weather conditions were appalling; I was absolutely soaked through when I reached the dressing-station, and, I must also say, really not sorry to have stopped that bullet.[15]
>
> Lieutenant Harding Farrow, 7th Royal Sussex Regiment, 36th Brigade, 12th Division

Ahead of them, in the absence of the rest of the battalion, Andrews was in a quandary as 06.50 approached, the time appointed for the second advance. He was also beset by a further threat: their neighbours in the 35th Brigade had been charged with taking Épehy itself, but the resistance was such that their attack had stalled. This left Andrews' men vulnerable to flanking machine-gun fire from the village.

> By then it was time for our second advance, and as the Battalion was still missing we decided that the only thing to do was to get on. Accordingly, Huggett took over the leading platoon and I followed with the remainder, our idea being to get to our objectives, and we hoped by that time that the others would turn up. We left a small post at the crossing to explain and guide the Battalion to our new position, which could just be seen. The mist was clearing by this time, and on our way from the railway line we were suddenly greeted with enfilade machine-gun fire and then a burst from the left rear. At the same time the leading Platoon, which was just nearing its objectives, met a heavy fire from front and flank, but succeeded in reaching some trenches. While the supports took cover immediately in rear in a sunken track lined on one side with low bushes. Here we established ourselves and soon found it necessary to form a defensive flank, as we were fired on from both front, flank, and left rear, and our two Lewis guns found plenty of work to do. Poor Huggett[16] was shot through the head while endeavouring to work way through the rough trench system in front of Malassise Farm, but our other casualties were very light in view of our position.[17]
>
> Captain Stephen Andrews, 7th Royal Sussex Regiment, 36th Brigade, 12th Division

Épehy would not be captured until 19.45 and the 7th Royal Sussex, which had been badly exposed to flanking fire for most of the day, failed to make any more progress. They suffered some 200 losses and only two officers were left unwounded. As fast as reinforcement officers arrived to join the Battalion, they were being chewed up by the fighting.

> Practically all the officers were new to the battalion and just after Nurlu we had a whole batch of officers, most of whom had been in the 11th, 12th and 13th Battalions – almost all of them became casualties by the end of the Épehy period. I remember one officer, whose name I cannot remember, coming fresh from Sandhurst. I

never saw him, for I was asleep when the rations came up, and the adjutant sent him to a company at once. By daylight he had been killed. There was, I know, a certain amount of difficulty in identifying him, as no one was quite sure what he looked like.[18]

Lieutenant Colonel Arthur Thomson, 7th Royal Sussex Regiment, 36th Brigade, 12th Division

During the night, the Germans pulled back from Malassise Farm and the advance continued. It was not spectacular, but eventually the British troops also attained most of their objectives. The scene was set for the great assault on the Hindenburg Line.

The American II Corps (27th and 30th Divisions) were being moved up into the line ready for their vital role in the planned attack on the Hindenburg Line. They were being used to augment the Australian Corps, as it was evident that there were not sufficient batches of fresh young Australians to restock their thinning ranks. Without conscription, voluntary recruitment in Australia had begun to falter in the face of the reality of the Great War. Monash was proud of his men and keen that they stay at the forefront of the battle, but his battalions were chronically understrength by the end of September. Indeed, it had been planned to reduce the Australian brigades to just three battalions, with the men of the disbanded fourth battalion being used to bring the others at least partially up to strength. Yet the issue of orders to that effect on 23 September had led to considerable disciplinary problems among the men, who had an emotional bond to the remnants of their old battalion. For the moment the idea was abandoned. In consequence, it was decided that the American divisions would provide the raw numbers needed to bolster the Australian Corps, while at the same time allowing the Americans to benefit from a close association in battle with such experienced veterans.

The reception of the 'Doughboys' as they reached the front was exactly as one might expect from the hard-bitten and downright cynical Australians – it was not only the British soldiers whom the Australians felt at liberty to mock and criticise.

The 'Doughboys' came into the line with all their gear up and looking like Christmas trees. They were led to their 'possies' in the lines and they made a great deal of noise, calling out to one another and generally acting like raw and over-confident troops. Lieutenant Wally Graham admonished them and told them not to make such a row, for, as he explained, Fritz was pretty good with his machine guns and the trenches and posts were hardly any protection against shell-fire. One of the Yanks replied: 'Don't you worry about us, Lootenant, we'll be okay!' They were! So much so that when I took some American officers to visit the same position only a few days later it was all I could do to find the site of the trenches. The whole place had been blown to bits and the posts wiped out. All the officers had been killed or wounded and the troops were badly shaken. Experience is always a costly thing to buy, as the 11th Battalion had found, but it is a commodity that is difficult to pass on to other people.[19]

Lieutenant Walter Belford, 11th (Western Australian) Battalion, 3rd Brigade, 1st Australian Division

After the handover, Belford rode back with a party of 11th Battalion officers, including their battalion commander Major Aubrey Darnell and his adjutant, Lieutenant John Archibald. All seemed well and they were looking forward to a period of rest after their great exertions in the recent attack on the Outpost Line.

'Archie' dropped back beside me and said, 'I feel so happy to-night. We have done a great stunt and the battalion has excelled itself. The only thing that spoils everything is that poor old 'Wally' Hallahan[20] and young 'Dud' Elliot[21] [Note says Dudley Archibald] were killed and the other lads. But for that I've never been so happy in my life. The 'good oil' is that we are going out for a long spell!' After some more general conversation Lieutenant Archibald rode forward and joined Major Darnell at the head of the party. The above conversation is recorded to show that not everyone had a premonition of his coming end. It was now well after midnight on September 23, and the party had just passed Roisel when I heard the drone of a German 'plane coming up behind. The German airman let go four small daisy-cutter bombs which fell right among the party of horsemen causing several horses to bolt. We found the C.O. and the adjutant lying on the ground. On dismounting it was seen that Major Darnell was quite dead, but that Lieutenant Archibald[22] was still moaning. A splinter of bomb had gone clean through his steel helmet, piercing his head. He never recovered consciousness again. The medical officer examined Major Darnell[23] and the latter's only wound was a tiny aperture over his heart where a piece of bomb had struck him. The fact that Major Darnell and Lieutenant Archibald were killed within a few minutes' ride from their camp and just when the battalion had left the line for the last time only proved what most of the troops had long realised: that a man can never escape his fate.[24]

Lieutenant Walter Belford, 11th (Western Australian) Battalion, 3rd Brigade, 1st Australian Division

THE MAIN THRUST OF THE ATTACK on the Hindenburg Line was entrusted by Rawlinson to Monash, who would also control the American II Corps which, although commanded by Major General George Read, would reside under Monash's overall command. Monash planned to use the Americans to capture the first objectives in the covered canal sector stretching from Gouy in the north to just beyond Nauroy in the south. This would encompass breaching both the Hindenburg Line and the Le Catelet-Nauroy Lines, entailing an advance of some 5,000 yards – an ambitious target. The Americans would then be leapfrogged by the Australian 3rd and 5th Australian Divisions for the assault on the Beaurevoir Line. Finally, the Americans would push on to exploit any further opportunities to both the north and south, while the British IX Corps would move through the gap created to move south and take the canal line from the rear. However, on reviewing the plans, Rawlinson intervened to order the IX Corps to instead attack the Hindenburg Line pushing straight across the open canal. This was a difficult task, one that Monash had considered far too dangerous, but Rawlinson wanted to widen the front attacked to complicate the deployment of German reserves and prevent the concentration of artillery fire from the flanks that always afflicted more localised attacks.

The artillery barrage would be crucial to success and it was decided that, in view of the brute strength of the German defences, a simple hurricane bombardment followed by a creeping barrage as the troops attacked would not be enough. A four-day bombardment was settled upon, to be fired by some 1,044 field guns and a further 593 medium and heavy guns which would add 'body 'to the bombardment. One new advantage was the long-awaited ability to deploy the BB gas shells, far better known as mustard gas, which the Germans had unveiled as far back as July 1917. Now at last some 30,000 BB shells had arrived, just in time for the Fourth Army attack. The German defences would be deluged with mustard-gas shells in the preliminary bombardment lasting from 22.30 on 26 September to 06.00 on 27 September. The physical damage done to the Germans would then have been done, but there would be time for the mustard gas to dissipate so that it would not affect the attacking troops. Then it was time for a spate of shrapnel and high-explosive shell to pound the key German defences as identified by a combination of captured plans and the photographic reconnaissance of the RAF. Particular care was taken to make sure that the German batteries had no chance to recover as they were to be liberally doused with phosgene gas shells. The Zero Hour creeping barrage would consist of 50 per cent shrapnel shell, 35 per cent HE and 15 per cent smoke shells. It would move forward at a rate of 100 yards in three minutes and would be supplemented by the fire of some 96 machine guns.

The American divisions were not ready for this kind of attack. They not only required support from Australian Corps artillery batteries, but also lacked the necessary experienced staff officers to draft and disseminate orders. The Fourth Army chief of staff wryly commented that, 'The arrangement was no doubt somewhat complicated, and might have led to difficulties, but for the loyalty of General Read and his subordinates, and the tact of the Australians.'[25] The Australians created a special liaison mission with the intention of explaining Australian methods, with

Australian officers and NCOs attached to the American units right down to a company level. Rawlinson understood the problems of entrusting such a major task to inexperienced troops, but he really had little option. The Fourth Army had suffered terrible casualties during the August and September battles; now it needed the fresh blood offered by the gigantic double-sized American divisions – whatever the risks.

> With new troops like the Americans, one has, of course, anxious moments. For instance, today it was quite impossible to find out just where they were. Alarmist rumours came in from the front, and the evidence seemed to show that they were not on the Gillemont Farm line, where they should have been, but the airmen repeatedly reported that they were. It was just the same on the Somme. New troops never know just where they are.[26]

> General Henry Rawlinson, Headquarters, Fourth Army

Yet he was still confident. After all this was not an isolated battle; it was part of the greater series of offensives orchestrated by Foch. The other attacks had been successful and there were grounds for optimism.

> Douglas Haig came to see me. He is in great form, delighted with the way things have gone in the north, and with the First and Third Armies. He thinks we shall finish the war this year, and I hope he may be right, but it is no certainty. If we can drive the German armies out of France before November, there may be a good chance of it; but we must send troops to march through Germany and enter Berlin. Turkey and Bulgaria are done, and Austria is very near the end. I should like to see Clemenceau and Foch now; they must be proud men. The guns are thundering. I have 1,600 for the battle, and I go to bed feeling 30 years old.[27]

> General Henry Rawlinson, Headquarters, Fourth Army

The scene was set.

RAWLINSON MAY HAVE BEEN CONFIDENT, but the American II Corps would have a terrible time in the attack on 29 September. They may not have faced an open canal, but the German defences were very strong. There was also the problem that when the British III Corps had handed over the sector to them, they had not yet been able to reach the start line intended for the 27th Division. This meant an immediate additional operation by the American 106th Regiment to capture the neighbourhood of Gillemont Farm on the morning of 27 September. Little progress was made and it was decided that the 107th and 108th Regiments would start early at 04.50 on 29 September, to fight their way forward to attain the originally intended start line by the Zero Hour, before then progressing as planned. This was not a matter of an extra few yards – they had to advance nearly a mile. To make matters worse, owing to confusion over the location of advanced parties of troops from the earlier attack, the barrage would start some 1,000 yards ahead of the start line.

The Australian liaison officers attached to each American battalion soon proved their worth, as the battalions began to move forward to their jumping-off positions in a very confused situation against a tight timetable.

> Lieutenant Sheldon, the Australian officer, had just returned from a trip over the ground which we were to cover between 3.00 am and 5.30 am the next day. He was to be the 'eyes' of the battalion. He had been fighting over this sector for two years and knew the ground thoroughly. We were to 'step off' at 5.50 on the morning of September 29th under the protection of a barrage which was to lift its fire 100 yards every five minutes until 10.30 am. My battalion was ordered to make arrangements for an advance at 3.00 am. This left two hours to issue rations, water bottles, shovels, hand grenades and to get the water carts up, and it seemed an impossible task. But Lieutenant Sheldon took charge and by 2.30 am we were ready. It was a heart-chilling morning; a heavy fog enveloped us and the air was gas laden. It was impossible to march over the ground in gas masks and it was left to each man to judge when to use his mask. Most of us breathed through our mouth-pieces

without putting on the mask. We reached our rendezvous at the ordered time under Lieutenant Sheldon's guidance, the Germans shelling us incessantly. Each company commander was ordered to place his company in yawning holes made by the shells. I shuddered to think that if a shell should strike in one of these holes a whole company would be wiped out.[28]

Captain Henry Maslin, 1/105th Regiment, 53rd Brigade, 27th Division

And then all they could do was wait.

When at last the time came, the men of the 107th Regiment came under terrible fire as they advanced towards Gillemont Farm at 04.50, in an unforgiving mixture of fog and darkness. They had a task that would have tested any troops – no matter how experienced. They had a terrible fight on their hands just to reach the notational start line.

Believe me it was some experience to go over. It was an awful sight – seeing some of our lads all blown to pieces. I thought that I would go all to pieces, but I was just as calm as could be. The funniest part was, just as our barrage opened up we all lit up a cigarette. We lost quite a few men, but I happened to come back safe and sound, but the shells and bullets were shrieking and humming past my ears. Henry Reed[29] was killed. I will have to find a new chum, for him and I used to chum around together.[30]

Private Fred Pierce, 2/107th Regiment, 54th Brigade, 27th Division

Lieutenant Ralph Polk Buell was commanding C Company of 1/107th Regiment. His men came under the imminent threat of exposure to heavy machine-gun fire and in such a pressurised life or death situation – where there was no obvious 'right' course of action – he was not quite sure what to do for the best.

All of a sudden, I saw in front of me a trench manned by three Germans with a machine gun, perhaps 40 yards away and back of them, in an angle in the trench, a group of about fifteen more Germans, with what appeared to be two machine guns. The ground between us was being heavily swept by machine-gun fire from the left, and the one gun in front of me was just commencing to fire to my left. The Germans apparently had not seen me, as there was some haze. My first impulse was to drop down, let the line come up and flank this position; but I was afraid that my men might stop if I did, all along the line, and might also mistake my motive, lose their confidence in me, and with it much of their morale. So, I decided that the best thing to do was to go right at it, hoping that if I could get through the enfilading fire the Germans would be disturbed by the show of force and quit. It took me perhaps half a minute to come to this conclusion, and I started to run toward the trench.[31]

Lieutenant Ralph Polk Buell, 1/107th Regiment, 54th Brigade, 27th Division

Against the odds, Buell managed to get as close as about 20 feet from the German machine gunners before he came under direct fire.

I took a shot at the man with the rifle and put him out of action. I later saw him dead in the trench. Just at this moment I was hit in the shoulder and nearly knocked off my feet. I did not realize that I was badly hit, and tried to keep going, taking several steps and bringing me probably 10 feet away from the machine gun, which was spitting all the time, but for some unknown reason was not hitting me. I tried to shoot the gunner, but had apparently exhausted the clip in my automatic, for it would not go off, and as I was vomiting blood and apparently about to go down I tried to throw my automatic at the man, hoping to put him out of business. My recollection is that just as I got my arm back I spun around and went down on my back. I do not remember anything more until I came to a few minutes later, lying there with a very vigorous fight going on over me. In a few minutes my men managed to clean the position out and went on.[32]

Lieutenant Ralph Polk Buell, 1/107th Regiment, 54th Brigade, 27th Division

The German defence system was not based on a single line, but rather a layered system of defensive positions. They were willing to fall back if necessary, with troops held ready to counter-attack if the opportunity arose. One of those forced to fall back was Leutnant Stoffel.

> The enemy succeeded in pushing into the forward zone, whose garrison, in accordance with orders, fought their way back step by step. From the Chalk Trench, use of hand and rifle grenades, together with light machine-gun fire, prevented the attack from being developed frontally. In the meantime, the forward zone troops of 84 Infantry Regiment had pulled right back without informing us. As a result, the enemy was able to push forward without opposition and suddenly we were completely outflanked on the right. When on top of this a formation of tanks appeared, I gave orders to withdraw to the Vendhuille position. We had a tough time pulling back across level ground under fire from the tanks.[33]

Leutnant Stoffel, Reserve Infantry Regiment 2/27, 108th Brigade, 54th Division

Then, as planned, their resistance stiffened in front of the advancing Americans. It was soon evident that the Germans had the skills and weaponry to defend themselves against the oncoming tanks. Hauptmann Jahns was one of those to swing into deadly action.

> At 6.30 am the Americans, assisted by smoke, appeared. Immediately the reserve guns of 1st Machine Gun Company, which had been kept in the Battalion command post, were deployed. The entire Battalion staff manned the trench left and right of the machine guns and through rapid fire prevented the enemy from advancing any further. As visibility improved, strong attacking columns, supported by two tanks, could be seen in the low ground. Destructive rifle and machine-gun fire was brought down by 1st and 3rd Machine Gun Companies, as well as that of 11th Company. The two tanks were halted and destroyed by the grenade launcher platoon and the anti-tank battery which had been subordinated to [me]. Shortly afterwards two more tanks appeared from behind the hill east of Lempire and descended into the hollow, so as to assist the hard-pressed American infantry to break through the Vendhuille position. The first went up in flames forward of our position,

while the other was knocked out just in front of the anti-tank gun. Enemy aircraft machine-gunned our trench from low level. It was most unpleasant, but one was brought down 30 metres from the command post by small arms fire. One occupant was killed, but the other, an English officer, was captured by Leutnants Herpolzheimer and Seinfoth, despite all the small arms fire. We retained contact with 90th Reserve Infantry Regiment, but lost it to 84th Infantry Regiment, so the commander of the forward troops had to order a counter-attack to guard our right flank.[34]

Hauptmann Jahns Headquarters, Reserve Infantry Regiment 2/27, 108th Brigade, 54th Division

The battlefield was in chaos as the American 105th Regiment began to advance. They were meant to be following up behind the leading troops to form a protective screen on the left flank, thereby securing the advance of the rest of the division. In addition, as they pushed forwards they found themselves in a dangerous position, sucked into the confused fighting. A further problem was that much of the expected support from twenty-three tanks had evaporated. Some were knocked out of action in an old British minefield, there were mechanical breakdowns, some were ditched in old trenches, and many more were knocked out by fire from the German infantry or artillery. Men like Leutnant Steiner were experienced in coping with tank attacks.

The tank fire did us no harm. Because of their lurching progress the rounds went high. We all fired at the observation slits and brought the monster to a halt. That improved our men's morale greatly. The other tank received a direct hit and burnt fiercely. There was indescribable jubilation on our trench. Once the tanks had been dealt with, the Americans took cover helplessly in shell holes just before our positions. Our men stormed forward in a grenade attack. The grenade launchers made them run for it and our weapons tore great holes in their ranks. It was simply one great hare shoot. Very few escaped unscathed; only the ones who stayed down in their holes and later surrendered.'[35]

Leutnant Steiner, Reserve Infantry Regiment 3/27, 108th Brigade, 54th Division

The advancing American troops suffered a complete breakdown in communications with the supporting tanks – a common problem if tanks and infantry had not had a proper opportunity to train and work together. Captain Henry Maslin found that the tank assigned to 105th Regiment had not arrived, but then recalled a frustrating encounter.

> We met a tank and the officer in charge had inquired where the 107th Infantry was; that his orders were to report to that regiment. I could give him no information, and he said: 'For God's sake, Captain, attach me to your unit! I have been wandering around all morning and don't know where to go!' but I could not order him to attach himself to my battalion. It was likely our tank commander was looking for us, but the smoke screen had upset a lot of carefully laid plans.[36]

Captain Henry Maslin, 1/105th Regiment, 53rd Brigade, 27th Division

Maslin was fast realising that the whole situation was out of control. Absolutely nothing seemed to be going to plan – to his intense frustration.

> The Lieutenant Colonel said that this ground would be 'mopped up' and that I would meet no opposition until the afternoon, when I was to fight for the villages, but at 10.00 am we had taken prisoners and the ground we had passed over was filled with scattered Germans from the trenches and it was certain that machine gunners were in our rear. Sent a runner to the Lieutenant Colonel with a message, giving my position and reporting, 'Have taken seventy-seven men and two officers prisoners; the tank has not reported; the ground has not been mopped up; probably machine gun nests in our rear. Suicidal to advance. Send instructions by messenger.' I do not know if this message reached Duncan's Post. After a few minutes, I sent a runner to Captain Bulkley,[37] who had established his headquarters in a shell-hole abreast of and at the left of his battalion trenches, to find out if he had received any information from regimental headquarters, and shortly thereafter my Adjutant went over to Captain Bulkley. The firing had again ceased and after another fifteen minutes' delay I decided to go

over and confer with Captain Bulkley myself, but instead of going obliquely to my right, the quickest way to reach his headquarters' shell-hole, I went to see if I could do anything for the wounded German I had noticed. Then I walked along the front of the 3rd Battalion trenches to reach Captain Bulkley. When about to step into the headquarters shell-hole, machine-gun fire opened and I was shot by a sniper and fell in.[38]

Captain Henry Maslin, 1/105th Regiment, 53rd Brigade, 27th Division

He would lie in that shell hole for some twenty-seven long and painful hours.

I was afraid that they would never get me out of that shell-hole. Shelling commenced again and it seemed an age until I heard voices – quarrelling – in German. It appeared that I was to have unpleasant visitors, but my fears vanished when someone called out, 'It's me, Captain; everything is all right!' and a pale-faced German came into the shell-hole and sat down near my feet. He was followed by one of our men who had gone for hot tea and I noticed that he had on the German's steel hat. I asked him why he had brought that fellow in and he said it was to help carry me back on the stretcher; that he was coming back with the tea and saw the German standing near a dugout. He had told the German to come along, but instead of doing so the German had thrown a potato-masher hand-grenade and had run into the dugout. He had dodged the grenade and had followed the German and had given him a good licking. The tactical way to invade an enemy dugout was to invite the occupant to, 'Come up, or be blown up!' If no one appeared on this invitation a couple of hand grenades were thrown in, and after the explosion the dugout was entered. This young American, however, with a canteen of hot tea in his hand had chased a German into his own dugout – with the possibility of there being a number of other Germans there – had beat him up with his fists and then had brought the German and the hot tea to me. The Yanks had original ways of doing things in the war.[39]

Captain Henry Maslin, 1/105th Regiment, 53rd Brigade, 27th Division

Original, true, brave too, but still symptomatic of a paucity of hard practical experience and – in this case – a lack of common sense.

The American 27th Division had been given a nigh-on impossible task by Monash and had accordingly failed. The overall perception from the men on the ground was that they did not know what exactly had happened, but they knew things had gone wrong – and they had no idea how to redress the situation. The men were confused, lost in the pervasive swirling smoke clouds, surrounded by intangible but deadly enemies and often lacking leadership, given the terrible casualty rate among their officers – as typified by the fate of both Lieutenant Ralph Polk Buell and Captain Henry Maslin. The ability to efficiently 'mop up' parties of Germans hidden away in dugouts was crucial, and the Americans found it hard to achieve. Yet this was not the whole story: in many cases the German soldiers counter-attacked hard, using the lessons gleaned from years of combat experience. Among them was Leutnant Nowakowski.

> While the assault group worked its way forward, one platoon of the company under Unteroffizier Dietz moved to secure the right flank. Taking under fire enemy machine guns on the opposite hill, he suddenly noticed a line of about fifty riflemen closing in on the rear of the company. He was just in time to redirect the fire of his machine guns and to cause the enemy heavy casualties. He also passed the word to the heavy machine guns which were able to provide timely support. Very few of the enemy escaped. The company was thus spared serious damage. A short while later the company came under machine-gun fire from a knocked-out tank which was located in rear of the company. Dietz pulled together an assault group under Gefreiter Schindelies. They closed up and threw hand grenades at the tank. At that the crew withdrew.[40]

Leutnant Nowakowski, Reserve Infantry Regiment 2/27, 108th Brigade, 54th Division

It was these localised counter-attacks, launched to capitalise on the increasing disorganisation of the Americans, that seem to have caused many of the problems.

On the American right flank the 30th Division advanced at 05.30, pushing out from the intended start line and at first made more progress. Although they were hampered on their left flank by the failure of the 27th Division, they moved forward, supported by some thirty-three tanks and crashing through both the Hindenburg Line and the Hindenburg Support Line to reach the village of Nauroy. However, they too were unable to mop up properly and the machine-gun teams rose phoenix-like behind them. Many advancing Americans were taking casualties without realising that the fire was coming from beside or behind them. Soon small parties of Americans were cut off, no longer advancing as units but simply sheltering from the storm that surrounded them.

The American disarray caused problems for the 3rd and 5th Australian Divisions who were supposed to leapfrog over them to assault the Beaurevoir Line. The Australian veterans soon realised that things were not proceeding according to plan.

Suddenly a machine gun rattled, then another and another. Several men dropped, writhing. We took cover in shell-holes. All the troops to the right and left had done the same. A breath of wind blew away the thinning strands of smoke and let in a brief gleam of sunlight. We advanced warily from cover to cover. Men dropped in their tracks, a few for every hundred yards. We could not at first understand it. The Americans had gone forward, yet now there was no sign of them. They had not come back. They had not been wiped out, for we had not seen any bodies. They seemed to have had an easy passage, so why were the enemy here? The bullets were coming from left and right, but not from in front. We advanced by sectional rushes, a few dashing forward at a time, while the remainder gave covering fire, but we could see nothing to fire at. We heard a flurry of fire from our Lewis guns on the left, then our neighbours began running forward by twos and threes. Some of them got into one end of a trench. We saw and heard bombing. Then the remainder of them dashed forward. There seemed to be some kind of a scuffle, then our men passed over the place. We could not see what they had done to the Germans. We could guess. Much the same was happening far on the right. At length, pushing through the desultory fire, we entered Bellicourt. It was full of Americans. What had occurred was now apparent. Following the custom of most troops with more spirit than experience, they had gone as far as their feet would take them, and in their impetuous haste had neglected either to throw bombs down the dugouts or to capture their occupants. Consequently, the enemy came out of the earth and cut them off.[41]

Sergeant Walter Downing, 57th Battalion, 15th Brigade, 5th Australian Division

The Australians eradicated the German pockets of resistance to secure a solid base, before trying to push on. The British Mark V tanks, which were meant to be in their support, were with great difficulty slowly making their way across the battlefield.

Our path lay across a sunken road; one tank was already ditched and another in lesser difficulties. Our officer and crew were outside. I was alone in the driver's seat. Noting the troubles of those two who preceded us I almost despaired of getting across safely. Selecting a suitable spot, I drove forward, when, notwithstanding the utmost care, the tank slid down the slippery side with a crash upon the bottom, our fascine grating and grinding like a ship's revolving capstan. To our great relief we crossed all intact, proceeding up the rough surface of a hill and nearing a bend in the road. Suddenly I heard a tremendous clatter of chains overhead, above the noise made by the engine and internal gears. Casting my eyes upward through the still open ports, I saw our fascine slipping forward. Striking the revolving tracks it was pitched on the left side with a terrible thud; the fellows walking on that side jumped away just in time to prevent being crushed by our derelict fascine. The retaining bolt had broken in two by sheer strain, one half still remaining in the hole.[42]

Private Arthur Jenkin,[43] Tank Corps

Pushing on regardless, they passed through the rear areas of the battle, where they found the Australians moving forwards, while the wounded and German prisoners were making their way back. The German artillery posed the greatest threat to the tanks as they crested a rise and came under direct observation.

> The enemy used gas shells, gas masks having to be worn. This was a very trying ordeal inside the tank, the heat given off by the engine being intense, and the petrol fumes produced a semi-suffocating feeling, much relieved after passing this gas-shelled territory by the removal of the mask. Coming out upon a hillside and being observed by the enemy, who must have had it under close observation, we got a bunch of high-explosive shells all around which fortunately left us unhurt, although splinters, earth and stones fell in showers. At the foot of this hill we turned to the right across a flat burrowed with trenches and large bomb-holes. Into one of these old trenches we slid, its wet decayed sides giving way beneath our weight. Successful in getting out, we negotiated another maze of pitfalls.[44]
>
> Private Arthur Jenkin, Tank Corps

Finally, they caught up with the leading troops.

> We soon entered a wrecked village crowded with troops, some preparing to go on with us in the advance, others consolidating the ground already taken. Having parted from the rest of our Company farther back, only two other tanks beside ourselves were here lined up in single file in the village street, protected from shell-fire by the ruins on either side. Against these ruins crouched hundreds of infantrymen seeking shelter from German machine-gun fire which swept over the village. Opening the man-hole cover overhead I looked out for a little fresh air. No sooner was my head above the cabin roof than an enemy aeroplane flying low, covered by the smoke which still hung like a pall over the village, emptied his machine gun among the troops below, who rushed madly about seeking shelter from the rain of bullets that ricocheted on the stones.[45]
>
> Private Arthur Jenkin, Tank Corps

The three tanks split up and began to push further forward. By this time the terrible conditions experienced within a tank were beginning to have their coruscating effect on the crew.

> I was tired, hungry, and exhausted by heat and fumes. The driving of a Mark V tank is laborious work; the steering-levers, counteracted by strong springs, require much effort to move, while the clutch-lever and left-foot brake also require considerable energy to operate properly. Each man was now at his gun, three of which were already sending forth a deadly hail. Enemy machine-gun bullets could be heard tapping against our sponsons like hailstones upon glass roofs, while notwithstanding the new splinter-proof protectors which had been specially fixed for this action, our faces got marked with fine hot splinters, producing a sensation similar to pinpricks. This induced me to wear the splinter mask with which we were provided; this is a steel mask padded in leather, the eyes protected by small flat steel bars one-sixteenth of an inch apart, and a steel chain about 6" by 3" hangs over the mouth and chin, very similar to the face armour worn by knights in the Middle Ages. After ten minutes' going – the enemy in full flight – I heard groaning. Looking across the tank I saw one of the gunners lying full length on the floor with blood running fast from his nose. Satisfied that he was not wounded, I returned to my gun.[46]
>
> Private Arthur Jenkin, Tank Corps

A few minutes later the situation got worse still as the tank juddered to a stop.

> I found the officer was beckoning me to come up into the driver's seat again. I obeyed, and went forward once more. Turning hastily around, I saw the driver who had just vacated the position I held sitting on the gear-box cover and vomiting as a consequence of the poisonous fumes he had inhaled. It was now a veritable hell inside; machine-gun bullets beat like hail upon the outside, from which hot splinters pricked the gunners' faces, while shells could be heard bursting in close proximity. Inside, above the noise of the engine,

was heard the sharp cracking of our own machine-guns, mingled with the groaning and whining of the gunner who lay stretched along the blood and oil-saturated floor; this, with the vomiting of our second driver, intense heat, exhaust petrol fumes, and nauseous vapour from the guns made an inferno that no outside observer would have thought possible to exist within those steel plates. The whinings of the sick man increased like the howling of a dog by night; his groans were piteous, his nerves seemed to have become entirely unstrung, and it was beginning to affect the morale of the others. The crisis came; he appeared either to be dying or going insane. Then the officer ordered two men to put him outside. The tank was stopped, and he was laid upon the grass in No Man's Land.[47]

Private Arthur Jenkin, Tank Corps

They found themselves facing a concentration of German troops in a village, with both Australian and American troops scattered around alongside them. Somewhere there was also a German field battery that had been missed by the British barrages. It soon made its presence felt.

I well remember the terrific explosion near my head and the sickening smell of the explosive gases, then nothing more until some minutes later, when consciousness returned, I found myself leaning forward against the front. It was a little time before I recollected what had happened, then the blood dripping from the severed artery of my right arm upon the steel plates reminded me of my injuries, for as yet I felt no pain whatever, nothing but a numbness produced by the concussion. When sufficiently recovered I looked around; everything was now still inside, the tank was deserted, the engine silent. I was alone and nearly helpless; my right arm was powerless; there was a big gaping wound on the first finger of my left hand, blood leaked from my chin from wounds the whereabouts of which I did not then know; my trousers were torn in several places where steel fragments had entered. With an extreme effort I pulled myself up with my only, half-disabled hand, and with great difficulty succeeded in getting outside. Lying exhausted and alone upon the grass, the pain commenced, and for the next two hours it was agony, increased by the indescribable feelings produced by fumes upon an empty stomach. I really thought I was dying, and gave up hopes of ever seeing home again.[48]

Private Arthur Jenkin, Tank Corps

Jenkin lay *in extremis*, his wounds being tended by an Australian soldier, before he became aware that the rest of the crew – less the officer – had returned. When they left, promising to return, Jenkin was left behind with two badly wounded soldiers.

We lay under cover of the tank for the next five hours, during which the tank was repeatedly shelled by the Germans in the hope of totally destroying it, these shells falling all around, sometimes spraying us with earth and small stones. We were momentarily in expectation of one dropping among us, making a finish once and for all. Hour after hour we watched for the promised assistance, but in vain; not a man saw we during that interminable afternoon. We were in No Man's Land; the ceaseless click, click of German machine guns from the village was plainly heard; overhead aeroplane combatants could be seen fighting with their guns, but our fighting was done. There we lay, like many thousands of other poor soldiers stricken on the field, hoping against hope for the help.[49]

Private Arthur Jenkin, Tank Corps

He was eventually picked up and evacuated, but his arm would be have to be amputated.

Overall, nothing could be done by the Australians to rescue the situation on the 27th Division front, and they finished the day preparing for a resumption of the assault by units pushing north from Bellicourt towards Le Catelet and Gouy. Afterwards there would be considerable Australian criticism of the American performance. This was not entirely justified, but taken from the Australian perspective it is understandable, as they suffered considerable casualties in their attempts to rescue the situation.

It was tragic to observe the state of disintegration which existed among the American troops. Probably as individuals they were not to be blamed, but their behaviour under fire showed clearly that in modern warfare it was of little avail to launch an attack with men untrained in war, even though the bravery of the individual men may not be questioned. In effect, so far as the Americans were concerned, it was a case of a mob let loose, all plans forgotten and no definite objective in view.[50]

Captain Oliver Woodward, 1st Australian Tunnelling Company

All told, the Americans had not done that well, but it was not their fault. They had fought to the best of their ability to achieve objectives that were unrealistic. They were too inexperienced in combat to make such an ambitious advance against strong German defences. It may well be considered that more criticism should be directed at Monash, rather than the hapless men of the 27th Division who had to advance a mile before they even reached the start line and then cope with a badly disrupted barrage plan. As to the grim business of 'mopping up', the necessity was easy to grasp, but it was difficult to achieve in practice – especially in conditions of terrible visibility. Even when the 'Doughboys' did try to mop up, it is evident that the German defenders were often simply too well prepared in their concealed positions, too strong, too experienced and too cunning to be overwhelmed easily. From the German perspective, General Ernst Kabisch was, with good reason, proud of the resistance put up by the men of his 54th Division.

The regiments performed brilliantly. Everywhere 27th and 90th Reserve Infantry Regiments threw back the Americans who had broken in. Nevertheless, in the evening we had to order them to pull back to depth positions because, to our south, the neighbouring division had to withdraw in all haste, having courageously held their positions until the afternoon. Towards evening I visited the wounded in the main dressing station and found them in good heart – tough men full of courage and self-confidence.[51]

General Ernst Kabisch, Headquarters, 54th Infantry Division

This was a German success rather than just an American failure.

TO THE SOUTH OF THE AUSTRALIAN CORPS was the IX Corps sector, where the 46th Division (Major General Gerald Boyd), had been given the intimidating task of leaping across the gaping St Quentin Canal. The canal emerged from a tunnel some 400 yards south of Bellicourt village. Here the Hindenburg Line bent back to the east and ran along the eastern bank, allowing the water to act almost as a moat, with a series of concrete walls erected across the canal by the Germans to prevent the water being drained away by any catastrophic breach in the canal bank. Although the canal was still not overly deep, it nevertheless represented a serious obstacle for heavily laden soldiers. The initial assault between Riqueval Bridge and the Bellenglise village was to be made by the 137th Brigade – the 1/5th and 1/6th South Staffordshire Regiment, and the 1/6th North Staffordshire Regiment. They were to cross the canal, capture Bellenglise and consolidate their position, before the 138th and 139th Brigades pushed through to capture the small villages of Magny la Fosse and Lehaucourt. Many considered this task near impossible and there was understandably a considerable amount of apprehension among the men of the 46th Division. Some feared their role was little more than a diversion for the main attack to be conducted by the Australians and Americans to the north. Yet others saw it as a challenge that they must rise above.

> I wish I could tell you all that's happening, but I can't. But perhaps there's no harm in telling you – seeing that you haven't any idea where I am – that I'm on the threshold of the greatest adventure of all just now. If the Fates are kind and we do what we're asked to do, I shall be happy, whether I survive or not. If the Fates are not kind – well, I shall have some good memories to relieve the gloom of the long sleep.[52]
>
> Lieutenant Colonel Thomas Evans, 1/6th North Staffordshire Regiment, 137th Brigade, 46th Division

Captain George Thomas wrote a touching quick note to his parents, which must have worried them far more than if they had been left in a state of blissful ignorance.

My Dear Mamma and Papa, I am going to take part in a very big
battle. I hope to get out OK and that my luck holds good and acquit
myself well. Will write to you as soon as possible after. Much Love
to all, George.[53]

Captain George Thomas, 1/8th Sherwood Foresters, 46th Division

Once the operation had been sanctioned by Rawlinson, plans were put
in train to overcome the obstacle in their path. The sappers did everything they could to make the canal crossing a feasible proposition. Masses
of bridging materials were dragged forwards; collapsible boats and rafts
assembled from disparate sources. As a last resort, some 3,000 lifebelts
were brought up. Furthermore, a river-crossing demonstration and exercise was arranged in the waters of the River Somme. This had not gone
well, as the somewhat jaded men saw it as a somewhat tiresome joke. They
could, however, have confidence in the demonstrable power of their artillery. The gunners were raining down shells all over the German positions,
cutting off the front-line trenches, preventing the garrison from being
relieved, blocking the arrival of reinforcements or rations and severing
all communications with the rear. In the final hours, the assorted Staffordshires gathered in their jumping-off trenches, ready for the attack
scheduled at the Zero Hour of 05.50 on 29 September. As the moment
approached there was a deepening fog hanging over the sector, restrict-
ing visibility in some places to just a few yards. This contributed to the
sombre mood as many officers were haunted by the fear of losing their
compass bearings in the murk; but at least they hoped the Germans would
not see them as they approached.

In an attack such as this the barrage was crucial, and the gunners
recognised their responsibility to keep up the firing rate required under
the bombardment plan.

We were firing at a steady rate of three rounds per minute – rapid
– and at 180 per hour the ammunition at the guns soon dwindled
and we had to start carrying shells from all the various places where
they had been dumped. Then the fog came down and I could barely
see the lights at the aiming posts. The gun required at least three

men to work it and there were only four of us, so I spent a lot of
the time searching for ammunition and then carrying four rounds
at a time (92 lbs) back to the gun which I could only find by the
flash when it was fired. When I wasn't carrying ammunition, I was
loading and this went on for hours.[54]

Gunner Rollin Brierley, C Battery, 231 Brigade, Royal Field Artillery

Their efforts were certainly impressive to the infantry crouched in their
jumping-off trenches.

An enormous barrage opened. It was tremendous. Everything possible was rained on the rear of the canal to prevent their reserves
being brought up. The other side knew something was on by the
intensity of our barrage, so, up went their flares, green and gold,
and over came the counter-barrage. The racket was awe-inspiring;
it was impossible to hear, even if orders were given.[55]

Corporal George Parker, 1/8th Battalion Sherwood Foresters, 139th
Brigade, 46th Division

The shells were augmented by a concentrated Vickers machine-gun
barrage which hosed bullets across the German positions. At Zero Hour,
the troops emerged from their trenches and advanced in waves, overwhelming what little remained of the German outpost line, until they
came to the canal. Here there was a drop of 5 feet to the stagnant black
water, which was up to 15 feet deep in places. Where there was no option,
the men entered the water, helping each other across, using cables and
rafts, but they also took advantage of several surviving small foot-bridges,
the small dams and – best of all – the Riqueval Bridge itself, which the
Germans had primed for demolition but failed to destroy.

It had been assumed that the Germans would have already blown
it up and we went over the top equipped with lifebelts and were
supposed to swim the canal: I was mortified to find out that I was
the extreme left hand man in the attack. We were instructed to
keep moving, as others would 'mop up'. It was not very long before
I had lost touch with my Platoon due to the smoke and a ground

fog, which made visibility Zero – and which turned out to be a blessing. I eventually found myself on the bridge and was scared stiff that it would blow up at any minute, so I returned to our side of the canal. After walking south about 20 yards I bumped into my company commander, Captain Humphrey Charlton, and about ten men from my company. They were just lining up to go down the canal bank and Captain Charlton was amazed to hear that the bridge was intact – the visibility was still almost Zero. I led the party back to the bridge and we moved slowly over to the German side meeting only slight opposition, as they were taken by surprise and had no idea our penetration was so deep. Captain Charlton then went down the bank and cut the wires, thus saving the bridge from demolition, which without doubt saved countless lives.[56]

Private Alexander Shennan, 1/6th North Staffordshire Regiment, 46th Division

Led by Captain Charlton, they rushed a defending machine-gun post and shot down the demolition party before they could set off their charges.

Despite all the natural trepidation, the 137th Brigade succeeded in getting across with very few casualties. The barrage and the fog were doing their work. After a brief reorganisation behind the defensive 'wall' of shells created by a standing barrage, they charged forward again at 07.30, breasting a set of unmanned trenches before attacking the main German defences. As the mist began to lift, the Staffordshires could see the line of shells that marked their creeping barrage moving slowly forward. Most of the German defenders were trapped in their dugouts and, shell-shocked by the British bombardment, they emerged as a bedraggled rabble to be taken prisoner. Those that did not emerge voluntarily would be despatched by hand grenades rolled down into the depths – once a haven, but in that moment a slaughterhouse.

The Bellenglise Canal tunnel was a veritable underground town equipped with railways, lit by electric light and with ventilation shafts. Here an army of men could shelter, immune from the heaviest of shells. Clearing this underground complex seemed an intimidating prospect, yet the illusion of security seemed to have undermined the resolve of the German garrison. In effect, they were caught in a trap and some 800 Germans surrendered with very little resistance. The German electrical staff were then swiftly inveigled – with menaces – into revealing the existence of booby-trap mines that would have been triggered by the restarting of the generator system. Even more curious was the discovery made in a hidden chamber; here it seemed there was 'evidence' that justified a favourite British propaganda slur.

> It contained three large cauldrons: one empty; one with a few inches of filthy grease at the bottom, from which emerged a blackened human hand; while the third held the cut-up portions of several human bodies. On the floor were a dozen other bodies, while a row of tins containing a disgusting-looking grease were ranged along a back wall. An appalling stench pervaded the whole place. A sort of trolley-way led down to this place from the trenches above. All who saw this at once rushed to the conclusion that they were beholding one of the much-talked-of German 'corpse factories' in which bodies were said to be melted down for their grease. It takes something to make an Australian soldier sick, but this sight turned some of them up. There was a small opening in the brick work near the top of the chamber and we were informed afterwards by a prisoner that a small shell had come through this, killing all these men and throwing some bodies into the coppers. The place was actually a kitchen supplying the trenches above.[57]

Captain John Marshall, Headquarters, Royal Engineers, 46th Division

Once Major General Gerald Boyd was certain the assault battalions were safely across and secure, he ordered forward his 138th and 139th Brigades.

During the attack, Lieutenant Herbert Boucher was a forward observation officer with 231st Brigade, Royal Field Artillery, which was responsible for firing the barrage for the second wave as they leapfrogged the 137th Brigade.

> There was a thick fog, and as I walked behind waves of infantry, out of the mist appeared four Germans! Boy was I scared, I hadn't even got my revolver out. Fortunately, they were disarmed

prisoners being sent back without escort. I had five telephonists walking behind me carrying field telephones and laying wire. When we reached the canal the Riqueval Bridge was still intact. As fast as we laid the phone wire it was blown up and cut behind us. To maintain contact the telephonists had all gone back to repair the breaks and I was on my own. My orders were to 'stay put' and gather information until told to return.[58]

Lieutenant Herbert Boucher, C Battery 231 Brigade, Royal Field Artillery, 46th Division

Back at the C Battery gun positions, the gunners were still sweating over the guns.

The range gradually increased and then the 18-pounder batteries behind us started moving forward to take up new positions and provide cover for the infantry who were still advancing. It was a remarkable experience to see this two-way traffic and still keep on blasting away. The range eventually became so long that we got to the end of the range drum and had to put on more elevation by angle of sight in degrees and minutes. After that the elevation of the gun became so extreme that the piece would not run up to the firing position and two of us had to stand in the hole we had dug for the trail and catch the piece at the end of its recoil and push it back into position. At last we got the order to 'Cease Fire' and the full range was calculated at over 9,000 yards – we had started at 2,400 yards so the advance had made up to 7,000 yards – nearly 4 miles. We had fired 750 rounds per gun at rates from 3 per minute down to 1 per two minutes without stopping and the gun was nearly red hot. The breech had to be left open to let the air blow through before we could clean up.[59]

Gunner Rollin Brierley, C Battery, 231 Brigade, Royal Field Artillery

As the 138th and 139th Brigades pushed forward, the men were delighted to see evidence of the earlier success of the Staffordshires.

Prisoners were passing back at this time, one of whom was in a very merry mood singing and waving his arms about as if he was returning from a wedding party: someone remarked that Fritz evidently received a larger rum ration than we did![60]

Private Charles Hufton, 1/6th Sherwood Foresters, 139th Brigade, 46th Division

There was no one spare to guard the prisoners, but they were mostly more than keen to escape the dangers of the battlefield.

Swarms of prisoners, waving their arms, were seen coming from various trenches and the village; no one was looking after them, we were all much too keen on getting forward. Here and there, when a few Bosches showed signs of getting into a trench instead of keeping to the open, some soldier would administer a friendly jab with the bayonet to show them what was expected of them.[61]

Major John Hills, 1/5th Leicestershire Regiment, 138th Brigade, 46th Division

Veterans did not waste time on the niceties of requesting and accepting surrenders while mopping up, but tended to take no chances.

We passed Jerry dugouts galore; of course they were packed with square faced bastards. Mills No. 5 were lobbed down, but even the rattle of these could not drown Jerry's pitiful appeal: 'Mercy Kamarade!' 'Comrade be buggered!' said Lance Corporal Janner and forthwith trained his Lewis gun down the steps of one dugout and emptied the pan without even a No. 1 stoppage. After that the Jerries were allowed to file out, which they did in close column and as they marched the lot were relieved of their booty in the way of Iron Crosses, cigars, revolvers, etc.[62]

Private Charles Hufton, 1/6th Sherwood Foresters, 139th Brigade, 46th Division

One feature of the battle was the relative failure of the tanks, which had been despatched round from Bellicourt to the north to assist in the second phase of the 46th Division advance. The German artillery concentrated much of their fire on these easy targets. Not all the German batteries had been cowed into submission and as usual tank armour provided no defence against field artillery. Many tanks were knocked out during their efforts to support the infantry, who were generally ungrateful, as they considered the tanks to be a dangerous magnet for German shellfire.

> Our casualties had been very light indeed, but it was not long before we got some bad news. On our right flank the tanks had suffered heavily at the hands of the German gunners on the Le Tronquoy high ground, and one of them, disabled and on fire, was a mark for several German batteries. Some of the crew managed to escape, but others, too badly wounded, were left inside; one crawled to our aid post. Padre Buck heard of this and at once went off to the rescue. The shelling was very heavy, and he was hit almost at once and wounded in many places. He was carried back to the aid post, but died soon afterwards, conscious to the last, but not in great pain. The Padre[63] had been with us two years, and during all that time there was never a trench or outpost that he had not visited, no matter how dangerous or exposed.[64]
>
> Major John Hills, 1/5th Leicestershire Regiment, 138th Brigade, 46th Division

On the right of the 139th Brigade front, the 1/6th Sherwood Foresters, led by Lieutenant Colonel Bernard Vann, pushed on towards the final line of objectives, overcoming the inconvenience posed by a German battery to the south of the canal which was on their right flank. Vann was an intriguing figure: a 'muscular Christian', he had joined up in the first flush of enthusiasm for the war in August 1914. He was a much respected, much wounded and much decorated officer – and many credited him with providing the drive that made all the difference when the attack might otherwise have become bogged down. His personal example acted as both a spur and inspiration. During a pause, Private Charles Hufton and his fellow signallers were asked by Vann to send some messages back to headquarters. They were interrupted by a British contact patrol aircraft hawking out a loud signal on its klaxon horn.

> 'Send a flare up!' yells the Colonel – and then commenced a hasty hunt among us for a flare. Eventually one was found in the corner

of someone's pocket where it had been hidden away among Mills No. 5, SAA, salvaged watches and biscuits etc. It was lit and put on top of the trench. 'Take it off the top, you bloody fool,' yells the Colonel, 'the enemy is only a few yards away and will see it!'[65]

Private Charles Hufton, 1/6th Sherwood Foresters, 139th Brigade, 46th Division

After sending Vann's messages back to battalion headquarters, the signallers were pressed into more urgent action as Vann led the attack into the southern end of the Lehaucourt village.

'Follow me!' Wind was 'vertical', but off we went just three of us – Lance Corporal Whitworth, Broughton and myself – all hampered with a lamp and pip-don as well as the ordinary gear. Jerries began to come out now with their hands up; they wanted no escort to take them down, however they knew the way back better than we did and ran off on their own. 'Come on, Signallers!' shouted the Colonel and off we went on the trot after a German gun team. Imagine us with all our signalling stuff hung round our necks trying to chase Fritz and fire our rifles at the same time. The Colonel got in front of us firing his revolver point-blank until he had finished up all his ammo, after which he threw his stick at them, saying, 'B**** you!'[66]

Private Charles Hufton, 1/6th Sherwood Foresters, 139th Brigade, 46th Division

By 16.00, both Magny la Fosse and Lehaucourt had been captured by the 138th and 139th Brigade, so they turned their attention to establishing firm defensive flanks to the north and south. The 32nd Division moved forward and made a little more progress towards Le Tronquoy and Levergies as dusk fell.

Collectively, the hitherto unremarkable 46th Division had taken 4,200 prisoners, captured 72 guns and taken over 1,000 machine guns. This was an amazing accomplishment, especially as they had suffered under 800 casualties, which, in the circumstances of the attack, was acceptable. As such, the 46th Division has become the standard bearer for the qualities of the unsung British divisions that made up the bulk of the British Armies on the Western Front. Given the backdrop of a crushing artillery bombardment, disillusioned German troops, the right weapons, better leadership and the tactics of the 'All Arms Battle' they could punch as hard as anyone. Claims as to their performance should not be exaggerated, but the improvements collectively achieved in an 'ordinary' division, which had previously performed indifferently at Gommecourt on the Somme on 1 July 1916, were quite evident.

DESPITE GLITCHES INEVITABLE IN HUGE OPERATIONS undertaken against German troops occupying strong defences, Rawlinson's Fourth Army had achieved considerable success. They had not just broken the Hindenburg Line, but in places the Support Line had been overwhelmed as well. True, the Beaurevoir Line still lay ahead, but that was a far less formidable defensive work. The French First Army had also begun supporting attacks, although too slowly for Haig's liking – he wanted a far more energetic performance. Indeed, as a result of British complaints, Foch once again had to admonish Debeney in an effort to get his First Army moving. On 2 October, the French captured St Quentin and crossed the canal, but were then held back as the German resistance solidified in front of them.

Over the next few days, as Monash attempted to gain his original objectives and Rawlinson sought to widen the breach achieved in the Hindenburg Line, the attacks continued. Finally, on 3 October, they were ready to launch an assault on the rest of the Beaurevoir Line. This proved a desperate fight, during which Lieutenant Colonel Bernard Vann[67] was killed at Ramicourt as his battalion again set a splendid example at the forefront of the attack. He was awarded a posthumous Victoria Cross for his leadership and courage that day. Luck was a precious possession to those that seemed to have it: doubtless to his parents' relief, Captain George Thomas had survived two vicious battles, although his breezy letter may not have entirely reassured them.

I have had most marvellous escapes both times. On the St Quentin Canal a shell landed near me and killed an officer I was talking to and blew a leg off my runner. I was covered with blood and only got hit in the face with a stone. On the second occasion, I had one bullet through my sleeve that just cut my arm, another through my pack and another through my field glasses.[68]

Captain George Thomas, 1/8th Sherwood Foresters, 46th Division,

A see-saw battle for Montbréhain ended when on 5 October the Australian 2nd Division made a final effort to capture the town. This proved to be the swansong of the Australian Corps. They were worn down to the bone and not even Monash could keep them in the line, so they were at last withdrawn to rest and recuperate. But the Australian achievements since the Battle of Amiens assault on 8 August were admirable: collectively they took some 22,854 prisoners and captured 332 guns, in the course of which they suffered a terrible 25,588 killed, wounded and missing. The exhausted survivors little knew it, but their war was done.

IN PREVIOUS WARS THERE HAD OFTEN BEEN A LULL in the fighting, a period of calm that could last for months. A chance for men to recharge their batteries, for units to restock their ranks, for supplies and ammunition to be built up for the next effort. But the Western Front in the Autumn of 1918 was unremitting. Battle followed battle, often blurring together with a complexity that was only unravelled – in theory at least – by post-war deliberations of the Battles Nomenclature Committee, which struggled valiantly to define the difference between phases, operations, battles, actions and miscellaneous incidents. For the men who fought face to face on the ground, the chance of even a couple of days while not actually under fire was a blessed relief.

Walked into Havrincourt and gathered mushrooms. It struck me as incongruous, picking mushrooms 'midst almost perfect peace, whereas only a few days ago – less than a week – this village must have been a veritable inferno, judging by the wreckage on all sides.

Still, it is not so utterly levelled as other villages, but somehow the sight of one blown up, shell-torn house after the other, with all the timber lying about in most grotesque shapes and forms, makes one realise the wreckage more vividly than where just a patch of overgrown bricks and iron meet the eye. Another remarkable sight, yet somehow in keeping with the surroundings, was the carrying of a piano through one of the main streets by a party of men who had discovered it among the ruins. How it remained untouched and unhurt is a marvel. Whenever this party halted for a rest, one of them started to play and the others danced around like so many street urchins. The sight of this piano being played in the middle of the street, these men dancing round and the ruins around was a very striking picture which yet seemed to be quite the natural order of things where, at present, the unnatural has become the natural.[69]

Corporal Vince Schürhoff, Signal Service, Royal Engineers, Headquarters, VI Corps

Some of the wilder spirits among the men grasped any opportunity for mischief that arose. Canadian Private Pat Gleason was out on rest with 46th Battalion, when he and two friends came across a rum jar while watering the battalion transport animals. It was a chance they simply could not resist.

This was a hot day, we were hungry and it didn't take much of that stuff until I had more than I should! The other two were pretty well loaded also. The last I remember, Dune was sitting on the ground, hanging on to two horses. I said, 'Where's your other horse, Dune?' He looked around and said, 'Oh, hell, one horse more or less don't matter in a war this size!' We managed to get back to camp okay, but I passed out on arrival. I just might have gotten away with it, had Captain Lett, the adjutant, not chosen that particular hour in which to inspect transport lines.[70]

Private Pat Gleason, 46th (South Saskatchewan) Battalion, 10th Brigade, 4th Canadian Division

Next day, Gleason was the first of the three to be called to a defaulters' parade in front of the august presence of Lieutenant Colonel Herbert Dawson.

> I was paraded into the colonel's tent first, leaving the two older chaps outside. The charge was read and I pleaded guilty. Then Colonel Dawson asked me what I had to say for myself. On the spur of the moment, I told him that three of us had gone to water our horses, and while there a couple of chaps from our home town of Yorkton came along and produced a bottle of some kind of liquor. Having scarcely ever tasted any before in my life, I told him I didn't know what the stuff was, but I had a couple of drinks of it, and that was the last I could remember. He turned to Lieutenant [George] Gilbert, OC of Transport, and asked him how long he had known me. George really went to bat for me and informed Dawson that he had known me since I was a small boy, which was partly true in that he had seen me a couple of times when I was 8 or 9 years old when he had come to see my dad concerning a team of mules. He told Dawson he had never known me to take a drink in all the years he had known me. Dawson turned to me and said, 'Will you take my punishment or will you elect a court martial?' I said, 'I'll take your punishment, Sir!!' 'Very well, fourteen days Field Punishment No. 1.' As I emerged from the tent and passed Dune, he said, just loudly enough for me to hear, 'You young bugger! You bull-shitted him out of fourteen days! I was sure we'd get twenty-eight!'[71]

Private Patrick Gleason, 46th (South Saskatchewan) Battalion, 10th Brigade, 4th Canadian Division

In the newly captured ground, the scale of the destruction was almost more shocking once the fighting had moved on. Major Charles Dudley Ward pondered on the debris of war as he and the Welsh Guards rested behind the new front line.

> One would scarcely credit it. They live in holes in the ground with bits of tin over the top. Of course, there is nowhere else for them to be – the one and only feature of this country is desolation. It is

awful. For miles, there is not a house, a barn, a roof of any kind. Piles of crumbling brick, mostly turned to dust, mark the spots where villages once stood. There is no sign of cultivation. All one finds on the ground is waste: mostly shells that have not gone off, bits of some that have, and confused heaps of some that have never been fired. Then rusty barbed wire, bits of clothes, boots, broken rifles, bayonets, scabbards, old dusty bombs, caps, steel helmets, dead horses, mounds with little tumbledown crosses, old half-filled in trenches, paper, rags – and over it all tonight the most glorious sunset.[72]

Major Charles Dudley Ward, 1st Welsh Guards, 3rd Guards Brigade, Guards Division

Lieutenant Burgon Bickersteth found himself based with the headquarters of the 6th Cavalry Brigade in the Bellenglise tunnel complex. It was still very evident that just a few days before it had been in German hands.

The entrance was unassuming. Steps led down about 40 feet as into any ordinary dugout. At the bottom of the steps one found oneself in a long passage, doors opening out on either side into different rooms. The air was somewhat musty, but not so as to be unpleasant. Mess rooms for officers and men, kitchens, offices, telephone exchanges, long rooms full of bunks succeeded one another. After walking 40 or 50 yards we came to more steps – about forty – and descended still more into the earth. Here one found the same thing – more passages, more rooms, turning to the left and to the right, sign-boards 'Nach Magny-La-Fosse', 'Nach Bellecourt', and a light railway with sidings. We were allotted two rooms by the officer commanding the tunnel – a Scottish captain, who told us that the engines for the electricity were still manned by the four Bosches who had worked it when the tunnels were German.[73]

Lieutenant Burgon Bickersteth, Headquarters, 6th Cavalry Brigade, 3rd Cavalry Division

The transport lines and rear headquarters of the 2/6th King's Liverpool Regiment had been set up next to Bourlon Wood. During the night of the 6/7 October they were bombed by a German aircraft.

The destruction caused by these terrific explosions was very considerable. One man was killed and seven wounded; while among
the transport itself, which received the brunt of the bombing, eighteen animals were either blown to pieces or so maimed that they
had to be shot. It was a horrible business digging out the wounded
men and putting the mutilated and screaming animals out of their
pain, and in the morning the place looked like a shambles.[74]

Captain Charles Wurtzburg, 2/6th King's Liverpool Regiment, 171st
Brigade, 57th Division

For the men caught up in this seemingly never-ending cycle of fighting,
danger seemed to be everywhere and their thoughts could not but drift
towards the idea of a nice 'Blighty wound'; an injury bad enough to get
the man sent back home, but not permanently crippling, or disfiguring.

The one large dugout was occupied by the officers; we servants were
in a bit of a shelter in a ditch covered only by sheets of corrugated
iron. The guns were in the open. Shellfire was almost continuous,
I must have dropped off and was awakened by a shell that dropped
just in front of our shelter, I felt something hit my foot and did it
sting. I jumped up coughing, it was a gas shell, killing the sentry
who was on guard outside. My first thoughts were to dash into the
officers' dugout. Major Campbell[75] found that I had been hit in the
stomach, also in the leg and foot. When the stretcher arrived and I
was being carried away, Major Campbell came to me and said, 'You
are a lucky lad, I wish it was me. Best of luck!'[76]

Gunner Jack Robey, C Battery, 231 Brigade, Royal Field Artillery, 46th
Division

Robey was evacuated back to the dressing station. It is often forgotten that
comparatively minor wounds could still kill in the days before antibiotics.

A deep dugout was full of wounded troops, so I was left out in the
bitter cold with only one blanket over me. A soldier came up to
my stretcher and asked where I was wounded, I told him. 'Never
mind, I will go and try to get an ambulance', he said, which he did.
About three hours afterwards I was moved to a field hospital tent.

I asked for a drink but was told not until I had been X-rayed. I was
so cold and I suppose a bit frightened; they put me on a stand and
turned on the steam, or at least I thought it was. I soon got warm.
The Roman Catholic priest came round and gave me the last rites,
Holy Communion. He said 'All operations are serious so it's as well
to be prepared!'[77]

Gunner Jack Robey, C Battery, 231 Brigade, Royal Field Artillery, 46th
Division

The ever-present risk of infection – especially from stomach wounds
– could lead to deadly complications like septicaemia or tetanus that
threatened an early grave.

The rapid progress since the start of the 'Hundred Days', back on 8
August, meant that all along the Western Front soldiers were beginning
to get just an inkling that the war might not last forever. They had been
almost devoid of hope but now there were glimmerings of optimism.

The military news seems almost incredibly good, however. It is
something to know one has played a part, however small, in securing this dramatic swing of the pendulum, and that on some of the
most famous battlefields of the war. It is like a game of chess. The
players have reached that part of the whole game known as 'the
end game'. We have the advantage in pieces and in position, and a
referee would award the game to us. Germany may choose to play
on, in which case the game may last for a long time, but only a
stupid blunder could rob us of the final checkmate.[78]

Lance Corporal Lawrence Attwell, 1/15th London Regiment (Civil Service
Rifles), 140th Brigade, 47th Division

The question was, could they live to see it? But still the idea of a renewed
life after the war was beginning to bubble to the surface. How could it
not? One such was Driver John Whitehead who had been on leave in his
home town of Huddersfield – his first for fourteen long months.

We had felt ever since our great advance started, that this was
the final advance, and that we were now really winning the war.
During this leave, I was engaged to Lucy, but not before a lot of

hesitation and the changing of mind. First, there was the 'Popping the question'! What a nervous chap! However, that hurdle safely negotiated, and the hope for 'Yes!' received as answer, I began to doubt the wisdom of our engagement. The war was not yet over, and anything might happen to me before it was. I did not want Lucy to be bound to a cripple, perhaps, or even something worse. So, I said, 'Let's wait until the war is over, and see how we are fixed then!' That day we hiked and rode on tramcars to Manchester, and, on our journey, we saw lots of John Bull's posters, which read, 'What a mistake!'. I applied it to my decision to wait, with the result that next morning we paraded at a jeweller's shop and from then we were engaged to be married.[79]

Driver John Whitehead, 168th Brigade, Royal Field Artillery, 32nd Division

Sergeant Charles Templar had come to the same kind of conclusion. He too had decided that the time had come to take the plunge.

The Allies were going forward and I thought there was a chance I might survive. So I wrote home to my lady love's father, told him that I'd been in love with her for four years and I would like to know whether he would have any objection to me as a potential son in law as I wanted to ask her to marry me! He wrote back and said, 'No!' Except one little stipulation, which was I should take out an insurance policy on my life for £100 made out in favour of his daughter! Now £100 was a lot of money! I acknowledged the responsibility and that I would see to it when I came home on leave. So, I came home on leave in the 2 October 1918. I went to Baker Street where my parents were living and I rang Daisy in St John's Wood at her home. She said, 'I'll come down on the bus', which stopped at Baker Street tube station! There was a blackout and I met her there as she got off the bus. She walked straight up to me and she said, 'Charles, are you quite sure, I'm the one you want?' And I kissed her for the first time – and that was it![80]

Sergeant Charles Templar, 13th Gloucestershire Regiment, 197th Brigade, 66th Division

The idea of survival was pervasive; the temptation to take things easy, to reduce the personal risks taken in action.

> While I was over on that leave my mother told me that my uncle, her brother who was my godfather, was in hospital with cancer and very ill. So I went to see him. I walked in there to his room and the first thing he said to me was, 'Charles, don't get yourself killed now, the war won't last much longer – the country will need young men like you!'[81]
>
> Sergeant Charles Templar, 13th Gloucestershire Regiment, 197th Brigade, 66th Division

But there would be plenty more fighting in store for them on the Western Front. Could they survive?

6

ADVANCE TO THE SELLE

Our General said, 'You're doing fine! I've just come along to congratulate you on the good job you're doing. I want you to hit him! You're hitting him now – don't think I don't know – you are – you're going like hell! And I want you to hit him, hit him, hit him! And keep hitting him! As soon as he stands, I'll relieve you – your job's done – I'll pull you out!' We kept hitting him right up to the last minute![1]

Private Leonard Hewitt, 7th Leicestershire Regiment, 110th Brigade, 21st Division

IN OCTOBER, FIGHTING WAS RAGING up and down the Western Front. Foch's strategy of four successive linked attacks was proving successful and the intensive fighting that followed on each of these sectors was stretching the German Army to its limits. It was evident that the five British armies were all making impressive headway. By contrast, Foch was not happy with the progress made by the French attacks, especially the performance of General Henri Gouraud's Fourth Army, which was attacking immediately to the north of the American Meuse-Argonne offensive. The irascible Foch proved a hard taskmaster; for in places Gouraud's men had advanced up to 8 miles. Indeed, in retrospect, it is clear that the French Army was playing a full part in the overall operations; it was just that for once it was not centre-stage. Almost everywhere the Germans were either retiring, or making serious preparations to fall back. However, the success of those retirements depended on the centre of their line holding firm – which meant those German divisions having to stand and fight for as long as possible. As such, attention began to focus on the push by the British Fourth and Third Armies towards Cambrai and beyond. This would be the scene of the next great effort.

Both sides were now struggling with the scale of losses suffered in 1918 and manpower was becoming critical. The German policy was clearly designed to minimise losses, as they used machine guns and artillery to hold up the advance. The British GHQ monitored the German tactics closely, with staff officer Lieutenant Colonel Cuthbert Headlam conducting several interviews with men fresh from the front to determine what was going on and to consider possible responses.

> The Germans have developed machine-gun tactics into a fine art and their best men are in their Machine Gun Corps. They stick to their guns splendidly and the damage machine guns can do is enormous provided they are well-sited and well-manned. If only we had twice as many men troops and better weather, the war might soon be on its last legs.[2]

Lieutenant Colonel Cuthbert Headlam, Training Branch, General Headquarters, BEF

The German artillery had also modified its tactics to take advantage of the fact that single or paired gun positions were difficult to pinpoint in a fluid situation where the British had insufficient time to allow for proper aerial reconnaissance.

> The enemy reply was heavy, and little counter battery work was possible against it owing to lack of knowledge of the enemy position, which had been withdrawn some distance. The enemy method was to fire with all guns for about the first half hour, then, if the attack

was not held up, all guns bar one per battery would retire. The single gun would continue firing as rapidly as possible, using up the battery ammunition dump. The crew would then destroy the gun and retire.[3]

Lieutenant Colonel Charles Hudson, 2nd Sherwood Foresters, 71st Brigade, 6th Division

The overall German intention was to delay the British advance, allowing time for further defensive works to be constructed.

On 8 October, the British Third and Fourth Armies and the French First Army launched a new offensive, with the intention of finally taking Cambrai and then pushing on to reach a line stretching through Valenciennes, Le Cateau and Wassigny. This attack was generally successful, but there was much hard fighting. On the right flank of the Third Army, V Corps was still faced with the continuation of the Beaurevoir Line which was still held by the Germans. A preliminary attack was therefore to be launched at 01.00 by the 38th Division, who would attack towards the village of Villers Outréux. The 115th Brigade would send the 17th Royal Welsh Fusiliers and the 10th South Wales Borderers forward on either side of Villers Outréux, while the third battalion, the 2nd Royal Welsh Fusiliers, was assigned to mopping up, aided by the 11th Tank Battalion. Things went badly wrong in the face of unbroken barbed wire defences covered by German machine guns. Captain John Nickson of the 2nd Royal Welsh Fusiliers found that they would have to take the village themselves.

Colonel Norman met us at the end of the sunken road. He told us that the attack had failed, that our supporting tank had not turned up, but B Company was to go ahead and do its best to get into the village. The Company pushed off. It was organized as two Platoons. There was no time to make any elaborate plan of advance, and no object in doing so; we did not know what to expect, and we were not being fired on. Leading to the village was a long straight piece of pavé road alongside which was a light railway. The ground along the railway was very broken, so we marched straight up the road in fours, fixing bayonets as we went. Ware's[4] platoon, which was leading, got right up to the wire across the road. Suddenly German SOS rockets went up all round and we were fired on heavily from a trench just ahead. Almost at the same moment our belated tank came lumbering up behind, spitting fire into our backs. We scattered in all directions, taking cover as best we could. The tank came right into the middle of us and circled round, shooting at anything moving it could see. A lot of our men were hit. 'Uncle' was lying on the ground riddled from the trench in front and the tank behind, but he kept on shouting to the men to, 'Get on with it!' and to the tank to get elsewhere. He is so large that he could harbour a good many missiles without any important part being touched. By this time Fritz was barraging the road heavily with howitzers and trench-mortars. The shells burst with tremendous crashes on the hard pavé; one of them hit the tank and, most happily, put it out of action.[5]

Captain John Nickson, 2nd Royal Welsh Fusiliers, 115th Brigade, 38th Division

Nickson was lightly wounded in the leg but carried on with his men. Amidst the chaos, grizzled veteran Private Frank Richards witnessed a courageous display by the Wesleyan chaplain, Reverend William Evans-Jones, who had recently been attached to the battalion. He had become popular by frequently helping the men carry their heavy equipment.

I liked him very much, although he had chastised me several times for my language! I told him the attack would start in about five minutes and he told me that he was going over with the first wave of attacking troops, so that he could attend the wounded as soon as they were hit. I told him that he was different from all the chaplains of my experience and that I admired his pluck, but not his sense. It would be far better if he waited a few minutes until after the first wave had gone over; then he would be able to go forward and attend the wounded. But if he went over with the first wave it was quite possible he would get knocked out himself and would not be able to attend anyone. He would not take my advice and

went over with the first wave, dropping dead[6] before he had run
ten paces.[7]

Private Frank Richards, 2nd Royal Welsh Fusiliers, 115th Brigade, 38th
Division

Others had a different impression of the chaplain's motives, including the
somewhat cynical battalion historian, Captain James Dunn, 'He was told
that he would be an embarrassment to them; but he was impulsive, he
insisted on going, and was killed when seeking a Military Cross to please
some fool of a girl in Liverpool who had taunted him with having no deco-
ration.'[8] Meanwhile, Second Lieutenant William Ware pushed on into
Villers-Outréux. After a short interval spent gathering up his somewhat
scattered men, Nickson followed him.

> We found quite a number of Germans in the cellars of houses.
> Why they were there, and the entrance to the village not more
> strongly held I don't know, unless they relied on their exceedingly
> strong flank positions to cover the direct approach, and thought
> an attack up the main road impossible; or they may have thought
> that only the usual early morning strafe was going on, and didn't
> bother to come up. As it was still rather dark, and difficult to keep
> control in the streets and houses, we of B Company decided to
> get out and work our way along the light railway round the north-
> west outskirts until we could see better. Turner arrived now with
> C Company, and made off towards the south-eastern part of the
> village. By the time we reached the railway station it was begin-
> ning to be light. We were fired on from Pierre Mill, on the left,
> and from the trenches directly behind us, which the 17th Battalion
> had attacked unsuccessfully earlier; so, turning round and taking
> cover behind the railway embankment, we returned the fire with
> our Lewis guns. It was rather an open question then if we, or the
> enemy, were surrounded.[9]

Captain John Nickson, 2nd Royal Welsh Fusiliers, 115th Brigade, 38th
Division

In this kind of action, it is evident that however experienced or well-intentioned a unit might be, the random factors thrown up in the hurly-burly of warfare could cause chaos. No time for reconnaissance, planning and the proper dissemination of orders; the late arrival of key components of the attack; confusion caused by darkness – in such circumstances war became little more than survival and reacting to the press of events – and the casualty rate rose accordingly. This, in essence, was what had happened on 29 September to the Americans – but it could have happened to anyone. Eventually the situation was stabilised, although Nickson had to be evacuated, as it became apparent that his leg wound was bad enough to need proper medical treatment. Despite such isolated hold-ups, the overall results of the day were very satisfactory for the Third Army, as they had collectively smashed through the Beurevoir-Masnières Line with an advance that stretched up to 5,000 yards in places, while on the right of the advance the 63rd (Royal Naval) Division of the XVII Corps was well positioned to threaten to outflank Cambrai from the south.

To the south, the Fourth Army also had a successful day. It is perhaps interesting to view the advance from the perspective of an artillery officer, Major Joseph Rice. It was apparent that they would all have to get used to a new form of open warfare. The gun positions would no longer be permanent, but merely stations on a journey to who knows where, with no time to dig in properly with gunpits, shell stores and dugouts. This left them vulnerable to either counter-battery fire, or a sudden air attack.

At about 10 am we advanced through Beaurevoir, not being sorry to leave our last position. We came into action about three-quarters of a mile north-east of Beaurevoir as ordered, and had just got the lines of fire laid out and the camouflage nets put up, when Colonel Thorp, who had been up forward on his horse, galloped back to say that the enemy's resistance was less than had been expected. He therefore sent Battery commanders forward to look for positions about a mile and a half ahead in the direction of Serain. The enemy were obviously retiring rapidly, and it was most cheering to go forward into practically undamaged country on a lovely sunny day with hardly a sound of enemy shelling. I soon found a suitable position about three-quarters of a mile west of Serain, and sent an orderly back to guide the Battery up. We got into action in the afternoon, and the light went pretty soon afterwards. On this evening the noise of rifle fire almost died away and there was practically no shellfire, but the Bosche seemed to have detailed every aeroplane in his army to drop bombs on the advancing XIII Corps! Everyone in a large area round about us seemed to get a taste of it. Our three 18-pdr batteries were close together, and between 7.30 and 10.30 pm we had several visits from the Bosche aeroplanes. A/82 had a gun and dial-sight hit, and we had two bombs very close, one nearly hitting the culvert which was the only place the officers of C/82 could find in which to spend the night. We had a cold supper that night as we dared not light a fire![10]

Major Joseph Rice, C Battery, 82 Brigade, Royal Field Artillery, 18th Division

Next day they moved further forward to Serain, where they found more proof that the war was changing.

We had some breakfast at this spot, and had the unusual experience for gunners of capturing two prisoners. Some of the gunners, wandering about the nearest house, found two Germans in a cellar, and brought them out to me. One was ugly and big, and the other good looking and quite a boy. With the aid of the few German words I knew, I found out their regiment and division, and then, strange to relate, chiefly because of the young boy, I gave them some bread and treacle! Just then an orderly arrived with orders for a bigger advance than we had expected, so we got the Germans to give a hand in sorting the ammunition in the wagons and limbers, and then handed them over to two military police.[11]

Major Joseph Rice, C Battery, 82 Brigade, Royal Field Artillery, 18th Division

For the Germans, this was a grim period. As the British shells set fire to the buildings of Cambrai, a general retirement was ordered on 8–9

October. They were to fall back to the newly constructed Hermann Line, running through Tournai, Valenciennes and Avesnes. Among those the Germans forced to retreat was Corporal Frederick Meisel.

> Our division passed through Cambrai. British shells had set it on fire. The air was acrid with black smoke, the heat intense. Our pace increased as the danger from falling timbers became evident. Scurrying down the endless streets, Otto tried to light a cigarette, 'Anybody got a match?' Pointing to a smouldering telegraph pole, Paul replied, 'There, help yourself!' Eyes and throats were beginning to burn, lips becoming parched with the heat. Just as I thought we were doomed to be burned alive, the outskirts of the town were reached. A short rest was ordered while we filled our lungs with sweet fresh air. A wind had sprung up, driving away the thick clouds of smoke, showing the burning city clearly, the flames lighting the landscape.[12]

> Corporal Frederick Meisel, Infantry Regiment 371, 43rd Ersatz Brigade, 10th Ersatz Division

As the pace of the Allied advance was increasing, they found that they had broken through into 'clean' country, with open fields, natural vegetation and small towns still inhabited by the French civilians. But there were also frequent reminders that, while the terrain looked more friendly, and the inhabitants were welcoming, this was still a war zone.

> I shall never forget the march through Bertry and Troisvilles. The former was populated by old men, women and children. The men lifted their caps to us as they had been made to do to the Bosche. There were one or two of our cavalrymen lying dead in the streets, and we also passed a number of them and their horses before reaching Bertry. All the civilians waved or cheered or cried, and lots of houses had a French flag flying. The inhabitants must have hidden these flags for four years. The same sort of thing happened in Troisvilles, but, while we were marching through, a Bosche shell crashed through the wall of a house just in front of us, and as we passed an old man came out, wringing his hands which were

ADVANCE TO THE SELLE

covered in blood, and two soldiers carried out a girl who was apparently badly hit, but we could not see whether she was dead or not. It was a terribly sad sight.[13]

Major Joseph Rice, C Battery, 82 Brigade, Royal Field Artillery, 18th Division

As a matter of policy, the Germans attempted to destroy anything of value before evacuating the area. Just a couple of miles to the north of Troisvilles, the New Zealanders were shocked by what they found as they entered the town of Caudry. A shell randomly killing civilians could be understood as an accident of war, but the events in Caudry indicated a more disturbing wanton cruelty.

The place had not been knocked about by the Hun until a few days ago, when parties of men were detailed to go through the factories and deliberately smash the machinery with hammers. I saw the results: cogs and wheels broken everywhere. Six men smashed all the machinery of a cotton mill in one half-day. Windows, clocks, ornaments and furniture had in many cases been treated in a similar way. Between 2,000 and 3,000 refugees were left in the town. Women, children and old men. The Huns had lived there so long, they had all learnt to speak German. They were delighted to see us. The French Tricolour was flying from nearly every window. The people waved their hands, doffed their caps, threw kisses, came to the car and shook hands and showed in a thousand ways by smiles, expression and otherwise how grateful they were to be liberated from slavery. All men between 15 and 60 had been taken away. Most of the population had been induced by promises, alternating with threats, to leave at various times during the four years, and were employed in munitions, roads, railways, etc. The people were not starved. They had continued growing their crops and vegetables and managed for the most part to keep themselves in food. The women apparently were not much molested while they were able to remain in their own homes with the family complete and intact. Once they left their homes, for work or under compulsion, they lived lives of enforced prostitution. There were a number of cases of raping just as the Hun was about to leave. It was a fatal thing for a woman under such circumstances, having a pretty face.[14]

Brigadier General Herbert Hart, Headquarters, 3rd New Zealand (Rifle) Brigade, New Zealand Division

War crimes occurred on both sides including cases of rape and the murder of soldiers attempting to surrender. Soldiers tend to notice only the crimes committed by the 'other' side.

As usual, the plentiful booby traps threatening soldiers and civilians alike needed to be cleared away. These took many forms and Hart employed an unethical, but highly effective, method of dealing with the menace.

The roads in and around Caudry were blown up at all junctions and all important points. Half a dozen minenwerfer or large shells are buried, then exploded by electric batteries. Booby traps are placed in dugouts, houses, roads and wells, but we now keep Hun prisoners and make them go in these places first, either remove them or themselves cause the explosion and get blown up instead of us![15]

Brigadier General Herbert Hart, Headquarters, 3rd New Zealand (Rifle) Brigade, New Zealand Division

Up and down the line, this was a common approach to the problem. It may have been against the rules of war, but it was seen as a quick, effective and sure method of avoiding casualties.

Last night we stopped at a village which had been evacuated at 11 the previous morning. The streets had all been sown with mines; but fortunately some of the German engineers who fixed them up were captured, and when we left this morning they were going round under escort picking them out again – that's the stuff to give them.[16]

Captain Joseph Maclean, 1st Cameronians (Scottish Rifles), 19th Brigade, 33rd Division

The 5th Connaught Rangers were in reserve on 9 October, and thus had the pleasure of watching a busy day of fighting unfold in front of them.

The 66th Division were pushing hard along the main road to Le Cateau on the River Selle.

> When the fog lifted, the 197th and 198th Brigades could be seen entering Maretz and advancing on the woods south of the village under frequent machine-gun fire. Then the field artillery dashed at top speed over the fields, the guns bounding like toys on the stubble, while the Germans shelled them by fits and starts. Later, the aeroplanes made an appearance in very large numbers and fired thousands of rounds at one another, while the anti-aircraft guns nearly blotted out the blue with smoke. In the afternoon, the German guns almost got our range. Later in the afternoon, masses of cavalry came up and changed into various formations before charging over the ground in front of us. There was a lot of machine-fire and a few riderless horses came back. Early in the evening, nine German aeroplanes suddenly appeared, and tried to machine-gun the battalion, but they were driven off with some hearty firing, in which all ranks joined with great goodwill. Some armoured cars also made an appearance, so, if the Navy could only have done something, it would have been a nice full day. [17]
>
> Lieutenant Alan McPeake, 5th Connaught Rangers, 199th Brigade, 66th Division

At times, there was a strange resemblance to at least some of the tactics of 1914, as cavalry provided a light screen reaching ahead of the infantry as they advanced. One of those feeling his way along the road to Le Cateau was Lieutenant Burgon Bickersteth in his role as acting intelligence officer to the 6th Cavalry Brigade. He was with the 1st (Royal) Dragoons as they took up dismounted positions on the high ground east of the village of Reumont, where they were spotted by a German reconnaissance aircraft and soon came under a barrage of shells.

> Ellis, who had brought his two Vickers guns up to consolidate the position, was in the next shell-hole to mine, with a Corporal, a Private and a gun. The Bosches got a direct hit on them and killed all three. I did not realize this for about a quarter of an hour and

began calling out to Ellis. No answer – and then I caught sight of his body thrown half out of the shell-hole. I crawled across to the hole and found him, one half of his head entirely blown away.[18] The corporal[19] had his left arm and side entirely blown off – there was no sign of his arm at all – and Private Harris[20] lay there just breathing, a thick red slime welling out of his throat. He died while I was crouching in the hole with them.[21]

Lieutenant Burgon Bickersteth, Headquarters, 6th Cavalry Brigade, 3rd Cavalry Division

Up above them their own 'cavalry of the clouds' was carrying out a series of low-level reconnaissance flights in an effort to locate the exact positions of the German rearguards.

Visibility was only about 400 yards, and the cloud base was down to about 300 feet. I took off and flew just above the tree tops down the long, straight road that ran from north of St Quentin to Le Cateau. There were three or four roads running out of Le Cateau to the east, and I flew along each of these in turn until I found myself shot at from the ground, at which point I rapidly turned around. After marking on my map the spot where I had been fired at I made my way back to Le Cateau and repeated the process along the other roads. Having collected this information, I then groped my way back to my own aerodrome by contour-chasing with my map on my knee. When I got there and gave the information to our intelligence people they were able to join up the points that I had marked, and through that they were able to gain quite a fair picture of the location of the German front line.[22]

Major Sholto Douglas, 85 Squadron, RAF

On 10 October, it was the turn of the Connaught Rangers to take up the lead. They pressed forwards and soon came under heavy shellfire as they reached the outskirts to Le Cateau. Out in the open as they were, at the very forefront of the advance, and with no idea of where the Germans were, then casualties were inevitable. Suddenly the howl of shells announced they had run into German resistance.

I will never forget the look of horror on the face of one of my men, as
a splinter of shell disembowelled him, in the seconds, or moments,
before he died. Another had one of his legs almost amputated just
at his knee, and I, with my penknife, severed the few scraps of flesh
and sinew which held it together before tying him up and sending
him back on a stretcher.[23]

Captain Charles Brett, 5th Connaught Rangers, 199th Brigade, 66th
Division

At 17.00, the Connaughts were ordered forward to take the town. They
were exhausted and hungry, but nevertheless dragged themselves up from
the shallow holes they had scraped out for shelter. Before they had gone
100 yards, the German artillery once more burst into life.

It sounded as if express trains were crashing through space and
blowing the roadway into a ceaseless fountain of dust, smoke and
blazing light. The leading platoon was almost destroyed by one of
these shells and the dead bodies came rolling down the high banks
at the side of the road.[24]

Second Lieutenant Alan McPeake, 5th Connaught Rangers, 199th
Brigade

By the time they got into Le Cateau it was dark. Soon many of the platoons had become isolated. Captain Brett led a small party across an iron
footbridge that spanned the River Selle and was approaching his objective
– a railway embankment on the eastern outskirts of the town. The men
rushed through the deserted streets, fearing a burst of fire at every twist
and turn. Suddenly it happened.

A machine gun opened up on us, from the top of what appeared to
be an obstacle across the road, 50 or 60 yards away, and the bullets
made bright sparks as they hit the granite setts of the roadway.
We all took cover in doorways and the machine gun stopped. My
subaltern said, 'Come on, we can't stop here!' and we all started
up the street. A German shouted, 'Wie geht?' to which I replied,
in elementary schoolboy German, 'Was ist das?' which apparently
satisfied the German who replied, 'Gans recht!' So we went on and

found the obstacle across the street to be an iron railway bridge, which had been blown up and tipped sideways. On top were several Germans with the machine gun – we climbed up and disposed of them. Having done so, we looked down into the roadway on the German side of the bridge and saw below us 50 to 100 German soldiers standing and looking up at the top of the bridge to see what it was all about. It was pretty dark but one could see the serried rows of white faces looking up. At my command we leapt down among them, killed and wounded several, and captured two, all the rest turned tail and fled. It was well for us that they were very poor class troops.[25]

Captain Charles Brett, 5th Connaught Rangers, 199th Brigade, 66th Division

Brett did not have enough men with him to hold defensive positions along the embankment, so he quickly fell back to the River Selle, where, to his alarm he discovered the footbridge he had crossed had been partially demolished. Brett didn't think long before leaping into action.

The iron handrail still ran across several feet above the water. I handed my rifle to the man immediately behind me and set off across the river on the handrail. It was a bit wobbly, but bore my weight all right, so I ordered the others to come over one at a time. The first man over handed me back my rifle – and I was interested to see that he was one of our German prisoners! We staggered back to the place we had started from. I collapsed into one of the little holes we had dug, utterly exhausted, and went to sleep at once. When I woke next morning I found there was something with me in the hole – it turned out to be the leg I had cut off the evening before, with its boot and puttee complete![26]

Captain Charles Brett, 5th Connaught Rangers, 199th Brigade, 66th Division

For the moment, the Selle marked the limit of the British advance.

On 10 October, in the midst of successful British operations in the centre of the overall front, Foch issued another directive to his armies.

This had to some extent been overtaken by events, but showed that he was still intent on maintaining a constant unified pressure on the Germans within a coherent overall strategy. He envisioned three converging attacks: the Flanders Army Group to strike towards Ghent; the British to advance on Maubeuge; the French and Americans to continue to push forwards on Mézières. Foch now saw the British thrust as being possibly the most advantageous. This was partly because, despite the encouragement from Foch to speed the advance of his armies, Pétain was still keen to reduce the risk of mass casualties. The consequent reliance on prolonged artillery preparation and the overall cautious approach naturally slowed up French progress.

The next directive from Foch came just a few days later, on 19 October, reflecting the fast-moving pace of events on the ground. The Flanders Army Group were now to march on Brussels, the main British force would push through Maubeuge and drive the Germans back into the Ardennes region, the French First Army was directed towards Hirson, while the French Fifth and Fourth Armies, with the American First Army, were to carry on battering their way to Mézières. As a final blow, Foch also planned a major new offensive in Lorraine, envisioning an advance from Mangin's Tenth Army from Nancy towards Morhange – a new Battle of the Frontiers some four years after the first. Only the end of the war thwarted this attempt at closure.

7

BATTLE OF SELLE

The Enemy has not the means, nor the will-power, to launch an attack strong enough to affect even our front line troops. We have got the Enemy down, in fact he is a beaten Army, and my plan is to go on hitting him as hard as we possibly can, till he begs for mercy.[1]

Field Marshal Sir Douglas Haig, General Headquarters, BEF

THE RIVER SELLE THAT STILL LAY AHEAD of both the British Third and Fourth Armies in the centre of the Allied advance on the Western Front was a considerable obstacle to progress. The Germans had done everything that time allowed to strengthen this section of the Hermann Line. Gentle slopes stretching down to the river from the west provided ideal fields of fire for the German machine gunners, while the German side was far more suited to defence with a steeper rise to a ridge line, cut by valleys draining down to the Selle. In places, the Germans had dammed the Selle, thereby flooding the bottom of the valley. The ground was enclosed with hedges and dotted with orchards, farms and villages, which all provided an excellent basis for an improvised defence. The town of Le Cateau, only briefly penetrated by the Connaught Rangers, also acted as a useful anchor to the defensive line. To crack this 'nut', the Allied attack was planned in two main phases: first, on 17 October, the Fourth Army would attack south of Le Cateau in conjunction with the French First Army. Then, when the right flank had been secured, the Third Army would attack north of Le Cateau. Rawlinson knew the scale of the task before his Fourth Army, so had wisely paused to bring up his medium heavy guns, replenish his ammunition supplies and allow for the partial reorganisation – and some rest – for his tired infantry. The overall objective was for a 5-mile advance to the Sambre-Oise Canal and the western edge of the Forêt de Mormal. This was ambitious, but reflected Haig's confidence that the German defence was crumbling. Risks had to be taken; they could not lose the momentum.

At 05.20 on 17 October, the Fourth Army infantry went over the top on a 10-mile front, stretching south from Le Cateau to Riquerval Wood. The River Selle itself was not too serious an obstacle in the southern sector of the advance, certainly not to the men of the 46th Division who had so recently braved the St Quentin Canal. Yet once they got up on the Belle Vue ridge line behind the Selle, German resistance stiffened appreciably. Lewis gunner Corporal George Parker was attacking with the 1/8th Sherwood Foresters to the right of the town of Vaux Andigney.

> We managed, with great loss, to get over some pontoon bridges which the engineers and pioneers had miraculously rigged up over-night, cleared some trenches there, with bayonets and grenades, took more prisoners, mostly boys younger than me. In front of us across a flat area was a ridge, which, as we approached, erupted with tremendous machine-gun fire. Our officers were killed in getting to that ridge and by the time we reached its shelter all NCOs but myself and another Corporal were either dead or wounded. My team, now only three, and I set up our Lewis gun on the top of the ridge, keeping heads well down. Suddenly lines of grey figures swarmed over towards the ridge. They were putting in a counter attack! I opened up with my gun, traversing left and right over the plain. I could actually see men falling like ninepins, but still

they came on, reinforced by more and more waves of field grey. I
thought we had had it! Suddenly firing started to come from the
side of our position, then almost at the back of us. It didn't need
brains to know what that meant: we were a few men on a bit of
a hill, being gradually surrounded – we hadn't a hope in hell of
getting out of it. We kept up our fire, and our artillery opened out
on the rear of the German hordes, but it was too late, no one could
get to us in time to help.[2]

Corporal George Parker, 1/8th Battalion Sherwood Foresters, 139th
Brigade, 46th Division

As Parker tried to crawl back to get some instructions, he was suddenly
hit.

It seemed as though I had been kicked by a horse on the left knee,
it gave way and down I went, rolling down the bank. The only thing
I thought of then, was to get out of it, before the only gap in the
circle closed. I crawled; dragging that blasted leg, in between hundreds of our dead, towards what I hoped was the right way. I was
more scared then than when I was behind my gun – so helpless.
Even then Jerry gave me a parting gift – a bullet in my hip – I don't
think he liked me![3]

Corporal George Parker, 1/8th Battalion Sherwood Foresters, 139th
Brigade, 46th Division

Bleeding profusely, Parker managed to make his way back to the first aid
posts and was safely evacuated. His war was over.

Not far to the left of the 46th Division was Second Lieutenant Clifford Carter of the 2nd York & Lancasters who went over at 07.00 with
the second wave. He had an easier time of it, thanks to their supporting
artillery.

The guns put up a perfect barrage – a real wall of fire – just ahead.
It was too near to be pleasant and we had to lie flat with our faces
in the grass. After a few minutes the barrage advanced 100 yards
and we were just preparing to follow it when a great shout went
up from behind and three tanks came lumbering out of the wood.

We dashed after them seeing nothing but fog, fog, fog, fog and not knowing when we should come across the enemy. But the guns had done their work and only a few Germans popped up here and there out of shell holes and dugouts. If they seemed prepared to put up a fight our fellows gave them three rounds 'rapid' – most of them just put up their hands and surrendered, crying 'Kamerad!' We soon collected a score or so, and after depriving them of bayonets, knives and so forth, I sent them marching off with an NCO and two men. Suddenly ahead I saw a German officer preparing to fire with his pistol. I quickly aimed at him and he quickly put up one hand, still holding his pistol in the other. We shouted to him to drop it – and seeing he had no chance, he did so. I pinched his field-glasses and iron-pointed stick and still prize them as mementoes of the occasion.[4]

Second Lieutenant Clifford Carter, 2nd York & Lancasters, 16th Brigade, 6th Division

The guns did not go unscathed though. On 19 October, Gunner Rollin Brierley and the rest of C Battery 231st Brigade had arrived at Bohain, and billeted in an old warehouse which they used as the battery stables. The reception from the civilians had been ecstatic, but the men were worried by the occasional large German shells that were still crashing down around the town. They were well advised to worry. Long-range shells posed a threat even when well behind the front.

We had just turned in for harness cleaning when a shell landed in the larger room. I was flattened out by people falling over me as they dived for cover and when I got up there was a thick pall of smoke and dust coming through the doorway of the other room. I got to the entrance just as the Battery Sergeant Major arrived and we found the body of a Sergeant, who had only joined us the night before and I had never seen him or knew his name. A man with a severed artery in his leg was screaming out, 'I'm dying!' and the BSM went to help him and told me to push on. I found another man with the back of his head blown off. He was Gunner Gibson[5] from Hull who had come out on the same boat as I did in July

1916. A stretcher bearer said, 'Leave him and let's look after the living!' A stretcher party went by with Sergeant Laurence,[6] a Mons veteran with his right arm blown to bits. After finding another dead man, I joined a party who were looking after a shoeing smith whose arm and leg had gone and they wanted someone with a knife to cut his clothes away. I had my knife handy so I did what was necessary and they put on shell dressings and whipped him off to the dressing station. That meant six dead, or dying, and there were about sixteen less seriously wounded, including George Thomson, just back from leave in England.[7]

Gunner Rollin Brierley, C Battery, 231 Brigade, Royal Field Artillery

Over two days of hard fighting, Fourth Army achieved its objective, cracking the difficult nut of Le Cateau, reaching the Sambre at the town of Catillon and establishing a defensive front stretching back to the Third Army lined up along the Selle. For the moment their work was done.

Third Army would attack on 20 October, pushing across the Selle, then a series of ridges and valleys until they reached high ground between the Harpies and St Georges rivers. There would be no preliminary bombardment, and Zero Hour was set at 02.00 to gain the best advantage from what was nearly a full moon. The men of the 1st Welsh Guards were getting ready for the attack when their adjutant, Major Charles Dudley Ward, became deeply suspicious of the antics of one of his officers.

[Anon officer] is playing the fool. He scrimshanked home once before and Bill winkled him out again. Now he is trying all he knows to do it once more. Having tried to get home on the grounds that he has served 31 months out here and failed, he went up to the battalion today and signed a paper saying in effect that his nerve had gone and that he is willing to be sent permanently to the base. From there he hopes to 'swing' home! I never thought very much of him. Of course, in character he is contemptible – but there are quite a number as bad as he.[8]

Major Charles Dudley Ward, 1st Welsh Guards, 3rd Guards Brigade, Guards Division

Others might have been more sympathetic for an officer that seemed broken by his experiences, and indeed there is no trace of such a negative attitude towards this individual in Dudley Ward's own *History of the Welsh Guards*. The officer's record shows that he had been invalided back in England for just a few weeks in 1917 and that he had also been awarded the MC. It shows the pressures that men were under in these final months of the war. Not everyone could take it and there was a considerable resentment for those whom it was believed – rightly or wrongly – could not maintain the standards expected.

When the attack came, the Guards Division crossed the Selle by means of eight floating footbridges, while the artillery would follow them across as soon as possible, by means of two rapidly installed trestle bridges. It would prove to be an exciting day for young Second Lieutenant Alexander Stanier of the 1st Welsh Guards.

> They were holding the high ground beyond the River Selle, in strength. It was therefore decided to put in a brigade attack by night. During the day, sappers came up and taped out the ground down to the river itself, under cover of fire, as close as they could get, and bridges were made of petrol cans, lashed together with ropes. At midnight, the most spectacular barrage I have ever seen opened up. It was pouring with rain, very dark, and suddenly this terrific bombardment came down on the Germans. Single file across the little bridges, then halted on the far side. When the last man had come, we started up. We advanced, I came up the hill in the leading company, great difficulty in finding my way – it was so dark, it was pouring with rain, it was slippery and muddy – there weren't any particular tracks. I had my compass, but it seemed to be whizzing round, with all the steel about. There was barbed wire all over the place. So many people were in the wrong place, people from the flanks had moved in and across. There was a terrible lot of shouting and cursing! They opened up with machine guns quite a lot. Small trenches, nothing continuous, just what they'd had time to dig. We captured a certain number of Germans, including one with an anti-tank rifle, which we'd never seen before. They

put their hands up straight away directly they saw us. The war was coming to an end and they knew it. Once they saw it was up, perhaps they would surrender quicker than before, but they were still ready to fire – they were brave men.[9]

Second Lieutenant Alexander Stanier, 1st Welsh Guards, 3rd Brigade, Guards Division

They pressed on to the top of the ridge about 1,000 yards in front of the small River Harpies. At this point, Stanier's company commander ordered him to take out a reconnaissance patrol. He was to check whether there was any serious German opposition on the far bank of the river and furthermore, discover whether it was possible to cross the Harpies, i.e. to get information about the width, depth and banks of the stream. By this time it was almost dawn, but there was a slight mist in the air that restricted visibility. Stanier collected six men, including Corporal William Gam and his servant, Private William Lakin, for a patrol that would be plagued by an unfortunate series of events.

I told them to follow me, there was no time to give any further instructions – I knew what we had to do myself. We walked down the sloping hillside, which was quite bare stubble. We came to a little hedge, which I left the patrol behind and I and my servant went on across the meadow, about 200–300 yards. As we approached the river I saw a German with a machine gun between his legs, asleep, and a German NCO shaking him up and pointing at me! Where-upon, he let off the machine gun, but of course it wasn't properly aimed and the bullets went over my head. My servant and I then jumped into the river, so that he couldn't see us and waded up the stream until we came to a little ditch that ran into the river.[10]

Second Lieutenant Alexander Stanier, 1st Welsh Guards, 3rd Brigade, Guards Division

Stanier and Lakin crawled up the ditch, heading back towards where he had left his men behind the hedge, but on getting to a point about 100 yards away, he saw more trouble unfolding in front of him.

By this time, the Germans had started firing, having been woken up, and the patrol found that they couldn't see to fire from behind the hedge, so that they had to move out into the open before they could fire – some of them got shot for their trouble. I ought to have put them in a fire position before I left. After a time, I decided I must just run across to them, which I did. Thinking that my servant would see me and follow me, but he didn't – he stayed in the brook. I got behind the hedge and all went quiet. We saw some of the Germans withdrawing up the hillside.[11]

Second Lieutenant Alexander Stanier, 1st Welsh Guards, 3rd Brigade, Guards Division

Stanier fanned out his men and set off back up the hill to report the situation to his company commander. They had only got about halfway back when they discovered that not all the Germans had retreated, some still lurking within range the other side of the river.

The Germans opened up and the other members of the patrol were all hit, including the corporal in the arm, who fell on the top of me into a very small shell-hole! The Germans went on firing, put one through the rim of my tin hat, which was rather too close for my liking. Anyhow we lay there and at about 12 o'clock it seemed to go quiet and some gallant stretcher-bearers came out – the Germans must have withdrawn – and took them down to Battalion headquarters. One of the guardsman was asked by the adjutant, 'Where's the officer?' To which the guardsman said, 'He's been very badly wounded in the upper leg and is covered in blood, so badly hit he can't walk – and we've had to leave him behind at company headquarters.' The Adjutant said, 'Thank you very much!' and filled in the casualty report that had to go in at 12 o'clock, saying, 'One officer seriously wounded, upper leg!' Actually, what had happened was that the Corporal Gam's arm had bled on the top of my mackintosh, and of course made the most awful mess on me! But other than being hit in the hand I was all right and remained at duty. Next day, we were relieved and I reported to the Adjutant and said, 'I think I'm due for leave in England!' He said, 'Good God, I thought you were there already, I've reported you as being seriously wounded!'[12]

Second Lieutenant Alexander Stanier, 1st Welsh Guards, 3rd Brigade, Guards Division

Private William Lakin later wrote to Stanier from the East Leeds War Hospital at Killingbeck in Leeds.

Just a line to let you know I have arrived in Blighty as per above address and am pleased to say I am going on well. I am hit in the head, shoulder, back, leg and arm, quite a few, but I am smiling. There is one consolation I have, that is I am well out of reach of those whistling machine-gun bullets. I met Corporal Gam at casualty clearing station, but have not seen him since. I did not notice you go from that brook where we were lying-in, so I decided to hang on a bit. The suspense began to get on my nerves and not knowing whether Fritz was not working up those bushes I decided to run the gauntlet. I started. I managed to clear the brook and field and got past the hedge when one of our shells caught me in the back and shoulder. Down I fell, then Fritz contributed one through my arm and one through my leg. Thinking I had not enough he loaned me another – in the head. After this quite exciting period here I am, happy at the prospect of being once again in Blighty. I am quite well at present despite my wounds and hope my letter finds you in the very best of health. I must close now, wishing the Battalion the very best of luck.[13]

Private William Lakin, 1st Welsh Guards, 3rd Guards Brigade, Guards Division

The adjutant in question was the somewhat acerbic figure of Major Charles Dudley Ward, who later made some critical remarks on the conduct of Stanier's patrol in his *History of the Welsh Guards*.

The way in which the patrol worked, gallant and successful though its efforts were, is open to criticism. It is suggested that as soon as Second Lieutenant Stanier received his orders, he might have spent a few minutes in reconnoitring the country before him with his field-glasses. By so doing he might have discovered at once the answer to the question of whether the Germans were holding the far bank, and secondly, he might have found a covered line of approach to the river, possibly on the flank of the company front. The ground, however, was singularly devoid of cover, and 2nd Lieut. Stanier was probably right to make the bold advance he did, as the early morning haze still hung about and he was not moving on a skyline. But before moving forward he gave his patrol no chance to look at the ground nor did he give it any orders as to its task or the way in which he proposed it should be carried out. It was fortunate, therefore, that Stanier was able to get back himself from the river; it was unfortunate that the patrol had not been left in a fire position at the willows to cover its leader or that some arrangements had not been made in the company to cover the withdrawal of the patrol should it get into difficulties as, in fact, it did.[14]

Major Charles Dudley Ward, 1st Welsh Guards, 3rd Guards Brigade, Guards Division

Also in the attack that morning was Private Horace Calvert of the 2nd Grenadier Guards, who, although only 19 years old, had joined up while well under age and had been serving out in France since 1916. As such he was now a veteran. That morning he was digging with the rest of his platoon.

We got to the other side of the village, early morning and started digging in! The young fellow who was with me I was telling him how to dig a bit of a foxhole to get himself down for daylight proper. There was a small wood about 300 yards away, and what I judged to be a farmhouse or something there, the other side of it – and that's where the Germans were. As we started digging in they were sending over small shells – 'appen a 'Whizz-Bang' type of thing. One landed just in front of where I was and I got a right bash on the side of head. Got a black eye and I couldn't see – full of dirt! Sergeant said to me, 'It's no good you stopping here, you'd better go out and have that attended to!' There was always the fear of getting tetanus, the soil was full of it – it paid you to get an injection. I set off and I dropped all my equipment and rifle, because you always left it behind for whatever was in there could be used by the chaps left behind – if there was any food or water. The young fellow I left behind – he'd only just come out the day before and joined us previous to the attack. He was from Northumberland way – I never had time to get his name! He was a right nice young chap about 19. He'd been pulled out of the mines. He was killed a few hours after I left. They dropped one straight in the place and that was the end of him. Funny thing how these people join you and before you know them they've gone. You can't get to even know their full name.[15]

Private Horace Calvert, 2nd Grenadier Guards, 1st Guards Brigade, Guards Division

Every attack had its teeming casualties, each an individual tragedy buried within the overall narrative of successful military operations.

THE BRITISH WERE ITCHING TO ATTACK AGAIN in the centre of the Allied front, to capitalise on their successful assault on 20 October. Yet, despite the best of intentions, it had proved impossible owing to a shortage of ammunition for the voracious guns required to power them forward. The railheads were dropping ever further behind the advancing front and this acted as a brake to progress. The Allied commanders knew that every day's extra delay gave the Germans more time to reorganise their troops and improve their defences, yet they had no option but to wait. At last, on 23 October, they were ready: this time the First Army in the north, the Third Army in the centre, and the Fourth Army in the south would make the next advance which sought to push forward to reach the German Herman II Line that ran along the Sambre Canal. The attack was scheduled to commence at 01.20, when once more the guns blasted out. Major Joseph Rice and the 82nd Brigade, RFA, were occupying gun positions close to Le Cateau.

1. Field Marshal Sir Douglas Haig

2. David Lloyd George became Prime Minister in December 1916 following the resignation of Asquith on 5 December 1916.

3. On 19 February 1918 Field Marshal Sir Henry Hughes Wilson, 1st Baronet, was appointed Chief of the Imperial General Staff (CIGS) and was the principal military adviser to Lloyd George in the last year of the First World War.

4. General Henry Sinclair Horne, 1st Baron Horne GCB, KCMG was the only British artillery officer to command an army in the war.

5. Horses pull a 60-pounder gun through the captured
village of Bertincourt, 8 September 1918.

6. Canal du Nord

7. A German machine-gun position at Grevillers, France, photographed just after its capture by New Zealand troops in August 1918. A New Zealander inspects the trench in which lays a dead German soldier. Sheets of iron and pieces of timber are strewn around the nearby dugout. Two stick hand grenades are visible in the foreground.

8. General, later Field Marshal, Julian Hedworth George Byng, 1st Viscount Byng of Vimy. Byng is remembered for his role in the Battle of Vimy Ridge in 1917.

9. General Sir Arthur William Currie had the unique distinction of starting his military career on the very bottom rung as a pre-war militia gunner before rising through the ranks to become the first Canadian commander of the Canadian Corps.

10. General of the Armies John Joseph 'Black Jack' Pershing served as the commander of the American Expeditionary Force on the Western Front from 1917 to 1918.

11. Major-General Robert Alexander commanded the 77th Infantry Division on the Western Front.

12. Major General John Monash, General Officer Commanding, 3rd Australian Division.

13. Major General Joseph E. Kuhn was the Commanding General 79th Division, here pictured at Troyon-sur-Meuse, France, on 23 October 1918.

14. Major General William Haan commanded the 32nd Division of the US Army.

15. Captain Eddie Rickenbacker proved to be an exceptional fighter pilot and rose to command the 94th Aero Squadron and became the leading US ace with twenty-six confirmed victories.

16. Renault FT light tanks of the 337th Company, 13th Battalion, 505th Regiment US Army pictured passing Rampont, 10 October 1918.

17. Horse team of the Royal Field Artillery pulling an 18-pounder field gun up the slope of a cutting through the bank of the Canal du Nord, near Moeuvres, 27 September 1918. Note the destroyed bridge.

18. One of the mortars has been marked by the 4th Battalion, Australian Imperial Force, which captured it. Units typically chalked captured guns, mortars, and machine-guns as signs of their victories.

19. Men of the American 30th Division and Mark V tanks of the 8th Battalion, Tank Corps, with 'cribs' fitted, advancing near Bellicourt, 29 September 1918.

20. Brigadier-General John Vaughan Campbell VC addressing men of the 137th Brigade (46th Division) on the Riqueval Bridge over the St Quentin Canal which they crossed on 29 September 1918.

21. General Paul von Hindenburg *(left)* and General Erich Friedrich Wilhelm Ludendorff *(right)*

22. Marshal Ferdinand Jean Marie Foch was a French general and Marshal of France, Great Britain and Poland, a military theorist and the Supreme Allied Commander during the war.

23. Maximilian Alexander Friedrich Wilhelm Margrave of Baden was a German prince and politician. Heir to the Grand Duchy of Baden, he briefly served as Chancellor of the German Empire.

24. Crown Prince Rupprecht or Rupert was the last Bavarian crown prince. During the first half of the First World War he commanded the German Sixth Army on the Western Front.

25. A German pill box taken during the advance of the 79th Division, Haucourt, Meuse.

26. Sergeant Alvin C. York, 328th Infantry, who, with the aid of seven men captured 132 German prisoners, pictured on the hill on which the raid took place on 8 October 1918 in the Argonne Forest, France.

27. Troops on lorry, near Joncourt, 9 October 1918

28. New Zealand gunners manning an 18-pounder gun during
the fighting near Le Quesnoy, 29 October 1918.

29. Infantry waiting in the New Zealand front line prior to their successful attack on Le Quesnoy. Note the dead horse on the left and the mortar on the right.

30. German soldiers captured in the fighting for Le Quesnoy, November 1918, are pictured awaiting examination at Brigade Headquarters in Pont-a-Pierre, 3 November 1918. The PoWs are being held at a large farm in Pont-a-Pierre which is a hamlet in the town and administrative district of Beaudignies, not far from Le Quesnoy.

31. Divisional commanders on horseback, entering Le Quesnoy, in the early morning, after its capture by New Zealand troops on 4 November 1918. The building on the left is the city hall which was destroyed by bombing.

32. British soldiers, part of the first British Army of the Rhine, marching across the Hohenzollern Bridge in Cologne.

33. A British Army band, one small part of the British Army of the Rhine after the signing of the Armistice in 1918, parades in Cologne.

34. A farmer who has returned to his war-ravaged home ploughs around the remains of a British tank, numbered as C-31, which awaits removal from the battlefield after the Armistice. Note the grave marker in the foreground.

35. Accompanied by a military band, US soldiers of the 803rd Pioneer Infantry Battalion on the deck of the USS *Philippine* during their return trip from Brest to the US, for demobilisation.

36. British troops work to remove a knocked-out tank from the battlefield after the end of the end of the fighting in 1918.

A big barrage at night is a wonderful sight. As I blew my whistle for my guns to start, the whole countryside suddenly became covered with little darting points of flame, and this was immediately followed by the heavy deep thunder of the guns, which was accentuated by the proximity of the buildings of Le Cateau. Coloured lights, mostly red, immediately flared up from the German lines.[16]

Major Joseph Rice, C Battery, 82nd Brigade, Royal Field Artillery, 18th Division

The Germans responded with heavy return fire which soon started a serious blaze through the centre of Le Cateau. Once they had completed their scheduled barrage, Rice's guns had to get ready to make the next move forward; as ever, they needed to stay close to the infantry to provide immediate support should they encounter serious opposition.

We began to form up on the road, and I was just making sure that everyone had either a horse or a seat on a vehicle, as I intended to trot through the town, when a single stray shell landed among the outriders. Two sergeants and one or two men were wounded and several horses were hit. Among the horses hit was the one I had ordered to be brought up for me instead of one of my chargers. I never had a charger of mine hit during the War as a result of not riding my own during advances. It was incorrect procedure, no doubt, but the staff had most of the good chargers, and it was largely a matter of luck whether a regimental officer got even a reasonable good charger from Remounts to replace a casualty. Also, one got fond of one's chargers![17]

Major Joseph Rice, C Battery, 82 Brigade, Royal Field Artillery, 18th Division

Rice grabbed his groom's horse, a recently captured German charger that had also suffered slight wounds in the shelling, and set off with his battery.

It was a never-to-be-forgotten ride. The town was still being shelled, and was on fire, and it was still dark. No shells came near us till we were nearly through the town, and then, as we were leaving it by a narrow street leading to the railway on the north-east of the town, a hail of 77mm H.E. came over, as if some battery was trying to fire off as many shells as possible before retiring. They came from our right-front, hissed over the road, and crashed over or into the houses on the left-hand side. Only one fell short, i.e. to the right of the road, about 10 yards from it, but as the road was luckily sunken, all the bits went over us. We all crouched down on our horses' necks, but no one tried to quicken the pace, which I think was a good test of discipline, although it would certainly have done no individuals any good to quicken the pace unless those in front had done likewise! To my amazement no man or horse was hit. By this time, the wound on the horse I was riding was making him tremble all over from exhaustion, so I told my groom to wait with him till the first line arrived, and I took his horse and pushed on.[18]

Major Joseph Rice, C Battery, 82 Brigade, Royal Field Artillery, 18th Division

His battery went as far as the Richemont stream before pausing awaiting the arrival of the sappers with the necessary bridging materials to get the guns and limbers across.

Colonel Thorp and I loosed off odd rounds, with a dirty rifle we found, at small parties of Bosche in the distance, and I captured a Bosche medical man! He suddenly bobbed up about 20 yards away so I put the German rifle to my shoulder, whereat he flopped down and pointed at his stomach to indicate that he had been wounded. I went up to him to have a look, and I think he was untouched. As there was no one handy to take charge of him, and as we wanted to push on reconnoitring, I made him march off westwards, and I don't know what happened to him.[19]

Major Joseph Rice, C Battery, 82 Brigade, Royal Field Artillery, 18th Division

As they tried to get their guns as far forward as possible the Royal Artillery officers were not greatly impressed by the performance of either the tanks or the infantry.

One of our tanks came along about a quarter of a mile behind us, and began loosing off its 6-pdrs indiscriminately all over the place. I think the advance must have gone to its head! As one or two shells came fairly close to us, Colonel Thorp and I walked up to it and made a few suitable remarks through one of its 'windows'. Some of our junior infantry commanders were not very pushy just about now, and were rather more inclined to dig in than to push forward. I don't think our infantry were in close touch with the Bosche in Bousies because, after passing odd posts of infantry, we went on still farther and met no one at all. In the very enclosed country in which we now found ourselves we did not know when we might run into the enemy, and when we got some of our own 6-inch howitzer shells all round us, two very close, we thought we had gone far enough![20]

Major Joseph Rice, C Battery, 82 Brigade, Royal Field Artillery, 18th Division

It should be remembered in assessing such criticism that soldiers of different arms often criticise each other's performance in action; they understand their own 'trade', but rarely have the empathy or knowledge to understand someone else's problems.

Among the infantry pressing forwards was one officer who certainly did not lack in 'push'. Lieutenant Colonel Harry Greenwood was commanding the 9th King's Own Yorkshire Light Infantry when they led the 64th Brigade attack through Ovillers in an advance on Vendegies au Bois. They had been subjected to a considerable amount of artillery and machine-gun fire, which caused occasional hold-ups. Early on, Greenwood, a believer in leading from the front, rushed a machine-gun post single-handed, killing all four crew members; and later, with his runners, he overwhelmed a second post on the outskirts of Ovillers. The 9th KOYLI moved on, leaving the German garrison still occupying Ovillers, then helped beat off a counter-attack before leading the charge to capture their final objective in Dukes Wood. Here they captured 150 prisoners, eight machine guns and one field gun. All in all, it represented a fine day's work for his battalion. A letter he wrote subsequently revealed a slightly chilling edge to his thoughts:

I did really nothing save drive on, kill a few Huns and cheer our own fellows on a bit when they flagged. It was topping fighting really and I would not have missed it for anything. Lots of Bosche to kill and plenty of time to kill them in, in fact one could almost always choose one's bird. Our fellows were splendid and with any kind of leadership would have gone anywhere. It is a great shame of course that you were not there to get a little of your own back.[21]

Lieutenant Colonel Harry Greenwood, 9th King's Own Yorkshire Light Infantry, 64th Brigade, 21st Division

Following up behind the 9th KOYLI were two companies of the 15th Durham Light Infantry who were to 'mop up' the Germans still ensconced in Ovillers, before pushing through the KOYLI to complete the capture of Vendegies au Bois.

We had information that on a main road there would be a bridge which most probably would be mined, which we had to cross. By this time there was only the Company Commander and me among the officers – the other two had been hit or killed – I never did know. Well, the Company Commander said, 'Go on, Chappie, get 'em up!' So I rushed this considerable bridge and got over that. Nothing went up. Facing the bridge, just off the road there was a street of houses. On the right-hand side there was a building like an annexe, built on the end of the house, which was sand-bagged, obviously a strongpoint. I managed to get a No. 5 Mills bomb in it. We had to fight our way up this street. You were trained that when you were attacking up a straight street to keep on the right-hand side, so that if an enemy is firing a gun, he's got to bend right out of the window to get at you and you can get him. That's how we did it. From time to time a German would appear at a window – we'd get shots – and our Lewis gun men would shoot in the bedroom window. Going up this street I heard a door bang behind me. And I thought, 'That's funny!' I collected a few men – the door wasn't solid wood; it was panelled with opaque glass on the top part. We broke the door down. We heard a scuffle. I had my revolver in my right-hand and a bomb in this damaged hand – it had been hit in the shelling. I'd drawn the pin, which means that within five seconds of loosing the hammer, within five seconds that bomb explodes. Well I went into this room with my revolver and there was nobody in. And I could hear a sciffle in the next room. I thought, 'Yes, that's where they are!' I thought of throwing this bomb in – there was no door – just a doorway. So I went gingerly in with my revolver-arm perched. That's what they saw first – my revolver. I peered in. It was full of French people. They were mostly old French people and children. All I could do was say, 'Vive la France!' I couldn't talk French. And they exploded – poor things. The old ladies came and kissed me. And the old men tried to do the same and I had to point to my bomb to get out. That was a very moving occasion.[22]

Second Lieutenant William Chapman, 15th Durham Light Infantry, 64th Brigade 21st Division

Ovillers was secured by the 15th Durhams and indeed they captured a German regimental commander and his staff. Here Chapman momentarily gave way to temptation.

We captured a German headquarters and they came out with their hands up. Quite a number of them were wearing Iron Cross ribbons. I thought, 'Oooh! What marvellous souvenirs!' They used to have the ribbons stitched on their uniforms and I took four or five of them, plucked them like that. Then I took another one and then the chap looked at me as if to say, 'Well, you call yourself a man, do you?' I said, 'Here you are Fritz, I'm sorry!' And gave it back. I think most people would do that. I mean I was armed and I had men round me armed. They were not.[23]

Second Lieutenant William Chapman, 15th Durham Light Infantry, 64th Brigade 21st Division

The next day they were ordered to attack again, pushing towards the next objective of Poix du Nord. This time Chapman was not quite so lucky.

We'd started with 134 men and four officers. I had twenty men for the last attack. I spaced them out as well as I could. It was absolutely open country, there wasn't a house; our objective was a long way off – I guessed 500 yards – more than that. There was a clump of trees, that was our objective which may or may not be a strongpoint. The artillery barrage was getting rather light – we'd lost guns as well as men – and 'We'll come down at five o'clock – when they lift you get on with it – wait till they lift!' The barrage came down and quite a bit of it landed on us. They were dropping short – there's no worse experience in life than to be shot at by your own guns. Anyway, they found their range eventually. We got over, according to my cheap French watch, which unfortunately, gained about a minute and a half, or two minutes, and I got over in front of the rest of the Brigade. We took the initiative and had to keep the initiative. The instructions were that if you had open country, and you were making an attack, you went until you became more or less breathless. Then you got down – the officer got down – everybody else got down. Run about say, 100 yards, then get set down and turn your guns on where you felt the enemy might be. If he showed his head, you'd try to get him. This happened again and again, and I was losing a few men who were very spaced out. Then I was knocked down: I got a bullet in the foot and fell forward. It knocked me down. And everybody else got down. The whole Brigade got down! I shouted, 'I'm hit, get on with it!' But nobody, perhaps heard me. Eventually, I hobbled to my objective. It was getting dim light by that time and I consolidated – I had very few men to consolidate – but I put a sentry out here, one out there, and made contact with the companies right and left. I took my runner to try and get back and left the whole Company in the charge of a Corporal.[24]

Second Lieutenant William Chapman, 15th Durham Light Infantry, 64th Brigade, 21st Division

Limping badly, Chapman was helped back, sheltering and falling asleep at one point in a German artillery dugout. He was then picked up by a couple of stretcher-bearers.

We got an occasional shell, it didn't come too near but the ground was a little bit pock-marked and they stumbled a time or two. But we got out. Eventually, we came to some broken-down farm buildings and we got behind them and out of sight of the enemy. Followed our noses. We came to a dirt track and there were a couple of army photographers, they said, 'Could you raise your head a bit, Sir?' And they took my picture but I've never seen it since – never heard about it.[25]

Second Lieutenant William Chapman, 15th Durham Light Infantry, 64th Brigade, 21st Division

Chapman was safely evacuated.

During this period, the weather was not generally kind to the airmen, who were thwarted by days of mist, low cloud and rain. However, on 23 October the skies had at last cleared. Lieutenant Ralph Silk was flying as the observer in an RE8, piloted by Lieutenant Ralph Cresswell. After taking off, they passed over Le Cateau and headed east.

I was at the height of about 2,500 feet; the sky was clear with the exception of some cumulous clouds, which rather worried me because they were always a hiding place for the Huns. I was waiting for the signal from our leading machine to dive in, drop my bombs, make our reconnaissance and get what information we could. The roads below were absolutely chock-a-block. The Germans were retreating left, right and centre. I waited in vain for the signal – something had gone wrong. But then out of the clouds, like a flash of lightening, dived a Fokker machine. I didn't see him – he was almost on my tail before I realised it! The frontal area of a Fokker machine is so small and he came in out of the sun which makes it more difficult. He fired a burst at me and I almost felt the bullets whizzing past my head. I replied by giving him two short bursts, but he seemed to be encased in a cast-iron shirt – for I knew my shots were good, but still he came on – they didn't have any effect. With his speed he passed me and as he passed I saw the red flash and realised I was scrapping with one of the German aces. He was so near I could see the rims of his goggles! Then in a moment after, another machine was on my tail. Again, I fired a short burst of ten to twenty rounds – and again I heard the tat-tat-tat-tat passing me and I felt my machine lurch. I turned my head over my shoulder and I saw that my pilot was slumped over the controls. Then there was a gasping sound – and an awesome silence – the machine had stopped. There was I suspended in the air with a dead pilot – Huns, bullets, wings all around me. I looked up to the Heavens and I said, Oh, God, help me! The next thing I remember was having a sledge hammer blow to my head. I put my hand to my helmet and I found it all jagged and torn with a certain amount of blood. Then I had a blackout. I fell through the air like a falling leaf and I think it was the upward rush of the air that brought me to my senses. By the grace of God, I had the presence of mind to pull on the joystick to break the fall and the machine staggered, stalled and fell on some trees. I just remember, very faintly, the Germans letting me down by rope then I lost consciousness again.[26]

Lieutenant Ralph Silk, 6 Squadron, RAF

His pilot, Second Lieutenant Ralph Cresswell,[27] had been killed. Silk had been incredibly lucky to survive.

AS THE MEN OF THE 2ND DIVISION advanced, their commander, Major General Cecil Pereira, moved his headquarters forward to St Python. Here he was presented with an analysis of the German prisoners they had captured over the last few days that had been carried out by his divisional intelligence officers.

We have captured men from the 21st Reserve, 9th Reserve, 4th, and 113th Divisions, and from eight different regiments of these divisions. We have got two battalion commanders. The 21st Reserve Division was completing a relief when we attacked, and one of their regiments – 168th – had just been transferred to them from the 25th Division which had been broken up. The feeling of the prisoners is 'What is the good of going on, as we are beaten!' The officers say Germany has agreed to Wilson's Fourteen Points, but, 'We must be allowed to evacuate occupied territory for the honour of Germany and the army'. Many prisoners still believe we shoot prisoners in cold blood, but the belief cannot be very strong, as they surrender so easily! [28]

Major General Cecil Pereira, Headquarters, 2nd Division

The Allies may have been 'winning', but there is no doubt that the British Army was also approaching the end of its tether. Private George Kidson was disarmingly frank in an oral history interview when discussing the incident for which he was awarded the Military Medal.

We had an officer in No Man's Land. He shouldn't have been out there until it was time to go, but he was just showing off I think! Of course, he got sniped, wounded in both arms. They shouted, 'Stretcher bearers!' Well I didn't want to go – I was frightened – you know? But if I hadn't have gone all the others would have said, 'Wind up! Windy!' Frightened see! Of course, I went. I pulled myself through the long grass until I got to him. There was another three besides me, they were doing the same. When we got to him, we couldn't put him on a stretcher, we put him on an oil sheet and we were crouched low carrying him. The sniper killed the fellow at that corner and the bullet hit me in the back of the neck. Another fraction and I'd have had it! That was the finish of me! I said to the Sergeant, 'I'll send you some Woodbines!' I was that pleased to get away. Everybody was wanting to get a nice wound so that they could get away. Champion![29]

Private George Kidson, 9th Yorkshire Regiment, 74th Brigade, 25th Division

In an effort to spread the load and reduce battle fatigue, the British divisions were regularly rotated, each taking it in turns to lead the attack.

You must not imagine every company was engaged in front every time the division made a move forward. Brigades took it in turns, or battalions took it in turns, so that it was only at intervals that we had to push out in front. We leapfrogged alternately with the 42nd Division. The attack of a division was something like a series of waves breaking on the shore – one battalion after another pushing on and the whole sweep up the beach gradually losing its momentum.[30]

Second Lieutenant Reginald Richards, 2nd Battalion, 3rd New Zealand (Rifle) Brigade, New Zealand Division

At that point another division would take over advance. Richards had the misfortune to be part of an operation in the Le Quesnoy area, which could be considered the last trickle of advancing 'wave' as they reached the next line of German defences on the Sambre. On 26 October, while leading a recce towards the walled town of Le Quesnoy, Richards' platoon was badly harassed by strong German positions located somewhere in the triangle of railways just north-west of the town.

There were machine guns firing at us from three sides. Well we moved out into the open in scattered formation, trying to get cover from view from a few bushes and pollarded willows. But the Bosche soon got onto us. As I ran forward through the wet grass I could see the paths of bullets knocking the water off the grass – and the bullets were going both ways. However, we progressed some way without casualties, surprise I suppose. A little way on I saw some Bosches running down to take up another position, and I had the satisfaction of seeing one of my Lewis guns in front get onto them in a moment. I was just going up to join them when I took it bang in the throat – the first in my platoon to be hit. I was surprised more than hurt. One moment I was trotting along – the next I found myself on all-fours with blood spouting from my mouth and both sides of my neck. I heard one of my men call to another, 'Poor old Richie! His jugular's gone!' They tied me up and stopped the outside wounds, but blood was still pouring down my throat. [31]

Second Lieutenant Reginald Richards, 2nd Battalion, 3rd New Zealand (Rifle) Brigade, New Zealand Division

He was unceremoniously dragged back under the shelter of a low bank behind a line of willow trees, but even then was still trying to give orders to his men, trying to ensure they were pulled back out of danger, before he found himself fast losing consciousness.

I became very faint and fell off the bank face downwards into some blackberries. I had a bit of luck as the blood drained away out of my mouth and did not choke me. Also, my being unconscious kept me still and gave the internal wound a chance to congeal and stop bleeding. I remembered nothing until I was aware of two men pulling me out. They were Bosche privates and grinned in a friendly way. I was still somewhat fuddled. It was now some time in the afternoon and it was clear that during my quiet slumbers we had been heavily shelled, for as the two friendly Bosche carried me off, I saw great shell holes quite close. I never endured such a shelling with such composure![32]

Second Lieutenant Reginald Richards, 2nd Battalion, 3rd New Zealand (Rifle) Brigade, New Zealand Division

Richards was carried back and given urgently needed medical treatment. He had been very lucky, for the bullet had managed to just miss not only his jugular vein, but also his carotid artery and windpipe. Throughout the early stages of his captivity he was well treated by the Germans – and indeed felt a twinge of guilt.

The Colonel then came and apologised for going through my pockets. I said I quite understood and turned out everything for them. They kept my pay book and one or two letters, but returned everything else: cigarettes, money, watch, knife and so on. When I remembered how some of our New Zealand soldiers used to rifle prisoners' pockets, my own treatment made me feel rather ashamed.[33]

Second Lieutenant Reginald Richards, 2nd Battalion, 3rd New Zealand (Rifle) Brigade, New Zealand Division

As the lines solidified once more in front of the new German defensive line along the River Sambre the British artillery was slowly moved up and beginning the task of preparing for the next lunge forward. As ever, observation was key.

We found a deep pit in which we cut a step at a suitable height for looking over the edge, and used this as a brigade observation post.

This was about half a mile behind the front line. Unfortunately, it was impossible to get much of a view beyond the front line owing to the presence of Mormal Forest. However, we did some useful observed shooting: one case in particular I remember; our orders were not to shoot at buildings unnecessarily as many of them were occupied by civilians, but one day Colonel Thorp thought he had spotted a sniper firing from inside the roof of a house where a tile appeared to be missing, and he got me to put a shell through the roof which I did in about four rounds – a fluke after one bracket.[34]

Major Joseph Rice, C Battery, 82 Brigade, Royal Field Artillery, 18th Division

Content in his work, Rice went back to the battery waggon lines in an effort to secure a good night's sleep. On his return, he found that the German artillery was also going about its business to considerable effect.

As I was entering Bousies I met Carey, our American doctor, who told me the terribly sad news that Colonel Thorp has been killed. He had been walking through Bousies with a Colonel Burnyeat this same afternoon, and there was no hostile fire at all in the neighbourhood. Colonel Burnyeat[35] had his leave warrant in his pocket. Suddenly a salvo of three 10.5 cm shells arrived, and one of them landed almost at their feet. I don't think either of them can have known anything about it. It was most cruel luck so near to the end of the War. And what a loss to us all! Colonel Thorp[36] was the ideal brigade commander; we realised it so well when other people took on his job in his absence, and I, for one, am thankful he was not taken from us earlier in the War. I was now the only officer left in the brigade who had come to France with the Division and had not been killed or wounded, or gassed, or evacuated sick, and I felt that if the War did not end pretty soon I was just about due to join the majority in some way or other.[37]

Major Joseph Rice, C Battery, 82nd Brigade, Royal Field Artillery, 18th Division

They all still had one last battle to fight.

8

CATCHING UP

I am presently still alive. I can't tell you what is happening here on the German side. There is no quiet moment any more. We had to move back more than 100 kilometres within a few days. Whoever can't run is taken prisoner. Please don't be upset. There's nothing we can do. There are no men left. It won't take long this way.[1]

Gefreiter Hans Spieb,[2] Machine Gun Sharp-Shooter Detachment 2, 2nd Bavarian Division

THE FOCH SERIES OF OFFENSIVES LAUNCHED during the last week of September 1918 has come to be seen as the point of no return for Germany in the Great War. With an ever-changing focus, the attacks had battered away at the German Army all along the Western Front, from the Meuse to Flanders. With the Hindenburg Line broken, the Germans had no great defensive lines left that could realistically hope to stem the Allied onslaught, no masses of reserves left to reverse the tide of battle. The German casualties were horrendous: all told, since the launch of the Spring Offensives on 21 March to 1 October they had lost 40,722 officers and 1,181,577 other ranks. This mass leaching away of

German strength had coincided with the utter collapse of the Bulgarian and Turkish allies. The Bulgarians had held their own in the Salonika Campaign from 1915 deep into 1918, but an Allied campaign launched in September 1918 had finally flung them back, triggering their surrender through an Armistice signed on 29 September and taking effect the next day. The Turks had hoped to profit from the collapse of their eternal enemy Russia by advancing into the Caucasus, but they had been under severe pressure in both the Palestine and Mesopotamian campaigns since 1917. Early successes like Gallipoli had converted to a cycle of repeated defeats, while events on the Western Front made it obvious to the Turks that with Germany herself on the rocks there was no hope of relief. In October, the Turkish government were to start the process which would ultimately lead to an Armistice with the Allies, signed on 30 October. Germany's final ally, Austro-Hungary, the fading empire that had provided the genesis of the war, was also clearly approaching the end of her military resources. Hindenburg summed up the dreadful situation of the German Army.

> What terrible demands were made in these few weeks on the physical strength and moral resolution of the officers and men of all staffs and formations! The troops had now to be thrown from one battle into another. It was seldom that the so-called days in rest billets were enough to allow us to reorganise the decimated or scattered units and supply them with drafts, or distribute the remains of divisions we had broken up among other formations. Both officers and men were certainly beginning to tire, but they always managed to find a new impulse whenever it was a question of holding up some fresh enemy attack. Officers of all ranks, even up to the higher Staffs, fought in the front lines, sometimes rifle in hand. The only order issued in many cases was simply, 'Hold out to the last!' We had not the men to form a continuous line. We could only offer resistance in groups, large and small. It was only successful because the enemy, too, was visibly tiring. He seldom attempted a large operation unless his tanks had opened a way or his artillery had extinguished every sign of German life. He did not

storm our lines directly, but gradually slipped through their many gaps. It was on this fact that I based my hope of being able to hold out until the efforts of our enemies were paralysed.[3]

Field Marshal Paul von Hindenburg, Headquarters, Supreme Army Command

As if this was not bad enough, the news from the Salonikan front dragged him even further into the pits of despair. He could see no way out of the multiple problems that surrounded Germany on every front.

Who would close the gap if Bulgaria fell out once and for all? We could still do much, but we could not build up a new front. It was true that a new army was in process of formation in Serbia, but how weak these troops were! Our Alpine Corps had scarcely any effective units, and one of the Austro-Hungarian divisions which were on their way was declared to be totally useless. It consisted of Czechs, who would presumably refuse to fight. Although the Syrian theatre lay far from a decisive point of the war, the defeat there would undoubtedly cause the collapse of our loyal Turkish comrades, who now saw themselves threatened in Europe again. What would Romania, or the mighty fragments of Russia do? All these thoughts swept over me and forced me to decide to seek an end, though only an honourable end. No one would say it was too soon.[4]

Field Marshal Paul von Hindenburg, Headquarters, Supreme Army Command

His First Quartermaster General, General Erich Ludendorff, had been his comrade in arms since their joint triumph over the Russians on the Eastern Front at the Battle of Tannenberg in August 1914. At their meeting on the afternoon of 28 September it was evident that the two had come independently to the same conclusion.

The Field Marshal listened to me with emotion. He answered that he had intended to say the same to me in the evening; that he had considered the whole situation carefully and thought the step necessary. We were also at one in the view that the Armistice

conditions would have to provide for controlled and orderly evacuation of the occupied territory and the possible resumption of
hostilities on our own borders. We did not consider any abandonment of territory in the east, thinking that the Entente would be
fully conscious of the dangers threatening them as well as ourselves
from Bolshevism.[5]

General Erich Ludendorff, Headquarters, Supreme Army Command

It is fascinating to note that these warlords had still not entirely conceded
defeat, both explicitly referring to the possibility of a future resumption
of the war.

The Armistice is militarily necessary to us. We shall soon be at the
end of our strength. If the peace does not follow, then we have at
least disengaged ourselves from the enemy, rested ourselves and
won time. Then we shall be more fit to fight than now, if that is
necessary.[6]

Field Marshal Paul von Hindenburg, Headquarters, Supreme Army
Command

Ludendorff was in a febrile mood, seeming to have suffered from some
kind of a nervous breakdown under the huge stress imposed on him over
the last few weeks. His memoirs are an unreliable source, but he claims
that, while they had to sue for peace, if those overtures were rejected,
then he was still confident that the challenge of defending the German
homeland would revitalise his battered armies.

If the war should approach our own territory, if the feeling that
he was protecting home and all that word meant, entered into the
heart of each man at the front, who knew full well the meaning of
such terms as 'theatre of war', 'battlefield' and 'lines of communication', if the war with all its destruction threatened German
soil, then I felt our seventy million Germans would stand like
one man, determined and ready to sacrifice for their country all
the mighty strength that still remained to them. Whether France
herself, bled white and suffering worse than we were, would
remain in the field for long after her territory was evacuated, also

was doubtful. In any case, our position was not so bad that we could have justified a capitulation to our people or descendants; on the other hand, we plainly must sue for peace if peace could be had.[7]

Quartermaster General Erich Ludendorff, Headquarters, Supreme Army Command

This though, is *not* what he said at the time – when it mattered.

On 29 September, a Council of War was held to consider the earth-shattering news that both of Germany's great military leaders were requesting an Armistice. Present was the Foreign Minister, Admiral Paul von Hintze, who bluntly reported Ludendorff as saying, 'The situation of the Army demands an immediate Armistice to save a catastrophe'.[8] It was suggested that an approach should be made to the American President Woodrow Wilson, based on the Fourteen Points he had first put forward to the Congress on 8 January 1918. The Fourteen Points were a somewhat idealistic attempt to set a course for global harmony between nations. Given the often pernicious nature of America's relationship with Central American countries, there was more than a whiff of hypocrisy about this assumed position of moral superiority.

Summarised,[9] the Fourteen Points were as follows:

1. Open publication of all peace treaties.
2. Freedom of the seas.
3. Removal of all economic barriers between nations.
4. Reduction of armaments.
5. Thorough examination of all colonial claims.
6. Evacuation and re-establishment of Russia.
7. Evacuation, re-establishment and guarantee of the sovereignty of Belgium.
8. Freeing and re-establishment of the occupied territories of France, as well as the making good of the injustice done by Prussia to the French fifty years ago as regards Alsace-Lorraine.
9. Adjustment of the Italian frontiers according to national populations.
10. Autonomous development of the peoples of Austria-Hungary.

11. Evacuation of Romania, Serbia and Montenegro and the res-
     titution of occupied territories.
12. Independence of the Turkish portions of the Osmanli Empire
     and the assurance of the lives and property of the other nation-
     alities living under Turkish rule. Freedom of the Dardanelles.
13. Creation of an independent Polish State, with inclusion of all
     the districts inhabited by an undoubted Polish population and
     the assurance of free access to the sea.
14. Formation of a League of Nations.

The original wording reveals a surreal naivety in the very first point: 'Open covenants of peace, openly arrived at, after which there shall be no private international understandings of any kind but diplomacy shall proceed always frankly and in the public view.' Some of the points were also contentious to America's own co-belligerents, as for instance, in the trenchant British objections to Point 2: 'Absolute freedom of navigation upon the seas, outside territorial waters, alike in peace and in war.' This would have debarred any blockade operations as a method of war – but this was a key plank of British wartime strategy. However, acceptance of the Fourteen Points would have devastating consequences for the Germans and the decision to use them as a basis for the first exploratory peace talks via Wilson was a sign of just how desperate their situation had become.

Yet this was not the only momentous decision of the Council of War, for it also accepted Admiral von Hintze's strange concept of a 'revolution from above'. In essence, the Kaiser was to bestow representative parlia-mentary government, thereby ceding power to the Social Democratic Party, which was the largest party in the Reichstag. This was not a grand democratic gesture, but rather a cynical ploy designed to draw the SDP into government just as the scale of the imminent national defeat became obvious – with the hope that they could be saddled with much of the blame. It was also felt that Wilson would have more trouble resisting a call for peace from a fellow democratic leader than the autocratic Kaiser. The rigid conservativism of Chancellor Georg von Hertling made him unsuit-able to handle this tricky situation, so he was replaced on 3 October by the far more liberally inclined figure of Prince Max von Baden. Max von Baden was an inexperienced politician, but he was no fool and perceived the 'elephant trap' laid in front of him when he was informed that he would be responsible for requesting an Armistice. It was only after the intervention of the Kaiser himself that von Baden accepted the office of Chancellor. He would have been well advised to follow his instincts, as the Kaiser and the military junta still controlled most of the real levers of power. To make things worse, von Baden's modest efforts at introducing liberalising constitutional changes did little or nothing to satisfy the surging forces of the left that were beginning to gain momentum behind the scenes in Germany.

Max von Baden was unwilling to seek an immediate Armistice, as he recognised that this sign of weakness would undermine their position in the negotiations that must follow. He therefore sought written confirmation from the Supreme Army Command that this truly was the only option. The answer he received provided little real detail.

> The Supreme Command maintains the demand made on Sunday the 29th of September of this year for the immediate issue of the peace offer to our enemies. The German Army still stands firm and victoriously repels all attacks. The situation, however, is becoming more acute every day, and may compel the Supreme Command to take vital decisions. In these circumstances, the proper course is to break off the struggle in order to spare the German people and their Allies useless sacrifices. Every day's delay costs the lives of thousands of our brave soldiers.[10]

> Field Marshal Paul von Hindenburg, Headquarters, Supreme Army Command

Chancellor von Baden then tried to fortify his position by putting five specific questions in writing to Ludendorff. His motives were clear: he wanted to make it known that he was *not* initiating these peace negotiations, he was responding to the explicit demands of Hindenburg and Ludendorff.

1. How much longer can the Army hold the enemy beyond the frontiers?

2. Is the Supreme Army Command bound to expect a military collapse, and, if so, within what period? Would such collapse mean the end of our power of military resistance?

3. Is the military situation so critical that steps must be at once taken to secure an Armistice or peace?

4. In case the answer to 3 is in the affirmative, is the Supreme Army Command aware that the initiation of a peace step under the pressure of the military situation may lead to the loss of German colonies and German territory, in particular of Alsace-Lorraine and the purely Polish districts of the Eastern provinces?

5. Does the Supreme Army Command agree to the despatch of the enclosed draft?[11]

Chancellor Max von Baden

One can imagine his frustration when Ludendorff insouciantly evaded these questions – replying only verbally – to reiterate that the Supreme Army Command still demanded that the peace offer be despatched. It seemed there would be the bare minimum of paper trails for the subsequent allocation of responsibility. The new Chancellor considered he had no choice and the formal German request for an Armistice was drawn up on 4 October and forwarded to Wilson.

The German Government requests the President of the United States of America to take steps for the restoration of peace, to notify all belligerents of this request, and to invite them to delegate plenipotentiaries for the purpose of taking up negotiations. The German Government accepts, as a basis for the peace negotiations, the programme laid down by the President of the United States in his message to Congress of January 8, 1918, and in his subsequent pronouncements, particularly in his address of September 27, 1918. In order to avoid further bloodshed the German Government requests the President to bring about the immediate conclusion of a general Armistice on land, on water, and in the air.[12]

The deed was done.

Unsurprisingly, neither Wilson nor the Allies were over-enamoured with either von Baden or his request for an Armistice. The politicians recognised him as a scion of the ruling house of Baden, who owed his position to his royal connections, hardly a democratic leader to inspire any great confidence. The Allied military commanders were unanimous in their scorn for the German peace proposal. They were certain they were winning and saw no need to grant any favours to the Germans.

> The German is awfully put to it to find men to hold the length of line which he now occupies, and he must shorten it, I feel sure. That means that he must give up the Channel Ports, as otherwise he cannot shorten the line to any great extent, so I think we shall soon hear of his giving up Ostend and Zeebrugge and probably going back to Ghent, or even Antwerp. He is evidently in a very bad way and that is why he is asking for peace but I cannot think it is sincere. Why should he ask President Wilson? He is fighting the allies, he ought to address the allies, or at any rate the French as he is in their country. I fear that he is only trying to gain time to carry out his retirement unmolested. No one can believe a German nowadays. Also while he is asking for peace he is busy burning the mines east of Lens and devastating the country. They really are the limit and there is only one thing for them, and that is 'Force'. I do hope that the Governments concerned will stand fast in that way, and reply that there can be no talk of peace until the Germans have withdrawn their troops to within their own frontiers. We can only dictate terms of peace on German soil. If this is not impressed upon the Germans they will think that they have won the war.[13]

General Sir Henry Horne, Headquarters, First Army

Foch and Haig both considered that nothing should be left to chance. Their intention was clear: an Armistice would only be granted with concessions that were sufficiently stringent to render the German Army incapable of any resumed resistance.

Foch gave me a paper which he had handed to the Allied Conference in Paris on the subject of an Armistice. His main points were:

1.   Evacuation of Belgium, France and Alsace-Lorraine.
2.   Hand over to Allies to administer all country up to Rhine with
     three Bridgeheads on the river. The size of each of latter to be
     30 kilometres from the crossing drawn in semi-circle.
3.   Germans to leave all material behind, huts, supplies, etc., etc.,
     railway trains, railways in order.
4.   Enemy to clear out in 15 days from signing of agreement.

    I remarked that the only difference between his (Foch's)
conditions and a 'general surrender' is that the German Army is
allowed to march back with its rifles, and officers with their swords.
He is evidently of opinion that the Enemy is so desirous of peace
that he will agree to any terms of this nature which we impose.[14]

Field Marshal Sir Douglas Haig, General Headquarters, BEF

Henry Rawlinson expressed the same kind of robust views.

The Bosche is really squealing now, but I am not sure that he
will not wriggle out of the hole we have got him into, unless we
Allies, and especially the Americans and ourselves, keep a stiff
upper lip. We must follow him up to the frontier with our armies,
and only discuss terms of peace when we have the Allied troops in
Germany. I fancy you will have to march to the Rhine before you
will really bring down the German edifice, and it is right that Allied
troops should enter Germany. Personally, I think representative
detachments should continue the march and enter Berlin.[15]

General Henry Rawlinson, Headquarters, Fourth Army

Worried that the peace rumours might tempt his men into fraternisa-
tion, Major General Sir Torquhil Matheson issued a stern order to his
Guards Division, warning them of what he believed to be the real German
motives in seeking an Armistice.

All our troops will be warned against paying any attention to
rumours of this kind. They are intended not to shorten the war,

but to save the German Army from the consequences of defeat this year and to preserve its strength for the defence of German soil next year. Any attempt made by the enemy to fraternise in the field will also be disregarded absolutely. It is our intention to beat the enemy as fast as we can, not to allow him to recover his strength.[16]

Major General Sir Torquhil Matheson, Headquarters, Guards Division

The American president realised the value of maintaining a common front with his allies and in a peremptory reply, received by the Germans on 9 October, Wilson demanded that von Baden not only accept his Fourteen Points, but also the evacuation of all occupied territory as a preamble to any negotiations. Everyone could perceive that this was merely another way of describing unconditional surrender.

By this time Ludendorff was thrashing around, lost in a world of frustration, casting around for solutions, but perhaps more importantly seeking someone to blame for the disaster that had befallen Germany. He demanded more troops, then baulked at the extreme measures that would be necessary to raise them, then, equally abruptly, accepted their necessity. When von Baden challenged him, asking for a second opinion on the real military situation from other sources within the Supreme Army Command, he was slapped down.

The Prince also wanted to hear the views of other high officers on the situation. Only Supreme Army Command, however, had a view of the whole position. The conditions were different with each army. Deductions as regards one army do not apply to the entire front. I refused his request. The Field-Marshal and I had alone to bear the responsibility. His Majesty could demand explanations at any moment, but not the Chancellor. The army was still subject to the Emperor as War Lord.[17]

Quartermaster General Erich Ludendorff, Headquarters, Supreme Army Command

On 12 October, the Germans accepted the evacuation of occupied territory as a preamble to negotiations. Behind the scenes, though, the 'blame

game' still seemed to occupy at least as much of the German political and
military elite as did the search for a path to peace.

In the interim, the Supreme Army Command considered it essential
that Germany's armies should not take a single step backwards. Earnest
entreaties were issued, appealing to every soldier to do their best to hold
back the Allies to facilitate the best possible terms for an Armistice.

> Diplomatic negotiations aimed at ending the war have begun. The
> outcome will be most favourable the more the army succeeds in
> remaining cohesive, maintaining captured territory and inflicting
> damage on the enemy. In particular:
> - Should there be breakthrough of the Hermann-Gudrun Posi-
>   tion, it is essential that the thrust be halted as soon as possible.
> - The construction of the Antwerp-Meuse Position and the
>   backloading of all stores and equipment that can be spared is
>   to be accelerated.
> - Each withdrawal is simply a costly makeshift measure. It is
>   damaging to the morale of the troops and means the loss to us
>   of irreplaceable stocks.
> - We should not underestimate the enemy. However, we must
>   not overestimate them.[18]
>
> Field Marshal Paul von Hindenburg, Headquarters, Supreme Army
> Command

It would all be to no avail – nor could it be. These were just words –
what was needed was hundreds of thousands more German boots on
the ground. Talk of numerous German divisions still on the army lists
concealed the fact that many had been reduced to a shell, some as low as
just a thousand or so men – nearer to the peacetime strength of a single
battalion. Regiments were being reduced from three to two battalions,
while in turn the number of companies was cut from twelve to just three.
Often companies were down to just twenty to thirty men – rendering
them no longer a serious military formation.

The riposte from Wilson to the German reply was a second diplomatic note on 15 October, which emphasised the weakness of the German
position. This time, Wilson demanded the immediate cessation of U-boat

warfare and cessation of 'wanton destruction' by the Germans. By now Max von Baden had realised the awful truth of his position.

> I could have recoiled in horror when I saw that there was no military force to back my policy, that we had already gone bankrupt on the battlefield. I believed that I had been summoned at five minutes to twelve, and find out that it is already five minutes past.[19]

Chancellor Max von Baden

On 17 October, at a meeting in Berlin of the German War Cabinet with the Supreme Army Command, there was another vigorous clash between von Baden and Ludendorff on the question of a wider representation of military views within the German armies. Hindenburg was not present, but it was also evident at this meeting that Ludendorff was fast changing his tune; now he was talking of continuing the fight in the face of the intransigence of the Allies in the Armistice negotiations. In his view, the new government was entirely to blame for everything – including considering withdrawing divisions from the Eastern Front, for wavering over the occupation of the Ukraine, for failing to counter Bolshevism effectively, for failing to promise the undying commitment of the whole German people, and for failing to send the reinforcements he demanded. Next day, the discussions went on in Berlin, this time without Ludendorff. As the politicians wavered towards accepting the abandoning of U-boat warfare, Ludendorff sent a cable proposing a rallying cry to the people of Germany.

> The question to be asked is, will the German people fight for their honour not only with words but actually to the last man, and thus ensure the possibility of recovery; or will they allow themselves to be driven to capitulation before making a supreme effort? By consenting to the abandonment of U-boat warfare as agreed in the Note, we enter the latter path.[20]

General Erich Ludendorff, Headquarters, Supreme Army Command

This from the man who had poured scorn on the idea of such a rallying call to the German people on 29 September. Then the final cynical attempt to wash his hands of all blame.

Supreme Army Command does not regard itself as a factor of political power. It bears therefore no political responsibility. Its political consent to the Note is not necessary.[21]

General Erich Ludendorff, Headquarters, Supreme Army Command

At the end of all this juggling for position, the German government sent a note which accepted an end to the German submarine warfare campaign as a precondition of negotiations.

Whatever Ludendorff might think, there *were* other views from senior German commanders on the Western Front. That same day, Crown Prince Rupprecht summed up the reality of their military situation in a letter to the von Baden.

Our troops are exhausted and their numbers have dwindled terribly. The number of infantry in an active division is seldom as many as 3,000. In general, the infantry of a division can be treated as equivalent to one or two battalions, and in certain cases as only equivalent to two or three companies. Quantities of machine guns have been lost, and there is a lack of trained machine-gun teams. The artillery has also lost a great number of guns and suffers from a lack of trained gun-layers. In certain Armies 50 per cent of the guns are without horses. There is also a lack of ammunition, and particularly for the most important kind of guns, such as the 77-mm field guns, the light field howitzers and the 10-cm guns, which can no longer be adequately kept supplied from home. Apart from the commanders, regular officers are now only to be found occasionally in the higher regimental staffs. The morale of the troops has suffered seriously and their power of resistance diminishes daily. They surrender in hordes whenever the enemy attacks and thousands of plunderers infest the districts round the bases. We have no more prepared lines, and no more can be dug. There is a shortage of fuel for the lorries, and, when the Austrians desert us, and we get no more petrol from Romania, two months will put a stop to our aviation. I do not expect much from a *levée en masse* on the model of Carnot's at the beginning of the French revolutionary wars; it meant much then, because it was put into

force at the beginning of a war; but we are already in the fifth year
of the war, and our reserves in men are already exhausted to breaking point. Further, how are the war industries to carry on in face of
a *levée en masse,* when they are not even now in a position to fulfil
completely the demands we make on them? We cannot sustain a
serious enemy attack, owing to a lack of all reserves. If we succeed,
by retreating behind the serious obstacle of the Meuse, in shorten-
ing our front considerably, we can hold out there under favourable
circumstances for one or two months, but only if the enemy does
not violate Holland's neutrality or drive her to take sides against
us, and if the Austro-Hungarian troops are not withdrawn from
the Western Front. I should like to add that in every fresh retreat
we always have to leave a good deal of material behind. I do not
believe that there is any possibility of holding out over December, particularly as the Americans are drawing about 300,000 men
monthly from beyond the ocean. I should like to add that our
situation is already exceedingly dangerous, and that under certain
circumstances a catastrophe can occur overnight. Ludendorff
does not realize the whole seriousness of the situation. Whatever
happens, we must obtain peace before the enemy breaks through
into Germany; if he does, woe on us![22]

Crown Prince Rupprecht, Headquarters, Army Group Rupprecht

No-one seemed to be listening, or if they were, there was nothing they
could do. Germany fought on with little or no hope.

Meanwhile on 19 October, Haig was reflecting on the nature of the
terms that should be offered to the Germans. He had backed Foch to the
hilt in driving his armies forward to ensure that the war did not drift into
1919. Now he was minded to accept marginally less stringent terms than
Foch – if that enabled peace to be attained at once. He may have been
reputed to be inarticulate, but this consummate staff officer could express
himself clearly on paper.

The Prime Minister asked my views on the terms which we should
offer the Enemy if he asked for an Armistice. I replied that they
must greatly depend on the answers we give to two questions:

1. Is Germany now so beaten that she will accept whatever terms the Allies may offer?

2. Can the Allies continue to press the Enemy sufficiently vigorously during the coming winter months as to cause him to withdraw so quickly that he cannot destroy the railways, roads, etc.?

The answer to both is in [the] negative. The German Army is capable of retiring to its own frontier, and holding that line if there should be any attempt to touch the honour of the German people.

The situation of the Allied Armies is as follows:

French Army worn out, and has not been fighting latterly. It has been freely said that 'war is over' and 'we don't wish to lose our lives now that peace is in sight'.

American Army is disorganised, ill equipped and ill trained. Good officers and NCOs are lacking.

The British Army was never more efficient but has fought hard, and it lacks reinforcements. With diminishing effectives, morale is bound to suffer.

French and American Armies are not capable of making a serious offensive now. British alone cannot bring the Enemy to his knees.

In the coming winter, Enemy will have some months for recuperation and absorption of 1920 class, untouched as yet. He will be in a position to destroy all communications before he falls back. This will mean serious delay to our advance next year.

I therefore recommend that terms of Armistice should be:

1. Immediate evacuation of Belgium and occupied French territory.

2. Metz and Strassburg to be at once occupied by the Allied Armies, and Alsace-Lorraine to be vacated by the Enemy.

3. Belgian and French rolling stock to be returned, inhabitants restored etc.

The Prime Minister seemed in agreement with me. Wilson urged 'laying down arms'. Lord Milner took a middle course between my recommendations and those of Foch, i.e., in addition to what I lay down he would occupy the west bank of the Rhine as a temporary measure until the Germans have complied with our peace terms. I was asked what the attitude of the Army would be if we stuck out for stiff terms, which Enemy then refuses, and war goes on. I reminded the PM of the situation a year ago when there were frequent demands for information as to what we were fighting for. He (the PM) then made a speech and stated our war aims. The British Army had done most of the fighting latterly, and everyone wants to have done with the war, provided we get what we want. I therefore advise that we only ask in the Armistice for what we intend to hold, and that we set our faces against the French entering Germany to pay off old scores. In my opinion, under the supposed conditions, the British Army would not fight keenly for what is really not its own affair. Mr Balfour spoke about deserting the Poles and the people of Eastern Europe. But the PM gave the opinion that we cannot expect the British to go on sacrificing their lives for the Poles! Admiral Wemyss, First Sea Lord, then came in and the views of Navy for an Armistice were stated. They seemed most exacting and incapable of enforcement except by a land force.[23]

Field Marshal Sir Douglas Haig, General Headquarters, BEF

Rawlinson came up with an analogy for the process that Haig, as an old cavalry officer, would surely have approved of.

The Bosche answer to Wilson is another squeal for an Armistice, the result of our latest successes. The negotiations are like selling a horse. We have got to fix the reserve price. If it is too high, the Bosche won't buy, and we shall have to go on fighting. If he continues to destroy all railways, as he has done, we shall not reach the German frontier before February. Even so, I would rather go on another three or four months than have an unsatisfactory peace. We have spent so much, that we must not haggle at the little bit extra to get all we want.[24]

General Henry Rawlinson, Headquarters, Fourth Army

However, Foch was resolute, and it would be his vision of the Armistice conditions that was eventually agreed.

Having consulted his allies, on 23 October Wilson sent his third diplomatic note. This indicated a willingness among the Allied governments to agree to an Armistice, but insisted on two conditions. First, hostilities must not be resumed, and second, the Allies would only negotiate with genuine representatives of the German people. Only outright surrender was on offer to the Kaiser and his military supreme commanders. This, as might be expected, triggered an immediate conflict between Chancellor von Baden's new government and the Supreme Army Command. Now Hindenburg and Ludendorff wanted to fight on: the final rupture came on 24 October, when Hindenburg issued an Order of the Day to the army. This order had been countersigned by Ludendorff, but without any consultation with von Baden – although the press had been informed. The contents were outrageous:

> Wilson's answer means military capitulation. It is therefore unacceptable to us soldiers. Wilson's answer can be for us soldiers only a challenge to continue resistance to the utmost of our power. When the enemy realises that the German front is not to be broken through in spite of every sacrifice, he will be ready for a peace which ensures Germany's future. [25]
>
> Headquarters, Supreme Army Command

Their *volte face* was complete. Max von Baden was understandably furious. It was clear that the warlords were confident that they had done enough to shift the blame for imminent defeat to the civilian government. Ludendorff and Hindenburg went to Berlin for a showdown, intending to report to the Kaiser – a meeting that did not go quite as they expected. The Kaiser had been infuriated by their inability to maintain a consistent position on whether an Armistice was – or was not – necessary, coupled with hurt pride over their failure to consult him before issuing their contentious Order of the Day. As Hindenburg put it somewhat disingenuously, 'It was too late. Politics demanded a victim. The victim was forthcoming.'[26] The Kaiser had made up his mind and told Ludendorff of his misgivings, before pointedly informing him that he was inviting two senior generals to report on the state of the Army to the Chancellor and the War Cabinet. This triggered the intended resignation from Ludendorff, but when Hindenburg also offered to resign it was rejected. Hindenburg was distraught.

> I left the capital, whither I had gone with my First Quartermaster General to confer with our All-Highest War Lord, and returned to Headquarters. I was alone. His Majesty had granted General Ludendorff's request to be allowed to resign and refused my own. Next day I entered what had been our common office. I felt as if I had returned to my desolate quarters from the graveside of a particularly dear friend.[27]

Field Marshal Paul von Hindenburg, Headquarters, Supreme Army Command

He was not the only German soldier that was upset by this news. German propaganda had built up a legend of Ludendorff, dating back to his involvement in the capture of Liège in 1914, the subsequent forging of the partnership with Hindenburg and the triumph at Tannenberg, their string of victories in the East, and the accession to the Supreme Army Command. Now, suddenly, he was gone. Leutnant Herbert Sulzbach was devastated at the news – and at the rumours that the Kaiser himself was to abdicate.

> A piece of news has come in today which really was too much and too unexpected: Ludendorff has gone; that greatest among commanders of armies, the man of iron energy, has been unceremoniously relieved of his post. And Kaiser Wilhelm is to follow him. For us fighting men of the front line, these are the two most terrible events which could possibly occur. Ludendorff was our idol, and the Kaiser our supreme commander in the field. Now it is really hard to preserve any confidence.[28]

Leutnant Herbert Sulzbach, No. 5 Battery, 5th Field Artillery Regiment, 9th Division

A far more realistic view of the overall German situation was held by Leutnant Eugen Kaufmann.

We heard details of the enormous scale of the enemy offensive – also about events in Bulgaria and the fateful political changes at home! I forced myself not to speculate about the possible repercussions on our own sector of the front! After a few days in a reserve trench near Bétheniville we were relieved and ordered to march further back to Annelles where there was time enough to refresh ourselves with thorough ablutions and changes of underwear. Our retreat – for that was what we were now engaged in – was so orderly that nobody seemed to be very worried about it! Foremost in our minds was what was happening in Germany and what may be the result of Germany's latest peace proposals – no one seriously believing they could still be successful! On October 10th we further retreat – across the River Aisne – marching most of that day and the following night in mist and very low temperatures as far as Machéroménil. There we had to make the best of what this village had to offer. Another example of a place just recently evacuated and left in the sad condition which such a situation usually brought about! So I finally decided to put my Company into the local church! The necessary clear space in the nave was created by piling up the benches in the choir! There was plenty of hay and straw to be found in the barns and stables of the farmsteads! Masses of soldiers, horses and vehicles in the village street. I managed to secure for myself a snug, warm room, where I was able to collect my thoughts and to consider our situation and the tremendous events we were right in the middle of! I could not then believe that we might have to accept the humiliating peace conditions drawn up in Wilson's latest offer! By the 19th October we had moved further back to Auboncourt, expecting the Armistice to be declared at any moment. Instead we only heard of a new set of conditions drawn up by the American President – which were in tone and content, even more humiliating than the present ones! I did not dare to hope or fear for any rejection or acceptance – instead I tried to push all these feelings aside by trying to concentrate my attention on Dostoevsky's *Brothers Karamazov* and to accept that great writer's view that the sense and purpose in life is not, or should not, be dependent on external happenings, successes and impressions so much as on works and on love for all mankind![29]

Leutnant Eugen Kaufmann, Infantry Regiment 165, 14th Brigade, 7th Division

The Germans would fight on, but with no real hope in their hearts.

The senior generals selected to provide an alternative source of advice to Max von Baden were General Max von Gallwitz, the commander of the eponymous Army Group Gallwitz on the Argonne front, and General Bruno von Mudra commanding the Seventeenth Army facing the British First Army. In the event, they could offer little of practical value, recommending a retirement to a shorter line of defence, and more reinforcements. Ludendorff himself was replaced as Quartermaster General by General Wilhelm Gröner on 29 October.

All this political wrangling leaves an unpleasant taste in the mouth when one considers that men were being maimed and dying in huge numbers with every day that passed. By this time, most soldiers and civilians wanted as early an end to the war as possible. They wanted victory, but, like Haig, were willing to surrender the 'perfect triumph' for a swift and certain victory. The French had suffered terrible casualties in the Great War and Corporal Louis Barthas had been badly wounded before being posted to act as a training instructor with the Vitré garrison in 1918. He had served through most of the war, was present at the great slaughterhouse battles and had even been a passive mutineer in 1917. His thoughts reek of a cynicism inculcated by his mordant experiences of the generals and politicians who would decide their future.

War had to end with total disaster for the German Army, against which Jena, Waterloo and Sedan would be mere skirmishes. Thousands of captured cannon, hundreds of thousands of captured Bosches, shattered enemy forces streaming back across the Rhine bridges, pursued with bayonets at their backs by our soldiers, our regiments entering the great cities beyond the Rhine, flags fluttering, bands playing – here was the apotheosis dreamed of not only by our great warriors, but also by the government, almost all the press, and, back in the rear, all those who had nothing more to lose, or who had more to gain by continuing the war. What did a 100,000, 200,000 more cadavers matter; a few more months of unimaginable suffering to bear?[30]

Corporal Louis Barthas, Vitré Garrison

9

AMERICANS ON THE MEUSE

Shells brought names and numbers down that night. They killed
off men who had hope of Armistice – tomorrow. So many died that
night, short hours away from Armistice. They had held on to hope
in spite of everything.[1]

Private Elton Macklin, 1/5th Marines, 4th Marine Brigade, 2nd Division

THE AMERICANS WERE GEARING UP for a great attack in the Meuse-
Argonne campaign to be launched on 1 November. It had been a long
hard autumn, but now they had finally fought their way clear of the
confines of the Argonne Forest and had battered their way through the
Kriemhilde Stellung. Ahead of them still lay the River Meuse, which had
gradually encroached on their right flank as they pushed forward, and
which was now lying diagonally across the line of their advance. Yet there
was to be no let-up: John Pershing was a very hard man, determined to
push forward, desperate to press home their advantage. This was no time
for hesitation, they must seize the moment – no matter what the cost.

Now that Germany and the Central Powers are losing, they are begging for an Armistice. Their request is an acknowledgment of weakness and clearly means that the Allies are winning the war. That is the best of our reasons for our pushing the war more vigorously at this moment. We must strike harder than ever. Our strong blows are telling, and continuous pressure by us has compelled the enemy to meet us, enabling our Allies to gain on other parts of the line. There can be no conclusion to this war until Germany is brought to her knees.[2]

General John Pershing, Headquarters, American Expeditionary Force

Although a Second American Army had been created in mid October, it was not yet ready for serious operations, so it would again be the First Army, now under the command of General Hunter Liggett, that would carry out the advance up to and then across the Meuse. One of his subordinates, Major General William Wright, had no illusions as to what lay ahead.

We can expect bitter fighting – many machine guns. To overcome this we must have full development of fire action, great development in depth and resolute determination to go forward at all costs. The more we hesitate the greater will be our losses. The halts on our objectives are taken according to the best previous experience in order for the infantry to be coordinated with the barrage. All other halts should be avoided. Troops must drive on and leave strongpoints to be mopped up by the support detachments. This mopping up must not be neglected, however; special detachments are detailed for it, but the assault elements should pass on and gain the main objective. Don't forget your communications. Send back reports of how you are getting along. Then we can help you. Then we can keep the attack going. If your phone doesn't work, try the buzzer. Remember you will have pigeons and runners. Infantry must never be advanced in the open without a tremendous fire of machine guns or artillery. You must organize for this. Move your supporting machine guns when your infantry is halted. Then move the infantry forward under their fire. Machine gun officers must study the terrain and study the maps of the forward areas in great detail, deciding where they can best site their guns to accomplish this mission.[3]

Major General William Wright, Headquarters, 89th Division

Wright appreciated the military necessity of seizing bridgeheads across the Meuse while the German defence was relatively weak. After all, the much-anticipated Armistice could still fail to materialise.

Unsurprisingly, many of the 'Doughboys' were less than enthusiastic as they considered what might lie ahead of them. Rumours of peace were spreading like wildfire and nothing could prevent the men from speculating about their likely fate. Chatting with friends one night, Private Horace Baker put his views explicitly.

I said, 'Fellows, I don't want to go back to the lines again, for next week is going to be the last week of the war and I don't want to get killed that late in the game.' One of the fellows said, 'Yes, if a man had been over here three years ago – or even one – and had got killed, it would have been a mercy, for he would have been saved all this suffering, but now it's different.' Banholzer[4] added, 'You are right! I wouldn't mind having been killed away back then, but it would be terrible to get killed the last week of the war, and if I were to get knocked off the last day, why, I'd never get over it!' This raised a laugh of course.[5]

Private Horace Baker, 3/128th Regiment, 64th Brigade, 32nd Division

Whatever they thought, or hoped, however, one last great battle still lay ahead of them.

In the days before the planned attack, Wright attended a V Corps meeting where he found himself attempting to temper the enthusiasm of Major General Charles Summerall, for what Wright perceived as an over-decentralisation in the control of artillery in battle.

I told him that I didn't think the paragraph in his order, which stated that 'Commanders of assault Battalions should have complete control of the barrage', was practicable, that I did not see how it could be done, as they might have different views. One might want to stop his barrage, while the other one might want to have his barrage go on. I suggested that the question of the barrage be left up to the Brigade commander. He stated that he had no objection to this provided proper liaison could be obtained, but he saw no objection to the commanders of the assault Battalions having charge of their respective barrages, as the front of a battalion would cover at least 1 kilometre, and if one battalion stopped and the other went on, the advancing Battalion would invariably pull the other one along with it, and if one stopped and the other did not go on, the barrage would be stopped anyhow. [6]

Major General William Wright, Headquarters, 89th Division

There was merit in both sides of the argument, for the Americans were struggling to find a workable methodology to allow their 75mm guns to get forward and be more responsive to the pressing needs of advancing troops. The possibilities of this had been made evident by British, French and German gunners, but the question was how best to retain control?

On 1 November, the barrage roared out above them ready for the assault. As ever, to the men watching and listening, it seemed that nothing could ever have matched its raw power.

I shall never forget this day. At 3 o'clock our barrage started and I believe that there has never been such a great artillery demonstration in the world's history. Lieutenant Bennet commanded load and the deafening roar broke forth, not only from our guns, but from thousands, for it had been so wonderfully well timed that the fury was loosed on the dot. Our position is so far forward that a battalion of machine guns operated behind us and their cracking was so monotonous and intense that actually at times they seemed to drown out the noise of our powerful howitzers. The good old 75s too were everywhere, spitting out their destruction. Tongues of flames leapt from the mouths of such numberless guns that the heavens were lighted as by electricity. For a time, Fritz bombarded us but his bursts could hardly be distinguished in the turmoil. [7]

Corporal Elmer Sherwood, 150th Field Artillery, 67th Artillery Brigade, 42nd Division

Colonel Conrad Babcock was also greatly impressed by the bombardment, especially the indirect fire of massed machine guns pumping a deadly staccato hail across the German lines and all the immediate hinterland.

> I have no adjectives to describe this man-made flying death, the appalling noises of the shells as they swept over us in one continuous flight. In some respects, the machine-gun bullets were, to us, the most terrifying. My recollection is that the machine guns fired from 3.30 am to 6.30 am, then those assigned to the attacking battalions caught up with their organisations and went forward as previously described. The machine-gun barrage was terrific. The bullets, following one another in thousands of files, sounded to me like giant shears cutting a mile-wide sheet of tin. Although these bullets were clearing the trees under which we waited H hour, it really took quite a bit of mental effort to stand up; it was hard to believe those bullets weren't flying right past one's head. For two hours, we sat or lay down under this torrent of lead, steel and high explosive; then, at 5.30 am, on the minute, the infantry whistles blew and the assault battalion went forward behind the rolling barrage.[8]
>
> Colonel Conrad Babcock, Headquarters, 354th Regiment, 177th Brigade, 89th Division

If anything, this bombardment had just an aperitif to the creeping barrage that erupted as the troops moved forward. The Americans had now learnt many of the artillery techniques required: their barrage mixed a rolling wall of bursting 75mm shells, with the heavier medium and heavy guns that fired on a series of pre-identified targets. The machine-gun fire hosed across the German positions, while the trench mortars added to the sound and fury.

The practical problems facing detached guns assigned to work closely with infantry units, were soon all too apparent to Captain Robert Casey. He had been ordered to take forward two 75mm guns, to follow immediately behind the first wave in order to assist the 353rd Regiment in their attack, pushing towards the corner of the Bois de Bantheville. There is no doubt that right from the start Casey was deeply concerned by the nature of his task.

Artillery has no business in front of infantry. The horses can't live more than a few minutes under fire. The enemy doesn't have to be told what will happen to him with 75mms smashing him at a range of a few hundred metres direct laying. So he never lets it happen.[9]

Captain Robert Casey, A Battery, 124th Field Artillery, 33rd Division

As they approached the jumping-off line, the gun teams were harassed by German gas shells and general shellfire, while trying to avoid the shell craters spattered across what remained of the road. Their intended route, via a firebreak through the woods, had been totally blocked off by the German shells and they had no option but to travel up the Bantheville road.

I don't suppose there was ever a stranger procession through No Man's Land. The shells of the Bosche were lighting with beautiful precision in the middle of the road, and it's a poor fuse that won't explode when dropped on concrete. Parachute flares – a thousand of them – floated over us and made the road as bright as Broadway! Overhead travelled bullets that cracked and snapped and others that swished with the frou-frou of a silk skirt. Trench mortar projectiles made a whispering passage and smashed in the bank.[10]

Captain Robert Casey, A Battery, 124th Field Artillery, 33rd Division

They were taking more and more casualties. As their horses were killed, it was becoming difficult to keep the guns and limbers moving with the few that remained.

We were still mobile – but not much more. As we started up the hill we had four horses to the carriage instead of six. Three of our caissons were missing. About half our men were lying back there in the woods. One of the horses in the lead team of the first piece was bleeding from six wounds. He had lost an eye, the remnants of which hung in an oystery mass over his nose. I felt like shooting him but he was still pulling and we needed his help![11]

Captain Robert Casey, A Battery, 124th Field Artillery, 33rd Division

As if in compensation, Casey then witnessed an incredible vista of the battlefield – its beauty in shocking contrast to the deadly scene around him.

> Dawn had come up like thunder. The light had struggled briefly to penetrate the pall of battle and then had given up the effort. A cold white mist, choking with mustard, rolled northward with the wind. New shell craters added wisps of smoke to the noisome vapours. The sun hung like a red lantern over the woods. Ahead the entire panorama of battle was spread in the dim light – a line of infantry, slowly advancing in extended order. The line of the barrage was just ahead of them – plainly marked by churning earth, smoke puffs whiter than the morning mists, and the drums of melanite rolling and echoing. The flat top of the hill was an abattoir. The barrage had fallen squarely upon three lines of machine-gun trenches running east and west. A headless body lay in the road. The trenches were filled with a hash of blood and entrails that looked like the offal of a packing plant. There were no wounded men – few corpses that one could identify as such. Probably not a man in this part of the rearguard action was alive five minutes after the start of the advance. On the other side of the barrage line the Germans were falling back.[12]
>
> Captain Robert Casey, A Battery, 124th Field Artillery, 33rd Division

When they were finally in place to open fire themselves, he contacted the nearest infantry officer to offer his close support fire. The ungrateful response made the stultifying futility of their efforts all too obvious.

> We found the infantry Colonel crouched with his adjutant in the shelter of a bank along the road. He looked as if he had suddenly received a visit from smallpox. 'Keep moving,' he ordered. 'Don't stop here. You'll attract fire.' 'What targets do you want us to shoot at?' I asked him. 'None,' he declared. 'There's a patch of woods 2 kilometres ahead. Get cover on the south edge of that and keep out of sight. You'll attract fire!' Once more I could have laughed, but the man was a Colonel. We had sacrificed most of the best men

in A Battery to say nothing of some thirty horses for the privilege of being ordered off the road. Gerry was in a column of squads squarely under our sights not 3 kilometres away. But we weren't to be allowed to shoot at him. We might attract fire! And here we are. The great adventure is a dud![13]

Captain Robert Casey, A Battery, 124th Field Artillery, 33rd Division

Close infantry–artillery cooperation demanded training and practice for both sides of the equation if it was to be a success. The idea wasn't stupid, but the execution was ill-considered.

One of the men opposing the Americans was Leutnant Otto Lais and the Baden Infantry Regiment 3/169 which had moved into the Landres et St Georges sector in front of Bayonville. They were facing the men of the American 2nd Division.

During a pitch-black, rainy night, the regiment arrived and began to dig into the open fields and meadows. No sooner had they started to dig when a storm of heavy artillery fire descended upon them. Within two hours, over one hundred American heavy tanks and countless light tanks emerged to roll over, crush, and wipe out the regiment completely. The majority of the officers are dead or severely wounded. The machine-gun crews, the anti-tank crews, and the hand-grenade troop of the infantry have all been eliminated after a brave defence. Superiority of force has prevailed. Out of the pale grey mist of the dawn come row upon row of grey monsters with the rumbling of motors towards us. The heavy tanks move up to the machine-gun nests and the anti-tank guns. The turret gun is lowered – there is a flash of fire and a report. The defenders are swimming in their blood. 'Move out!' The tank rattles on.[14]

Leutnant Otto Lais, Baden Infantry Regiment 3/169, 84th Brigade, 29th Division

It is noticeable that Lais attributes the American success almost entirely to tanks, as if divorcing the human element. This is a misrepresentation of the fighting, but perhaps understandable; beaten by machines, not men, is the unsubtle sub-text here.

Overall, the attack was indeed a considerable American victory. Major General William Wright was just one of several relieved generals who had just cause to be proud of his men who had advanced some 4–6 miles to capture the Bois de Barricourt and the Barricourt Heights. It left the Germans in some disarray, retreating to the River Meuse.

> I, of course, am delighted with what has been accomplished. It is a great source of satisfaction to me to feel that General Summerall is pleased. All in the division have done well. Babcock and Reeves have led their regiments gallantly and successfully. Winn has handled his job with his usual thoroughness. It is reported that the Division captured over 1,000 prisoners, over 300 machine guns, a battery of 88mms, known as 'Whiz-Bangs', and one 77mm field piece. They took all of their objectives on schedule time, a fact to be proud of.[15]
>
> Major General William Wright, Headquarters, 89th Division

As they advanced, there were still many dangers. The German rearguard units were well capable of striking back hard, before rapidly withdrawing again. A sudden flurry of shells or burst of machine-gun fire could cause severe casualties in moments. Sergeant Lynwood Downs of the 305th Field Artillery witnessed an example of men willing to respond to the 'call to duty' during such an incident, even though they knew in their hearts that the war must surely be over soon.

> The battery was lined up along a hedge behind a low bank. The Germans had hastily vacated the position leaving two 77s behind, but they were now attempting a stand. Shells were dropping in unpleasant proximity and the 'cannoneers' had been ordered to seek what little protection the bank offered. Altho' there had been several narrow escapes, the battery had as yet not suffered, altho' a 6-inch had exacted a large toll from the 'Doughboys' who in unbroken stream were filing past. The phone rang and word came that artillery was needed to clean out several troublesome machine-gun nests. The executive, Lieutenant Stribling,[16] called to the section chiefs, 'I want three volunteers from each gun crew to work the

guns!' Crouching low, the men ran to their posts and when the firing data arrived, not a single man was missing from his post.[17]

Sergeant Lynwood Downs, 305th Field Artillery, 77th Division

On 5 November, the American advance guards reached the town of Stonne. Here Captain Walter Rainsford had a poignant reminder of what they were all fighting for.

The town was filthy with a litter of garbage and refuse strewn broadcast about it; and packed in the church and the graveyard was a crowd of civilians, gathered together for the hour of their deliverance. As the first American troops came down the street, close along the house-walls, in one tide of hysterical joy they streamed forth to greet them. Four years of bondage, in hatred and in fear, and these were their deliverers, a people whom they had never seen before, but had been taught to love, and the French do not try to conceal emotion. Old men, old women, and girls, their arms were around the necks of the soldiers, and their poor pillaged homes were ransacked for some token, some hidden treasure of food, to press, laughing and crying, into the hands of the hungry and tired men. It was worth much of hardship and of suffering to have been among the first troops into Stonne; not often is the fruit of victory spread at one's feet in such a harvest of human hearts.[18]

Captain Walter Rainsford, 3/307th Regiment, 154th Brigade, 77th Division

That same day a farcical incident occurred, which shows that human rivalries and unnecessary frictions can exist in even the closest of alliances. The French had wanted the honour of entering Sedan, a city which had much historical and symbolic significance to them, being the site of the most humiliating defeat of the Franco-Prussian War in 1870, a date then still within living memory. However, Pershing wanted the honour for the Americans, which would involve his troops encroaching within the assigned French area of operations. That would have been bad enough, but indirectly or directly inspired by Pershing, an unseemly 'race' to Sedan then began, triggered by the American 1st Division, which swerved across the established line of advance of the 42nd Division, thereby causing utter chaos. Soon everyone was furious with everyone else; the wayward 1st Division was duly recalled, and it would indeed be the French who ultimately exercised their right to enter Sedan in triumph.

Collectively, the generals were now pondering the best method to force a crossing of the Meuse river. This was no easy matter for it was deep and up to 300 feet wide, as was demonstrated in a tragic incident that occurred when the 3/356 Regiment reached the river. Captain Arthur Wear had asked for volunteers to swim the river and scout out how well-defended was a village on the other side. Unfortunately, the river was in spate, with the result that several of the volunteers were swept away and drowned as they lost strength in the freezing waters, while others were shot by the Germans on the far bank. When the survivors reported to Wear[19] that they had been able to discover nothing of value, he was so distraught that he walked into a nearby wood and shot himself in the head.

> We had been advancing night and day for five days. The pace was killing and the strain on him with the responsibility of the whole battalion must have been terrible. We were trying to cross the river, but the Germans had blown out all of the bridges and it was impossible. The battalion was in an exposed, dangerous place. Captain Wear gave the order to withdraw the battalion, then shot himself. I am positive in my mind that he believed that he was saving his men at the cost of his own life. I was nowhere near him at the time. He sent word to me by his orderly to write his brother, Jim, and say simply that he was 'Weary and tired'.[20]
>
> Lieutenant Joseph Hook 3/356th Infantry, 178th Brigade, 89th Division

As they neared the Meuse, Major General William Wright found himself beset by complications, typical of the lot of a divisional commander at this stage of the advance. There were the usual logistical problems, niggling difficulties in getting the artillery far enough forward, hordes of French refugees to cope with – and most annoying of all – he had no faith in the command skills of one of his subordinates, Brigadier General Thomas Hanson, whom he considered lacked the requisite drive.

The orders given Hanson to make reconnaissance and force the bridge apparently petered out, so that when it got down to the officer commanding the operation nothing was done. It is another one of those cases where the Colonel and the Brigadier have not been out on the job; if they had been, something would have been accomplished, instead of sitting back on a wire and trying to act. I don't believe Hanson has been to his front line since he has been here. The orders given were not obeyed, and the entire effort was unsatisfactory. I am rapidly reaching the end of my patience with Hanson, and although I believe he tries hard, he has not the ability to handle his job. His viewpoint in regard to the methods to be adopted to accomplish his mission is wrong. He is entirely too much inclined to sit back on the wire, and rest easy and conduct his operations from there instead of going out with his men and putting things over.[21]

Major General William Wright, Headquarters, 89th Division

Hanson would be summarily dismissed on 9 November. He was not alone, as several other officers were found wanting and sacked, even at this late stage of the battle. Wright himself would be rewarded for his performance by news of imminent promotion to command the I Corps.

On 7 November, the 128th Regiment had been attached to 5th Division which, although having already forced a crossing at Dun sur Meuse, required support for a final push on Brandeville. As they moved into Brandeville Woods, the fighting became disjointed. After coming under fire from massed machine guns, Corporal Horace Baker and his section (he had been recently given acting corporal status) had fallen back in total disorder, before an officer stepped in to stem the retreat and order Baker back up the hill. Suddenly, he had to make a simple life or death choice.

I looked down the hill, straining my eyes through the fog. Somehow there was a blur in the little thicket at the far side of the field. I looked again and, horrors, it was a line of German soldiers, not less than two hundred strong, standing or walking about. It will be difficult to tell my emotions then. Will say that my hair stood on end as it does when I see a snake. I raised my rifle and took deliberate aim. Thinks I, 'I can get one now and know I got him!' But just as I was ready to pull the trigger I thought of something else, 'I can get two at least before they can tell where I am!' So, I aimed again, but failed to shoot again for a pesky thought almost knocked me down. It was, 'What if I do kill two or a half dozen and they swarm over the field and kill me, how much will that profit me?' So, I decided to let them live![22]

Corporal Horace Baker, 3/128th Regiment, (attached) 5th Division

Further north the swollen Meuse still lay ahead of the Americans. The war was not over yet.

10

BATTLE OF THE SAMBRE, 4 NOVEMBER

'This is going to be my last battle.' It was Geoffrey Gunther who spoke. 'It's going to be the last battle,' I replied, looking up. 'Well, it's going to be my last battle anyway; I'm sick of the war!' 'Yes', I agree. 'Mine too. We'll simply refuse to fight any more!' But I did not like that word 'last'. It stuck. It made me apprehensive.[1]

Lieutenant Carroll Carstairs, 3rd Grenadier Guards, 2nd Guards Brigade, Guards Division

THE LAST BATTLE FOUGHT BY THE BEF in the Great War should surely be a much-celebrated affair. This was an enormous clash of arms involving thirteen British divisions fighting on a 20-mile front – a battle to match the scale of the ill-fated opening attack of the Battle of the Somme on 1 July 1916. The reasons for the scandalous neglect of this battle are manifold. Authors who have slogged through the whole war, or even just the tumultuous events of 1918, are often by this stage of the story suffering from either writer's cramp, or, understandably, fear that yet another offensive, yet more barrages, the men going over the top 'one more time', might test the reader's patience. Yet, although the outcome of the war was decided, the details of the timetable of the defeat of Germany were still cloudy. One by one, Germany's allies had collapsed, yet it was not this that doomed Germany to defeat; it was Foch's relentless series of attacks up and down the Western Front. The only question was when? But the ultimate German collapse was nearer than might have been imagined. It started with a series of disturbing small shocks which were reported to General Max von Gallwitz on 30 October.

> In a regiment belonging to the 18th Landwehr Division, which was due to relieve 10th Infantry Division, a very large group of men from Alsace-Lorraine led by an officer deputy declared that they did not want to fight here and had marched back without permission to Thionville. A criminal investigation is under way. That evening it was also reported that a battalion of another regiment of this division had refused to move forward into the positions. This was something that was unheard of in the German army. A trainload of reinforcements intended for the Saxon 241st Infantry Division had been the scene of ugly disturbances, such that one hundred men had to be arrested. 1st Landwehr Division which had always fought well reported that recently many men had deserted to the Americans. They were mainly from Alsace or belonged to the latest batch of young reinforcements.[2]

General Max von Gallwitz, Headquarters, Army Group Gallwitz

As if this was not bad enough, the Imperial German Navy then were all at sea – or rather they were not. Orders had been issued to the High Seas Fleet for a final desperate mission into the North Sea to face the assembled might of the Grand Fleet, now reinforced by the arrival of a strong American dreadnought squadron. This was nothing but suicide, so on 29 October some of the crews began a slow-burning mutiny. The situation was gradually exacerbated as more and more ships mutinied. When troops were sent to restore order, they joined the mutineers. By 5 November, the whole of the Kiel area was in the hands of revolutionaries.

An extreme word, but one which reflected the situation. As a further complication, on 3 November, Austro-Hungary, Germany's last remaining ally, had signed an Armistice. Now Germany was alone.

By this time General Wilhelm Gröner was desperate. His assessment of the situation indicated that they must achieve an Armistice within a matter of a few days or face a total military collapse. The German armies had no reserves, their main rail communications were directly threatened, their divisions were disintegrating about them. The Supreme Army Command were left with no choice but to accept any conditions to secure an Armistice.

Meanwhile, Foch met with Haig, Pétain and Pershing to finalise the demands they intended to put to the Germans. As a start, the Germans would have to evacuate all occupied territory in Belgium, France and Alsace-Loraine within fourteen days. Then the Allied generals were determined to ensure that the Germans would be crippled as a military force. Thus 5,000 artillery pieces, 30,000 machine guns, 3,000 trench mortars and 2,000 aircraft would have to be surrendered. German military logistics were to be hamstrung by the demand that over 5,000 locomotives, 150,000 railway coaches and 10,000 lorries be handed over. The Allies also wanted to prevent any resurgence of naval power, demanding the humiliating surrender of six Dreadnoughts, 160 U-boats and eight light cruisers. Until the peace treaty – not the Armistice – had been signed the British naval blockade would continue. To prevent any thoughts of the German Army creating a near impregnable line of defences along the Rhine, the Allies would occupy the Rhineland west bank, with strong bridgeheads and an enforced neutral zone on the eastern bank. They would demand all this just for a *temporary* Armistice. The German government was powerless. Revolution seemed to surround them, but one huge impediment remained to any possible settlement – the fate of Kaiser Wilhelm. Meanwhile the war went on.

In attempting the next step of their long advance to victory, the British had one great advantage. The German defence works along the Sambre were not the awesome constructs that had plagued the Allies over the past two years, for there had been no time to construct the trenches, the reinforced concrete pill boxes, the deep dugouts, or even to lay the masses of barbed wire. Instead the Germans had to use the landscape as they found it; employing rivers, canals and forested areas to slow down attacks, and using any natural cover to hide the machine guns and guns that were the *de facto* backbone of the defences. Villages could be quickly fortified by employing buildings and cellars to create improvised forts. With determined troops this method of fighting could be effective, but it could not hope to hold out against a full-scale assault backed by almost unlimited artillery resources.

However, the British had also been forced to modify their tactics as a result of more open warfare, as more emphasis had to be placed on flexibility. The Battle of Amiens had demonstrated that with the 'All Arms Battle' the British had mastered trench warfare, but this open warfare was very different. Many elements of the successful equation were also absent. Indeed, the supply of tanks had eroded to almost nothing, while the heavy artillery could no longer keep up with the pace of the advance. The new circumstances caused some unit commanders to flounder as they carried on applying the methods and thinking of the trenches to the new conditions, typically, by demanding full-scale artillery barrages before advancing, when there was no real necessity. This naturally slowed progress to a crawl. However, more often a refreshing flexibility in overcoming the new tactical problems was demonstrated at all levels of command. For instance, they had worked hard to overcome the difficulties in getting field guns forward in support of the infantry – the very concept that was still baffling the Americans.

> The chief lesson learnt during these times was in the cooperation of the field artillery with the infantry. In long advances the infantry very soon got beyond the support of the heavy artillery and depended entirely on the lighter arm for support. Undoubtedly the field artillery, long accustomed as they had been to the system of barrages – so essential in an attack on a limited objective – were somewhat at sea and rather 'sticky'; when confronted with the problem of supporting infantry in the open. They very quickly adapted themselves to the changed conditions. Indirect fire could

still have been employed where necessary, and fire brought to bear over open sights when opportunity offered. Some portion of the guns in an advance of this kind should be far enough forward to be able to take advantage of opportunities, which may be fleeting ones, for energetically supporting the infantry.[3]

Brigadier Hanway Cumming, Headquarters, 110th Brigade, 21st Division

Despite the obvious risks of being caught in the open without gunpits, many of the younger artillery officers actually found this new freedom of action very exhilarating.

If you can imagine having been penned into trench warfare for years, getting up, doing terrific bombardments, taking 100 yards of trench, being pushed back; the flow of war going back and forward for very little gain and terrific casualties. To suddenly find yourselves out on the open country, grassland, being able to gallop over the place, take your guns over at a reasonable lick – it was a changed world altogether. We had our 'tails' on the ground, oh, four or five times a day, which is a very unusual thing for a field battery. One move might be enough. But we were moving on for quarter of a mile, half a mile – something like that – down we'd go again, shoot up on the instructions of a galloper who'd been in touch with the battalion coming back telling us what targets he wanted us on. Then off we'd go again; horses up, limbers up and off we'd go. Oh, it was a great exciting time, very exciting![4]

Captain George Jameson, C Battery, 72nd Brigade, Royal Field Artillery

The use of the heavy Vickers machine guns was also devolved, allowing the experts to maximise the firepower potential in the cause – but not the direct control – of the infantry.

The machine guns during this period had made great strides. Their tactical handling was getting more and more understood; they were no longer tied to the apron-strings of the Brigadier or Battalion commander, but were given a definite place in the general scheme and allowed to carry out their role without being hampered or fettered with unnecessary orders and instructions. Their chief *raison d'être* is to support the infantry wholeheartedly and to the last man and gun, and it was now clearly understood that this support could be obtained, not with the infantry, but by pursuing their own tactics for the infantry. Here again close support is essential, and this was obtained by the principles of echeloning in depth and continuous leapfrogging in the advance. Their performance was excellent but, to be hypercritical, it seemed that freer and better use of limbers might have improved it.[5]

Brigadier Hanway Cumming, Headquarters, 110th Brigade, 21st Division

Tactically, the situation of 1918 was unrecognisable from that of 1914. Then, at the Battle of Mons, each BEF infantry battalion had fought as a separate entity, lined up behind the Mons-Condé with no idea of inter-arms cooperation; even simple tactics such as the siting of machine guns in defensive locations were applied wrongly. Now it was the German Army lined up behind improvised defences along the Sambre river and canal. The tables had turned, but the war was not yet over. The question was whether they could finish the job in 1918 – and it was evident that the Allies were certainly trying their best.

The attack is to be on a huge scale, the Armageddon of the War: three British Armies, First and Third and Fourth attacking the centre of the German line, and French and American Armies pushing up from the South on both banks of the Meuse. The fighting spirit of the enemy is broken; the only obstacles in the way of a complete breakthrough to the Rhine are communications, supplies and the weather.[6]

Brigadier General Herbert Hart, Headquarters, 3rd New Zealand (Rifle) Brigade, New Zealand Division

More sensitive souls found their minds fixated by the strange juxtaposition of life and death that hung over them. Death was all around; yet the chance of a happy fulfilled post-war life shone brightly just over the horizon. One such thoughtful young man was Second Lieutenant Alan Bullock, who had pondered much upon his fate while on leave in mid October.

Quite a space has elapsed since last I wrote; a period full of excitement and life – and death. Hitherto I haven't understood the value of life; our natures are such that we do not recognise the value of anything until we stand in danger of losing it. I have dared and risked a good deal, and now that I'm on leave the retrospect is almost pleasant; the workman has earned his hire. Often we realise that war has lost its glamour – there is no array, no banners, no glorious investment of a battle. War is sordid and grim and utterly loathly, but, until military dominance is crushed, entirely necessary. Realising this we do not count the price; we only carry on as best we may, and trust in God's love to spare those whom He will, and to take to Himself those others who offer their all. Though war is so brutal and harsh, yet men's natures are not changed. The happy boy remains a happy boy – if he can grasp something of the meaning of Eternity and Value; his soul is white and clean, and his hands are clean though bloody.[7]

Second Lieutenant Alan Bullock, 1st/4th (Royal Fusiliers), London Regiment, 168th Brigade, 56th Division

When Bullock rejoined his battalion a few days later, the war was almost over. While his battalion paused at Douchy on 1 November, Bullock expressed his thoughts in writing for one last time. When reading the letters of the deeply religious, there is sometimes a feeling that they are in some sense bargaining their piety with their creator in the unspoken hope that others – less worthy – will be chosen for the ultimate sacrifice.

•

If you don't receive a letter in the next few days, don't worry. Of course, there are many things which can happen in a 'show'; but be assured that I don't fear that which supreme love ordains as my lot. We learn, some of us, how great is our dependence on the Infinite out here, where life and limb are not worth a moment's purchase.[8]

Second Lieutenant Alan Bullock, 1st/4th (Royal Fusiliers). London Regiment, 168th Brigade, 56th Division

Like so many others he would only discover his fate on Monday 4 November.

EVERY BATTLE OF THIS SIZE exists in the context of supporting operations that are interconnected or that prepare the way. Thus, the air war
boiled up into a bloody frenzy during the preparations for the Battle
of the Sambre. During open warfare there was often not enough time
painstakingly to identify the German batteries, machine-gun posts and
headquarters from photographic interpretation, as had become routine
during trench warfare. In these circumstances, the ground strafing role of
the RAF had become increasingly important. The intention was to harass
the Germans at every possible stage of their retreat.

> We used to carry four 20-pound Cooper bombs in the undercar-
> riage. Then we had your two machine guns. If you could shoot up
> transport and block the road that was a fine thing – you stopped
> the whole lot. Personally, I used to try and attack them from the
> front, not from the back. If you could manage to shoot up a couple
> of transport wagons the whole road was blocked for some time, then
> they were just cold meat. You went along with the bombs, pulled a
> plug and away they went. After you had been flying for some time
> you knew roughly what speed you were flying and just how far you
> had to be away to release your bomb. But they were really only a
> great success when you had a line of transport or a block of stuff. If
> you tried to bomb a motor-cyclist, for example, you wouldn't stand
> a chance in hell of getting him! If you could get transport in line on
> a road you could hit something somewhere.[9]
>
> Second Lieutenant James Gascoyne, 92 Squadron, RAF

Wednesday 30 October proved a dreadful day for both sides in the air
war. Although they claimed to have shot down some sixty-seven German
aircraft, the British had lost forty-one themselves. One of the victims was
Second Lieutenant Howard Andrews who was acting as observer in an
RE8 with South African pilot, Lieutenant Eric Goodwill. They were on
an artillery observation mission, sending down corrections to the batteries
below, when disaster struck.

> We turned back home and there was suddenly an appalling crash.
> Part of my machine gun seemed to disappear, the spade grip shot

off and disappeared over the side. I thought, 'Oh! We've been hit!' We started diving and I thought the pilot was trying to get out of trouble. When the engine started screaming a bit, I looked over the top and he was obviously badly injured, he was lying on one side with a lot of blood about. So I stretched myself out and shut the throttle. It was very difficult because you're against the wind and you have to come out to your waist to bend forward. In front of me was a joystick in clips. I took it out and put it in a hole through the flooring. Then I slowly pulled the joystick back against the pressure of the wind. Round the side of me ran two wires with wooden handles, so we could fly the machine by holding the joysticks and at the same time juggling with the side wires to the rudder bar – I got the wings fairly straight and got it about on level keel. I stretched myself up to have a look forward. By that time, I was absolutely scared stiff. We were down to 400 or 500 feet. I think by then I was committed. I don't think I could possibly have got to the throttle in time, so I looked forward and in front of me was a big army camp – tents everywhere – nearly in the centre was a strip like a landing strip, absolutely perfect grass verge – all the way along. By a bit of juggling with the controls I got it level, coming down right in the middle of this strip, perfect. Of course, I was still very frightened – out of my mind, I didn't know what I was doing quite! But I slowed down, slightly pulled the stick back and I felt the wheels just touch the ground, beautiful landing. I ran straight along, all sorts of soldiers running away, out of the way. But, unfortunately, I had a bad bit of luck – at the end was a big trench – impossible to avoid it – the front wheels dropped, the engine dug itself into the ground, turned itself upside down and that broke the back of the aircraft. Within a few seconds dozens of soldiers were around. I asked them to get the pilot out first, as he was hurt. They got him out and tried to get me out but I couldn't unwind my legs from round the stool, I'd round them round so tightly. In the end, I got out and crawled to see the pilot; he was obviously very badly hurt. For some reason, I couldn't keep still – I was shaking all over.[10]

Second Lieutenant Howard Andrews, 42 Squadron, RAF

Lieutenant Eric Goodwill[11] died of his wounds. Andrews wasn't physically
hurt, but he was left suffering from 'shell shock' and had to be evacuated
back to England.

THE PRELIMINARIES WERE OFTEN A BATTLE in themselves. At
05.15 on 1 November, First and Third Armies launched a series of attacks
designed to capture the great railway centre of Valenciennes. The town
itself was full of refugees and French civilians, so it could not be bombarded, while the situation was further complicated by the flooded area
alongside the Schelde Canal, which protected the town from a direct
approach from the west. It was therefore decided to outflank the town
from the south, as here the XXII Corps had already got across the Schelde.
The XXII and Canadian Corps would attack across the River Rhonelle,
taking the dominant ridge that lay behind before moving on to capture
the town. Among those attacking was Sergeant John Stephenson, a Lewis
gunner with 1/6th Duke of Wellingtons.

> Three of my team were killed right away. Just a little way out, we
> found some hidden machine-gun posts fully manned. We dealt
> with them promptly. There were no barbed entanglements. Our
> next obstruction was the Rhonelle river which we crossed by means
> of the trees which the Lancashire Fusiliers felled for us. We caught
> up to the barrage in which there was a break, but my team were
> all knocked out except Smailes and myself. We went through
> that break in the barrage and were now ahead of it. We got to
> the sunken road before the barrage and found it full of Germans.
> We jumped straight into the trench-like road. The Germans who
> first saw us looked bewildered, but others started grabbing their
> rifles and grenades. I swung my Lewis into action from the hip,
> while Smailes let off a few telling shots with his rifle – at which
> they flung down their weapons and raised their arms in surrender,
> many crying out, *'Mercy, Kamerad!'* I continued using the Lewis
> gun where any groups of opposition formed. Some of them started

running across the road to the rear and I had then to let them know quickly that what I said I meant.[12]

Sergeant John Stephenson, 1/6th Battalion, Duke of Wellington's Regiment, 147th Brigade, 49th Division

Further to the south, the 61st Division were successful in taking the town of Maresches. Here the 2/5th Gloucestershire Regiment had been ordered to carry out a secondary attack on a crossroads at St Hubert about a mile further to the east.

The objective was to be marked out for us by our artillery firing star shells, and we were to have a protective creeping barrage. At 7.30 pm we moved forward into a void of darkness – our only means of keeping direction was by compass, except for the bursting of the star shells. We were unable to keep up with the barrage; moreover, we lost touch with one another. We moved through the advanced line of our Divisional troops, over a field of turnips, in what was supposed to be diamond formation. I remember plunging through a hedge with the men and landing in an orchard, where we came under enemy fire. We rallied the men, fixed bayonets and charged into the darkness. We were certainly very far short of our official objective. Forms of Germans loomed up at us; some of us got in front of our own Lewis guns; some succeeded in bayonetting a few Germans. I deflected a German thrust with an ash stick – my revolver was clogged with mud – and things seemed to be in a pretty state of chaos. We took about eighteen prisoners, who were sent to the rear. What exploits B and C Companies performed I do not know to this day. Things quietened down after this scrap and we dug ourselves in, having not the foggiest notion where we were or who was on our flanks or where the enemy was or what had happened to the rest of the Battalion. We were very much 'in the air'.[13]

Captain Ronald Sinclair, 2/5th Gloucestershire Regiment, 184th Brigade, 61st Division

Meanwhile, on the left flank of the attack, the Canadian Corps had done well, managing to partly capture Valenciennes, a process they completed early next morning, prior to pushing east towards St Saulve.

THE BATTLE OF THE SAMBRE posed many problems for both the British and German high commands. For all the evidence of a collapse in German morale, the British were also aware that many of their own divisions had been fighting hard for the best part of eight months. Between August and November 1918 they had suffered some 360,000 casualties. The British battalions had been generally restocked to maintain a strength of between 500–700 effectives, but new arrivals would take time to settle in, and during that period could easily disrupt the existing established patterns of command and control within a unit, particularly if they were replacing NCOs and officers of long standing. In war, the most testing arena of human relationships, men needed to know, understand and trust each other.

The reinforcements were also sometimes of dubious quality, with a lot of young inexperienced – or worse still – unwilling soldiers. It was certainly evident that Private Jim Fox and his friend Charlie Ford had no appetite for front line service.

We were wondering what to do and I said to Charles, 'I tell you what, we might get two or three more days here if we report sick!' So, next morning the usual request, 'Anyone, sick, two paces forward!' Charlie and I stepped two paces forward. There was about forty or fifty others. All different regiments, all congregated together and the sergeant in charge marched us to the medical hut at Étaples. He asked every one of us to strip. We waited about five minutes and the medical officer, who was an old Colonel who had been in 20 to 30 years, a fellow in his sixties. A very gruff old fellow. He just came down the line and he didn't stop very long at any one person. I was just before Charles. He said, 'Fox, what's the matter with you?' I said, 'Sir, I've had trouble with pains in the back, they recur!' He said, 'Whereabouts!' I put my hand behind my back and said, 'About here, Colonel!' 'You say they recur quite frequently?' I said, 'Yes!' 'When are these pains the worst, morning, the afternoon, or during the night?' I said, 'They're not all the time, but the greater part of the time, morning, noon and night! The pain is there then!' He paused for about five seconds, which seemed like five minutes, then he said, 'Look, there's only one thing the matter with you, Fox!' I said, 'What's that Colonel?' He said, 'You want your bloody hair cut!' So, we got no sympathy at all – that was a waste of time![14]

Private Jim Fox, Base Depot, Étaples

Fox was an intelligent man; his fears were, after all, entirely rational. He knew what he was – and most of all he entirely grasped what he wasn't.

There are professional soldiers who seem to be born to be a soldier. They were very brave soldiers, men of that calibre. No doubt about that, I was never born to be a soldier. I was not of that frame of mind. I was never cut out to be a soldier. I didn't want to be in the front line, didn't want to serve as a soldier. As a boy, I went to Sunday School, I regularly went to Chapel. My grandfather was a local preacher all his life. They were very Christian people. As a young boy, I was brought up in that way, to respect Christianity and I believe that had a lot to do with it.[15]

Private Jim Fox, Base Depot, Étaples

Many of the men who had already been wounded were also reluctant to be sent back into the fighting. Corporal Dennis Price had been taken back to hospital at Boulogne after being hit during an attack on 8 October. The wound looked bad, but from Price's jaundiced perspective, it was healing far too quickly. He had loyally served with his regiment on the Western Front for three years, and now he considered he had done his 'bit' for King and Country. Price decided to try to postpone his return to the front.

The bullet had gone right round the bone and blew a hole right out of the back; it didn't even crack the bone! I was a very, very healthy lad and my wounds were healing too quickly! So I decided to keep the wound open. I tried to keep the back open, knocked the scab off one or twice and used my toothbrush to rub the scab off. But I healed very quickly; the whole thing was healed. I was limping a bit about the 10th November and that was about all![16]

Corporal Donald Price, 13th Royal Fusiliers, 112th Brigade, 37th Division

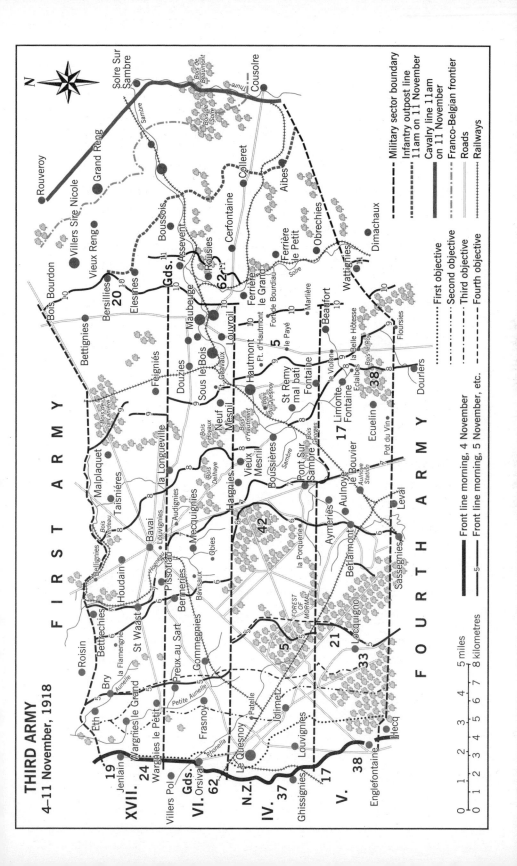

THIRD ARMY
4–11 November, 1918

Military sector boundary
Infantry outpost line 11am on 11 November
Cavalry line 11am on 11 November
Franco-Belgian frontier
Roads
Railways

First objective
Second objective
Third objective
Fourth objective

Front line morning, 4 November
Front line morning, 5 November, etc.

FIRST ARMY

FOURTH ARMY

And of course, men at the front were every day forced to grapple with the dichotomy between their duty and their personal safety.

> We were advancing and we had a rather close shave from a shell in a field of cabbages – and I thought, 'Oh my God, I don't want to get killed now – the war's coming to an end!' It made it more difficult. I don't know to what extent I evaded the risks, but I know that it was harder to do it. You knew jolly well what you ought to do – and I didn't want to when it was dangerous! I had always this consciousness that any moment might be your last. It was never away from my mind – even when I was enjoying myself my ears were attuned to the sound of a shell.[17]
>
> Second Lieutenant Cyril Dennys, 212 Siege Battery, Royal Garrison Artillery

Yet some of the original BEF were still on their feet: Private William Holbrook had been at the Battle of Mons on 23 August 1914, and indeed he was present when Lieutenant Maurice Dease and Private Sidney Godley won the first VCs of the war defending the Nimy bridge on the Condé Canal.

> Sooner or later the law of averages I should 'have it'. Eventually, I would get badly wounded, or wounded – the only thing I worried about was getting blinded. I thought it was just a matter of luck. You couldn't get much sleep; you got tired and weary. Sometimes, I didn't care one way or another. It seemed to drag on and on. You didn't take risks so much. It seemed to be going on for ever; you seemed so weary. You didn't expose yourself much.[18]
>
> Private William Holbrook, 4th Royal Fusiliers, 9th Brigade, 3rd Division

It was not surprising that, after four years of fighting in the front line, Holbrook was increasingly aware of his own mortality.

Yet whatever problems with morale lurked beneath the surface of the BEF, the German Army was still in a far worse state. The Second Army assessed only three of its divisions as fully fit for combat, seven were judged still capable of combat, five thought in need of immediate relief and four were described as not operational.[19] The Seventeenth Army was in a similar state of disrepair. As a general point, the clear signs of diminishing morale were exemplified by the increasing lack of potency in German counter-attacks. In previous years, the result of a day's fighting could not be judged until the counter-attack divisions had intervened in the battle. The most impressive-looking Allied gains could be overturned in a matter of hours. But now German counter-attacks were far more localised and often aimed at mere disruption, rather than hurling attackers back from whence they came.

The most serious problem facing the BEF in early November was simple logistics. This had threatened trouble before, but could no longer be ignored. The railheads were still not moving forward fast enough to keep pace with the rapidity of the advance, while the damage done to the infrastructure by the fighting had left a wide band of devastation that had to be bridged by roads and railways rebuilt almost from scratch, a tremendous undertaking demanding a substantial allocation of scarce manpower and resources. Beyond the area afflicted by years of trench warfare the Germans had destroyed everything they could: railways were an obvious target, but the roads were disrupted by huge craters at crossroads, hundreds of trees were felled across the highway, culverts blown up or mined, and houses pulled down across the road. The creation of new tracks and roads, the repairs of all these demolitions, took the involvement of skilled personnel and could not be done quickly enough to keep pace with the advance. Worse still, the Germans had concealed timed explosive charges on the embankments, bridges and viaducts, which, if not located, would explode up to eight weeks later to devastating effect after a route had been considered 'repaired' and open for use. Gradually the railheads fell further and further behind, while those few roads that had been repaired were simply incapable of transporting the scale of supplies and munitions needed by the armies. Horse transport and waggons were impractical so there was a great reliance on motor lorries, which, although almost unknown at the start of the war, were now proving their value in no uncertain manner. Nevertheless, the roads could not cope; often a whole corps was restricted to a single road for its lifeline supply route. It was inevitable that traffic jams clogged the key routes, while the road surfaces, not designed for such heavy traffic, soon began to deteriorate, requiring yet more repairs. Poor road conditions in turn led to breakdowns among the lorries, which imposed a fantastic strain on the vehicle maintenance teams, who soon began to run out of spares. All this against the background of a very wet and cold autumn.

It was soon evident that only railways and, to a lesser extent, the Decauville light railways, offered the bulk capacity necessary to provide the food for hundreds of thousands of men, to transport the shells to feed the voracious guns, the tons of small-arms ammunition, the hand grenades, the fuel, the fodder and all the other requirements and impedimenta. It has been estimated[20] that the Third Army alone needed some 33,000 tons of supplies, which required more than 100 trains, or a staggering 10,000 lorry loads on a *daily* basis. This did not take into account the thousands of tons of stone ballast and other materials required for the construction and repair of the roads and railways themselves. The British just about coped, but occasionally the tempo of offensive operations was disrupted by delays imposed by the failing logistical supply lines. And the situation was deteriorating with every mile they advanced.

As for weaponry, the two sides remained evenly balanced when it came to artillery, mortars and machine guns. Here it was far more the case that the British had caught up with the German provision rather than significantly overtaking them. In the air the Germans were badly outnumbered, as indeed they had been for most of the war. Their Fokker DVII was a fine scout aircraft, but the assorted hundreds of only marginally inferior scouts such as the Allied Sopwith Camel, the SE5a and Spad were more than capable of holding their own. The crippling shortage of aviation fuel was also beginning to have a restrictive impact on German flying operations. The late German conversion to tanks meant that they had far more captured British tanks than their own lumbering A7Vs. However, by November the British were also facing a crippling shortage of tanks ready for action, so that they had to be conserved in order to maximise their impact. The situation is evident when one realises that for this – the last major tank action of the war – the Tank Corps could only muster some thirty-seven tanks for an attack on a 30-mile frontage – and that these had been 'scraped up' from the surviving elements of several Tank Battalions. To put this in context, they were deploying fewer than those originally sent forward in the very first tank operation on 15 September 1916. This surely indicates that the secret of the British Army success in the 'Hundred Days' was not based on tanks – they were *part of* rather than the *main* component within the overall weapons mix. Tanks were welcome when they were available, but if not, the levels of tactical sophistication in many units was such that they could deploy other forms of firepower to overcome German resistance. In the absence of massed barbed wire – which did require tanks or a barrage – the tanks could be replaced by the flexible usage of forward detachments of field guns, gas and smoke shells, Stokes mortars, rifle grenades, machine guns and hand grenades. One additional complication was the continued presence of civilians in the battle area, which precluded the over-liberal use of high-explosive ordnance. Flexibility would be the key to success; indeed, it was at the heart of the 'All Arms Battle'.

The final orders for the Sambre attack had only been issued by Haig on 29 October, but, in accordance with the now established principles of good staff work, various plans and preparatory arrangements had already been started.

> Fourth, Third and First Armies will be prepared to resume the offensive on or after 3rd November with a view to breaking the enemy's resistance south of the Condé Canal and advancing in the general direction towards Avesnes-Maubeuge-Mons.[21]
>
> Field Marshal Sir Douglas Haig, General Headquarters, BEF

Physically, this was a challenging area for an attack. In the north, facing First Army, there was a network of canals and irrigation channels including the Mons-Comdé Canal, while between Valenciennes and Condé was another maze of irrigation channels and rivers draining to the River Scheldt. Facing the Third Army was the dark mass of the Forêt de Mormal, which was well suited to defence, with its maze of dense undergrowth cut by deep-cut watercourses. Further south on the Fourth Army front was the canalised menace of the Sambre river itself – up to 40 feet wide and 6 feet deep. On low ground beside the canal, the Germans had deliberately released water to create a shallow quagmire across which progress was difficult. Finally, the French First Army was attacking in support further south and driving towards La Capelle.

On the Third Army front, the VI Corps was to advance through a typically 'close' country, divided into small pastures and orchards, slightly rising upwards and cut by stream beds. At 06.00, the Guards Division would attack half an hour after their neighbours of the 62nd Division. Although there had been a flurry of late changes in the corps orders, they were all assimilated successfully without too much drama, as the opposition proved negligible. The 3rd Grenadier Guards was in the second wave of the 2nd Guards Brigade attack. Lieutenant Carroll Carstairs relates an account typical of the fighting experienced.

> The Germans were shelling the wood and a shell struck a tree on our immediate right with a mighty crash – like a giant axe splitting it at a stroke. Clouds of shrapnel bursting high scudded before the wind as though the elements were bent on minimising their effect. The men moved forward with heads slightly bowed, like people going through a heavy downpour. Passing through the wood without casualties, we continued to advance until we reached a ridge. From this elevation, the ground fell away to a road, about 1,000 yards off, running along our front. From the road, the ground rose again to a ridge opposite, perhaps 3,000 yards from where we stood. Quarter right and on the road itself lay a group of three or four houses – a big farm. For a few seconds, I noticed the country spread before me, and then we came under heavy machine-gun fire. I withdrew the men behind the ridge until the bullets whipped overhead. We decided the houses on my right front were occupied by the enemy and concealed machine guns. I determined to attack them, half the men advancing in short rushes while the other half covered their advance with rifle fire. We started out, but came again under so heavy a fire that a half dozen men were hit at once. Both the men on either side of me fell wounded – one was Corporal Clark, the

smartest soldier I have seen. I realised that at this rate we could soon be wiped out, and so retired again to comparative safety behind the ridge. The experience of having one's men hit and hearing their groans and being responsible for it turned me sick for a moment. The instinctive antidote was action, and I decided to attack the houses from a flank, making a detour to our right and taking advantage of every rise in the ground. When about 100 yards from the houses we rushed them. I shouted to the men to scatter into the different houses and dashed into one, revolver in hand. Not a German was found. Either they had seen us and retired, or else they had never occupied the houses but had been firing at us from other 'hidden machine-gun nests'. Rather relieved, we lined the road. The main thing was to advance, whether we met Germans or not, and that we were doing.[22]

Lieutenant Carroll Carstairs, 3rd Grenadier Guards, 2nd Guards Brigade, Guards Division

After the sudden crash of a shell, the deadly chatter of machine-gun fire, a cautious advance to contact, it seemed that the German rearguard had evaporated before them. The ground was ideal for defence with a series of buildings and thick hedges interspersed with open ground that provided a clear field of fire for the defenders.

We came across an empty trench, and finally to another field. Here we found a gap in the hedge. We went through and found ourselves at once under direct machine gun fire 200 yards from our left front. We could see the Germans and opened fire with rifles and Lewis gun. Meanwhile I thought to attack it at the same time from a flank, and leading a detachment to my left started along the hedge. I had hardly run 20 yards, however, when I was hit and fell forward into the beginning of a trench a foot deep. Here I lay for perhaps an hour. The pain was in the right hip. Gunther ran out to me. As I looked round he fell and I saw the rip at the back of his jacket where the bullet had gone out. He died almost at once. A private soldier shot through both arms fell at the same time, and together we lay until the battle had gone on ahead and stretcher bearers turned up. I was in too much pain to be picked up, and dragged myself on to the stretcher.[23]

Lieutenant Carroll Carstairs, 3rd Grenadier Guards, 2nd Guards Brigade, Guards Division

As he had feared, Second Lieutenant Geoffrey Gunther[24] had indeed fought his last battle. For Carstairs it would be touch and go, but he would survive his wounds to write one of the classic memoirs of Great War literature, A *Generation Missing*.

One of the most interesting operations on the Third Army front was the attack by the New Zealand Division to capture Le Quesnoy, which required a considerable degree of tactical flexibility in difficult circumstances. This picture-postcard fortified town was still encircled with a set of star-shaped Vauban ramparts, with a series of additional detached bastions and (mostly dry) moats culminating in a final high brick wall with protruding redoubts stationed every 200 yards, which would allow a deadly flanking fire from machine guns. It could have been blown away by the British artillery, but, as many of the French civilian population were still in residence, it was impossible to contemplate a frontal assault behind the usual deluge of shells. As such, Le Quesnoy represented a serious obstacle, so a plan of envelopment was devised and assigned to the New Zealand Rifle Brigade.

The enemy was holding strong positions in front of the town, mainly on the railway line, which crossed our whole frontage. We had first to storm and capture these positions before we reached the town. This first effort yielded several hundred prisoners as the enemy was holding out in considerable strength. Each Battalion then proceeded steadily and surely to invest the town. It was completely surrounded by 8 am and then our men manoeuvred forward from position to position, behind trees, mounds, outbuildings, anything that would give concealment from which fire could be brought to bear upon the garrison. The advance of our men in the early morning was covered by the usual field artillery barrage, one gun to 30 yards upon which was superimposed the fire from twelve 6" medium and sixteen light trench mortars, and in addition, smoke and burning oil were projected on the ramparts. The ramparts presented a vertical face of brickwork 50 feet high, having grass-covered mounds on top, and completely surrounded by a wide deep moat, which fortunately was empty except for a small running stream. The enemy had field guns, *minenwerfer*, and dozens of machine guns mounted on, in and around the ramparts and these had to be put out of action before the assault could be made.[25]

Brigadier General Herbert Hart, Headquarters, 3rd New Zealand (Rifle) Brigade, New Zealand Division

Although the walls were to be heavily bombarded, no shells were aimed to fall inside the town itself.

About midday the effect of our fire began to make itself felt and several attempts were made to steal into the town. One man tried to crawl up a tree, which had fallen against the wall, and a few others tried to rush a bridge, but failed. Shortly afterwards, this bridge was blown up by the enemy to prevent any similar attempt being repeated. Later, three of the prisoners captured that morning were sent into the town from various points to demand the surrender of the place, and a message making a similar demand was dropped from an aeroplane. Before any reply was received however, one storming party succeeded in getting a scaling ladder into position against a part of the ramparts.[26]

Brigadier General Herbert Hart, Headquarters, 3rd New Zealand (Rifle) Brigade, New Zealand Division

The New Zealanders were forced back to the methodology of old-fashioned siege warfare. They deployed a mass of heavy small-arms fire, by about 12.00 successfully reducing the amount of German fire emanating from the walls. This gave Second Lieutenant Leslie Averill, the intelligence officer of the 3rd New Zealand Rifle Brigade, his chance, and he moved forward to reconnoitre a possible route through the bastions and up on to the ramparts.

Fortunately, the possibility of wall climbing had been foreseen and a ladder had been provided by the engineers. The CO was anxious that these bastions should be explored and so, with five to six men, I put the ladder against the wall, we climbed it and drew up the ladder behind us. We took the ladder down on the third and sloping grassy side of this first bastion only to find a similar fortification straight ahead of us. The wall climbing of this second bastion had to be repeated and from the top of this outlying rampart I could see that we could now approach the main and final wall of this well-fortified town. The 30-foot ladder was too short to reach from the bottom of the moat to the top of the final wall but there was one place where the ladder could be placed to reach the top. This was on a narrow stone bridge, about a foot wide, which spanned the moat and was connected with a sluicegate. After crossing this bridge and sluicegate a narrow ledge ran for some 10 yards beside the wall to an arched opening, giving entrance to the town, but which – needless to say – had been completely blocked by the enemy to deny us access through the wall. It was only on this narrow wall above the sluicegate that the ladder could reach the top.[27]

Second Lieutenant Leslie Averill, 4th New Zealand Rifle Brigade, 3rd New Zealand (Rifle) Brigade, New Zealand Division

After returning to report progress and the possibilities to his colonel, Averill and Second Lieutenant H. W. Kerr returned to lead a small assault party from Kerr's platoon up the ladder, covered by lashings of Lewis gun fire sweeping along the parapet in that section of the walls. Averill went first, expecting at any moment to hear the rattle of a German machine gun, or the blast of a grenade, but there was no sign of resistance from the walls above and he reached the top safely at about 16.00. All he could see was two Germans running off in a panic-stricken manner and a pair of abandoned machine guns overlooking the moat. The bulk of the German soldiers in the locality had scuttled off to take shelter in a underground chamber concealed beneath the ramparts without making any further resistance. Averill's small incursion was all it took to crack

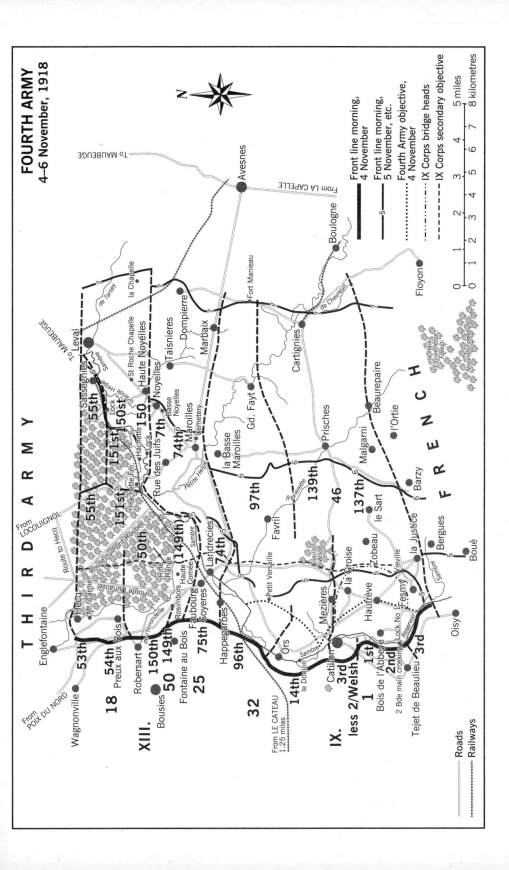

FOURTH ARMY
4–6 November, 1918

Front line morning, 4 November

Front line morning, 5 November, etc.

Fourth Army objective, 4 November

IX Corps bridge heads

IX Corps secondary objective

0 1 2 3 4 5 miles

0 1 2 3 4 5 6 7 8 kilometres

To MAUBEUGE

From LA CAPELLE

Avesnes

Boulogne

Fort Manieu

Floyon

de Chevreuil

Dompierre

Marbaix

Cartignies

Beaurepaire

l'Ortie

la Haie Equiverlesse forest

Nouvion forest

Taisnieres

Noyelles

Haute Noyelles

Basse Noyelles

Cemetery

Maroilles

la Basse Maroilles

Gd. Fayt

Prisches

Magarni

Barzy

FRENCH

St Roche Chapelle

la Chapelle

de Tarsy

To MAUBEUGE

To Leval

Sassegnies

55th

150st

150st

150

7th

74th

Rue des Juifs

Hachette Fm

Lock

Lock

Grande Helpe

Petite Helpe

Sambre

55th

151st

151st

50th

(149th)

74th

Landrecies

97th

139th

46

137th

le Sart

la Justice

Bergues

Boué

From LOCQUIGNOL

53th

54th

150th

50 149th

25

32

18

XIII.

IX.

less 2/Welsh

1

3rd

1st

2nd

3rd

Englefontaine

Preux aux Bois

Robersart

Bousies

Fontaine au Bois

Wagnonville

From POIX DU NORD

From LE CATEAU
1.25 miles

Hecq

Mt Carmel

Route du Pont Roullier

Rifle Range

Rosimbos

Faubourg

Comée

Soyeres

Haute

Happegarbes

96th

14th

le Donjon

Catillon

Bois de l'Abbeye

2 Bde main crossing

Lock No 1

Reservoir

Tejet de Beaulieu

Oisy

Route to Hecq

de l'Hirondelle

Route du Nauvel

From LOCUUIGNOL

Favril

Petit Versailles

Touillon Wood

Mezières

la Groise

Hautrêve

Fesmy

Vieville

Zobeau

la Justice

Reyterette

75th

Ors

Sambre

Sambre

T H I R D   A R M Y

Roads

Railways

open the fortress and he was followed by the rest of his battalion – all climbing up that single ladder. Once the façade had been cracked the mass surrender of the garrison swiftly followed.

> They quickly put several gun crews out of action, whereupon the remainder held up their hands, followed soon afterwards by the surrender of the garrison of about 1,000. 1,600 French civilians were in the town – women, children and old men – and they gave a wonderful demonstration of welcome to our men. They cheered and laughed and wept with joy, clasping all and sundry around the neck, kissing and hugging them with joy at being liberated. I entered the town at about that time and it was indeed a very stirring scene, one not to be appreciated and realised except by those actually taking part. The position appears so very strong I marvelled at what had been accomplished. The men showed great gallantry, keenness and determination throughout and their skill and cunning in using cover and concealment was equal to that one reads of in Red Indian warfare.[28]

> Brigadier General Herbert Hart, Headquarters, 3rd New Zealand (Rifle) Brigade, New Zealand Division

This was a major achievement by the New Zealand Division, who went on to secure all their objectives, pushing deep into the Forêt de Mormal. In just 24 hours they had advanced 5 miles, captured some 2,450 prisoners and an impressive 60 guns. One slightly sour note was struck due to the death of Major Hugh McKinnon, commanding the 2nd Wellington Regiment. He had been killed alongside his adjutant by a shell, but afterwards it was found that his corpse had been stripped of all personal valuables – 'ratted' as the Kiwis called it.

> Our padre spoke very strongly and feelingly about the desecration of our dead. When the body of the CO was brought in yesterday morning, the puttees and boots had been 'ratted' and his pockets rifled. This was a beastly act and is decried by all. Though he was a 'hard' man and not loved by the men, he was a game soldier and as

such should have been respected in his long last sleep. His death[29] is a great loss to the Battalion.[30]

Private Neil Ingram, 2nd Wellington Regiment, 2nd New Zealand Brigade, New Zealand Division

Major Hugh McKinnon had landed with the Wellingtons at Gallipoli back in April in 1915. After surviving so much deadly fighting, he died just a week from safety.

Not far to the south, the 37th Division were attacking towards the villages of Louvignies-Quesnoy and Jolimetz, before looking to penetrate the western edge of the Forêt de Mormal. During these operations, the 13th Rifle Brigade was required to attack a railway line running along an embankment into a cutting, before moving on to take a couple of strongly held orchards at Louvignies-Quesnoy. Here was an illustration of how many battalions responded to the challenges of open warfare, capable as they now were of independent action, not just by companies, but right down to platoon attacks split into three sections and manoeuvring to great effect under the command of their experienced officers and NCOs. A different set of skills from trench warfare was required: the ability to navigate across open country, to keep going despite intermittent fire, to swiftly adapt a plan to the circumstances found, and throughout to try and maintain communications back to headquarters. Individual initiative could be at a premium, it being vital to seize the moment to resolve a situation before the opposition could gather their thoughts. In command of 15 Platoon, D Company, 13th Rifle Brigade was Lieutenant Richard Blaker who, at 39, was a good deal older than most officers. He had already had a successful career as a county cricketer playing for Kent (for whom he had scored 120 runs in just 75 minutes against Gloucestershire in 1905). Blaker was no fool. Although his unit had been supplied with good aerial reconnaissance photos, he had personally carefully reconnoitred the intended 'jumping-off' positions in No Man's Land in front of the 8th Lincolnshire Regiment who were holding the front line. When the attack was launched, he gave a superb display of individual initiative.

At last I managed to get the section in position, and just before 5.30 am the barrage started. It was supposed to land on the railway, but it turned out that it was about 6 yards too far and went over the railway. It was a grand sight. The whole front along the railway seemed to be one vast sheet of flame, and earth, etc., was flying about. We immediately advanced so as to get up close to the barrage, so that when it lifted we could be on the enemy before he could resist, but unfortunately there was a thick hedge with barbed wire between us and the cutting, which was not touched by the barrage, and when I got there it was difficult to see any opening, as it was still dark, but I ran along the hedge and found a small gap near the ground and scrambled through on hands and knees. Sergeant Packer was just ahead. As I went down the cutting – which was 15 foot – two Germans came out of a dugout almost under my feet. I managed to kill them both, then I went over the single line and a German officer came out of a dugout and fired at me from 5 yards but missed. I then killed him and went up the bank the other side and found my Sergeant there firing at some Germans who were running away towards the orchards. I could see the outlines of the orchards about 180 to 200 yards away across a turnip field, and as there was no cover I at once made up my mind that if we went across the open we would be wiped out – in my opinion – before getting there.[31]

Lieutenant Richard Blaker, 13th Rifle Brigade, 11th Brigade, 37th Division

He resolved to go it alone. While Packer brought the men up to the railway line, he pushed on towards the orchards, relying on the fading darkness to be enough to conceal a single figure where a platoon would have been obvious. He also resolved to take his chances with the British creeping barrage – to catch the Germans still sheltering from the line of shell bursts moving towards them.

I had to walk through our barrage, which was going at the rate of 100 yards per four minutes, but although I had some extremely narrow shaves and a very unpleasant time I managed to get there safely. I had studied the positions where the enemy were likely to put machine guns and I now found this very useful. It was still fairly dark but beginning to get light. I immediately saw in a corner of an orchard a place where it was practically certain there would be a machine gun and got there without being seen, and my surmise was right as I got right up to a machine-gun dugout with two Germans on the look-out, but they had missed seeing me in the dark and also no doubt they didn't expect anyone so soon and were doing more sheltering that watching. On seeing me they immediately tried to put their hands down for their revolvers, but I killed them both before they could do so, as I was right close on them; thereupon yells came out of the dugout and I shouted, 'Come out!' and out came five pretty scared looking Germans with hands up. I motioned them to go back through the barrage towards our lines, and after a slight hesitation, they had to do so. I then went to another likely place on my front and managed to do exactly the same as before to another machine-gun crew. I then looked about but could see no more machine guns on my front.[32]

Lieutenant Richard Blaker, 13th Rifle Brigade, 11th Brigade, 37th Division

The remaining Germans that Blaker found in and around the orchard put up no resistance, clearly unnerved by the power of the barrage. He swiftly disarmed them and sent them back. All the fight had gone out of them and few – if any – tried to escape. Unarmed, and in the middle of their enemies on a deadly battlefield, they had little choice but to obey. Most were delighted to be out of the war.

It was practically light now and the barrage was very hot. I had some extraordinary narrow escapes – being blown along about 5 yards by a shell which pitched very near indeed and half-deafened me for a minute, but on the whole I considered that the method of getting onto the enemy while they were still sheltering seemed so successful that it was worthwhile going on a bit and risking it, especially as my men were coming along. So on I went disarming and sending back Germans here and there – but there were not so many beyond the orchards – until I came to the main road leading from Louvignies to Le Quesnoy, and on this road I came on a solitary house standing right on the road. I came from the back of it and went round to the front, where there was no door, and peeped inside a room which opened into the road and saw there a crowd of Germans, some sitting down and some standing. I don't know who was more surprised – they or I. Anyway I managed to pull myself together a bit quicker than they did and advanced just under the doorway holding a Mills bomb in my left hand and my revolver in my right, the only thing I could think of to say was '*Kamerad!*' and so I said it, at the same time menacing them with my revolver, they didn't seem very willing to surrender, so I repeated '*Kamerad*', and to my surprise and delight they '*Kameraded*'! Two officers and twenty-eight other ranks. Both officers and three of the other ranks had Iron Cross ribbons on![33]

Lieutenant Richard Blaker, 13th Rifle Brigade, 11th Brigade, 37th Division

Blaker pushed on, gathering more prisoners. But he was awfully reliant on the Germans all around him remaining quiescent.

At last to my relief I saw one of our men dodging along just by the road, and then another. I waved to them and think they saw me as they went back, and then the rest came along onto the road about 100 yards off with Second Lieutenant Dion, 'A' Company, and Sergeant Packer, together with about fourteen men of my Platoon. I immediately marched the prisoners up to them and sent them off to the rear under escort and told Second Lieutenant Dion that there were some revolvers and arms in the house and he went off with a few men and got them. I have in my possession now one of the German officers' revolvers from these![34]

Lieutenant Richard Blaker, 13th Rifle Brigade, 11th Brigade, 37th Division

As it turned out, the main risk to Blaker had been from the British barrage and indeed, some pieces of shrapnel had scored across the back of his leather jerkin, just missing his spine – and he also had a hole blown through the top of a torch he had strapped to his belt. His initiative had probably saved the lives of many of his men, for the neighbouring companies suffered bad casualties; indeed the battalion still lost 157 killed, wounded or missing that day. An extremely strong position had been taken through a combination of Blaker's imaginative tactics and the Germans' evident poor morale and unwillingness to make a fight of it.

On the Fourth Army front, the XIII Corps was directed to advance on Locquignol. Private Harry Bashford played a small part in this attack: a quote from his oral history interview recorded in 1987 gives us an idea, not of tactics, but of the unbearable poignancy of the loss of friends so close to the end of the war.

> A white tape had been laid, well in advance of our front line positions, and at the appointed time we crawled out and waited for our barrage to open up. When it did, all hell was let loose. Our instruction as always was to keep as close as possible to the creeping barrage. It was like walking behind a wall of fire. What effect it had on the enemy you could only guess, but it was the nearest I ever came to losing my nerve. Under these conditions, there is bound to be some confusion and I got mixed with another section, and later saw some of my platoon evidently caught by machine-gun fire, lying in a little semi-circle. The gun that had caught them was about 100 yards away and slumped over it the gunner, with his face cut clean away; not a pretty sight, and one not easily forgotten. It was here in our last engagement that one of our men suffered a stomach wound from which he had no chance of recovery. From the first days of war until the last, men will die, and to those concerned an equal misfortune, and yet there must be more sympathy for those who so nearly finish the course, but fall at the last fence. As far as we were concerned, the war was now over.[35]
>
> Private Harry Bashford, 2nd Bedfordshire Regiment, 54th Brigade, 18th Division

The coruscating emotional impact cannot be forgotten in analysing these horrendous battles.

Next in line to the south, the IX Corps of the Fourth Army was faced with the task of forcing a crossing over the Sambre-Oise Canal. Two bridgeheads were to be attempted by the 1st and 32nd Divisions respectively. At 05.45 on 4 November, the 2nd Royal Sussex Regiment moved forward in the pouring rain and thick mist to capture a key lock south of Catillon. They would be reliant on help from the 409th Field Company, Royal Engineers.

> We knew the end was very near. When dawn broke, we could see the outline of the canal and we could see the trees. We knew what we were up against then – we knew the Germans had got a machine gun in the lock house. Before we got on to the canal itself we had to get across a dyke and they had got duckboard bridges that we were supposed to cross on, but they were too short when the first chaps got there. We were the second line. So they were waiting for the next lot of duckboards to come up – all bunched up – all piled up on the bank. Over came a salvo of shells amongst us – that's where we lost a lot of men. Then at last, the engineers managed to get these longer boards on which we got across. Then they threw the bigger ones across the lock itself. I had a bullet go right through our Lewis gun that I was carrying. As we were going across I heard a 'Ping!' but during all the rattle of machine guns and shells I didn't take much notice. I always carried something in front of me and I was carrying this gun – that bullet would have gone through me if it hadn't been for the Lewis gun. They found out where the strongpoint was and they put two or three shells through it – and that's when the Germans gave up.[36]

Private Walter Grover, 2nd Royal Sussex Regiment, 2nd Brigade, 1st Division

Lieutenant Colonel Dudley Johnson was a key figure in the final stages of the attack. When his men hesitated and fell back in the face of a withering fire, he reorganised them and led them forward to achieve the objective. He would be awarded the VC for his actions. Once the brittle German defence had been cracked, resistance collapsed and the bridgehead was soon secured, so that the 1st Division could push on to their next objectives.

The other bridgeheads across the canal was to be forced by the 32nd Division. Here the 16th Lancashire Fusiliers and 2nd Manchester Regiment were two of the battalions charged with making the initial dangerous assault. The commanding officer of the 16th Lancashires was a fascinating personality: Lieutenant Colonel James Marshall. His pre-war life was a little murky, but he had ended up buying horses for the army in Argentina before enlisting with the Irish Guards. By 1918 he was in his prime as a soldier, much decorated and thriving despite suffering numerous wounds in various hard-fought battles. He was more than willing to lead from the front when necessary – and he was emphatically not a man to suffer fools. Captain Gordon Potts had been recently appointed to the challenging role of being his adjutant.

> Marshall's own reputation with the division is probably best illustrated by the fact that he was asked to do the reconnaissance of the divisional front by the divisional staff. This was surely a tribute to his courage and experience as an infantry battalion commander. One would have thought the staff would have themselves studied the front before preparing the orders.[37]
>
> Captain Gordon Potts, 16th Lancashire Fusiliers, 96th Brigade, 32nd Division

It was therefore an unwelcome surprise when Marshall and Potts saw the role the staff planned for the 16th Lancashire Fusiliers in the attack.

> The GSO1 of the division came to battalion headquarters and I well remember listening to the discussion between Colonel Marshall and the GSO1, at which Marshall criticised the orders on the grounds that on his own battalion front it was going to be virtually impossible for the attack to succeed at all, as the troops had first to cross the Sambre-Oise Canal, and then climb a gently rising slope, which was obviously pitted with machine-gun positions.[38]
>
> Captain Gordon Potts, 16th Lancashire Fusiliers, 96th Brigade, 32nd Division

The response of the GSO1 stuck in the memory of Captain Potts.

'You will find the weight of the artillery behind you will blot out all the opposition!' Now, to my mind, this was an extremely bad thing for any staff officer to say to any infantry battalion commander. It is never true and the suggestion quite clearly was that the infantry hadn't to do anything at all except walk behind the barrage. The upshot was the attack was an entire failure.[39]

Captain Gordon Potts, 16th Lancashire Fusiliers, 96th Brigade, 32nd Division

At 05.50, the 16th Lancashire Fusiliers rushed forward to the canal bank, where they provided covering fire to the efforts of the 218th Field Company, Royal Engineers, to get two bridges across the canal. It proved a disaster as one bridge was hit by a shell and the other covered by German machine-gun fire. Private Samuel Hudson was badly hit.

I was one of the ones who did get across the bridge. The bridge *was* fastened on the German side, but received a direct hit from a shell just in front of me as I rushed across. I jumped for the side, but was hit by machine-gun fire and fell into the water near the bank. I was picked up by the Canadian stretcher-bearers late on 6th November and lost my leg with other wounds.[40]

Private Samuel Hudson, 16th Lancashire Fusiliers, 96th Brigade, 32nd Division

Marshall himself rushed forward, organising parties to repair the bridge and then led a renewed, but equally doomed, assault. Throughout he demonstrated the great leadership qualities and courage which would win him a Victoria Cross. Sadly, it would be posthumous as he was fatally wounded at the head of his men.[41] The headquarters of 96th Brigade then issued orders that the 16th Lancashire Fusiliers were to sidestep to the right, moving behind the 2nd Manchesters to cross the temporarily repaired bridge that had been captured by the 1st Dorsetshire Regiment near Ors. Here Potts himself ran out of luck.

I began to prepare new orders with the object of recovering our objective from the flank. I was wounded at that moment. For-tunately for me I was quickly carried across the stone bridge to an advance aid post nearby where there was a 'T' Model Ford converted to an ambulance with space for two stretchers. I was eventually X-rayed – and the bullet which had hit me in the back and was still inside was discovered – partly in the left kidney. I was evacuated to Rouen where the operation to remove the bullet was duly performed. The bullet had obviously hit me near the end of its flight and had turned down, and turned over. The base of the bullet was in the kidney.[42]

Captain Gordon Potts, 16th Lancashire Fusiliers, 96th Brigade, 32nd Division

In amidst the fighting, newly promoted Lieutenant Wilfred Owen of the 2nd Manchesters was killed as he, too, attempted to lead his men across the canal. This is insignificant in the context of the battle, but Owen[43] had a growing reputation as a war poet, and his death so close to the end of the war would resonate deeply in post-war years. Indeed, poems like *Anthem for Doomed Youth*, *Strange Meeting* and *Dulce et Decorum Est* have come to define one popular view of the Great War. What really mattered at the time was that, despite heavy casualties, the Fourth Army managed to breast the Sambre-Oise Canal to create a strong bridgehead some 15 miles long and up to 3½ miles deep, capturing some 4,000 German prisoners and 80 guns in the course of the battle.

Although the Battle of the Sambre had been a great triumph, many individuals paid the price for that success. On the First Army Front to the north, the thoughtful Second Lieutenant Alan Bullock was with the 1/4th (Royal Fusilier) London Regiment as they went into the attack at 06.00. They advanced some 2,000 yards across stubble fields to cross the Aunelle river at Sebourquiaux, before gaining the higher ground some 500 yards east of the village. As the leading troops began to approach Sebourquiaux the cloaking dank mist cleared, leaving them exposed to heavy German machine-gun fire. Not unnaturally, the troops dashed forward seeking shelter in the village – at which point the Germans lashed down a heavy artillery barrage. Despite their best efforts they could not make any more progress and by the end of the day the village was in ruins. The battalion was relieved by the London Scottish, but, somewhere along the way, Alan

Bullock was killed.[44] As he had feared, 'Life and limb are not worth a moment's purchase'.[45]

The Allied attack was a resounding success as the First Army, Third Army, Fourth Army and the French First Army all made significant progress. Sometimes there were hold-ups, which meant serious casualties, but for the most part the obstacles were sidestepped or overcome. The Hermann II Line, such as it was, had been breached. Next day, 5 November, the advance continued apace and gradually came to have the characteristics of a pursuit. At this stage, individual officers were expected and trusted to assess and act quickly on a situation as they saw it.

Meanwhile, the Whippet tanks of the 6th Battalion, Tank Corps, contributed to the advance of the 3rd Guards Brigade along the northern border area of the Mormal Forest in what would be the last tank action of the war. Tanks were scarce resources and the Whippets had been conserved to help disrupt the German retreat rather than waste them in the initial assault. Once a bridge across the River Bultiaux had been secured near the village of Preux, six Whippets pushed forward, cooperating with the 2nd Scots Guards as they moved towards Bermeries and Buvignies. Two broke down almost immediately, but the Whippets made themselves useful firing short bursts of machine-gun fire along the hedges and railway embankments, putting two machine guns out of action. Meanwhile, the Whippet commanded by Lieutenant H. F. Jones brought a German battery under fire. All told, they materially assisted the advance of the 2nd Scots Guards on Buvignies, but this achievement was relatively small beer on a hot day of fighting.

Late on the night of 5 November, the Germans were left with no option but to order another full-scale retreat, this time falling back towards the Antwerp-Meuse Line. Crown Prince Rupprecht summarised their predicament.

> The heavy fighting of 4 November on the fronts of Second and Seventeenth armies caused heavy wastage in personnel. Units on the front line, whose combat power had already been seriously reduced before the battle, have mostly been weakened to the limit by the losses they suffered in this heavy fighting. It is no longer possible to

supply combat-capable reserves to the front. The commanders of Seventeenth and Second Armies dutifully report that, because of exhaustion, low unit strengths, and particularly the limited steadiness of their men, they are not capable of withstanding a new major offensive. There is a danger that a new large-scale attack would break through, or at least cause us heavy losses, and that we would have to start the move to the Antwerp-Meuse position in considerable disorder.[46]

Crown Prince Rupprecht, Headquarters, Army Group Rupprecht

By this time very few of his divisions were fit to fight. German resistance declined, although there were still vicious little encounters with determined rearguards. The weather was awful and Captain Joseph Maclean, 1st Cameronians, sums up the depressing conditions of service that must have sapped the morale of both sides in the days that followed.

You have no idea of what the men have had to endure in discomfort, cold and wet, and general misery. We kicked off on Monday morning – so did the rain, which started as a steady drizzle, then increased to a downpour that lasted intermittently for three days and nights. As our fighting equipment includes a sleeveless leather jerkin, but no greatcoat, we were all soaked through right at the start. The approaches to the river which we had to cross became a marsh that took us up to the knees in water, so we were distinctly wet. So were the rations, and altogether I thought half of us might die from exposure, but it's wonderful what one can stand. During the three days' fighting I had no shelter from weather, day or night, except a waterproof sheet, and slept (or tried to) on the ground – on the first and third nights at the edge of a wood, and on the second in a muddy hole where we had 'dug in' in the middle of a ploughed field. However, we survived it, and came through all right. My food was of the most ragtime description – wet bread and intensely filthy cheese, and once or twice a mess tin of tea made over a candle.[47]

Captain Joseph Maclean, 1st Cameronians (Scottish Rifles), 19th Brigade, 33rd Division

What perhaps helped his men endure was the knowledge that at last it was undeniable that they were winning and the end was nigh.

> My company was in front at the beginning, and succeeded in taking its objective after fair resistance from machine-gun fire and field guns, at close range. It was sufficiently exciting. During the advance I got a bullet right into my respirator (which hangs in front of the chest). How it didn't go through I don't know, but I suppose it was turned by some of the metal parts of the respirator. Anyway, it's the nearest thing I've had. On our way back we crossed the river on a pontoon bridge which was being used for heavy transport and guns; but going out we crossed it on planks and duck boards. It really is marvellous how all the branches of the army follow up behind the infantry so quickly. Already some of these small towns and villages look as if we had been in them for the duration.[48]
>
> Captain Joseph Maclean, 1st Cameronians (Scottish Rifles), 19th Brigade, 33rd Division

Yet some men were – apparently – still desperate to get involved at the sharp end before the dawn of peace. One such was Lieutenant Alex Wilkinson. He had already been wounded twice, but managed to get back to his unit just in time for one last battle. In a letter to his father, Wilkinson expressed himself with considerable vigour in describing how his company was assigned to lead a Coldstream Guards attack on a village:

> We were right on top of the Huns before he could get his machine guns to work and we got a nice few prisoners and machine guns straight away – the same that had fired at us the night before. And a nice few Huns were killed here too. I had sworn to shoot the first one I saw, but I could not bring myself to it. I am a sentimental ass. Having sent the prisoners back, on we went at a tremendous pace, capturing numerous prisoners and machine guns as we went – and killing a certain number too. The men were perfectly splendid, and showed amazing skill in the use of their Lewis Guns and rifles.

Thanks to that we had very little machine-gun fire – before the Huns could do any harm everyone was pouring lead in their direction. I have never seen greater skill in the issue of weapons, nor a keener fighting spirit. Truly it was wonderful. But what I call the battle discipline left a great deal to be desired. The men got out of their formation unless carefully watched, and were inclined to lose direction. And too much time was wasted searching prisoners not only for arms but also for souvenirs. Even so it was amusing to see practically every man smoking a cigar after we passed the first objective. The battle was the best I have ever had, and I would not have missed it for anything. Thank goodness, I got back in time for it. I was a little anxious that it might all be over too soon. I don't mind so much of the war does end now.[49]

Captain Alexander Wilkinson, 2nd Coldstream Guards, 1st Guards Brigade, Guards Division

Many years later, one of his fellow officers, Captain Carlos Blacker, wrote a letter to Wilkinson, which expressed a more mature reflection on events that day. The difference in approach is fascinating.

I remember standing by you when you took off. You had been stamping your feet and saying loudly, so that the troops on each flank could hear, 'We are going to have a dammed fine battle this morning, aren't we?' If I may say so, I am glad that you did not kill those Germans who were not resisting. In my position, I should have done what you did. I disliked the idea of killing Germans – for three reasons. I had lived in Freiburg for short stretches before 1914 – my earliest memories are of Freiburg – and happy ones they are. I feel that if, by another dispensation of fate, I had been born and reared in Germany, I would have taken part in the war on the other side, where I would have as little to do with the outbreak as I had on our side. And lastly, I couldn't help feeling that dead Germans had mothers, wives, sisters etc, who mourned their loss no less than dead Englishmen. The dead man's relatives reacted as my mother reacted when my brother was killed. I never consciously killed a German, and looking back, I am glad that I didn't. The war would have been easier for me if I had your spirit.[50]

Captain Carlos Blacker, 2nd Coldstream Guards, 1st Guards Brigade, Guards Division

One wonders what Alexander Wilkinson thought when in later life he read the letters he had written as a youth?

The war may have been almost over, but the creaky wheels of military justice had turned too quickly for two British soldiers, Private Ernest Jackson and Private Louis Harris, who were both executed on 7 November. Jackson had been called up in July 1916 and served with the 24th Royal Fusiliers on the Western Front. His service record was adequate, until on 13 April 1917 he absconded from his unit for 28 hours, before he was picked up in St Pol. Unusually, he was then sentenced to two years imprisonment with hard labour, and then released in August 1918 after serving sixteen months. Undeterred by this experience, Jackson went missing again on 29 September, then, after being arrested, actually deserted while the 24th Royal Fusiliers were in the support lines at Noyelles on 4 October.

> I left because I could not stand the treatment I was receiving. I wanted to get away from everything. On joining the battalion after doing imprisonment the Company Sergeant Major, in front of everyone, called me a 'gaol bird' and said he would make my life a misery. I have been looked down on by everyone and that is the cause of me being here today. Both my father and mother died in an asylum. I suffer from the same mental trouble caused by worries.[51]

Private Ernest Jackson, 24th Royal Fusiliers, 5th Brigade, 2nd Division

He was soon picked up at Doullens and faced a court martial at which he was sentenced to death. The sentence was confirmed and at 06.10 on 7 November he was executed at St Python.[52] Just a few minutes later the shots rang out at 06.29 to end the short life of Private Louis Harris[53] of the 10th West Yorkshire Regiment at Locquignol. Harris had a record bespattered with offences since he had first joined his battalion in France in July 1916. On 2 September 1918, he was a member of a Lewis gun team moving forward during an attack on Rocquigny. Harris deliberately hung back, then dumped his kit and made his way to the rear areas. Next day he was arrested at Martinpuich. Harris had no defence acting for him and he failed to cross-examine the witnesses called against him. He may have considered his case hopeless, but the judicial process was surely weighted against him. In a damning assessment, Lieutenant Colonel William Gibson referred to his fighting value as 'Nil'.[54] The sentence was confirmed at every level – and so died the last man executed by the British Army for desertion.

IN GERMANY THE GOVERNMENT WAS COLLAPSING. Max von Baden had struggled to make Kaiser Wilhelm II realise that he could not remain on the throne if Germany was to have any chance of gaining the peace it so desperately needed. But the Kaiser was intransigent, insisting that the army needed him as Supreme War Lord to maintain any cohesion. The Kaiser left Berlin and moved to Spa, ostensibly to be alongside the Headquarters of the Supreme Army Command, but more probably influenced by the spread of revolutionary fervour on the streets of Berlin. Here he continued to refuse all demands that he abdicate to clear the way to an Armistice. He found little cheer at Spa. In fact, Gröner was almost cruel in advising the Kaiser to go to the front:

> Not to review troops or to confer decorations, but to look for death. If he were killed it would be the finest death possible. If he were wounded the feelings of the German people would completely change towards him.[55]
>
> General Wilhelm Gröner, Headquarters, Supreme Army Command

Even Hindenburg had now accepted that the Kaiser had to go, although he favoured exile in Holland rather than the martyr's death offered by Gröner. But the Kaiser was adamant – he would not abdicate. On 9 November, Max von Baden finally resolved the matter by unilaterally announcing the Kaiser's abdication and at the same time handing over the poisoned chalice of his position of Chancellor to the leader of the Social Democratic Party, Friedrich Ebert. Wilhelm II might rage, but the deed was done: Germany was a republic. The deposed Supreme Warlord was placed on a train and sent into exile in Holland. The road to peace was unblocked at last.

During these last fraught days, Wilson had sent a further diplomatic note on 6 November which indicated that the allied governments would allow representatives of the German government to meet with Foch to be told the terms of the Armistice. This was accepted by the Germans. Because of his experiences while on duty with the Royal Engineer wireless section attached to Haig's advance headquarters train, Private Edgar Cranmer believed he had a privileged perspective of the imminent Armistice.

> A German station came in and offered me a message. He'd been waiting for me! Of course, it was in German – that didn't matter – it was sent in Morse and I took it down. I signalled to my driver, get the Sergeant, because the Germans would never send more than eight words a minute, you could go to sleep taking his message! I said, 'It's Jerry!' He said, 'What have you had to drink?' He put the spare headphones on and he nodded to me. I finally took this message and none of us could read German so he said, 'All right, I'll take it up to the train!' He went up to the train, found the Intelligence Officer and he read it and said, 'Hmm, yes! In a few words, Sergeant, it's Jerry asking for an Armistice!' We then had to transmit a message to General Foch, called up the Eiffel Tower, call sign 'FL', we knew that, called him up, offered him this message. He took it then we could listen and hear him retransmitting to General Foch's headquarters.[56]

> Private Edgar Cranmer, Royal Engineer Signal Service, General Headquarters, BEF

At the Grand Quartier Général of the French Army the news was received with joy by the French staff officers.

I was going upstairs to the Third Bureau about 4 o'clock in the afternoon, when I met General Duval. He said, 'I am going to tell you the most amazing news. Pull yourself together!' I looked at him in astonishment, his eyes were shining and his hands trembling slightly. He continued. 'The Germans have determined to ask for an Armistice; a message from Berne informs us that they have made tentative inquiries of the Federal Government whether they would act as intermediaries.' I followed him into his room and he showed me the message. In spite of the innumerable false reports of this nature which had cropped up since the beginning of the war, the message was couched in such precise language that it demanded consideration. If only it were true! The rumour spread through GQG with unrestrained delight. Nothing else was spoken of, and we could hardly wait for the morrow to hear full details.[57]

Lieutenant Jean de Pierrefeu, Grand Quartier Général

Once Wilson's note was accepted, the composition of the German Armistice Commission was swiftly decided: it would be led by Matthias Erzberger (leader of the Catholic Party and Minister without Portfolio), General Erich von Gündell (Headquarters, Supreme Army Command), Count Oberndorff (Foreign Ministry), Captain Ernst Vanselow (German Navy) and Major General Detlev von Winterfeldt (former Military Attaché, Paris). In a manoeuvre that was entirely predictable, at the last moment von Gündell was withdrawn by the Supreme Army Command, to maintain the fiction that the army was not involved in the Armistice. On 8 November, the German delegation crossed the lines and were whisked to the meeting place in a railway carriage hidden from prying eyes in the Forest of Compiègne. Here they met the Allied team: Maréchal Ferdinand Foch, First Lord of the Admiralty, Admiral Sir Rosslyn Wemyss, Rear Admiral George Hope and General Maxime Weygand, Foch's Chief of Staff. Foch himself retained complete control of events and was determined to secure the agreed military conditions, leaving the Germans with no capability to restart hostilities.

The 'negotiations' were a painful experience for Erzberger. He had come to negotiate, but Foch was intransigent. The Germans must formally ask for an Armistice, and only then would Foch would reveal his conditions – these were set in stone and could not be altered in any meaningful manner. There would be no Armistice during the negotiations and the naval blockade would not be lifted until an actual peace treaty was signed. One quote sums it up:

> My responsibility ends at the Rhine. I have no concern with the rest of Germany. It is your affair. I would remind you that this is a military Armistice, that the war is not ended thereby, and that it is directed at preventing your nation from continuing the war. You must recollect a reply given by Bismarck in 1871, when we made a request similar to what you are making now. Bismarck then said, '*Krieg ist Krieg*', and I say to you, '*La guerre est la guerre*'.[58]
>
> Maréchal de France, Ferdinand Foch

Nothing Erzberger could say would shift Foch. In the end, Erzberger had no option, and at 05.15 on 11 November he signed the Armistice document. The Armistice would take effect from the eleventh hour of the eleventh day of the eleventh month.

RUMOURS WERE BEGINNING TO SPREAD that the war was almost over. This growing realisation was accelerated when on 9 November news reached them of the abdication of Kaiser Wilhelm II. However, it is fair to say that Brigadier General Bernard Freyberg may have been disappointed at the reception when he brought the news to the tough regulars of the 2nd Leinster Regiment.

> While on the march, the Brigadier had galloped up and yelled out, 'The war is over! The Kaiser has abdicated!' We were typically Irish and never cheered except under adverse conditions, such as shellfire and rain! Somewhat crestfallen the Brigadier rode slowly off to communicate his glad tidings to an English Battalion, who, no doubt, took the news in a different way. After we had narrowly

missed being mined at a crossroads, Private Flaherty calmly said, 'They do say the war is over!'[59]

Captain Francis Hitchcock, 2nd Leinster Regiment, 88th Brigade, 29th Division,

There was a wide variety of reactions to the possibility of peace. Many craved it, but a few still seemed to want to have their fill of killing before it was all over. Perhaps this was more common in the artillery, where they killed their opponents at a distance, over the horizon and not up close and personal, as was so often the case for the infantry.

A Bosche prisoner I spoke to yesterday told me that they all expected the war to be over in seven days. What we must do is bomb Berlin and all big towns in Germany both day and night. That will bring them to their senses quicker than anything. Meantime we will have a glorious time smashing him up – some of the finest times of my life. It's glorious to be in at the death – so to speak.[60]

Second Lieutenant Charles Bennett, 162nd Brigade Royal Field Artillery, 33rd Division

As the Germans continued to fall back towards the Antwerp-Meuse Line, the advance became more akin to a procession, not without danger, but unrecognisable to the fighting of just a few weeks before. However, in many areas over the last few days, British progress slowed to a crawl. The precarious logistical situation had finally collapsed. The already distant railheads had been left even further behind by the latest advance and the round trip for the lorries now exceeded 60 miles, which was asking far too much of worn vehicles travelling on atrocious road conditions in bad weather. The use of horse transport to bridge the gap was a poor and ineffective substitute. Crowded roads meant increasing difficulties in moving forward the medium and heavy guns – and of course the shell stocks they required. Although the advance was still under way, there was also a growing attitude that foolish risks should not be taken with the end of war so very close. With all these factors combined, many units lost contact with the Germans that were falling back in front of them. After the capture of Maubeuge on 9 November, the pursuit on the Third

Army front was left solely to the advance guards of the VI Corps, while the rest stood fast on the high ground to await the re-establishment of the supply chain.

There was little cavalry available right at the front, but what there was had a better chance of staying in touch with the German rearguards. Aware of the dangers of modern weaponry, they sought where possible to use flanking manoeuvres, coupled with sheer speed and aggression to counter the threat posed by machine guns.

> Positions were usually well concealed. But once these had been located a swift turning movement, when the country permitted it, invariably forced him to retire, sometimes with precipitation. The vital thing was to gallop fast. The comparative immunity of horsemen moving at speed, even when under machine-gun fire at close range, was strikingly shewn by the fact that in a running fight of 10 miles against an enemy who admittedly was only fighting a delaying action but who was in superior numbers we lost one man killed and one wounded together with five horses. Machine guns behind wire are fatal to cavalry; machine guns in the open are not. It is the man behind the machine gun or the rifle that matters. Rattle his nerves and you upset his aim. To rattle his nerves your attack must threaten him directly or must endanger his line of retreat.[61]
>
> Major Ralph Furse, A Squadron, King Edward's Horse

Although there was less contact on the ground, the RAF was still able to harass the retreating columns of Germans from the air. This was often a pitiless business, comparable to shooting fish in the proverbial barrel.

> We went out on a squadron sweep and found a long straight road filled with retreating German supply trains. We saw horse-drawn artillery, motor trucks, infantry and other military equipment of one kind or another. We formed a big circle and as we went down this road; we fired our machine guns, dropped out 25lb bombs. When we got through with that road it was one unbelievable scene of chaos, with dead horses, lorries and dead soldiers all over the

road. As I went down the last time to use up what was left of my ammunition and bombs, the two planes in front of me collided.

Lieutenant Richmond Viall, 46 Squadron, RAF

Low-level flying is never without risk and Second Lieutenant James Gascoyne was lucky to survive after committing a schoolboy error during the last couple of days of the war.

I was out ground strafing. I came across a village where the German troops were retreating – a whole line of transport was on a very straight street and at the end was a church tower. I was so intent in having a go at this transport I was not flying at more than about 200 feet – or less – and I foolishly went absolutely straight down this street. Suddenly there was a burst of machine gun fire right into my machine. One bullet came through the windscreen, hit my helmet, made a little hole, a mark on my head – it felt just like being hit with a brick. I put my hand up and found there was blood. I stuck my head over the side and I regained consciousness very quickly. I discovered where the firing was coming from. It was from the church tower at the bottom end of the village – at round about the height as I was flying – straight into him.[62]

Second Lieutenant James Gascoyne, 92 Squadron, RAF

By this time, almost everyone was thinking of the imminent Armistice and the chance of peace at last. But, despite the obvious temptation to evade danger, most men continued to do their duty. It is difficult not to feel great admiration for them.

The last few days before the Armistice were somewhat trying. It was impossible to keep your thoughts away from the possible termination of hostilities and all that that involved. The authorities, with what seemed a rather unnecessary lack of confidence in their troops, deluged us with advice to maintain our morale. In point of fact, there appeared no shred of evidence that anyone was in danger of losing his morale, or, for the matter of that, any particular reason why he should, even though one might be glad if the war was really over.[63]

Captain Charles Wurtzburg, 2/6th King's Liverpool Regiment, 171st Brigade, 57th Division

For the German soldiers, it was very different. True, the war might be nearly over, but often they had little awareness of the grim reality of the situation back in Germany. Leutnant Walter Rappolt had been wounded back in April 1918, while serving with the 1st Guards Foot Artillery Regiment, and had been recuperating from his wounds in Germany. It is fascinating to sense his gradual realisation that it was all over.

> I supervised the training of recruits. I was not aware of any unrest among the military. I got an order to return to the front which was dated 7 November. I sent a telegram to my parents in Hamburg telling them that I would leave for the front and asking them to see me off in Berlin. They answered that a sort of revolution that had broken out in Kiel some days ago had now spread to Hamburg, which was now under the control of a so-called Soldiers and Workers Council – and they couldn't come to see me off! I showed this telegram to my Battalion commander which was the first news he had of these things. There was no telephone connection between Berlin and Hamburg. On 9 November, I travelled from Döberitz to Berlin and on the platform at the main station I met my batman. We were waiting for the train. After a short while we were told that there were no long-distance trains leaving Berlin – in other words the revolution had spread to Berlin. I took the next available train back to Döberitz and brought the news to my commander. Late in the afternoon we were told that Fritz Eberhard, a Social Democrat, had been trying to form a government. In the evening the camp of Döberitz decided to support Eberhard against the revolutionaries who we regarded not only as Communist but also criminals of all sorts mixing in politics. The next few days there were some clashes with the Communists. My father managed to send an employee from our firm together with civilian clothes – and I always wore civilian clothes when I went to Berlin, because as a commissioned officer you were in danger of your

epaulettes being torn off. A sort of Soldiers Council started to reign at Döberitz, but you would scarcely describe them as revolutionaries. They behaved quite normally and with dignity, they were quite decent. They checked our passes when we left the camp and when we entered the camp, but they did not in any way resort to violence.[64]

Leutnant Walter Rappolt, Döberitz Camp

At the front, many German soldiers were stunned when they heard their first news that an Armistice was about to be declared.

At long last, on Sunday the 10th November 1918, the whole Regiment was ordered to assemble at 11 am in the local church, awaiting for delegates from the Reichstag to arrive and talk to us. The atmosphere in that church became thicker and bluer and mistier every moment from the tobacco smoke produced by the assembled soldiery, but the delegates never came. Instead the leader of the Regiment read out to us a declaration informing us officially that a revolution had taken place at home and the Armistice was to begin almost at once. We are to complete our retreat, which is to start homewards immediately and it must be accomplished in good order! All this was enough to make our heads swirl! All day one heard further rumours of mutinies and revolts at home and in the navy and did not know whether all this could really be true! But we at least still remained where we were that day and sought the company of comrades. We tried to digest what we had been told and think ahead – where all this might lead us to![65]

Leutnant Eugen Kaufmann, Infantry Regiment 165, 14th Brigade, 7th Division

Yet to the very end of the war, men were dying. The emotional impact of such late losses was enormously magnified on their comrades. Often it seemed an entirely random incident, a shell spinning from nowhere to snuff out a life.

I got the news by runner, that poor old Croft[66] had been killed. It is no use trying to tell you what that meant to the Battalion, or to me personally. He had not been back with us very long after

a prolonged absence, and I know he felt like coming home when
he re-joined us at Brias. He was always like a ray of sunshine if
there was anything doing. With him were two other good fellows,
Second Lieutenant King[67] and Sergeant Garbutt;[68] also a Lancer
with whom they were talking at the time; a stray shell fell in the
sunken road and killed all four of them.[69]

Lieutenant Colonel Robert Goldthorp, 1/28th London Regiment (Artists'
Rifles), 190th Brigade, 63rd Division

Everyone wanted to survive the Great War, to feel safe, to return to a
life not bound by trench walls, gas alarms, exploding shells and flensing
shards of steel. No more requirement to 'stand to' at dawn and dusk, to
dodge the sniper's bullet. No more friends to bury in the cold damp earth.
It was all so near – so close. Yet there was also a lurking awareness that
somewhere men would be still dying; men drawing the shortest straw of
all.

Everywhere the troops' hearts were filled with a sense of relief and
anticipation as the fateful hour drew near. George Waring echoed
all our thoughts at breakfast time when he exclaimed, 'I'll be sorry
for the poor devils up and down the front who will not live to see
it! It's just the luck of the draw.'[70]

Private Edward Williamson, 17th Battalion, Royal Scots, 106th Brigade,
35th Division

The war was not over yet. Not quite.

11

DAY OF DAYS, 11 NOVEMBER 1918

My mind goes back to the last few pals that I knew that were killed
in that fateful hour on the Sambre Canal. Just a few more days, just
a few more hours and they would have been alive. One fellow was
next to me in the trenches, a few yards away and he was looking
over the top, and a sniper caught him right in the head; he was
calling for his mother with his last words.[1]

Private Walter Grover, 2nd Royal Sussex Regiment

THE ALLIES HAD WON THE WAR. On 11 November 1918, there was
no doubt as to the magnitude of the German defeat. Such doubts would
come later, confusion created by nationalist politicians harbouring their
own agenda. At the time, there on the Western Front, it was evident
that the German Army had been comprehensively routed. This was not
a question of superior manhood; no army could have fought with more
determination and courage than that demonstrated by the Germans. It
was more the merciless application of the Allied superior numbers, greater
military resources and a tactical flexibility born of harsh experience. It had

further been a long-term process as the weaponry and munitions had to be manufactured to exacting standards and men trained in specialist roles. In the enervating chaos of battle, the generals, staff and signallers had to be trained to maintain two-way communication to allow all points within the command chain to respond to variable outcomes with the appropriate tactical response. This was easier said than done.

It is also important to note that, while the British Army had probably reached peak efficiency as a military force in 1918, this was not necessarily the most important factor on the Western Front. The French Army, although understandably more cautious after its excruciating casualties earlier in the war, was still a huge force that had developed a method of fighting that maximised the objectives achieved at the minimum possible cost in casualties. They had borne an enormous burden throughout the war and excelled in the defensive battles during the German offensives in 1918. If in the last two months of the war they had rather run out of steam, who can blame them? It was the earlier huge overall contribution that really mattered. In addition, French industry supplied 3,532 of the 4,194 artillery guns used by the Americans, 227 of 289 tanks and 4,874 of 6,394 aircraft.[2] This gargantuan effort may have hindered their own preparations for offensive action. In a sense, the Americans had stepped into the breach, providing the vigour that had begun to drain out of the French troops. The sheer size of the American Army was an imposing threat to the Germans, but, as we have seen, by late 1918 the American divisions were gaining valuable experience in the tactics needed for success on the modern battlefield. Their contribution was already very important, but would have been crucial had the war dragged on into 1919.

At the end of the war, Ferdinand Foch was in command of the largest and most powerful force in the world. As soon as he gained the strategic direction of military operations on the Western Front he began to prepare actively for the moment when he could turn to the offensive. As such he was the true architect of victory. Foch provided the drive and the intellectual coherence that bound together what might have been a series of disparate offensives into one coherent whole. He could not 'order' compliance with his grand strategy, but he could use his powers of persuasion, coupled with negotiation, and a willingness to compromise, or even at times, to conciliate, to achieve the overall effects he wanted. He set the agenda, but the details were left to Haig, Pétain and Pershing. Foch was blessed with a superlative Chief of Staff in General Maxime Weygand, who had been at his side since 1914. Far more than a mere amanuensis, Weygand had the knack of summing up clearly and concisely what Foch wanted, often clarifying the intent to eradicate confusions or future recriminations. Entirely attuned to Foch's military thinking, Weygand could anticipate his decisions, which saved much time in the command and planning process.

Foch also discovered a true comrade in arms in Douglas Haig. The two men may have argued at times, sometimes vigorously, but their underlying relationship was sound, based on mutual respect. Haig shared Foch's understanding of the overall war situation: above all the importance of striving with every sinew to attain victory before the Germans could 'drop anchor' and prolong the war deep into 1919. Haig was also willing to comply with the considerable role required of the British under Foch's plans. Although he always insisted on retaining a good measure of tactical control of the BEF, in practice this did not deflect him far from the path required by Foch. As the British Army took the 'lead' in the later fighting, it was a measure of Haig's determination that he did not let up, even when threatened by Lloyd George and the civilian politicians who looked to an 'easier' path to victory in 1919. On 11 November, the British Fourth Army commander, General Sir Henry Rawlinson, reflected the prevailing attitude among the British army commanders as to the importance of Haig's contribution.

> We owe it to three things: to the spirit of the troops – their recovery after the events of the spring is a glorious testimony to British grit; to the way old Foch pulled the operations of the Allies together; and to Douglas Haig's faith in victory this year – he believed in it long before I did, and when all the people at home were talking about plans for 1919. He not only believed in it, but went all out for it, and he must be a proud and thankful man today.[3]
>
> General Henry Rawlinson, Headquarters, Fourth Army

Foch's relationship with Phillipe Pétain was considerably more fraught. Perhaps this was inevitable; they were both after all French generals, and as the French Commander in Chief, Pétain had formerly had a measure of overall control over the Western Front. Now, he had to accept orders from Foch and it is undeniable that at times this was a difficult process. Pétain had his own strategic methodology, which was much more cautious, a result of his experiences at Verdun and his role in the rebuilding of the French Army after the disaster of the Nivelle Offensive in April 1917. Defensively, his tactics were sound, but he had proved himself unable to see the 'bigger picture' during the German Spring offensives. Subsequently, his grudging responses during the Foch offensives betrayed a failure to grasp the opportunity that lay before them. Yet Pétain and his staff still performed miracles in both the logistical arrangements and management of his precious reserve divisions, without which the Allied attacks would surely have petered out.

John Pershing was a different kettle of fish. He commanded the mighty American Expeditionary Force, a huge military resource that was expanding exponentially, but which had no relevant experience. Foch and the other Allied leaders were reliant on that manpower to win the war, indeed they pressed Pershing repeatedly over the timetable by which the divisions would reach the front – the target being a hundred divisions by July 1919. Given the vast size of their divisions this was a stupendous commitment. Yet Pershing took his responsibility as an American commander very seriously and prioritised the concept of American armies, fighting independent battles in their 'own' sectors of the front. Pershing was more than willing to play the role allotted by Foch to the Americans in the Allied offensives, but at times his inflexible approach to lending his divisions to the British and French caused irritation – especially given the munitions, artillery, tanks, aircraft and overall support that the French and British gave to the Americans. This was a very real frustration to Foch, who was exasperated by Pershing's seeming inability to grasp the reality of fighting on the Western Front, the complexity of the military tactics required to secure victory, and the suffering that had been undergone to gain that knowledge. Yet although Pershing may have been obdurate, he was at least stubborn in following a course devoutly supported by most of his contemporary Americans. They were not willing to see their men treated as raw cannon fodder, to be fed into battle under French, or British, command. In warfare, good morale is crucial and perhaps Pershing was sensible in allowing his men to fight as Americans. It may have been frustrating for Foch and Haig, but Pershing delivered enough in the last months of the war to justify his obduracy.

THE WAR WAS WON, but the final moments were tense as the clock ticked down slowly to 11.00 on Monday 11 November. On the Meuse front, in accordance with the uncompromising views of General Pershing, the Americans had ordered a far more aggressive approach to operations in the last few hours. However, Major General William Wright of 89th Division was greatly worried at the thought of risking unnecessary casualties by launching a questionable crossing of the Meuse, especially amidst the rumours that the Armistice might be close. The Meuse had already been crossed and large bridgeheads previously established owing to the efforts of the 5th and 32nd Divisions. There seemed to be no military need for additional bridgeheads. However, orders were orders. Wright did at least try his best to reduce the potential for mass casualties.

> Received notice that the 90th Division was coming up the Meuse on the right; they crossed yesterday in the vicinity of Ville Franche. This relieves the situation very materially, and I think that the plans for the crossing at Pouilly and vicinity should be cut out and the entire division should cross at Stenay and exploit northward in liaison with the Ninetieth. The more I think the plan over the better it seems to me. In the afternoon, General Summerall came in and I told him that I was apprehensive about this evening's work, and that I recommended the postponement of the entire movement and the concentration of the division in the vicinity of Stenay with a view of crossing there and exploiting to the north and opening up the country for the 2nd Division to cross. He said he thought this plan was the best one also, but that he had received

his orders to cross and he must do it. He left saying that he thought
everything was well arranged and would go all right.[4]

Major General William Wright, Headquarters, 89th Division

On the evening of 10 November, Wright began to hear news that the
end of the war was very imminent. It was too late. The offensive would
proceed as planned.

We got a radio flash to the effect that Germany had accepted the
terms of an Armistice as laid down by General Foch. About this
time I heard the guns of my attack commencing to fire. This news
may be a Bosche trick. I have received no statement from higher
authority to that effect as yet. This at 9.10 pm.[5]

Major General William Wright, Headquarters, 89th Division

That night, his 89th Division guns bombarded the German positions and
would ultimately launch an infantry attack, which managed to get across
the Stenay with very few casualties. One of the men making this attack
was Lieutenant Francis Jordan.

We were then ordered forward and came under close machine-gun
fire not more than 15 or 20 feet on our left. I received a minor flesh
wound through the shoulder, which bullet continued on to hit my
pack which was filled with cans of food. The impact tipped me
over backwards, and, in falling, I threw up my hand and received
a bullet at the base of my left thumb. The machine gun had been
shifted quickly and killed the First Sergeant immediately behind
me and the Sergeant immediately behind him. Our advance was
stopped for the time being. Corporal Wicker crawled up beside
me and put his rifle across my chest to fire in the direction of the
German machine guns. The return fire was so accurate that the
wood on the Corporal's rifle was splintered. Those of us who had
been wounded remained there for some time, while those who were
unwounded took up the advance to locate and kill the German
machine gunner.[6]

Lieutenant Francis Jordan, 2/356th Regiment, 178th Brigade, 89th
Division

Jordan was evacuated to safety – although wounded he would live. Back at 89th Division headquarters, Wright was mightily relieved as he received news of the operations.

> I consider the forcing of the crossing and the manoeuvre afterwards to have been very successful, and accomplished our purpose in the face of opposition with small losses. The entire division is crossed, or can be crossed, and we have taken our objectives. At 8.45 word was received that an Armistice had been signed and would take effect at 11 o'clock. I directed Colonel Lee to keep up the fighting until that time and that it would stop exactly at 11 o'clock and the men would dig in on the ground they occupied and that absolutely no communication with the Bosche under any circumstances or on any subject would be permitted, nor would there be any hilarity, or demonstration on the part of my troops.[7]

Major General William Wright, Headquarters, 89th Division

Next day he would leave his division to take up command of I Corps.

The 4th Marine Brigade of 2nd Division was much less fortunate in their attempts at crossing the Meuse. Their commanding officer, Major General John Lejeune, shared Wright's scepticism as to the necessity for any more river crossings. While two battalions of the 5th Marines attempted a crossing at Letanne, the 6th Marines would make the main crossing at Mouzon. Nobody thought it was a good idea, but somehow it still had to be done. The engineers would construct the bridges which would then be launched across the freezing cold, swirling depths of the Meuse. As the marines helped the sappers carry the bridge to the bank they had a moment of sheer terror as recounted by Sergeant Melvin Krulewitch, who was 'celebrating' his twenty-third birthday on 11 November.

> Suddenly there came a new note in the approach of a 'Whiz-Bang' – and every marine froze to the spot. Each knew from experience that this particular high explosive had his name on it. Even if cover had been available, none could have been reached in time. Fascinated, immobile, they could only await the end. The shell landed squarely in the middle of the Company. And in that fraction of

a second between hit and explosion, there was no thought as to past and future. Each soldier braced himself for the terrific impact of the next moment when the fuse would detonate the charge. Nothing happened. For that little group of men came the war's greatest thrill – and my best birthday present. The fuse was a dud.[8]

Sergeant Melvin Krulewitch, 2/6th Marines, 4th Marine Brigade, 2nd Division

Several shells were bursting on the west bank by this time. One rickety footbridge had been erected, but it was considered that a second was required, to at least split the focus of any German machine-gun fire, and give the Marines at least some chance of crossing unscathed. When the second bridge was delayed and with daylight fast approaching, it was decided to abandon the crossing – much to the relief of almost everyone.

They were not so fortunate at the 5th Marines' crossing of the Meuse at Letanne which went ahead as planned.

We moved down a deep ravine towards the river. In this we halted and sheltered by a hillside we waited till our own artillery opened up. 'Fritzy' started to retaliate with shells and machine guns with it seems some success. Protected by a heavy mist and smoke screen the 2nd Engineers succeeded in putting a pontoon bridge across. Our company emerged from the ravine, crossed the bridge in single file. Because of the mist Heinie's flare lights were of no avail and in spite of a sweeping machine-gun fire I got across. All night we marched along the river bank – now dropping behind the high bank as protection from a withering machine-gun fire then taking up the advance again until halted by a renewal of the fire. By daylight we halted, dug in, and tried to rest a little – our battalion had become separated and any German counter-attack was expected. After an hour's sleep I was called out to stand watch at a position on our right flank where we had set up a German Maxim. While I was still on this post – carefully looking for some sign of Germans ahead, I noted that the artillery had ceased firing – not a gun was being fired. Everything had become quiet.[9]

Private Harold Strickler, 2/5th Marines, 4th Marine Brigade, 2nd Division

This entirely pointless operation cost several casualties.

The Americans involved in such bouts of last-minute fighting were affected by a complex array of emotions. Many simply did not know how to respond in this strangest of circumstances. Vicious fighting would be replaced by peace at the stroke of 11 o'clock – an arbitrary moment in time that could mean life or death to individuals. Unquestionably, Major General William Haan of the 32nd Division was enthusiastic about committing his troops to squeeze in one last battle before peace.

> Yesterday we pounded them all day, driving them back everywhere. But they fought like the very devil still – had a new Division in front of us and parts of two other Divisions, but we punched them. This morning we resumed the attack at 6.30 which we had stopped last night after dark. At 7 we received orders to stop the battle. That was some job, too. We got it stopped entirely at 10.45, just fifteen minutes before the Armistice went into effect. One of my chaplains was killed at 10.40. Hard luck![10]
>
> Major General William Haan, Headquarters, 32nd Division

Despite the activities of the more bellicose American generals, there were quieter sectors on the front where many of the 'Doughboys' had time to think, to try and put in context their experiences.

> Something was in the air, for we didn't receive the usual orders to pick up targets and fire on them, but rather instructions were to record all information of this nature for future information if called for. When, at night, I heard the rumbling of heavy traffic on the roads across the river, but was told that we were not to fire upon it, I became an optimist myself, and joined in the speculations of the hour. I could not help but look back over the vista of the past months and marvel at the enduring loyalty to 'The Cause' that had characterised every man with whom I had come in contact. If it had not been for the pluck and spirit that thought nothing of the cost, so long as it was a job to be done, I doubt if lots of us would

be here today, for there is nothing like knowing the other fellow is
absolutely sure to deliver, to stiffen a bowing back.[11]

Captain Thornton Thayer, B, Battery, 305th Field Artillery, 77th Division

Although many did not really believe the fighting would actually end at
11.00, they could not help but start counting down in their heads. They
were so close, yet that was no guarantee of survival; they had all seen far
too much sudden death to have any illusions on that score.

> In three hours the war will be over. It seems incredible even as I
> write it. I suppose I ought to be thrilled and cheering. Instead I
> am merely apathetic and incredulous. The adjutant, 'Good! Now
> all we have to do is keep alive until eleven o'clock. I know where
> there's a culvert half a kilometre down the road. You'll find me
> under it if I'm wanted!' 10.37 am. A shell just lit in the old sawmill.
> Men are out in the road running madly about. Other men are stag-
> gering out of the wreck and dropping as they emerge. Ambulances
> have been stopped and litter bearers are on their way across the
> clearing. Twenty men killed – thirty-five wounded. The war has
> 23 minutes still to go. 10.38 am. An 11th Field Artillery kitchen is
> near the road to the south of us. The battery alongside our shack
> had dropped into silence when this new bombardment started.
> Most of the men had gone down to the kitchen for breakfast. A
> shell – short of the road – smashed into the soup cannon. Fourteen
> dead. Four wounded. In 22 minutes we shall have peace.[12]

Captain Robert Casey, Headquarters, 124th Field Artillery, 33rd Division

The cataclysmic arrival of the German shells on that field kitchen shook
many of them out of their apathy, and triggered a murderous response
to casualties which would have been accepted with relative equanimity
a few days before. It now seemed a horrendous blow just minutes before
sanctuary. In the next minute Casey could hear the roar of 155mm shells
screaming off towards the Germans as the 11th Field Artillery gunners
sought their vengeance.

They are seeking pay for fourteen lives. There is quite a jamboree about the 155mm gun pits. Adjutants, majors and volunteer workers of all ranks are howling, 'Cease firing!' Nobody pays any attention to them. Me? I'm all for the 11th. I'd be over helping them if I knew how to fire a 155mm.[13]

Captain Robert Casey, Headquarters, 124th Field Artillery, 33rd Division

Up and down the front soldiers could hear the gunfire and many began to think that it had all been just another stupid latrine rumour. This was not helped by the variable accuracy of their watches.

We almost held our breath as the time neared. The hand of the gunner's watch was on the verge of pointing to eleven, the far-flung battle line was silent, and we were breathless with expectancy, when over to our left loud explosions of bursting shells rent the air. Immediately a clatter of guns arose and the hand of the watch was past eleven. Was the watch wrong or the report false? We believed the latter.[14]

Private Horace Baker, 3/128th Regiment, (attached) 5th Division

One more man at least was to die in the very last minute of the war. Private Henry Gunther of 1/313rd Regiment in the 79th Division was advancing with his company towards a pair of German machine guns in the village of Chaumont devant Damvillers. Ignoring explicit orders from his sergeant, Gunther made a solo bayonet charge. As he approached, the German soldiers, who seemed well aware of the time, were unwilling to fire and indeed shouted out and tried to wave him away – all to no avail. When Gunther[15] started shooting he was cut down with a short burst of machine-gun fire. He was reputedly the last American soldier to die in action during the Great War.

Then the final moment of truth arrived at 11.00. In retrospect, it was an amazing demonstration of discipline.

10.59 am. The 11th has just fired its last shot. The guns are so hot that the paint is rising from them in blisters. The crews are sweating despite the autumn chill of the air. To them peace approaches as a regrettable interruption. 11.00 am. The silence is oppressive. It weighs in on one's eardrums. We have lived and had our being in din since we left the Forêt de la Reine. There seems to be something uncanny – unnatural in the all-enveloping lack of sound. A bird is singing in the tree outside our door.[16]

Captain Robert Casey, Headquarters, 124th Field Artillery, 33rd Division

Some of them soon found out how the Germans felt about the Armistice. Not to put too fine a point on it, they seemed ecstatic.

We were stupefied to see crowds of Bosche running over to us between the mine fields with their hands up and yelling like mad. They were crazy for cigarettes and chocolate. They had some cigars but they were awful. They were big fellows in sloppy uniforms, from the 328th Infantry. Some of them had been to America and talked English and, of course, many of our Reading crowd could talk to them in German. They said their food had been vile. We had some burned rice that our boys wouldn't eat and they fell on it like wolves. This getting together lasted for only about an hour when our officers stopped it and chased the Germans back to their lines. All that night we could hear them singing and burning Very lights and bonfires. There wasn't much doing with our crowd as they were all played out and wanted sleep.[17]

Private Carl Stuber, 108th Machine Gun Battalion, 55th Brigade, 28th Division

Even the gruff Major General William Haan was pleased that peace had been achieved, although in his case it was far more a celebration of victory than any celebration of international brotherhood.

I am glad the war is over. This is a day of celebration. We are now waiting for the enemy to get a little start and then we will follow him and before long we will establish 'Die Wacht am Rhein'. Isn't that grand? Anyhow, we licked the foe to a frazzle and the Hohenzollerns and the Hapsburgs are out of business for keeps.[18]

Major General William Haan, Headquarters, 32nd Division

One affecting memory from a young soldier indicated that the horrors of war would not fade rapidly, nor would the deeply troubled find peace. Private Arthur Yenson had been a waggon driver, not safe from shells, but well away from the terrors of the front line. Now he wanted to explore the scenes of the last battles. What he found repulsed him.

> I struck out to explore the heights along the Meuse River. Here I found several machine-gun nests, lots of dead Germans, and a few dead Yanks. In some places the men had been killed by bullets; but in others they were blown to pieces by shells; an arm here with the hand gone, and a leg there with the genitals hanging to it, or a solitary head which seemed to accuse civilization with its silence! In one place I found a stomach lost in the grass, while wound around the limbs of a nearby tree were the intestines. The whole ridge had a stench so horrible and so repulsive that all the ghastly sights seemed indescribably worse! Another place I found four Germans shocked together. Their stinking flesh had turned green and presented a spectacle so gruesome that I could see, smell, and taste them all at once! Sickening as it was, I hadn't seen anything yet. A little farther on was an American soldier stamping a dead German's face into a pulp. I suppose the Germans had killed one of his buddies.[19]
>
> Private Arthur Yenson, 7th Engineers Train, 5th Division

An ugly scene that showed peace would not immediately eradicate wartime hatreds.

The men of the French Army had more reason than most to celebrate. During the war, they had suffered an incredible 1,400,000 deaths among a total of some 4,700,000 casualties. It has been estimated that up to 18 per cent of those mobilised had been killed. The first news of the Armistice was thus a precious moment.

> The battalion was heading towards the rear and had arrived at Guignicourt, where we found the whole village still asleep. A cyclist went past and said, 'The Armistice has been signed'. 'God, let it be true!' 7.30 am. 'Armistice, Armistice!' That's what everyone was

saying. People were congratulating each other, asking each other, 'Who told you?' 'A cyclist!' 'A cuirassier Lieutenant!' 'A telephonist!' The soldiers had no need to ask more. Then a group of 93rd Régiment d'Infanterie arrived from the front, muddy and tired. 'It's over!' we shouted to them. 'It's signed!' Broad smiles lit up their faces. 'Thanks, old chap!' was all they could say. There was none of the noisy show of enthusiasm which greeted the declaration of War. They didn't throw down their weapons. They didn't break ranks; they just lifted their heads, the happy faces of brave men, incapable of disorder and excess, even in the midst of victory. My beloved France![20]

Lieutenant Maurice Laurentin, 219th Régiment d'Infanterie, 61st Division

Major Henri Desagneaux had a more pressing reason for celebration as his battalion was facing an imminent attack, which had already been postponed three times. They had known that their fate would be decided by Foch and the other negotiators.

This is the only thing in our minds at present. If the Armistice is signed, it's peace; if not, it's an immediate attack, and butchery in all its horror. There's been a real firework display going on over in the German lines all night long. They are letting off all their flares and rockets, green, red, yellow, they all mingle in the sky. A few Bosches try to come and fraternize with our troops, but they are chased off by rifle fire. Then we learn that Revolution is brewing in Germany, that the Emperor is abdicating. It's over, the Bosches are withdrawing everywhere. We are excited, we wait and hope. Firework display continued all night over in the enemy camp. At 6 am, we hear on the radio that the Armistice has been signed. The end of hostilities is fixed for 11 am. At 11 am it's all over, we are no longer at war. What joy – the champagne flows, the attack won't take place. There's a smile on everyone's lips, no more fighting, we'll be able to move without fearing a bullet, a shell, a rocket, or gas – the war is over![21]

Major Henri Desagneaux, 14th Régiment de Tirailleurs, 129th Division

Many celebrated with that most French of refreshing beverages – a glass of wine. Stretcher-bearer Ernest Brec, a cleric in his pre-war life, was certainly suddenly thirsty.

> Damn! A wave of joy swept over us. I don't know if I'd tears in my eyes. Like the others, I must have shouted '*Vive la France!*' For a moment, we were left breathless with happiness. Great sorrow is silent; so too is great joy. Then the shock passed; we recovered our power of speech and with it the reflex common to all Frenchmen, 'We'll have to drink a toast to that!' Yes, but with what? There was no red wine in this poor little place, just a bottle of lousy sparkling wine Bebert dug up in a shop, where the bastard made us pay 15 francs! We split it sixteen ways – hardly enough to wet your whistle! And that was how, on 11 November 1918, my battalion celebrated victory in a little town in the Meurthe-et-Moselle.[22]

Private Ernest Brec, 77th Régiment d'Infanterie, 18th Division

These French veterans were the unsung heroes of the war, the men that had faced the German Army for so long. Before the British or Americans had arrived, it was their efforts that had held back the mighty German Army at the height of its powers.

> It was noon when the news reached us in the Vitré barracks. There wasn't a single soldier left in the rooms. It was a devilish stampede down the corridors and down to the police station, where they had just posted a telegram announcing, in two laconic lines, the deliverance of millions of men, the end of their tortures, the imminent return to civilized life. How many times had we thought about this blessed day, which so many did not live to see? How many times had we peered into the mysterious future, looking for this star of salvation, this invisible lighthouse in the dark night? And now this forever immortal day had arrived! This happiness, this joy, overwhelmed us. We couldn't keep it in our hearts. We stood there looking at each other, mute and stupid.[23]

Corporal Louis Barthas, Vitré Barracks

Peace had come to France at last.

On the British front there was one flurry of activity as they strove to capture the town of Mons, the scene of the first British battle of the war on 23 August 1914. As his First Army troops approached Mons, General Sir Henry Horne relished the symbolism of both the location and date.

> It was on November 11 1914 that the I Corps, in which I held the appointment of Brigadier General Royal Artillery, defeated the great attack of the Prussian Guard. An attack which was planned to break down the British resistance and to open the road to Calais! Now the mighty German nation is completely humbled and the great German Army, which regarded itself as the most powerful fighting machine in the world, is in retreat to its own frontiers, broken and defeated. It is marvellous, and as I look back on it, my darling, I realize that it is the hand of God, and we cannot be suf-ficiently thankful to him for his mercy to us. We took Mons – we were well round it last night and early this morning we disposed of the Germans who made an attempt to hold it, and occupied the town. I am so very pleased. I began at Mons and I end the fighting at Mons![24]

General Sir Henry Horne, Headquarters, First Army

Horne had risen from an artillery brigadier general to full general since 1914, a rapid promotion which would have been impossible for a peace-time soldier.

As the Canadians moved towards Mons, there was some competition among the battalions as to who would relieve the town first.

> It did not take us long to get to the front line which was being held by the Royal Canadian Regiment, the supposed premier regiment of the 7th Brigade. Arriving in Cuesmes about 12.30 we took up position along the streets and acted as a support to the RCR. We had no special look out work so the time passed very dull for us. The Huns were very busy with their light guns and also machine guns – it was thought advisable to take all cover possible. The people of Cuesmes were throwing open their doors for us, and we

were only too pleased to enter their houses knowing full well the danger of the stray bullet that was aimed at no one in particular, but was meant for someone.[25]

Sergeant George Tizard, 42nd (Royal Highlanders) Battalion, 7th Brigade, 3rd Canadian Division

While the disbelieving soldiers were sheltering in the house a Canadian journalist, John Livesay, came in and told them that the war would be over next day.

He assured us that what he said was true. The French Belgians had been listening to our conversation but could gather nothing from it so I endeavoured to explain. That was the commencement of my trouble; the daughter of the house called a few neighbours in and explained all about the peace – and with one accord they all kissed me. My good luck was with me as our guns which were in the next street opened up a salvo, and everybody rushed for the cellar thinking that the Heinies were coming back. To quiet them I told them that is our guns sending peace messages to the Heinies. I had again pleased all the folks and again they showed their pleasure with their lips. I was getting fed up with their embraces. I did not mind the daughter, but I distinctly objected to all the neighbours.[26]

Sergeant George Tizard, 42nd (Royal Highlanders) Battalion, 7th Brigade, 3rd Canadian Division

Early next morning, they became aware that the Germans had pulled back from Mons.

Things had become suspiciously quiet during the last two hours with the exception of a little machine-gun fire. Our patrols that had been sent in the town sent word back that all was OK. By 4.00 the Battalion had entered Mons; a couple of hours later, the Royal Canadian Regiment woke up to the fact that the 42nd had gotten into Mons before them. Our Company marched up the Grand Boulevard of Mons. A halt was called and we sat on the sidewalk. Men, women and children came and embraced us.[27]

Sergeant George Tizard, 42nd (Royal Highlanders) Battalion, 7th Brigade, 3rd Canadian Division

There was subsequently a fair amount of acrimony with their rivals of the Royal Canadian Regiment, as both regiments claimed to have been the first to relieve the town. In truth, both regiments seem to have sent patrols and then advanced almost simultaneously into Mons. At 11.00, the Mayor of Mons presented the keys of the city to Brigadier General John Clark, commanding the 7th Canadian Brigade, to a backdrop of bands playing both the Belgian national anthem '*La Brabançonne*' and '*O Canada*'. The Canadian Corps had finished the war with a symbolic success, one which emphasised their status as one of the finest forces on the Western Front. Their performance throughout the 'Hundred Days' campaign had been outstanding, matching that of the Australian Corps. The regrettable habit of Canadian historians in ascribing every military innovation of the Great War to the Canadians, and the Canadians alone, should not distract from their success in battle. Since 8 August they had engaged some 68 German divisions, taken 31,537 prisoners, captured 623 guns, 2,842 machine guns and 336 trench mortars. But they had also suffered some 45,830 casualties; the quid pro quo of any assault force. Truly it was a magnificent achievement.

Elsewhere, some other units seemed determined to get into action one more time. Corporal Harry Hopthrow was witness to the commencement of a last dash for action made by the 7th Dragoon Guards.

> We had a wireless station by the side of the road and we knew what was going on – there were messages coming through from army headquarters saying that there was going to be an Armistice at 11 o'clock. The 7th Dragoon Guards were just coming up and they halted quite nearby; they were going to have their breakfast. I walked down to the roadside and I was talking to one of the men and I mentioned to him the war was going to be over in a few hours' time. He told an NCO, who told an officer, who told the commanding officer and immediately he gave the order to mount and he obviously intended to be in action before the war ended – and off they went![28]

Corporal Harry Hopthrow, Signal Service, Royal Engineers, 30th Division

The 7th Dragoons would indeed arrive just in time to fight a brief action in the last hour before the war ended. They captured the Belgian town of Lessines on the Dendre River, just ten minutes before 11.00, in which they took four German officers and 167 men prisoner.

Captain Gerald Wellesley of the Oxfordshire Hussars was rather more restrained in his cautious approach to the town of Erquellines.

> Both the advance troops had patrols well out in front, and – beyond a certain amount of desultory rifle fire – little opposition was met with. About 10.30 we came with the advance troop on the right under long-range machine-gun fire, and withdrew into some dead ground. A patrol under Corporal Stockford pushed on round the edge of Erquelinnes – immediately beyond which was our final objective, the main road. I followed the patrol, and on reaching the outskirts of the town was met by a cheering mass of inhabitants, some of whom sang, others wept, and others begged me to be careful as German machine guns were in position round the corner. To these civilians, of course, it was complete news that an Armistice was at hand. So great was the crush that, having sent back for the squadron to come on, it was with the greatest difficulty that I got down to the market-place on foot, only to find that the last of the enemy had just gone.[29]

Captain Gerald Wellesley, D Sqdn, 1/1st Oxfordshire Hussars, 4th Cavalry Brigade, 2nd Cavalry Division

Captain Wellesley struggled back through the teeming Belgian towns-people to reclaim his horse.

> I found her bestraddled by a huge fat Belgian who was address-ing the crowd from her back. Having kicked him off, I went on to investigate, charged through mobs of wildly excited inhabitants, and finally got through the town and out on to the main road beyond. Here I met the patrol, who had come round the outskirts, and we established a Hotchkiss post on the road and sent back for the squadron. Meanwhile, Stockford and I tried to round up some escaping Bosches, who finally jumped into the River Sambre!

Tompkins's troop arrived almost simultaneously on the road half a mile to our left, and reported having obtained touch with 'A' Squadron, who had also reached the objective. I sent a patrol down the road on my right to Solre only 600 yards away, but found the village full of Germans. On the arrival of the squadron, posts were put out along the road, and we began to take stock of the situation. At 11.15 it was found necessary to end the days of a Hun machine gunner on our front who would keep on shooting. The Armistice was already in force, but there was no alternative. Perhaps his watch was wrong, but he was probably the last German killed in the war – a most unlucky individual![30]

Captain Gerald Wellesley, D Sqdn,1/1st Oxfordshire Hussars, 4th Cavalry Brigade, 2nd Cavalry Division

As one might expect with the British Army, there had been one popular response to the imminence of an Armistice – several sweepstakes were launched requiring the participants to guess the exact day of the Armistice. Many otherwise well-informed officers would prove to be hopelessly wrong-footed by the pace of events since they made their predictions back in October.

We began to think it must be coming to an end but we couldn't believe it! We'd been chasing the Germans like mad, but then the 'so and sos' would turn round. We ran a sweepstake on the day the war would end. I chose December 25th as my day! Many people chose a day around Easter! The chap that got up the sweepstake – he was pretty cunning he won it – he said November 13th – clever fellow wasn't he? Early in November, I wrote home and said, 'We may have peace by Christmas, but this is not very probable! Easter should see the end of it all!' That was my view at the time. We just couldn't believe it could end! We were a bit overcome. Thrilled to bits, rushing off letters home, just saying, 'It's ended and I'm still alive!'[31]

Captain Marmaduke Walkington, 47th Machine Gun Battalion, 47th Division

Of course, the staff officers behind the line had known early on what was in the air. Australian staff officer Major Keith Officer was in the Brewers House at Le Cateau – a rather appropriate location as it had been used as Sir John French's headquarters at the time of the Battle of Mons.

> I was sitting at a table with an English staff officer. He had a large old-fashioned hunting watch which he put on the table. He watched the minutes going round. The only disturbing thing was that we kept on getting messages from a German unit who were afraid that the people opposite them hadn't had instructions that they were to stop fighting at 11 o'clock, because they said the British troops opposite them were very aggressive and were giving them a lot of trouble. Anyway 11 o'clock came and he shut his watch up and said, 'I wonder what we are all going to do next?' That was very much the feeling of everyone! What was one going to do next? To some of us it was the end of four years, for some three years, for some less. To some of us it was practically the only life we'd known – we'd started quite young![32]

> Major Keith Officer, Headquarters, Australian Corps

One officer summed it up very succinctly.

> I remember thinking, 'It's all over!' and to my complete amazement, 'I am alive!' I had always taken it for granted that I shouldn't be.[33]

> Major Wilfred House, Headquarters, 57th Brigade, 19th Division

The mechanics of stopping a juggernaut war machine at precisely 11.00 were difficult and varied greatly depending on location, communications and, of course, the attitude of the protagonists.

> Just before 11 am it occurred to us that it would be very annoying to be left with loaded guns which we couldn't fire! Because unloading is an awful nuisance with big guns and you have to be jolly careful what you do! What we did was to cock our guns up to an angle which we felt made it certain that no-one was going to get

killed because I think everybody at the final moment didn't want to slay somebody in the last few minutes.[34]

Second Lieutenant Cyril Dennys, 212 Siege Battery, Royal Garrison Artillery

That morning, the 2/15th London Regiment was released from the haunting prospect of an assault over the River Scheldt at Avelghem.

Well before 11 am our people decided to cease fire, but the Germans, for some Teutonic reason, kept shelling our positions almost up to 11 am. Then the noise stopped everywhere, and there came a silence which hadn't been experienced for four long years. We had a tremendous feeling of relief at the thought that we had come through alive, and would, in due course, return to Blighty. At the same time, we felt that it was no time for jubilation, but for sadness at the thought of so many of our comrades who would not be going home.

When this bloody war is over,
Oh, how happy I shall be,
When I get my civvie clothes on,
No more soldiering for me.

We never sang the above ditty joyously, because so far as we could see the war was never going to end. It was sung only on those occasions when, as a small carrying party for example, we waited at some dreary ration dump to collect rations and take them up the line, or, after having drunk more than enough *vin blanc*, we sat in some estaminet feeling doleful. And now, to our great surprise and joy, it was 'Après la Guerre'.[35]

Corporal Charles Hennessey, 2/15th (Civil Service Rifles), London Regiment, 90th Brigade, 36th Division

The army was not a uniform body of automatons. Hidden behind the khaki was a wide variety of personalities – all responding to peace in dissimilar ways – much as men had responded differently to the challenges of war. In a few moments, everything had changed.

It was a strange feeling to ride back to the battery in the quiet that followed 11 o'clock. One had got used to the background noise of shellfire. Near the front it seemed a continuous orchestration of deep and echoing sound, punctuated by the sharper rat-tat-tat of rifle or machine-gun fire. The landscape was different: no observation balloons to be seen, no plumes of smoke from the shell bursts or burning buildings, no aeroplanes glinting in the sky. Peace seemed a very strange and new experience.[36]

Major Richard Foot, 'D' Battery, 310th Brigade, Royal Field Artillery, 62nd Division

They had become accustomed to the roar of the guns, the rumble of transport wheels, the bellowed orders and the crunch of marching feet.

That quiet – that quietness – we couldn't get used to it. We'd been deafened by gunfire for years! We were never without the sound of gunfire; either in your sector, the next sector, or somewhere within ear range! Suddenly all was quiet! We wanted to talk in whispers as if we were in church or something.[37]

Private Donald Hodge, 7th Royal West Kent Regiment, 55th Brigade, 18th Division,

Many could hardly believe it. Their lives had been shaped by the war. Every day, every action, every thought was dominated by the requirement to somehow survive while carrying out their duties beneath the looming spectre of death. Then suddenly that shadow was lifted.

Nobody would believe it. The war couldn't be over. It had been on for years. It was so unreal, we had got into the habit of feeling, 'Oh well, I suppose sometime this show will end!' But we still didn't see the end in sight at all. We thought, 'Well, my godfather! The war's over!' Eventually of course it sunk in. Then naturally we thought, 'Oh, where do we go from here?' Just that sort of feeling that we'd been sacked, we'd been kicked out of a job. A terribly empty feeling.[38]

Captain George Jameson, C Battery, 72nd Brigade, Royal Field Artillery

One grim task still had to be performed that day. There were corpses still to be buried and the funerals proved a miserable experience for the witnesses as everyone was well aware that these last victims had so nearly survived.

> I do not know if I can describe the funeral of Ben Croft, King and Garbutt, but of course it was the first thing we did. As they were killed just outside the village, we decided to bury them at the side of the road where they fell, with such military honours as we could, their own Company finding the firing party, and the buglers sounded the Last Post. It was a sad little party that gathered round the graves of the last Artists to fall in action. A large number of officers and men came and the Brigadier found time to be present. I think these three were the last casualties of the war in our Brigade. It seemed so very hard, that it was only a matter of 24 hours, and all would have been well. The inhabitants of the village had given us some oak to make a cross from and someone else thought of flowers – and after doing all we could we returned to our billets.[39]

> Lieutenant Colonel Robert Goldthorp, 1/28th (Artists' Rifles) London Regiment, 190th Brigade, 63rd Division

Many accounts refer to a strange emptiness caused by the removal of war from their mental landscape. In consequence, with some units there was no discernible excitement when the news came through. This phlegmatic approach was partially a public demonstration of the legendary British 'stiff-upper lip', but it was also deep-rooted in the stultifying effect of entrenched war-weariness. Many men required to control their innermost feelings in battle had become emotionally desensitised. The Armistice was too big an event, just too important for them to properly process what was happening to them. They no longer had the emotional vocabulary to respond appropriately.

> We were too far gone, too exhausted really, to enjoy it. All we could do was just go back to our billets; there was no cheering, no singing, we had no alcohol at all. We simply celebrated the Armistice in

silence and thankfulness that it was all over. It was such a sense of anti-climax. We were drained of all emotion.[40]

Corporal Clifford Lane, 2nd Bedfordshire Regiment, 54th Brigade, 18th Division

Yet, for all that, many units responded with a riotous sense of release, once, that is, they had escaped the vigilant gaze of their officers. Private Norman Cliff soon found that even the Guards could be tempted to displays of excitement.

I rushed back to the billet and amid a din of riotous cheering seized my rifle, equipment and all my belongings and flung the whole lot in the air. Others followed suit. A kind of frenzied madness seized us and we were no longer responsible for our antics and foolery. All the frustration, resentment, exasperation, sorrow, hope and despair had been bottled up for long harrowing years. Sudden relief was bound to cause an explosion. As suddenly, quietness returned. Feelings welled up that were too deep for expression. A dumbness fell upon us, and a solemn thoughtful mood took over; but not for long. Our excitement could not be contained. I had renounced everything to become Guardsman Cliff 'for the duration of the war'. The war was over. I was 'Civilian Cliff' again. I had borne so much that I loathed for so long. I had accepted bullying, abuse, humiliation and degradation for the sake of the cause we had been fighting for. Not for another day, I avowed to myself, would I put up with this nonsense.[41]

Private Norman Cliff, 1st Grenadier Guards, 3rd Brigade, Guards Division

But even generals could be light-hearted, given the magnitude of the victory their armies had achieved. There is a strange air of the 'giddy aunt' to Haig's description of the antics of his army commanders as they were filmed after a conference.

General Plumer, whom I told to 'go off and be cinema-ed' went off most obediently and stood before the camera trying to look his best, while Byng and others near him were chaffing the old man and trying to make him laugh.[42]

Field Marshal Sir Douglas Haig, General Headquarters, BEF

Meanwhile, the lightly wounded Private Frederick Noakes of the 1st Coldstream Guards had been in a convalescent camp at Cayeux on the coast near Abbeville. Not having had the mixed blessing of a more serious 'Blighty wound' that would require hospitalisation back in England, meant that such patients were aware that after an all-too-short period of convalescence, they would be sent back to the line to rejoin their units. Their reaction to the good news was simply ecstatic.

> The pent-up cheers broke loose. Caps were flung in the air, hands were shaken on all sides, and everyone yelled to the utmost extent of their lungs, many with tears of joy running unheeded down their faces. It was the moment all had been waiting for, a moment of such undiluted happiness and emotion as I had never known and probably shall never know again – no longer an imagined hope for the future, but actually here![43]
>
> Private Frederick Noakes, No. 5 Convalescent Camp, Cayeux

Where there was the means – the drink and the music – the men could let rip. Certainly, Frederick Noakes would enjoy a riotous celebration that night.

> At 9 o'clock the CO applied a torch to the giant bonfire, which stood 20 feet high in the midst of the camp, surmounted by a rough effigy of the Kaiser, complete with bristling moustache and clad in a German uniform. As the flames soared upwards and the petrol-soaked wood crackled furiously, all restraint was flung aside, and the troops danced and whirled round the blazing pyre in an orgy of primitive self-abandonment. When at last the 'Kaiser' tottered to his fiery doom, there was a great outburst of cheering, and the band struck up popular tunes. We went through the whole repertoire, from 'Rule Britannia' to 'Dixieland', everybody singing whether they knew the words or not, for three hours, until we could sing or dance no longer. At last, there was a unanimous demand for 'Home, Sweet Home', and on that note, tired out, we gradually dispersed to bed![44]
>
> Private Frederick Noakes, No. 5 Convalescent Camp, Cayeux

Later that night, many men lay in bed trying to come to terms with the end of what for many would be the most significant – the most terrible – chapter of their lives.

> At last I lie down tired and very happy, but sleep is elusive. How far away is that 22 August 1914, when I heard with a shudder, as a Platoon commander at Valenciennes, that real live German troops, armed to the teeth, were close at hand – one has been hardened since then. Incidents flash through the memory: the battles of the first four months: the awful winters in waterlogged trenches, cold and miserable: the terrible trench-war assaults and shellfire of the next three years: loss of friends, exhaustion and wounds: the stupendous victories of the last few months: our enemies all beaten to their knees. Thank God! the end of a fright-ful four years.[45]
>
> Brigadier General James Jack, Headquarters, 28th Brigade, 9th Division

But it is an all-too-human trait that once something devoutly desired has been achieved, then the mind moves on with scarcely a pause. One question was seeping into many heads that night – drunk or sober. What were they going to do now?

> A clear vision of the future suddenly came to me. I said, 'Do you realise that we shall probably live to be old men!' The enormous change in our outlook, expressed by these words, may not be appar-ent to the present generation. For years we had been accustomed to look no farther than the events of the next day or two, to the next meal, the next rest and, occasionally, the next leave. There were no personal responsibilities, no striving to hold down a job, no income tax, no bills, no dependants to feed. The Army paid us however well or ill we did our jobs, fed us regularly, nursed us when we were ill, provided a dentist when we wanted one, supplied us with equipment, moved us about as by an inevitable destiny and buried us when we died. Our sole responsibility was fighting and all that appertained to it. Now, in a few months' time this tremendously organised backing would be no longer behind us. We should have to fend for ourselves

as individuals in a hard world, building up our own security and comfort and alone providing for our old age.[46]

Captain Eric Bird, 2nd Machine Gun Battalion, 2nd Division

The war was over.

12

AFTERMATH

The raging desire still continues to be demobilised quickly. Nevertheless, I feel pretty sure that, for many, there will be pathetic disillusionment. In the trenches the troops have had plenty of time for thought, and there has grown up in their minds a heavenly picture of an England which does not exist, and never did exist, and never will exist so long as men are human.

Lieutenant Colonel Rowland Feilding, 1/15th (Civil Service Rifles), London Regiment

WHAT ARE WE GOING TO DO NOW? The words might well have been a near universal refrain, but military service was not something that could be dropped at will. It was not a peaceful world and there were significant external and internal threats to the status quo. An Army of Occupation in Germany required contingents from Britain, France and America to make their way into the Rhineland. Elsewhere there were operations to stem the real, or imagined, threat posed by Soviet Russia; troops were needed to occupy key locations in Turkey; while substantial garrisons were still required across the British Empire. The men may have craved demobilisation, but they could not all be released at once, indeed most would have to endure months, if not years, more military service. Even when released they would return to lives that, seen from the grim perspective of the trenches, they may have idealised but which in reality were deeply unsatisfying. Mere schoolboys were now officers, or senior NCOs – trained for nothing but war and unsuited to the mundanities of civilian life. Working-class lads who had risen through the ranks would find themselves once more cast down to the bottom of the pile. Their education or trade apprenticeships had been interrupted. New generations of workers had taken root in the jobs of the serving soldiers. There was a right to return to pre-enlistment positions, yet for many this option was no longer desirable. But what else was there for them to do? Before 11 November they had been bound together in a gigantic communal endeavour; now they would be cast adrift in an unsympathetic world.

This applied even at the very top, as it was almost immediately apparent that Douglas Haig was nothing more than an embarrassment to Lloyd George. Haig was the living reminder of all the poor strategic decisions the Prime Minister had made throughout the war years: of every sideshow campaign where hundreds of thousands of troops had been stranded when desperately needed on the Western Front; of all the hundreds and thousands of casualties endured in needless attacks against the Turks and Bulgarians; of the rich humiliation of Lloyd George's backing of the Nivelle Offensive which had nearly destroyed the French Army in 1917; and he was a reminder that, even at the end, the Prime Minister and his allies had failed to grasp that victory could be achieved in 1918. Throughout, Haig, backed by most senior army officers, had opposed – to the limit of his powers as commander of the BEF – the whims of Lloyd George. From the moment peace was signed, Haig was a nuisance to be tolerated only on sufferance. Instead of being created an earl or duke, as might have been expected, Haig was only offered a viscountcy – equal to that given to Sir John French in reward for his minimal achievements during his tenure as commander in chief in 1914–15. In response, Haig adroitly grasped the high moral ground, rejecting any peerage until an allowance had been fixed for disabled officers and men. In the end Lloyd

George gave in, and Haig attained the title Field Marshal Earl Haig of Bemersyde.

Haig seethed at the various other slights offered to him, as he saw them as disrespectful to the achievements of *all* the men he had commanded. His irritation boiled over when invited to attend a parade organised in honour of a Foch visit to London scheduled for 1 December. He realised that Lloyd George, in a self-serving attack on Haig, was deliberately elevating Foch's role.

> I heard that I was to be in the fifth carriage along with General Henry Wilson. I felt that this was more of an insult than I could put up with, even from the Prime Minister. For the past three years I have effaced myself, because I felt that to win the war it was essential that the British and French Armies should get on well together. And in consequence I have patiently submitted to Lloyd George's conceit and swagger, combined with much boasting as to what he had accomplished, thanks to his foresight in appointing Foch as C-in-C of the Allied Forces, sent Armies to Egypt, Palestine, Mesopotamia, Salonika, etc., etc. Now, the British Army has won the war in France in spite of LG and I have no intention of taking part in any triumphal ride with Foch and a pack of foreigners, through the streets of London, merely to add to LG's importance and help him in his election campaign. So I had a message to the following effect sent by telephone to War Office. First that I could not come to London tomorrow to take part in any ceremonial procession unless I was ordered to do so by the Army Council (tomorrow is a Sunday). Second, was I wanted for any discussion by the War Cabinet or merely for a ceremonial pageant? General Lawrence telephoned to War Office on my behalf and later in the afternoon he stated that he had spoken with General Harrington who fully realised my views on the matter, and that this matter was closed so far as the War Office and I were concerned. Further details of the proposed triumphal progress show that the procession is to go to the French Embassy at Albert Gate for a reception to which I am not invited. A motor car, however, is to be in waiting for me there, to take me 'wherever I like!' Was there ever such an insult prepared

for the welcome of a General on his return from commanding an
Army in the field during four long years of war? Yet this is the
Prime Minister of England's view of what is fitting.[1]

Field Marshal Sir Douglas Haig, General Headquarters, BEF

In the end Haig did not attend.

Eventually, Haig and his army commanders made their official return
to England on 19 December. It is often forgotten just how well-regarded
Haig was after the war – he was a true popular hero. Met by a guard of
honour at Charing Cross station, Haig was then driven in royal carriages
to Buckingham Palace along streets lined with troops and thronged with
cheering crowds. After a royal reception from George V, Haig and his wife
Doris made their way to their Kingston Hill residence and here he found
his true redemption.

> I was hoping for a quiet evening with her but at 8.30 pm a mass
> of people, probably 10,000 in all, with torches, and three bands,
> mostly workmen and women from the Sopwith Aeroplane Works,
> came to salute me and welcome me home to Kingston. I was asked
> to go to the gate and say a few words and see them march past. I
> complied of course and thanked them for turning out to greet me.
> The people were all in their best clothes except some who were
> in fancy dress, and all were most orderly and cheery. Today was
> indeed a red letter one in my life. To receive such a *spontaneous*
> welcome all the way from the coast to my house at Kingston Hill
> shows how the people of England realise what has been accom-
> plished by the Army and myself. This more than compensates me
> for the difficulties put in my way and the coldness towards me by
> the Prime Minister.[2]

Field Marshal Sir Douglas Haig, General Headquarters, BEF

The rest of his life would be devoted to the cause of the British Legion,
a non-political organisation established to care for the needs of ex-ser-
vicemen. Haig's family would discover the penalty of his relatively early
death in January 1928, leaving the field clear for the self-serving memoirs
of Lloyd George and Winston Churchill, and the relentless attacks of

their willing acolytes all too willing to pollute the historiographical waters. By the 1960s they had succeeded in making Haig's name reviled; his reputation reaching a nadir in 1963, through the biting satire of Joan Littlewood's play, *Oh! What a Lovely War*. However, that was also the year in which the John Terraine biography, *Douglas Haig – The Educated Soldier*, was published, a key opening gambit in the move, supported by the majority of recent historians, to view Haig's career honestly, recognising his many strengths and ultimate triumph.

THE PERIOD IMMEDIATELY FOLLOWING the Armistice was a strange one in France and Belgium. Tragically, men were still dying. Wounds incurred days or even months before would doom a man irrespective of a state of peace or war. One among many was Captain Guy Dodgson, who had been badly wounded on 4 November during an attack that pushed forwards to the Forêt de Mormal. At first all seemed well, as he wrote home to his family from No. 3 Casualty Clearing Station at Caudry, near Cambrai.

> They haven't sent me on yet as they weren't sure whether there was going to be any abdominal trouble. They operated the first day here and found very little wrong and today the surgeon is going to have another look at me and I quite hope to get down to a comfortable base hospital and then across the Channel. I will let you know what base hospital I go to. Don't worry about me. I am getting better quickly and the wound (in the right side between the bottom and the stomach) was never really bad. A devil of a Bosche sniper just managed to catch me. My writing is a bit wobbly as I am practically on my back and have had hardly anything to eat except slops since the great event.[3]
>
> Captain Guy Dodgson, 1/1st Hertfordshire Regiment

An operation went well, and Dodgson was almost ready to be sent back to the coast by train when the Medical Officer became concerned by his persistent cough. Grim news would follow from a friend who had visited Dodgson at the clearing station on 14 November.

Although his wounds were progressing favourably, Guy had developed pneumonia and was dangerously ill. I started off early this morning but did not arrive before 11 o'clock and found the poor boy delirious. Everything that was possible was being done for him, including injections and oxygen, and the nurse and the doctor were working incessantly. He apparently had had a very bad night and was barely conscious this morning, although he had spoken a few words to the nurse about 8 o'clock. About 11.30, just for a few seconds, he opened his eyes and I hope and think just recognized me, as a smile, the most pitiable ghost of his own charming smile, swept over his face; and his upper lip twitched in the same old characteristic fashion that I knew so well. After that it was obviously only a question of a short time before he died and, I think purposely, everyone else left me alone with him. He died absolutely peacefully and quickly a few minutes after twelve. If I did wrong I hope you will forgive me, but shortly after he died I kissed him once on the forehead for his Mother and then left him.[4]

Lieutenant Colonel Henry Dakeyne, 8th North Staffordshire Regiment

Next day Guy Dodgson[5] was given a regimental funeral.

Guy was brought down from No. 3 Casualty Clearing Station on an ambulance and was lifted out and carried from there. His slight figure, wrapped in a blanket and covered by a Union Jack, being carried across the square to where we were drawn up waiting was I think the most pitiful sight I have ever seen, and one I don't think I shall ever forget. There seemed so little of him and I found myself wondering where he really was, and whether he had carried away with him all the boyish charm and genius that had been his such a short time before. We fell in behind him, and marched at a slow march to the cemetery, being met a few hundred yards away from it by the Chaplain, who then walked at the head reading the service. It may not have been a very 'showy' funeral, but it was a soldier's funeral and I don't know that anyone can ask for a higher honour than that at the end.[6]

Lieutenant Colonel Henry Dakeyne, 8th North Staffordshire Regiment

For families, the stark juxtaposition between joy at the news of the Armistice and the unexpected demise of their loved one was hard to bear. Guy's brother, Philip, was devastated.

> The bad news of poor Guy has indeed come as a terrible shock to me and I was, for a time, quite overcome by it. The loss of brothers and friends is one that can never be made good to the end of our lives and nobody can ever replace them. One's heart goes out in gratitude to them and it is a great consolation to know their lives have not been given in vain. Poor Mother: I'm afraid she will be broken-hearted and I hate to think of her having to go through such sorrow.[7]
>
> Lieutenant Philip Dodgson, A Battery, 235 Brigade, Royal Field Artillery

THE OCCUPATION OF GERMANY loomed large. The arrangements had been spelled out in the Armistice agreement, whereby the German forces must evacuate occupied France and Belgium within fifteen days, before falling back beyond the Rhine within a further sixteen days. As the march commenced, the spirits of the German soldiers began slowly to improve.

> Our long homeward trek got properly going! Compared to the marches prior to the Armistice the one which was now starting was like walking ever further away from hell and getting nearer to the heaven of a normal civilised existence – the realisation of hopes and expectations which for so long had been relegated to the world of unreality and of dreams![8]
>
> Leutnant Eugen Kaufmann, Infantry Regiment 165

Yet the returning troops soon found that they had plenty to worry about. Their homeland was undergoing a violent political upheaval that was spiralling out of control. The old certainties of life were eroding fast.

> I had to cross the railway line and to wait to let an endless goods train pass the protected crossing. Every carriage bore a stuck-on notice, 'This train must pass unhindered. Workers' and Soldiers'

Council Cologne'. This for me was the first visible proof of the revolution at home! It made a deep impression on me![9]

Leutnant Eugen Kaufmann, Infantry Regiment 165

They had no reliable sources of information as to what was really happening back in Germany, nor indeed anywhere else in the world. In these circumstances, rumours spread like wildfire.

I found some recent newspapers – though not the latest news. But they did contain authentic descriptions of the mutinies in Kiel, the beginnings of a Bolshevistic movement which seemed to be successful in seizing power in Germany. There were also unconfirmed rumours about revolutions in France and England – that Clemenceau, Foch and Lloyd George had been toppled (if not murdered), English and German seamen having fraternised on the High Seas under red flags! Also that the English and Belgian Kings had fled to Holland! I thought 'If this were confirmed then the Peace might still be more bearable than we had lately been led to believe!'[10]

Leutnant Eugen Kaufmann, Infantry Regiment 165

Such latrine gossip was clutching at straws – they soon discovered it had no factual basis. The reality was of a society where the basic tenets of their pre-war existence were now overturned.

We were commanded to assemble the whole Company so that they should, from their midst, elect a 'Council of Confidence' consisting of a non-commissioned officer, a Lance Corporal and two men. This Council was to receive wishes from the soldiers so that they could be duly passed on to the commander of the Battalion? I thought then, 'How quickly all these changes had been effected!' I was too untrained politically to allow myself to doubt the wisdom of anything that was now happening! What I did notice, however, was that our chaps were not in the least changed in their behaviour and discipline had so far not suffered at all! One instance: most of the Company were for that night to sleep on straw in a barn

– it was bound to become very cold toward morning. In contrast,
I myself, like all other officers, enjoyed their undisputed privileges
– a nice warm room, even with a bed to each of us! We get on well
– particularly because of the regimental band making music ahead
of us! When the music stops for a pause there was singing – not
on command – but spontaneous, loud and happy! I thought at the
time that I would remember this joyful march home from the war
for the rest of my life! These men really did not look or behave like
remnants of a beaten army in retreat![11]

Leutnant Eugen Kaufmann, Infantry Regiment 165

This was the product of wishful thinking. The German Army had been
comprehensively defeated in the field; the improved demeanour of the
men did not represent martial fervour, but rather the approach of their
imminent release from the colours and their return home.

Behind them, the British were making their arrangements. The
First, Third and Fifth Armies would stand fast, while Second and Fourth
Armies (rejigged with specially selected corps and divisions) would, after
a short delay, follow up the retreating German Army with the Second
Army moving over the Rhine to become the actual Army of Occupation.
The British were pondering what might await them when they got to
Germany. In several officers' messes there were edgy discussions as to
how their men might behave when exposed to revolutionary propaganda.

They have, as a start, a long and trying march before them, which
I am not afraid of. But if there are months of idleness in Germany
they will be anxious ones. What I fear is German propaganda
among our troops – infinitely worse than riots and street fighting.
The men hate the Hun now, but if he lives in peace with them that
hatred may give way to tolerance and so to friendliness and absorption of revolutionary doctrine, discontent and trouble. There is still
much serious work in front of us. I think we have in front of us a
starving people and they are always desperate and apt to be dangerous. Still things may turn out well.[12]

Major Charles Dudley Ward, 1st Welsh Guards

On 17 November, the British began to advance towards Germany. Even then, the logistical situation remained dire. There was a 20–30-mile gap between the British and German railheads that could not be bridged without considerable railway construction work which would take time to undertake. The only solution was the concentration of all possible lorries to assist the Second and Fourth Army advance to the German frontier. The 29th Division was honoured to be selected as one of the two leading British divisions, but it would prove a tough experience for them, perched as they were at the end of a very long supply line.

> Food and smokes were short all the way, the men were filthy and covered with lice, and utterly worn out. The marches were very severe – anything up to 20 miles a day, the roads bad, and the weather usually appalling. The food supplies for some 20,000 men depended upon one pontoon bridge across the Scheldt. I happened to be crossing this bridge on the occasion when it collapsed. It was crammed with heavy general service wagons drawn by mules. The whole structure groaned and cracked, and eventually sank into the river, the wagons, etc., just getting to the other bank in the nick of time.[13]
>
> Reverend Kenelm Swallow, 2nd South Wales Borderers

One compensation for many of the soldiers was the reception they received from the Belgian populace.

> Coming into Belgian villages was an absolute treat! They all knew we were coming and they frequently came about a mile to meet us and cheered. Every man had a Belgian flag stuck at the end of his rifle. Triumphal arches and bands meeting us. They were absolutely thrilled and it really seemed worth fighting the war to get Germans out of Belgium. The Belgians obviously had very little food and then after a bit we began to run out of food – by the time we reached Germany we were two and a half days minus in food. One cold and frosty morning we were going to march about 15 miles *and* do some work on a road. I told Colonel Crouch on parade that the battalion had no breakfast, the rations hadn't come. He said, 'I'll speak to them!' He spoke to them very effectively, 'Men,

you have just taken part in the most comfortable war in history!'
In many ways that was true, with concert parties and leave, toilet
paper and canteens.[14]

Second Lieutenant Charles Gee, 9th Durham Light Infantry

Ahead of them the Germans had finally reached their own borders.
Amongst them was Corporal Frederick Meisel.

The highways were crammed with moving men, endless lines
of men, war equipment, guns, pack trains, lorries and horses.
Through France and Belgium the grey columns moved. Nobody
knew what the future held, but everybody's mind formed a belief of
better days to come. Back to build up what was wrecked; back to a
country proud even in defeat. We crossed the border and were again
on German soil. Our road took us over German fields, through
German villages and towns. Flags were out in the buildings and
signs decorated with late autumn flowers carried the inscriptions,
'Welcome Home'. German faces greeted us smilingly, blond and
blue-eyed girls waved their handkerchiefs in glee, boys ran alongside us, eager to carry the rifles or equipment. Speeches were made
and through it all the church bells chimed, 'Peace at Last'.[15]

Corporal Frederick Meisel, Infantry Regiment 371

Ironically, most of these defeated German soldiers would be demobilised
long before their British counterparts.

My first meeting with my parents was a highly emotional event.
However joyful their feelings over my home-coming must have
been, their looks still betrayed their constant anxiety and worry
about me, which had lasted right up to the date of the Armistice!
I myself had, during the war, for so long trained myself to be ready
for anything that might happen to me, that I had not realised, as
I now did, that theirs had been the harder fate! This was clearly
visible in their faces, small and still drawn, even now when there
was no longer any reason for fear about me![16]

Eugen Kaufmann

Meanwhile, the British advance guard of the 1st Cavalry Division reached the German border on 1 December. There was then an obligatory pause for a couple of days to allow supplies to catch up. It was thus not until the 4 December that the infantry of 29th Division arrived at the frontier. It was a significant moment, but, at the same time, something of an anti-climax. The reception from the Germans was understandably muted.

> Near Malmedy we came to a place where posts about 6 feet high, painted black and white, ran through the fields at intervals of about 200 yards. This was the frontier. Not a soul was to be seen. There were two houses, one on either side. The Belgian house flew colours. That on the German side had all the blinds drawn down, like a house of mourning and death. When the battalion reached this point an hour or two later they marched over playing national and Welsh airs. Nobody came out to meet us at the first German village, Widerum. No one was to be seen save a few boys and girls. We came upon these somewhat unexpectedly round a corner, and they fled from us in terror. All the inhabitants evidently expected that unspeakable atrocities would be committed. We found them quiet, homely people, all of them hating the war, and most of them quite likeable. The battalion arrived soaked to the skin after a long march in a continuous downpour; hot drinks were waiting for them in every billet, and the men were provided with fresh clean straw in abundance. As we went farther, and came to somewhat larger places, proclamations in German, bordered in deep black, were to be seen on all prominent walls. These gave the Germans the official intimation of their country's humiliation, coupled with instructions as to how to behave during the occupation. We received throughout every possible assistance from all town and village authorities, and it was interesting to observe the accuracy and businesslike method which ensured that every burgomaster was in possession of all details affecting the billeting capacity of his town or village. These were invariably handed over to me in my capacity as interpreter of German.[17]

Reverend Kenelm Swallow, 2nd South Wales Borderers

The mechanics of the occupation wrong-footed many of the men. Having hated the Germans for so long, envisioning them as monsters, the rather more mundane actuality came as something of a surprise.

> I had serious misgivings before entering Germany. My comrades vowed such vengeance on the people that I anticipated something worse than war. In theory, no treatment was going to be bad enough and cruel enough for the German. We were out to wreak on him four years' war-weariness; we were ready to settle all the old scores of treachery on the field and mischance in the fight. What, therefore, was my surprise to find, after two or three days in Germany, all our roaring lions converted into sucking doves.[18]
>
> Private Stephen Graham, 2nd Scots Guards

This was not an isolated response. Almost everywhere, the troops found themselves greeted with an unexpected civility. Even the fearsome Lieutenant Colonel Ernest Crouch of the 9th Durham Light Infantry found himself mentally disarmed.

> When we got into Germany, a country village, we halted there and the Colonel Crouch disappeared. People came to ask me what was happening and I said, 'I don't know!' Eventually Crouch came back after quite a long time, turned me aside and said, 'Gee, I've been walking round a bit, the people look quite human – I think we must treat them nicely!'[19]
>
> Second Lieutenant Charles Gee, 9th Durham Light Infantry

The British had taken stringent precautions to prevent unfortunate incidents triggered by the mutual loathing that had been anticipated from both sides.

> Our authorities certainly expected a different attitude, for commanding officers had been asked to leave behind any specially bad characters who might be likely to get out of hand in enemy country, and we were all warned to stick to one another and not quarrel among ourselves, as we should need to preserve a united front in the country of the enemy. Every man in a billeting party was

obliged to carry a revolver. Some units, I believe, made their entry into all towns and villages with fixed bayonets. But public opinion and atmosphere was different from what had been expected. No, there was not much craft or cunning calculation in the German attitude to us. The same attitude was to be found in the smallest and remotest villages as in the large towns. His strongest feeling was one of relief that the war was over – on any terms. Our coming in was a secondary evil only.[20]

Private Stephen Graham, 2nd Scots Guards

Crossing the Rhine would be a key symbolic moment of German defeat. The Cologne Department contained about 1,250,000 inhabitants of which 600,000 lived in the city of Cologne itself. This was a modern Rhineland city, blessed with a healthy mixture of heavy industry and manufacturing factories; in addition, it was an important rail hub for western Germany. The British crossed the Rhine to take up occupation of the east bank bridgehead, which stretched from Benrath in the north to Bonn in the south, with a radius of about 18 miles from the Cologne crossing point.

We crossed the Rhine at Bonn. The salute was taken by General Sir Arthur Currie, the commander of the Canadian forces. He took the salute. In England at the time, there'd been a popular song called, 'When we Wind up the Watch on the Rhine' – and there were all the troops winding up their watches crossing over the bridge. I had no watch, but it made me laugh.[21]

Sergeant William Collins, No. 1 Cavalry Field Ambulance, Royal Army Medical Corps

The entrance into Cologne could easily have gone badly as some soldiers seemed intent on enforcing respect for the occupying forces right from the start.

At the head of the column escorts accompanying officers on horse-back amused themselves by knocking off the hats of onlookers who failed to remove them. The official record says they 'had much

pleasure in teaching them manners'. No comment. The people of
Cologne welcomed us as rescuers from anarchy. It was a city of
hunger and misery. One felt ashamed to see the damage to the
lovely cathedral, and even more ashamed to walk about well fed
while children begged for food. We were met not with hatred, but
with fear, and offered friendly hospitality that was not without a
tinge of not so admirable subservience. Despite their pitiable circumstances, lowly citizens invited us into their homes and pressed
us to share their meagre fare, and we were at once aware that the
Huns were not such bestial monsters as we had been led to believe,
but human beings sharing the same sufferings and decent feelings
as ourselves.[22]

Private Norman Cliff, 1st Grenadier Guards

The British moved to the limits of the bridgehead and immediately began
constructing basic defence works – battalion defensive positions that
were covered by a series of outposts situated on the perimeter of a 6-mile
neutral zone.

Behind the new defences, it was strange that hatreds bred during
wartime seemed to melt away. In the flesh, the inhabitants of Cologne
made very poor enemies.

We had come prepared for hostility, but were met with smiles!
Many men who had been loudest in their threats of what they
would do to 'the dirty Hun' when they got the chance, speed-
ily reversed their attitude. Later, when on sentry in the city, most
passers-by would give me a pleasant '*Morgen!*' or '*Guten nacht!*' and
I heard that men who had the luck to be billeted on private families were made extremely comfortable. In the shops, too, there was
little disposition to raise prices against us, or to take advantage of
the troops' ignorance of the rate of exchange. In fact, it was often
the other way about. German ex-soldiers, too, were often eager to
fraternise with our men and to exchange war-reminiscences, so far
as the language difficulty would permit. Was all this conciliation
no more than a cunning conspiracy to secure better treatment for
themselves? Perhaps – it's hard to be sure. But if it was deliberate, it

was remarkably unanimous and widespread. The people welcomed us, not as conquerors, but as deliverers from war. That was the universal feeling: relief that the war was over, at any price.[23]

Private Frederick Noakes, 1st Coldstream Guards

Many of the German civilians had a very real fear of a Bolshevik uprising. What they wanted was nothing more than peace and a return to some kind of normality, not a Communist nirvana.

They were pleased to see us! Funny thing to say, but there were revolutions breaking out – and there might be one in the Rhineland – and they knew that if we were there, there wouldn't be anything like that! I don't think the average British soldier in the front lines ever had any deep feelings regarding revenge or anything against the German – he admired and respected him! The French soldiers used to come in gangs of about four and they used to walk on the footpath. If there were German civilians – if they didn't step off the footpath – they pushed them off – shouldered them off. I didn't think that was the right thing to do![24]

Guardsman Horace Calvert, 2nd Grenadier Guards

However, the British were also capable of poor behaviour in their treatment of helpless civilians. One unpleasant incident took place on Christmas Day, when a group of Welsh Guards officers rather 'let themselves go'.

About 4 o'clock Ball,[25] Jackie,[26] Battye,[27] Copland Griffiths,[28] Evans[29] and myself went into the town to see if we could get some fun. Jack said he would take us to a good place and introduced us to a low café where dancing was going on. For some unknown reason the youngsters immediately started to 'rag' the place. They said it was because it annoyed them to see Huns dancing. Any how we all joined in and raced round in a ring, holding each other's hands with the Hun dancers in the middle. As we all wear enormous pistols here they were quite alarmed and the women began to squeal. Then someone let go and Ball swung round and knocked

over a table; fearful crash of glasses. Old Vickery[30] was there with
some of his staff and they began to utter fox-hunting yells. It was
really funny. The civilians went out in one stream followed by us.
In five minutes we had emptied the place and as Ball said, 'Once
more established our superiority!' We then had an excellent dinner
with Rhine salmon and lager beer – and got back by the last train
at nine. Everyone thought it a most successful day.[31]

Major Charles Dudley Ward, 1st Welsh Guards

This account does not sit altogether well with some of the claims that
Dudley Ward made in his published: *History of the Welsh Guards*.

The behaviour of the Welsh Guards in Cologne was, as it has
always been, exemplary. They had, no doubt, many temptations,
cunningly offered by the Germans; but their attitude was always
correct, and in all respects they proved themselves the smartest
battalion in the Guards Division.[32]

Major Charles Dudley Ward, 1st Welsh Guards

But perhaps Dudley Ward was only referring to the other ranks – not the
officers?

There must have been many cases where practical jokes and high
spirits that seemed hilarious to drunken young officers could be deeply
offensive to the German inhabitants. This kind of thoughtless behaviour
was typified by a wild officers' mess party in the town of Bickendorf which
was held to celebrate the departure of 4 Squadron, Australian Flying
Corps in March 1919.

The Australians decided to paint Kaiser Bill's gigantic eques-
trian status, nearly opposite our mess, with white aircraft fabric
paint. The Kaiser's charger, twice as large as life, was a stallion
and the sculptor, with true Teutonic thoroughness, had faithfully
reproduced every detail of the animal's anatomy to scale. After
the Australians had finished the job, the stallion possessed Zebra
stripes and huge white bollocks! To crown all, literally, the Aussies
borrowed our CO's enamel chamber pot and wired it on top of the

Kaiser's head. Like Queen Victoria, the Germans were definitely *not* amused when they beheld this ribald spectacle next morning. Furious protests were made, but the culprits were by then well on their way home. For several days afterwards the Germans had a party of charwomen with buckets of water and scrubbing brushes at work trying to clean up the statue. Alas the white 'dope' was both water and petrol resistant and when I left Cologne the Zebra stripes still showed up faintly despite all the efforts of the 'Seven maids with seven mops'![33]

Second Lieutenant John Blanford, 206 Squadron

Yet despite occasional incidents and flare-ups, generally the British and Germans found a way of co-existing without too much overt rancour.

The billeting of so many troops in the Cologne area required considerable organisation. The Germans were required to make available any suitable buildings such as former German barracks, public buildings and factory premises. Private Norman Cliff was more than satisfied with his billets, but outraged by the preparations for a particularly public private inspection.

We were billeted in the well-equipped buildings of a college on the outskirts of the city, in conditions that were luxurious by the standards to which we had been accustomed. No sooner had we settled in than an inspection by the Prince of Wales was arranged. All the usual paraphernalia of a royal occasion went into operation, and the pretence was made that the Prince would see us engaged in our normal routine. It fell to the lot of Guardsman Cliff to pose in a state of nature under a shower in a cubicle at the baths. For an unconscionable time, I shivered in the longest ablution of my life, and at length I heard the approach of the royal procession. Believe it or not, His Royal Highness swept past without even a glance at my magnificent physique, and I had made a full frontal exposure to no effect! I wiped down hurriedly, relieved but humiliated, and struggled into my uniform, nursing disloyal thoughts of the indifference of noble personages to the higher things of life![34]

Private Norman Cliff, 1st Grenadier Guards

The officers and many soldiers were also housed in hotels and private billets. Sergeant William Collins found himself billeted in the hamlet of Heppendorf and was mostly content with his lot.

> We were billeted with the local population in their homes. We were given a room – I had a very small room with a sort of bunk bed, but it was something after nearly four and a half years of sleeping on the ground – it was a luxury! I was billeted with a small holding farmer and he had two daughters. The elder one was quite friendly, as a matter of fact she washed all my smalls for me! Our uniforms were all smartened up, we were polishing our buttons and we were well turned out. I must say the young men of Heppendorf didn't take very kindly to us. One morning we came down and on the village pump was written a message in German, 'It took four and a half years for the brave British troops to conquer the German Army, but they conquered the girls of Heppendorf in one night!' That was a bit of an exaggeration, but there was no doubt about it that the attitude of the females in Heppendorf towards our troops in general was a very friendly one! I think a few bars of chocolate exchanged hands![35]
>
> Sergeant William Collins, No. 1 Cavalry Field Ambulance, Royal Army Medical Corps

This was a not uncommon situation. Captain Rymer Murray-Jones was organising the billets in a village about 5 miles out of Cologne, when there was an unfortunate misunderstanding.

> I'd put the major into the best billet. The major went there and had a talk with the two daughters. They weren't very lovely either! They said how they'd all got poison in bottles for when the brutal British came in – they were going to take poison. Instead of which she came down halfway through the night and said she was prepared to cooperate with the Major! At least half the men were immediately snuggled up with the German ladies. I think it was rather bad, but only to be expected. You can't keep the men away from it![36]
>
> Captain Rymer Murray Jones, A Battery, 74th Brigade, Royal Field Artillery

However, young Second Lieutenant Charles Gee received an interesting insight into at least one unexpected aspect of the German male sexuality, during what he maintained was an entirely 'innocent' tour of the facilities on offer in the inner sanctums of an officers' brothel in the Cologne area.

We told them quite clearly we didn't want girls – we wanted a drink. They were friendly and we went there quite often. They knew that we'd come for a drink and a chatter – they'd occasionally put on some sort of sex exhibition! One of the girls was very young, about seventeen, and was an Alsatian, i.e. French not German by race. She said to two or three of us one night, 'Come and see my room!' She showed us: there was a divan bed, 'That's where I go with people who want to sleep with me, but I hate the Germans. They don't ever sleep with me, some British do, but the German don't!' She opened the door to a room fitted out like a gym. They went there to be tortured; they got their sex from being beaten. There was a wire cupboard about 6-feet high. A naked man would be locked in it and poked with something that hurt until he got his money's worth! Presumably the girl would be naked. Also a thing where he would lie on a stretcher raised above the floor with a hole in the middle he put his privates through the middle and they were strapped somehow underneath. But what happened with the rings, parallel bars and horizontal bar – standard things from the old-fashioned gym that I'd been brought up with? I suppose they'd show off their manhood and skill![37]

Second Lieutenant Charles Gee, 9th Durham Light Infantry

All in all, this experience was probably quite enough to make any respectable young man's eyes water.

The apparently amorous feelings of many German women must often have been underpinned by a desperation for the necessities of life; a weakness of which the more unscrupulous soldiers were far too willing to take advantage.

It was full of ladies of easy virtue! Sex was freely offered for fruit, tinned fruit, soap, bully beef or anything in short supply. The naval blockade had done its business without doubt. They hung around the barracks and they'd offer you sex if you could supply them with anything. They were desperate.[38]

Guardsman Horace Calvert, 2nd Grenadier Guards

Before long the black market spread its tentacles. Activities would start on a small scale, with just a few cigarettes or tins of food, but would soon grow in both size and scope. Private Herbert Cooper became aware of the activities of a prominent black-market profiteer while he was working on the officers' leave train which plied backwards and forwards from Boulogne to Cologne. The opportunities were obvious.

A little racket began on the train because you could get anything from the German population for a couple of cigarettes. There was a chap, Private Sharkey, who wasn't content with taking a box of cigarettes. He started with cartons of cigarettes and it grew and grew, until he was going to the Navy and Army Canteen Board store places in Boulogne and he'd take a wooden case full of cartons of cigarettes! He used to pay so much to the store keeper and when the train was in the siding at Boulogne would drive up and he'd help him on with a case of cigarettes – then the door was closed. His customer in Germany was the station master at the Cologne sidings. He was a Jewish fellow, so there were no flies on him. When our train was in the sidings he would provide an engine and a van, the case would be transferred to it and up to the station master's place. How much he made out of that I don't know. The business grew and grew.[39]

Private Herbert Cooper, Officers' Leave Trains, Army Service Corps

The real black market was not an amusing little sideline run by the cheery 'duckers and divers' of legend, however, but rather a corrupt criminal enterprise taking advantage of German civilians' misery out of sheer greed.

The Second Army was renamed the British Army of the Rhine in April 1919. At this point, there was a period of mild tension, as plans and preparation were made for an advance into Germany should the German government fail to sign the Treaty of Versailles, which ultimately brought a formal end to the Great War on 28 June 1919. This was followed by another flurry of alarm when it appeared that the Germans might not accept the stringent terms imposed, before it was finally ratified on 10 January 1920. The British would stay in the Rhineland until 1929. They were within, but separate from, a Germany that was continually racked by economic, political and revolutionary turmoil throughout the 1920s.

Walter Rappolt had been demobilised at the end of November and returned home to Hamburg, where he studied law at the university before joining the family textile firm. For a commercial man like Rappolt, a natural conservative, what was happening in Germany was totally unacceptable. Like many ex-army officers, he was soon sucked into one of the para-military Freikorps which had sprung up all over the country.

> Germany regarded the terms set by the Allies as unacceptable. It was only in June 1919 that the peace treaty – I would put the word in inverted commas – was signed! The Germans did not regard that as a peace. We lost all our Colonies, had to pay huge reparations. The political situation was very unstable. At the beginning of 1919 there were fights in Berlin with Sparticists. There were revolutions everywhere, in Munich there was a Communist regime for some time. In the eastern part, there were fights with Poles in Silesia and Pomerania. As far as Hamburg was concerned, soon after the Armistice we formed a sort of citizens' guard, who patrolled the streets after nightfall against revolutionaries, criminal robbers and so on. A little later in spring a sort of Freikorps was set up at Bahrenfeld – which I also joined. They were all middle-class people who wanted to protect their homes from Bolshevists, Communists and so on. Practically all my friends of my age had joined. I used my old uniform, without my epaulettes. We all had our carbines and one cannon, which was attached to a truck. I don't think it was ever fired! It was organised in companies and the whole organisation was called Bahrenfeld Battalion. There were perhaps two or three thousands of us. Normally there were only a few at Bahrenfeld and we used to go to our offices and work there

as usual. When a telephone call arrived that we had been called up, whereupon I changed into my uniform and went to Bahrenfeld. There were fights in Hamburg. In one, I think about twenty-two of the Bahrenfelders were killed but I did not take part. There was also a one- or two-day war between Hamburg and the neighbouring town of Bremen which was ruled by Communists – who were chased out! [40]

Walter Rappolt

Germany would prove to be a cauldron of hatred, a breeding ground in which fascism could simmer, twisting perceptions of the war, of how Germany had been defeated, until a new reality had been carved out by Hitler and his Nazi Party. But that is another story.

WHEREVER THEY WERE, whether in Germany, France or Belgium, the troops found that time hung heavy on their hands. With the war over, their sense of common purpose was eroding away with every day that passed. It had always been a central tenet of the British Army that the officers had to keep the men busy or trouble would soon brew. Haig was well aware of this characteristic of the British soldier and on 11 November had warned his five army commanders of the problem they faced.

> I then pointed out the importance of looking after the troops during the period following the cessation of hostilities. Very often the best fighters are the most difficult to deal with in periods of quiet! I suggested a number of ways in which men can be kept occupied. It is as much the duty of all officers to keep their men amused as it is to train them for war. If funds are wanted, GHQ should be informed, and I'll arrange for money to be found. [41]

Field Marshal Sir Douglas Haig, General Headquarters, BEF

It was suggested officers avoid 'irritating restrictions' and there were suggestions for organised visits to places of interest, celebratory military parades and processions, military demonstrations of the new technology introduced during the war and lectures on 'after the war'. It was recognised that competitions and sports of all sorts would be a welcome distraction. Most of these were tried, but it was an uphill struggle – as even those responsible realised.

> Everything is as dull as ditch water and I can see that it is going to be difficult to keep the Army – officers and men – amused and happy if this interregnum lasts very long. It is all very well soldiering when a war is in progress and you feel that your presence is essential to victory – but quite another thing being obliged to hang about in a foreign country (which is getting a bit tired of you!) when someone else is at home trying to get hold of your job.[42]

Lieutenant Colonel Cuthbert Headlam, Training Branch, General Headquarters, BEF

The men were generally fairly understanding of the general situation, but at the same time they had their own agenda.

> We soon began to speculate as to how long it was likely to be before we got home and into our 'civvie' clothes. As individuals, we were quite ready to go home at once, but we appreciated that some time must elapse before we could all hope to be back in civilian life. In the meantime, we began to feel all dressed up with nowhere to go, in other words that we were now neither soldiers nor civilians. We hardly expected to be allowed to remain idle, but at the same time thought that the new situation called for a rather less strictly military attitude on the part of the higher ranks. As things turned out, the people who had ordered our comings and goings for the past few years struck a very fair balance, which left the troops very content.[43]

Corporal Charles Hennessey, 2/15th (Civil Service Rifles), London Regiment

In the desolate zone of destruction that stretched across France and Belgium there was a requirement for a great deal of battlefield clearance, but this was both gruesome and dangerous at times. Many troops were bitter at being assigned to such a role.

Instead of garnering the fruits of victory in Rhineland, we were set
to gather in the rusty aftermath of war which abounded on the fields
of combat. Miles and miles of barbed wire we must have reeled in,
hundreds and hundreds of tin hats – Bosche and British – were
picked up, and bombs, rifles, shells, guns, aeroplanes, ammunition
boxes, derelict wagons, loads of timber and every conceivable form
of war material accumulated pyramid-like in monumental mounds
along the sides of the roadways. The energy we expended on the
new task in the first few weeks was colossal. But the machinery for
getting the stuff away to Blighty was not conspicuously adequate,
and gradually it began to dawn on the consciousness of the sol-
dier-man that there was scant chance of much of the mouldering
stuff we had collected ever seeing the white cliffs of old England. It
seemed a poor job at the best to be left to scavenge the dirty mess
the Hun had made, and the victorious warrior came to the conclusion that someone was getting a bit of a rise out of him.[44]

Lieutenant Colonel Thomas Banks, 10th Essex Regiment

The problem was that as the wartime unity eroded, men sought reasons
why they should be exempt from work, and came to believe that other
men with less service at the front should take over. This was a pernicious
influence, but nonetheless also understandable.

We were then employed on a task which I thought was disgusting.
I had to take working parties out to clear up all sorts of rubbish,
dud bombs, dud shells, which were still killing men long after
the war was over. The whole countryside was littered with lethal
weapons which might go up at any time. We lost one or two men
through these shells; you don't know what's going to happen to
them. You wanted experts to clear them really. One day, a friend of
mine and myself, we decided we weren't going to do any more of
that, when they got men there who'd only been in France three or
four months. We refused to obey orders to go to this clearing up
and went out for the day from the Battalion. Of course, we were
hauled up before the company commander. He said to me, 'I could
have you court-martialled for this, but you've done some very good

work in the line and I'm going to simply reprimand you!' The other chap, I think he was reduced one rank.[45]

Corporal Clifford Lane, 2nd Bedfordshire Regiment

One of the trickiest tasks was the collection and disposal of cylinders full of poisonous gas. These were collected together in dumps, but the condition of the cylinders caused considerable concern as some were leaking. It was decided to despatch some 1,500 cylinders of phosgene back to Morecambe, where it was intended for use in the manufacture of dyes. This was easier said than done! The cylinders were carefully loaded on to a train, but, during the Channel crossing, some of the leaking phosgene made its way into the ship's engine room forcing the stokers to don gas masks. The offending cylinder was unceremoniously pitched over the side into the sea, but worse was to follow in the train journey to the northwest. Two more leaking cylinders had to be buried by the train track, but by now several cylinders were giving problems and the train crew was badly affected. It subsequently became apparent that the train was exuding a plume of phosgene which was reported to have killed several farm animals. After this chastening experience, the remainder of the gas cylinders were buried on a deserted section of the French coast – where perhaps they lie to this day.

If they were based in France or Belgium, then the men had the opportunity to visit the places where they had fought, perhaps to find the graves of old comrades they had lost in action. Others who had never been on active service in the war were keen to see the fabled battlefields. Colonel Rowland Feilding was rather reluctantly inveigled into taking an American Army doctor around the old Cuinchy-Loos trenches. Feilding recounts a story that rings across the years to our current era of battlefield tourism.

He is a good enough fellow, but was too entirely absorbed in the collection of souvenirs. I remember one of my officers – Barron, during the battle at Croisilles, telling a Private whom he found relieving a German prisoner in a dugout of his watch – if he wanted souvenirs – to go and get them in the firing line. How much less right has a mere sightseer to souvenirs? It is horrifying to see this sacred ground desecrated in this way, and still more so to think of what will happen when the cheap tripper is let loose. With his spit he will saturate the ground that has been soaked with the blood of our soldiers. This particular man, not knowing what he was doing, would pick up a bone and would call out, 'Oh, look, a human tibia!' It is the way of the world, no doubt, but I pray I may see no more of it. I know that these things will be collected, and hoarded, and no doubt boasted of, by tourists, things that no one who has fought would have in his possession.[46]

Lieutenant Colonel Rowland Feilding, 1/15th (Civil Service Rifles), London Regiment

His reactions were understandable, but then Feilding did something that – even a hundred years later – would be regarded as a highly dangerous and irresponsible in the extreme.

Before we left I thought I would give our visitor a respectable souvenir, and picked up a German hand grenade. It had been lying about so long that I did not think it could possibly have any sting left. However, I pulled the safety cord to make sure, and immediately there followed a hissing sound. I called to the two doctors to take cover and threw the bomb, which a second or two later went off with a loud explosion. A splinter drew a spot of blood from our visitor's hand, at which he said, jokingly, 'Anyhow, I shall be able to tell them at home that I've had a wound!'[47]

Lieutenant Colonel Rowland Feilding, 1/15th (Civil Service Rifles), London Regiment

They had been lucky! People are still badly injured in such incidents today.

There was one obvious answer to the lacunae in the lives of soldiers left by the end of the war: a programme of mass education for the men. Such a project was easy to conceive, but difficult in the extreme to deliver. Most units were faced with a daunting series of difficulties as they lacked enough qualified teachers, access to feasible classrooms, textbooks, writing paper, or even an agreed syllabus of what was to be taught. At times, the results could be almost farcical.

> It was very greatly a case of brick-making without straw. For the Armistice, like the War, caught England bending, and the hastily-worked-out scheme of Army education had little chance to come to bearing-time. We had instructions and admonitions on the subject months before any materials or books arrived, and one remembers the momentous day when the first educational material for the Brigade arrived – three 12-inch rulers for three thousand men! Yet more humorous was the arrival of one typewriter keyboard for the instruction of the Division in typing – 10,000 men spread over 20 miles of countryside![48]
>
> Lieutenant Colonel Thomas Banks, 10th Essex Regiment

Gradually, through extensive improvisation, they made some progress. It was soon evident that there was no point in teaching calculous to the innumerate, or simple spelling to a clerk or graduate. The average battalion was of true mixed ability.

> Each company in turn was set a simple examination paper, which consisted of a short précis, a short piece of dictation, the interpretation and correct use of half a dozen four-syllable words, and some simple questions in arithmetic. From the results obtained – and it should be stated that but for the cordial cooperation of all ranks the results would have been nil – we were able to grade the battalion into three classes in English and arithmetic, X, Y and Z. From this, again, we were able to divide the battalion into three main groups: the 'General Education Group', subdivided into elementary and intermediate classes for English subjects and arithmetic respectively; the 'Commercial Group', who did bookkeeping, commercial correspondence, shorthand, and languages, in addition to a restricted programme of general subjects; and the 'Preliminary Group', who were instructed in reading and writing.[49]
>
> Captain Charles Wurtzburg, 2/6th King's Liverpool Regiment

Units that invested effort in the project were often rewarded by a startling enthusiasm for education among the men, many of whom seemed to seek knowledge as dried-up plants thirst for water.

> Education became the motto, and the gentler ways of pen and plodding pencil sought to demonstrate their superiority to the erstwhile pastimes of tummy-thrusts and throat-jabs. No doubt this latter-day renaissance of learning served its purpose, for there was no ambiguity about the volume of keen interest it aroused among the men. Second Lieutenant Potter and Sergeants Hodges and Whittaker, aided by anyone who could resuscitate any lingering remnants of the lessons of boyhood's days, sought to instruct the eager proselytes in reading, 'riting and 'rithmetic, and a haphazard medley of subjects such as Shorthand, Political Economy, Agriculture, Music, Steam Engines and Art. We found one or two men who were completely illiterate, and they, at least, will be able to follow the racing news in the evening papers as a result of midnight oil at Ponchaux. The delight of one boy who told me that he had managed to write his first letter home to his mother had something touching about it.[50]

> Lieutenant Colonel Thomas Banks, 10th Essex Regiment

Overall, there was an acceptance that, however, makeshift and ill-considered, whatever was achieved was of value. Education is never wasted.

DEMOBILISATION WAS ALL MEN REALLY CARED ABOUT. They may have bided their time in educational classes, engaged in low-key tourism and countless football matches, but underlying everything was the desire to get home; the desire to be free of what they considered the petty restrictions of army life.

> We were all impatient to be freed from regimentation, to return home, to be free individuals again, to recover our dignity as human beings, to cast off uniforms, to be done with parades and bull, to cease to be bawled at, and ordered about; to get away from all

the noise of guns, and drums, and bugles, and barking NCOs; to possess our own souls and to be masters of our own lives. What unimaginably heavenly bliss awaited us once we could escape from this stifling machine. We thought of love and leisure, of work we could enjoy, of being in affectionate indulgent company again, surrounded by our dear ones in the quiet peace of home. We should miss the rough cheerful companionship of the chums we had learnt to respect in dire adversity, and on the brink of eternity, but how welcome the gentle feminine touch would be for a change. We discussed our prospects, the kind of jobs we hoped to secure, the things we felt would change for the better.[51]

Private Norman Cliff, 1st Grenadier Guards

One veteran summed it up in a poem.

When I put on my civvies,
How happy I shall be,
To hear no more the cannon roar,
And know that I am free.[52]

Major Edward de Stein, Machine Gun Corps

Yet demobilisation was a massive undertaking. The army had swollen from its pre-war strength of 400,000 to 3,800,000; now it would have to shrink back. The question was how was it to be managed without triggering civil and industrial chaos? The terrifying scale of the problem had to be acknowledged. This was an army of millions spread across three continents. It was, if anything, an even greater challenge than the wartime mobilisation had been, as the reverse process would have to occur over a far more compressed time frame. Optimism of being home in a few weeks was sadly misplaced. It was one thing to identify the difficulties, but quite another to solve them. Many of the men were deeply concerned as to their employment prospects on leaving the army. Assurances had been given by their employers and the government, but they could not help but worry. With the best will in the world there would still be injustice, winners and losers, whatever decisions were taken as to the order and manner of demobilisation.

The government decided to adopt a system of piecemeal demobilisation, with priority given to 'pivotal men' who had worked in professions essential to get the British economy working again. The idea was that the battalions would be gradually reduced to a cadre, with the first to go being the civil servants – 'demobilisers' – who would be needed to administer the scheme. Then the agreed priority groups were coal miners, agricultural workers, seamen and fishermen, shipbuilders, building trades, students and teachers. Then the early volunteers would be released, with the conscripts supposedly left at the back of the queue. Regular soldiers would be required to complete their period of service with the colours. Some 17,000 soldiers a day would be demobilised from the Western Front area. A soldier would be sent back via a Corps Concentration Camp, then a series of staging camps, an Embarkation Camp, a Disembarkation Camp and finally a Dispersal Camp – hopefully as close as possible to the soldier's home town.

The system adopted was a mixture of pragmatism and principle – and, as might be expected, satisfied almost nobody. Delays multiplied as the army struggled to identify its demobilisers and pivotal men. One huge problem was that the key industry workers had often only recently been conscripted to join the army, after being 'combed out' during the 1918 manpower shortage. Now they would be demobilised first! This caused considerable resentment and there were outbreaks of ill-discipline that shaded into outright mutiny. Private Horace Calvert witnessed a typical 'spot of bother' at the Harfleur Base Camp on 9 December.

> I saw these red-tabbed staff officers – one of them was a Brigadier – surrounded by a lot of troops – three or four hundred – all sorts of regiments. There were soldiers, very excited shouting, the main theme was they wanted to go into Le Havre – all restrictions lifted, they wanted money paid every week so they could enjoy themselves – they hadn't been paid for weeks. They wanted the Military Police easing up a bit on them and something done about demobilisation! The rumour was around that the last to be called up would be the first to be demobilised, because they were the key men to get industry going. Some of the chaps in this disturbance said

they hadn't been home for four years. Everyone was in agreement apparently because occasionally there was a shout, 'YES!' I was on the outskirts, I kept a few yards away; I didn't join in – I listened! I thought, 'I'm not getting mixed up in that lot!' There were two or three ringleaders, they were doing all the talking and waving every-one around to come and join them, there was two or three hundred there. It wasn't a mutiny – I would call it a disturbance! There was no officer injured; nobody was attacked.[53]

Private Horace Calvert, Grenadier Guards, Harfleur Base Camp, Le Havre

The camp was swiftly cleared and the troublemakers dispersed. There was also a major disturbance at Victoria Station in London, triggered by unrest among troops supposed to be returning from home leave to their units. This was part of a veritable rash of protests, strikes and demonstrations in the south of England in early January 1919. Private Alexander Jamieson was caught up in the disturbances while on leave.

Victoria Station there was a bit of a riot! Owing to storms in the Channel and I think a strike, there was no Cross-Channel services for those going back to Germany. Well 24-hours leave was all right for those who lived within a reasonable distance of London, they could just go home. But it was no good for us from Scotland and many other places. The result was the Railway Transport Office in Victoria Station was attacked, broken in to and blank leave passes stolen! Then a procession formed and marched to Whitehall, to the War Office! We got there and I remember hearing somebody smashing a window. We both said, 'Look, we're going to get out of this!' So we did! We went and got into a YMCA for the night and got away next day to Germany.[54]

Private Alexander Jamieson, 11th Royal Scots

The government responded by allowing soldiers on home leave to take up offers of work from their pre-war employers provided that the local employment exchange and the parent army unit agreed. Then, on 17 January 1919, a new system was brought in which prioritised the release of men who had enlisted before the introduction of conscription in 1916; with exceptions made for compassionate cases, men with three or more wound stripes, those over 41 years old, a limited number of just 250,000 pivotal men and the demobilisers to administer the system. Shortly afterwards a new act allowed the compulsory military service required from conscripts to be extended into 1920. At the same time pay rates were doubled to try and compensate men who wanted to be free of the army. Taken in total, the measures worked, and although there were still sporadic outbreaks of unrest, gradually the discontent ebbed away.

The demobilisation process was labour intensive, and every unit set up its own in-house organisation to process the men as their time for demobilisation grew nigh. Lance Corporal Walter Williamson was selected to run the scheme for the 1/6th Cheshire Regiment. Once they had grasped what they had to do, their work began. It is refreshing to note that many aspects of human nature had not changed.

Miners are first priority. I have evidently been misinformed in my early youth, when I was taught that Cheshire was an agricultural county, as I was surprised when a call went round the battalion for miners, about 50 per cent reported to the Demob Office. Then the fun started. When it was explained that they would be put into mines by the government, and would not be released until such time as their corresponding length of service men in non-priority classes were demobbed, there was a sudden reduction in the number of miners, and the 'Cheshires' reverted to a more agricultural flavour.[55]

Lance Corporal Walter Williamson, 1/6th Cheshire Regiment

The pace of the work gradually increased, and by late January 1919 they were struggling to keep up. When the men turned up at the orderly room, Williamson and his assistant had a well-practised drill as each 'victim' is stood before them.

Tommy with half a dozen small forms, me with that monumental and now famous form Z10 (Dispersal Certificate). Tommy snaps at him 'Number?' and I yell, 'Name?' and he gets a crick in his neck

and an impediment in his speech trying to answer us both at once.
I can go on filling my forms up from the information I have got
while I can hear Tommy at it, 'Have you a pair of socks?' etc., then
a pause, then the famous question 'Have you anything wrong with
you?' Instead of, 'Do you wish to claim for any physical disability
due to your military service?'[56]

Lance Corporal Walter Williamson, 1/6th Cheshire Regiment

Next morning, each of the men would report for the last time before
leaving their unit.

I grab ten bundles of papers and rush downstairs and hand them
a bundle each, and then give them another lecture on what has to
be done with each form, where they are to hand it in, which they
are to hand in and which they are to keep. Then one man will
chip in that he hasn't got two little 'uns like the next man, then I
find he has forgotten to get his louse – pardon – I mean medical
certificate and clothing certificate, then I get excited in a calm way
and fix him up with blanks to get signed on his way back past the
camp. I then warn them to get dressed as the CO will come and
say a parting word. I don't mean that they have forgotten to put
their trousers on or anything like that – the weather is a bit too
nippy for such forgetfulness – but just to get their equipment on
again and button their pockets up. By the time the CO has shaken
hands with them all and assured them that they will all want to
be back in the Army in a month, another allotment comes in for
the next day![57]

Lance Corporal Walter Williamson, 1/6th Cheshire Regiment

The procedure was much the same in every battalion. Some of the more
sentimental commanding officers found the actual moment of departure
of these men quite emotional. After all they had shared so much, and now
they were all dispersing, going off to an uncertain future.

Early in January the first envied drafts left for Blighty and the
looked-for joys of a civvie suit. There was little regret among the

men who went. But some of us had strange lumps in the throat to see them turn their backs on the unit which owed so much to their wondrous uncomplaining efforts. In company together we had faced unimagined hardships; in company we had learned to thresh the chaff from the grain, to face the grimmest things with a cheery laugh, to prize comradeship and manly worth above the trappings and the manifold delusions of life before the cataclysm. And now the arts of peace were claiming the flower of the nation's manhood again. Would they sink or swim in the struggles of peacetime? Would the lessons of common effort for the common weal be lost? Would all that wealth of comradeship be dissipated like the smoke of last year's barrages? So there was sadness in the final handshake as one passed down the ranks and wished each sterling fellow 'Good luck'. There was inadequacy in the simple words by which one strove to phrase the Nation's thanks. And when the band played them out on their homeward way with the Essex march and 'Auld Lang Syne', the family circle seemed bereft; and we turned sadly back to billets with heartfelt hope that all would be well with them in the heritage of peace which they had earned so nobly.

Lieutenant Colonel Thomas Banks, 10th Essex Regiment

Corporal Charles Hennessey was demobbed on 26 January 1919. He found the cross-Channel crossing was the very stuff of romantic songs. The men were desperate to be home and many were in a highly emotional state.

We took up positions on the deck where, in spite of the chilly breeze, we were determined to remain, so as to catch sight of the English coastline at the earliest possible moment. When it at last came into view I thought of the many writers who had described this moment as one which always aroused a feeling of great emotion in the breasts of people who had been long away from their homeland. I thought of the famous lines

Breathes there a man with soul so dead,
Who never to himself has said,
This is my own, my native land.

And they suddenly took on a meaning which I had never before fully appreciated. The other troops on deck were quietly watching the legendary white cliffs of Dover becoming gradually clearer, and I could see by the expression on their faces that their reaction to the sight of the welcome coastline was much the same as mine. Percy Eels, as I knew from my long association with him, was a case-hardened character, but I noticed that even he almost forgot himself for a few moments.[58]

Corporal Charles Hennessey, 2/15th (Civil Service Rifles), London Regiment

The excitement intensified as the moment of disembarkation drew near. This time they were not returning on leave, for just an all-too-brief taste of civilian life and safety, before the inevitable return to the front. This was the promised land: they would be free of the army.

The troops suddenly became their cheerful selves again as the ship slowly reached the Harbour. The gangplank was lowered and the troops streamed ashore like a crowd of schoolboys, quickly forming ranks and setting off for the camp at Dover Castle. Little time was wasted before the work of converting us from soldiers to civilians began. Not many men had so far passed through the camp, and as a regular stream would be arriving from now on, we had to be dealt with at once. First of all, we were required to hand in our rifles and equipment, which was indeed a moment to remember. We had carried these for many weary miles, and they had become almost part of ourselves, so each man made a small ceremony of the handing over, and delivered himself of the oath that seemed most appropriate to him. We had always been told that our rifle was our best friend, and I could certainly recall an occasion or two when this could very well have been the case, but even so, no-one shed any tears at the parting.[59]

Corporal Charles Hennessey, 2/15th (Civil Service Rifles), London Regiment

The men were trooped from hut to hut, completing the multifarious practical details of demobilisation.

It seemed to me that we were being dealt with in a very courteous manner – and this we liked. In one hut a Padre enquired about our future moral welfare, and in another a perfect stranger was desperately anxious to be sure that we had a job to go back to. From each of the huts we emerged with a piece of paper, and finally staggered from the last hut with a handful of assorted documents calculated to save us from all possible trouble when we got back into civvies. We had also been given £2 to show how anxious the authorities were for our immediate needs, while I got a further £1 as compensation for not wishing to retain my greatcoat, and £1. 18. 6 in lieu of a reach-me-down 'Demob' suit.[60]

Corporal Charles Hennessey, 2/15th (Civil Service Rifles), London Regiment

All told it was a laborious process; indeed there seemed to be far more administration involved in leaving the army than they had encountered upon enlistment.

We found ourselves feeling very hungry. We had had nothing to eat since our very sketchy breakfast so we were very glad to hear that a good meal could be obtained at the mess hall. This hall was a large, cheerful place, with cloths on the tables that were so clean we were half afraid to sit at them. The food was actually served by orderlies, and for the very first time in years we were informed that, 'You can have as much as you like mate!' This promise proved to be correct, and it occurred to us that it was faintly possible that the army might be trying to offer us an apology for the way they had treated our 'inner man' for so many years! The implied apology was, of course, accepted with thanks, and we proceeded to enjoy the meal, plus the unusual experience of a second helping.[61]

Corporal Charles Hennessey, 2/15th (Civil Service Rifles), London Regiment

Then they left the camp as civilians and began their journey home. Even this was an exciting 'new' experience to these erstwhile soldiers. A brief station stop, while en route to Victoria in London, seemed a thing of wonder to Hennessey.

Everyone was thrilled at once more seeing the old familiar layout of an English railway station. It was all there, laid out exactly the same as it was on numberless British railway platforms. W. H. Smith's bookstall alongside the ticket collector's box; the refreshment buffet further along, flanked by a parcels and porters' cubby-holes; and at the very end of the platform, the station 'Gents'. There was even the motionless figure of a porter, standing leaning on the handles of an empty truck, with a facial expression which clearly dared anyone to ask him to do anything.[62]

Corporal Charles Hennessey, 2/15th (Civil Service Rifles), London Regiment

Almost before they knew it they were pulling into the hustle and bustle of Victoria Station. Here it would be time for a more special parting as Charles Hennessey bade farewell to his best friend Percy Eels.

Carriage doors were flung open and the troops poured out, their heavy boots making the station ring as they clattered along the platform. At the barrier were about a dozen elderly ladies, obviously come to welcome the troops home. Their outstretched hand and friendly smiles were more welcome to us than the best brass band in the land. Percy Eels and I got through the barrier at last, and found ourselves saying goodbye to each other after being in close contact since 1916. He did his job as a stretcher-bearer with his sleeves rolled up to the elbows and a dirty stub of cigarette in the corner of his mouth, but never failed to cheer his patients up as he cursed them for being silly enough to get in the way of a bullet.[63]

Corporal Charles Hennessey, 2/15th (Civil Service Rifles), London Regiment

And then, after a bus ride on the No. 16 bus to Kilburn, it was almost an anti-climax as he got back to his front door – the prodigal returned.

When I reached my house, I found my mother and sister there, having no idea that I was about to descend on them at that particular time. I had three brothers, one of whom had been discharged from the Army after being badly wounded at Loos in 1915, and the other two were still in France. So my sudden arrival was only a part-family reunion, although it was good enough to be going on with. After a hot meal and a rest, then a bath, I felt much better, and since I had previously flung my uniform, underclothing, and socks into the garden to be burnt on the morrow, I really began to feel myself a civilian again.[64]

Corporal Charles Hennessey, 2/15th (Civil Service Rifles), London Regiment

Demobilisation would eventually embrace most soldiers as the army shrank from 3,800,000 to just 230,000 by 1922.

The question was: would there be anything soldiers would miss about their military service as they returned to civilian life? In Roland Feilding's opinion there were certainly advantages.

After all, there was a good deal to be said in favour of the old trench life. There were none of the mean haunting fears of poverty there, and the next meal – if you were alive to take it – was as certain as the rising sun. The rations were the same for the haves and the have nots, and the shells fell, without favour, upon both. In a life where no money passes, the ownership of money counts for nothing. Rich and poor alike stand solely upon their individual merits, without discrimination. You can have no idea, till you have tried it, how much pleasanter life is under such circumstances. In spite – or partly perhaps because of the gloominess of the surroundings, there was an atmosphere of selflessness and a spirit of camaraderie the like of which has probably not been seen in the world before – at least on so grand a scale. Such is the influence of the shells! The life was a curious blend of discipline and good-fellowship; wherein men were easily pleased; where there was no gossip; where even a shell when it had just missed you produced a sort of exultation; a life in the course of which you actually got used to the taste of chloride of lime in tea. In short, there was no humbug in the trenches, and that is why – with all their disadvantages – the better kind of men who have lived in them will look back upon them hereafter with something like affection.[65]

Lieutenant Colonel Rowland Feilding

This idea of an 'aristocracy of the trenches' was often twinned with the idea that the shared nobler values of military service could be harnessed to the good of society at large. Brigadier General Herbert Hart hoped that some good might have come from it.

> In a few days, we will be taking off these uniforms. Are we going to discard with them all the khaki has taught us, or are we going to draw from our experiences and utilise the knowledge it has given us in such a way that we will help make our glorious country better, brighter and a happier place to live in?[66]
>
> Brigadier General Herbert Hart

Such optimism as to the future was often overwhelmed by despair at the reality that awaited them once they got home. This was no perfect society; nor was it ever likely to be so.

> The England to which we have returned is so different from the England of our hopes and dreams; and when the boys say to me, 'I am sorry I came back; I would be happier lying under a little white cross in France!' What can I say, when I know it is true? If only the wonderful spirit of the trenches had been brought to England – but it has not. The world is more sordid and self-seeking than ever before.[67]
>
> Father Benedict Williamson

As a chaplain, the disillusioned Williamson had clearly idealised his tangential involvement with the soldiery. Far more men considered their lives in the trenches to have been a brutal, sordid and depressing experience, a long torture only relieved by the comradeship of their fellows. Most were delighted to 'escape' the army. The discipline, the awful privations, the dangers and risk of death or traumatic wounds. Civilian life offered the chance of more comfort, more freedom; they could see their friends, families and girlfriends. Perhaps the opportunity to carve out their own path in the world, start a business, follow the career they wanted, pursue academia; the world was – at least in theory – their oyster.

As we approach the end, in one sense, this book has elements of fraud.

The 'last battle' for these men was not fought in 1918. The soldiers would find that there was no brave new world awaiting them; indeed, a whole new arena of conflict lay before them when they got back to their homes. They had to fight for worthwhile, secure, well-remunerated employment in blighted economies all struggling to recover from the massive costs of a global war. Some had to suffer the after-effects of dreadful wounds or mental trauma – what we now know to be post-traumatic stress, surely not a 'disorder' but a quite natural reaction to what they had undergone. They had to strive to re-establish relationships with their families, their wives, their girlfriends – their workmates who had not gone to war. They had to try to bury the memories of the terrible experiences they had endured, and to avoid being corrupted by all the evil they had witnessed. Most of all they had to fight to retain their self-respect in a society that did not seem to care one iota for their welfare. For some these would be the greatest battles of all.

ACKNOWLEDGEMENTS

I would like to thank all the people who have helped me write this book. First I must acknowledge the men who created the personal experience accounts upon which this book is based. Their memoirs, letters, diaries and interviews are the bedrock of this book. Throughout, I have tried to preserve their original words, only lightly editing quotes for readability, removing unnecessary material while standardising spellings and, to some extent, punctuation. It has been a privilege to share their experiences and to pass them on in this book.

Then I must thank Cecily Gayford who was patience itself as my editor, my lovely copy-editor Penny Gardiner and all the rest of the Profile team. I am also hugely indebted, as they frequently remind me, to Phil Wood and John Paylor, who carried out a thorough review of the text, saving me from hundreds of stupid errors and offering much constructive advice. Thank you chums! At the Imperial War Museum I am grateful to Margaret Brooks, Tony Richards, Bryn Hammond and Carl Warner, who have all had the dubious pleasure of being my line managers over countless eons. All my colleagues have been nothing but supportive, but I must particularly thank the Sound Archive, Library and Documents Departments. Many thanks to Jack Sheldon for supplying some excellent German accounts.

While writing this book, several relatively recently published books have been invaluable: some for the incisive thinking that opened my eyes to new historical research; others as rich seams of personal experience quotations. I would thank them all and urge everyone to consider buying and reading the excellent books listed below. These are the true gateways to the past.

398 THE LAST BATTLE

Conrad Babcock, edited by Robert Ferrell, *Reminiscences of Conrad S. Babcock* (Columbia: University of Missouri Press, 2012).

Chris Baker, The Long, Long Train website. http://www.longlongtrail.co.uk/

Horace Baker, edited by Robert Ferrell, *Argonne Days in World War I* (Columbia: University of Missouri, 2007).

Charles Beresford, *The Christian Soldier: The life of Lieutenant Colonel the Rev Bernard William Vann* (Solihull: Helion & Company Ltd, 2017).

Jonathan Boff, *Winning and Losing on the Western Front: The British Third Army and the Defeat of Germany in 1918* (Cambridge: Cambridge University Press, 2014).

Carl Brannen, *Over There: A Marine in the Great War* (Texas AM University Press, 1997).

Derek Clayton was kind enough to give me an advance look at the text for his keenly awaited book on the Battle of the Sambre, *Decisive Victory*, to be published by Hellion in 2018.

George Clark, *Devil Dogs Chronicle: Voices of the 4th Marine Brigade in World War 1* (Lawrence, Kansas: University Press of Kansas, 2013).

Norman Cliff, *To Hell and Back with the Guards* (Braunton: Merlin Books Ltd, 1988).

Tom Donovan, *The Hazy Red Hell: Fighting Experiences on the Western Front, 1914–18* (Staplehurst: Spellmount, 1999).

Walter Downing, *To the Last Ridge* (London: Grub Street, 2005).

Reginald and Charles Fair, *Marjorie's War: Four Families in the Great War, 1914–1918* (Brighton: Menin House Publishers, 2012).

Mark Feldbin, Ryan's Roughnecks website: http://www.oryansroughnecks.org/buell.html

Great War Society Doughboy Centre website was invaluable in guiding me to numerous American accounts.

James Hallas, *Doughboy War: The American Expeditionary Force in WWI* (Mechanicsburg: Stackpole Books, 2009).

Hubert Hart, edited by John Crawford, *The Devil's Own War: The Diary of Hubert Hart* (Auckland: Exisle Publishing Ltd, 2009).

Frank Hawkings, *From Ypres to Cambrai: The Diary of an Infantryman, 1914–1919* (Morley: Elmfield Press, 1974).

Francis Hitchcock, *Stand To: A Diary of the Trenches, 1915–1918* (Norwich: Gliddon Books, 1988).

Peter Hodgkinson, *British Battalion Commanders in the First World War*. (Abingdon: Routledge, 2016).

James Jack, *General Jack's Diary: War on the Western Front, 1914–1918* (London: Cassell & Co, 2000).

Robert Laplander, *Finding the Lost Battalion* (Wisconsin: Lulu Press, 2007).

James McWilliams and R. James Steel, *The Suicide Battalion* (Stevenage: Spa Books, 1990).

Gary Mead, *The Doughboys: America and the First World War* (London: Penguin Books Ltd, 2001).

Frederick Noakes, *Distant Drum, A Memoir of a Guardsman in the Great War* (London: Frontline Books, 2010).

Peter Owen, *A Battalion of Marines in the Great War* (College Station: Texas A&M University Press, 2007).

James Parks, *No Greater Love: The story of Lieutenant Wilbert W. White* (Over the Front: Vol. 1, No. 1).

Peter Pederson, 'Maintaining the Advance: Monash, battle procedure and the Australian Corps in 1918', article in A. Ekins (editor), *1918 Year of Victory*.

Edgar Rule, *Jacka's Mob: A Narrative of the Great War by Edgar John Rule* (Melbourne: Military Melbourne, 1999).

Gary Sheffield and John Bourne, *Douglas Haig: War Diaries and Letters, 1914–1918* (London: Weidenfeld & Nicolson, 2005).

Walter Williamson, edited by Doreen Priddey, *A Tommy at Ypres: Walter's War* (Stroud: Amberley Publishing, 2011).

William Wright, edited by R. H. Ferrell, *Meuse-Argonne Diary: A Division Commander in World War 1* (Columbia: University of Missouri Press, 2004).

NOTES

Preface

1. IWM DOCS: H. B. Owen Manuscript account, p. 351.

1. Where are we?

1. J. B. Bickersteth, quoted by J. Bickersteth, *The Bickersteth Diaries* (Barnsley: Leo Cooper, 1998), p. xiii.
2. The War Office, *Statistics of the Military Effort of the British Empire During the Great War, 1914–1920* (London: HMSO, 1922), p. 241.
3. H. Gough, quoted by K. Jeffery, *Field Marshal Sir Henry Wilson: A Political Soldier* (Oxford: Oxford University Press, 2008), p. 189.
4. H. Maslin, quoted by R. S. Sutcliffe, *Seventy First New York in the World War* (New York: J. J. Little & Ives Co., 1922), pp. 66–7.
5. C. H. Scott, quoted by R. S. Sutcliffe, *Seventy First New York in the World War* (New York: J. J. Little & Ives Co., 1922), p. 210.
6. IWM DOCS: J. Nettleton, Typescript account, pp. 155–6.
7. S. Faison, quoted by M. A. Yockelson, *Borrowed Soldiers: Americans under British Command, 1918* (Norman: University of Oklahoma Press, 2016), p. 217.

8. J. de Pierrefeu, *French Headquarters, 1915–1918* (London: Geoffrey Bles, 1924), pp. 271–2.

9. H. von Kuhl, quoted by O. Korfes (translated by T. Zuber), *The German 66th Regiment in the First World War: The German Perspective* (Stroud: History Press, 2016), p. 283.

10. J. de Pierrefeu, *French Headquarters, 1915–1918* (London: Geoffrey Bles, 1924), p. 277.

11. H. Sulzbach, *With the German Guns: Four Years on the Western Front, 1914–1918* (London: Leo Cooper, 1973), pp. 201–2.

12. E. Morin, *Lieutenant Morin: Combatant de la Guerre, 1914–1918* (Besançon, Cêtre, 2002), p. 287.

13. E. D. Cooke, quoted by G. B. Clark, *Devil Dogs Chronicle: Voices of the 4th Marine Brigade in World War 1* (Lawrence, Kansas: University Press of Kansas, 2013), p. 224.

14. E. D. Cooke, quoted by G. B. Clark, *Devil Dogs Chronicle: Voices of the 4th Marine Brigade in World War 1* (Lawrence, Kansas: University Press of Kansas, 2013), p. 225.

15. H. Sulzbach, *With the German Guns: Four Years on the Western Front, 1914–1918* (London: Leo Cooper, 1973), p. 206.

16. H. Sulzbach, *With the German Guns: Four Years on the Western Front, 1914–1918* (London: Leo Cooper, 1973), p. 207.

17. F. Foch, translated by T. Bentley Mott, *The Memoirs of Marshal Foch* (London: William Heinemann Ltd, 1931), pp. 426–7.

18. F. Foch, translated by T. Bentley Mott, *The Memoirs of Marshal Foch* (London: William Heinemann Ltd, 1931), p. 428.

19. F. Foch, translated by T. Bentley Mott, *The Memoirs of Marshal Foch* (London: William Heinemann Ltd, 1931), pp. 428–9.

20. H. Wilson, *British Military Policy, 1918–1919* (PRO CAB 25/85 Pt 1), p. 5–6.

21. H. Wilson, *British Military Policy, 1918–1919* (PRO CAB 25/85 Pt 1), p. 8.

22. W. Churchill, quoted by M. Gilbert, *Winston S. Churchill, Volume IV 1917–1922* (London: William Heinemann Ltd, 1975), p. 122.

23. INTERNET SOURCE: J. F. C. Fuller, Plan 1919, http://www.alternatewars.com/WW1/Fuller_1919.htm

24. C. Headlam, edited by J. Beach, *The Military Papers of Lieutenant Colonel Sir Cuthbert Headlam, 1910–1942* (Stroud: Military Press/Army Records Society, 2010), p. 216.

25. R. Barrington-Ward, quoted by J. Baynes, *Far From a Donkey: The Life of General Sir Ivor Maxse* (London: Brasseys Ltd, 1995), p. 212.

26. E. Ludendorff, *Ludendorff's Own Story: August 1914–November 1918* (New York and London: Harper & Bros, 1919), p. 326.

27. H. Desagneux, edited by J. Desagneaux and translated by G. Adams, *A French Soldier's War Diary* (Morley: The Elmfield Press, 1975), p. 95.

28. D. Haig, quoted in G. Sheffield and J. Bourne, *Douglas Haig: War Diaries and Letters, 1914–1918* (London: Weidenfeld & Nicolson, 2005), p. 445.

29. D. Haig, quoted in G. Sheffield and J. Bourne, *Douglas Haig: War Diaries and Letters, 1914–1918* (London: Weidenfeld & Nicolson, 2005), pp. 445–6.

30. F. Foch, translated by T. Bentley Mott, *The Memoirs of Marshal Foch* (London: William Heinemann Ltd, 1931), pp. 446–7.

31. D. Haig, quoted by J. E. Edmonds, *Military Operations France and Belgium, 1918 Vol. IV* (Nashville: The Battery Pres, 1993), Appendix XX, p. 588.

32. H. Sulzbach, *With the German Guns: Four Years on the Western Front, 1914–1918* (London: Leo Cooper, 1973), p. 216.

33. D. Lloyd George, *War Memoirs of David Lloyd George, Vol. II* (London: Odhams Press, Limited. 1038), p. 1844.

34. D. Haig, quoted by G. Sheffield and J. Bourne, *Douglas Haig: War Diaries and Letters, 1914–1918* (London: Weidenfeld & Nicolson, 2005), p. 453.

35. D. Haig, quoted by G. Sheffield and J. Bourne, *Douglas Haig: War Diaries and Letters, 1914–1918* (London: Weidenfeld & Nicolson, 2005), p. 453.

36. D. Haig, quoted by G. Sheffield and J. Bourne, *Douglas Haig: War Diaries and Letters, 1914–1918* (London: Weidenfeld & Nicolson, 2005), p. 456.

37. A. N. Philbrick, quoted by C. A. Cuthbert Keeson, *The History and Records of Queen Victoria's Rifles, 1792–1922* (London: Constable & Company, 1923), p. 439.

2. Battle of Meuse-Argonne

1. R. J. Casey, *The Cannoneers Have Hairy Ears: A Diary of the Front lines* (New York, J. H. Sears & Co, 1927), p. 170.

2. R. Alexander, quoted in Anon, *History of the Seventy-Seventh Division August 25th 1917–November 11th 1918* (New York: 77th Division Association, 1919), p. 148.

3. C. W. Camp, *History of the 305th Field Artillery* (New York: Country Life Press, 1919), pp. 266–7.

4. J. M. Howard, *The Autobiography of a Regiment: A History of 304th Field Artillery in the World War* (New York, 1920), pp. 164–5 and 171.

5. W. K. Rainsford, *From Upton to the Meuse with the Three Hundred and Seventh* (New York: Appleton & Company, 1920), pp. 161–2.

6. Private Clarence Manthe of 'C' Battery, 304 Field Artillery, was killed on 26 September 1918.

7. P. Newberry, quoted by J. M. Howard, *The Autobiography of a Regiment: A History of 304th Field Artillery in the World War* (New York, 1920), pp. 169–70.

8. W. K. Rainsford, *From Upton to the Meuse with the Three Hundred and Seventh* (New York: Appleton & Company, 1920), p. 166.

9. W. K. Rainsford, *From Upton to the Meuse with the Three Hundred and Seventh* (New York: Appleton & Company, 1920), pp. 166–7.

10. W. K. Rainsford, *From Upton to the Meuse with the Three Hundred and Seventh* (New York: Appleton & Company, 1920), pp. 167–8.

11. W. K. Rainsford, *From Upton to the Meuse with the Three Hundred and Seventh* (New York: Appleton & Company, 1920), p. 169.

12. IWM DOCS: T. F. Grady, Manuscript diary, 26 September 1918.

13. W. K. Rainsford, *From Upton to the Meuse with the Three Hundred and Seventh* (New York: Appleton & Company, 1920), p. 171.

14. R. Alexander,, quoted in Anon, *History of the Seventy-Seventh Division August 25th 1917 – November 11th 1918* (New York: 77th Division Association, 1919), p. 148.

15. G. S. Patton, quoted by J. H. Hallas, *Doughboy War: The American Expeditionary Force in WWI* (Mechanicsburg: Stackpole Books, 2009), p. 245.

16. G. S. Patton, quoted by J. H. Hallas, *Doughboy War: The American Expeditionary Force in WWI* (Mechanicsburg: Stackpole Books, 2009), pp. 245–6.

17. C. H. Donnelly, quoted by G. Mead, *The Doughboys: America and the First World War* (London: Penguin Books Ltd, 2001), p. 304.

18. R. L. Bullard, *Personalities and Reminiscences of War* (New York: Doubleday, Page & Company, 1925), p. 270.

19. W. Hayward, quoted by E. J. Scott, *Scott's Official History of the American Negro in the World War in World War I* (Chicago: Homewood Press, 1919), pp. 205–6.

20. H. Davis, quoted by S. L. Harris, *Harlem's Hell Fighters: The African American 368th Infantry in World War I* (Dulles: Potomac Books, 2003), p. 240.

21. E. McCowan, quoted by E. J. Scott, *Scott's Official History of the American Negro in the World War in World War I* (Chicago: Homewood Press, 1919), p. 210.

22. G. Miller, quoted by E. J. Scott, *Scott's Official History of the American Negro in the World War in World War I* (Chicago: Homewood Press, 1919), p. 210.

23. D. Haig, quoted by G. Sheffield and J. Bourne, *Douglas Haig: War Diaries and Letters, 1914–1918* (London: Weidenfeld & Nicolson, 2005), p. 468.

24. W. K. Rainsford, *From Upton to the Meuse with the Three Hundred and Seventh* (New York: Appleton & Company, 1920), pp. 174–5.

25. T. C. Thayer, *History of the 305th Field Artillery* (New York: Country Life Press, 1919), pp. 319–20.

26. W. K. Rainsford, *From Upton to the Meuse with the Three Hundred and Seventh* (New York: Appleton & Company, 1920), p. 169.

27. W. K. Rainsford, *From Upton to the Meuse with the Three Hundred and Seventh* (New York: Appleton & Company, 1920), pp. 187–8.

28. J. W. Nell, quoted by R. J. Laplander, *Finding the Lost Battalion* (Wisconsin: Lulu Press, 2007), p. 312.

29. A. R. Looker, quoted by R. J. Laplander, *Finding the Lost Battalion* (Wisconsin: Lulu Press, 2007), p. 381.

30. R. L. Bullard, *Personalities and Reminiscences of War* (New York: Doubleday, Page & Company, 1925), pp. 270–71.

31. M. Maverick, quoted by J. H. Hallas, *Doughboy War: The American Expeditionary Force in WWI* (Mechanicsburg: Stackpole Books, 2009), p. 267.

32. M. Maverick, quoted by J. H. Hallas, *Doughboy War: The American Expeditionary Force in WWI* (Mechanicsburg: Stackpole Books, 2009), p. 268.

33. C. A. Brannen, *Over There: A Marine in the Great War* (Texas AM University Press, 1997), p. 47.

34. C. A. Brannen, *Over There: A Marine in the Great War* (Texas AM University Press, 1997), pp. 47–8.

35. J. McBrayer Sellers, quoted by G. B. Clark, *Devil Dogs Chronicle: Voices of the 4th Marine Brigade in World War 1* (Lawrence, Kansas: University Press of Kansas, 2013), p. 293.

36. C. A. Brannen, *Over There: A Marine in the Great War* (Texas AM University Press, 1997), p. 48.

37. W. J. Jackson, quoted by G. B. Clark, *Devil Dogs Chronicle: Voices of the 4th Marine Brigade in World War 1* (Lawrence, Kansas: University Press of Kansas, 2013), p. 304.

38. W. A. Francis, quoted by G. Mead, *The Doughboys: America and the First World War* (London: Penguin Books Ltd, 2001), p. 315.

39. D. Haig, quoted by G. Sheffield and J. Bourne, *Douglas Haig: War Diaries and Letters, 1914–1918* (London: Weidenfeld & Nicolson, 2005), pp. 469–70.

40. J. W. Nell, quoted by R. J. Laplander, *Finding the Lost Battalion* (Wisconsin: Lulu Press, 2007), p. 407.

41. R. E. John, quoted by R. J. Laplander, *Finding the Lost Battalion* (Wisconsin: Lulu Press, 2007), p. 408.

42. Research by R. J. Laplander, *Finding the Lost Battalion* (Wisconsin: Lulu Press, 2007), p. 589.

43. R. Alexander, quoted in Anon, *History of the Seventy-Seventh Division August 25th 1917 – November 11th 1918* (New York: 77th Division Association, 1919), p. 152.

44. Shot him!

45. INTERNET SOURCE: A. York, diary, 7 October 1918, http://acacia.pair.com/Acacia.Vignettes/The.Diary.of.Alvin.York.html

46. INTERNET SOURCE: A. York, diary, 7 October 1918, http://acacia.pair.com/Acacia.Vignettes/The.Diary.of.Alvin.York.html

47. E Rickenbacker, quoted by J. Parks, 'No Greater Love: The story of Lieutenant Wilbert W. White', *Over the Front*: Vol. 1, No. 1, p. 52.

48. J. Meisssner, quoted by J. Parks, 'No Greater Love: The story of Lieutenant Wilbert W. White', *Over the Front*: Vol. 1, No. 1, p. 54.

49. C. Cox, quoted by J. Parks, 'No Greater Love: The story of Lieutenant Wilbert W. White', *Over the Front*: Vol. 1, No. 1, p. 57.

50. J. Meisssner, quoted by J. Parks, 'No Greater Love: The story of Lieutenant Wilbert W. White', *Over the Front*: Vol. 1, No. 1, p. 53.

51. E Rickenbacker, quoted by J. Parks, 'No Greater Love: The story of Lieutenant Wilbert W. White', *Over the Front*: Vol. 1, No. 1, p. 53.

52. Lieutenant Wilbert White, 147 Aero Squadron, died aged 29 on 10 January 1918. He is buried in the Meuse-Argonne American Cemetery, Romagne.

53. J. Meisssner, quoted by J. Parks, 'No Greater Love: The story of Lieutenant Wilbert W. White', *Over the Front*: Vol. 1, No. 1, p. 52 .

54. Private Meria Shirey of 3/128 Regiment, died of wounds on 15 October 1918.

55. H. L. Baker, edited by R. H. Ferrell, *Argonne Days in World War I* (Columbia: University of Missouri, 2007), p. 62.

56. H. L. Baker, edited by R. H. Ferrell, *Argonne Days in World War I* (Columbia: University of Missouri, 2007), pp. 63–4.

57. W. G. Haan, quoted in C. Hanton, *The 32nd Division in the World War, 1917–1919* (Wisconsin, Joint War History Commission, 1920), p. 201.

58. P. W. Schmidt, *CO. C. 127th Infantry in the Great War* (Wisconsin: Press Publishing Company, 1919), pp. 124–5.

59. O. Lais, translated by J. Sheldon, *Ein Regiment stirbt den Heldentod* (Karlsruhe: Gutsch, 1936) pp. 181–2.

60. R. L. Bullard, *Personalities and Reminiscences of War* (New York: Doubleday, Page & Company, 1925), p. 284.

61. R. Alexander, quoted in Anon, *History of the Seventy-Seventh Division August 25th 1917 – November 11th 1918* (New York: 77th Division Association, 1919), p. 155.

3. Battle of Canal du Nord

1. IWM SOUND: AC 10768, J. Grainger, Reel 9.

2. A. Currie, *The Selected Papers of Sir Arthur Currie: Diaries, Letters and Reports to the Ministry, 1917–1933,* edited by M. O. Humphries (Waterloo, Ontario: LCMSDS Press, Wilfred Laurier University, 2008), p. 116.

3. F. Hawkings, *From Ypres to Cambrai: The Diary of an Infantryman, 1914–1919* (Morley: Elmfield Press, 1974), 24 September, p. 125.

4. IWM DOCS: C. Dudley Ward, Manuscript diary, 27 September 1918.

5. F. Noakes, *The Distant Drum: A Memoir of a Guardsman in the Great War* (London: Frontline Books, 2010), p. 168.

6. F. Noakes, *The Distant Drum: A Memoir of a Guardsman in the Great War* (London: Frontline Books, 2010), p. 169.

7. D. R. Stevenson, quoted by J. L. McWilliams and R. James Steel, *The Suicide Battalion* (Stevenage: Spa Books, 1990), p. 174.

8. F. Noakes, *The Distant Drum: A Memoir of a Guardsman in the Great War* (London: Frontline Books, 2010), p. 170.

9. D. McKerchar, quoted by J. L. McWilliams and R. James Steel, *The Suicide Battalion* (Stevenage: Spa Books, 1990), p. 174 and 176.

10. D. R. Stevenson, quoted by J. L. McWilliams and R. James Steel, *The Suicide Battalion* (Stevenage: Spa Books, 1990), p. 175.

11. S. Colbeck, quoted by J. L. McWilliams and R. James Steel, *The Suicide Battalion* (Stevenage: Spa Books, 1990), p. 175.

12. IWM SOUND: R. Sykes, AC 301, Reel 5.

13. IWM SOUND: R. Sykes, AC 301, Reel 5.

14. F. Hawkings, *From Ypres to Cambrai: The Diary of an Infantryman, 1914–1919* (Morley: Elmfield Press, 1974), pp. 127–8.

15. F. Hawkings, *From Ypres to Cambrai: The Diary of an Infantryman, 1914–1919* (Morley: Elmfield Press, 1974), pp. 129–30.

16. F. Noakes, *The Distant Drum: A Memoir of a Guardsman in the Great War* (London: Frontline Books, 2010), p. 170.

17. F. Noakes, *The Distant Drum: A Memoir of a Guardsman in the Great War* (London: Frontline Books, 2010), p. 171.

18. F. Noakes, *The Distant Drum: A Memoir of a Guardsman in the Great War* (London: Frontline Books, 2010), pp. 171–2.

19. Lance Corporal Thomas Jackson died aged 21 on 27 September 1918, the same day as the act for which he won his posthumous VC. He is buried at Sanders Keep Military Cemetery, Graincourt les Havrincourt.

20. F. Noakes, *The Distant Drum: A Memoir of a Guardsman in the Great War* (London: Frontline Books, 2010), pp. 172–3.

21. Private F. G Ransome, 1st Grenadier Guards, was killed aged 28 on 27 September 1918. He is buried at Beaumetz Crossroads Cemetery, Beaumetz les Cambrai.

22. N. D. Cliff, *To Hell and Back with the Guards* (Braunton: Merlin Books Ltd, 1988), p. 97.

23. IWM SOUND: AC 10768, J. Grainger, Reel 9–10.

24. IWM SOUND: AC 10768, J. Grainger, Reel 10–11.

25. Leutnant Baldamus, quoted by O. Korfes, translated by T. Zuber, *The German 66th Regiment in the First World War: The German Perspective* (Stroud: History Press, 2016), pp. 303–4.

26. F. Noakes, *The Distant Drum: A Memoir of a Guardsman in the Great War* (London: Frontline Books, 2010), p. 175.

4. Fifth Battle of Ypres and Battle of Courtrai

1. J. L. Jack, *General Jack's Diary: War on the Western Front, 1914–1918* (London: Cassell & Co, 2000), 28 September, pp. 273–4.

2. F. C. Hitchcock, *Stand To: A Diary of the Trenches, 1915–1918* (Norwich: Gliddon Books, 1988), pp. 280–81.

3. W. D. Croft, *Three Years with the 9th (Scottish) Division* (London: John Murray, 1919), p. 248–51.

4. J. L. Jack, *General Jack's Diary: War on the Western Front, 1914–1918* (London: Cassell & Co, 2000), 20 September, pp. 267–8.

5. H. G. Nelson, quoted by H. C. Sclater and H. C. C. Uniacke, in *The Royal Artillery War Commemoration Book* (London: G. Bell & Sons, Ltd, 1920), pp. 306–7.

6. H. G. Nelson, quoted by H. C. Sclater and H. C. C. Uniacke, in *The Royal Artillery War Commemoration Book* (London: G. Bell & Sons, Ltd, 1920), pp. 306–7.

7. F. C. Hitchcock, *Stand To: A Diary of the Trenches, 1915–1918* (Norwich: Gliddon Books, 1988), p. 285.

8. F. C. Hitchcock, *Stand To: A Diary of the Trenches, 1915–1918* (Norwich: Gliddon Books, 1988), p. 288.

9. G. H. N. Jackson, quoted by S. Gillon, *The Story of the 29th Division: A Record of Gallant Deeds* (London: Thomas Nelson & Sons Ltd, 1925), p. 207.

10. IWM DOCS: J. S. Blanford, Typescript manuscript, *Sans Escort*, pp. 16–17.

11. J. L. Jack, *General Jack's Diary: War on the Western Front, 1914–1918* (London: Cassell & Co, 2000), 29 September, p. 274.

12. Rupprecht, Crown Prince of Bavaria, quoted by J. E. Edmonds, *Military Operations France and Belgium, 1918 Volume* V (Nashville: Battery Press, 1993), p. 73.

13. IWM DOCS: W. Heavens, Transcript diary, 29 September 1918.

14. IWM DOCS: W. Heavens, Transcript diary, 29 September 1918.

15. IWM DOCS: W. Heavens, Transcript diary, 1 October 1918.

16. IWM DOCS: W. Heavens, Transcript diary, 1 October 1918.

17. IWM SOUND: AC 9254, V. Polhill, Reel 12.

18. IWM DOCS: W. Heavens, Transcript diary, 4 October 1918.

19. IWM SOUND: F. Burslem, SR 0007, Reel 2.

20. D. Walker, quoted by C. Falls, *The History of the 36th (Ulster) Division* (London: McCaw, Stevenson & Orr Limited, 1922), pp. 269–70.

21. IWM DOCS: G. Skelton, Typescript Account, p. 9.

22. I. L. Read, *Of Those We Loved: A narrative 1914–1919* (Bishop Auckland: Pentland Press Ltd, 1994), pp. 415–16.

23. B. Freyberg, quoted by P. Freyberg, *Bernard Freyberg, VC: Soldier of Two Nations* (London: Hodder & Stoughton, 1991), p. 136.

24. H. W. Weldon, quoted by S. Gillon, *The Story of the 29th Division: A Record of Gallant Deeds* (London: Thomas Nelson & Sons, 1925), p. 211.

25. B. Freyberg, quoted by S. Gillon, *The Story of the 29th Division: A Record of Gallant Deeds* (London: Thomas Nelson & Sons, 1925), p. 211.

26. IWM DOCS: P. A. Ledward, Manuscript account, p. 112.

27. IWM DOCS: P. A. Ledward, Manuscript account, pp. 112–13.

28. IWM DOCS: P. A. Ledward, Manuscript account, p. 113a.

29. IWM DOCS: H. T. Pope, Transcript diary, 14 October 1918.

30. C. F. Jones, quoted by J. Knight, *The Civil Service Rifles in the Great War: All Bloody Gentlemen* (Barnsley: Pen & Sword, 2005), p. 216.

31. W. Whigham Ferguson, quoted by J. M. Findlay, *With the Scottish Rifles, 1914–1919* (London: Blackie & Sons Ltd, 1926), pp. 181–2.

32. IWM DOCS: W. Heavens, Transcript diary, 15 October 1918.

33. IWM DOCS: W. Heavens, Transcript diary, 20 October 1918.

34. W. Law, quoted by A. Crossley, *Chin-Wag: Being the War Records of the Eton Manor Clubs, 1914–1918* (London: Christophers, 1930), p. 109.

35. C. E. Wurtzburg, *The History of the 2/6th (Rifle) Battalion, The King's Liverpool Regiment, 1914–1919* (Aldershot: Gale & Polden Ltd, 1920), pp. 236–7.

36. P. Dodgson, quoted by R. H. Fair and C. S. Fair, *Marjorie's War: Four Families in the Great War, 1914–1918* (Brighton: Menin House Publishers, 2012), pp. 393–4.

37. R. Feilding, *War Letters to a Wife: France and Flanders, 1915–1919* (London: The Medici Society, 1929), p. 333.

38. C. E. Wurtzburg, *The History of the 2/6th (Rifle) Battalion, The King's Liverpool Regiment, 1914–1919* (Aldershot: Gale & Polden Ltd, 1920), p. 241.

39. IWM SOUND: AC 11214, F. W. S. Jourdain, Reel 6.

40. Hénin-Liétard is now known as Hénin-Beaumont.

41. J. B. Platnauer, quoted by D. Richter, *Chemical Soldiers, British Gas Warfare in World War One* (Barnsley, Pen & Sword, 2014), p. 210.

42. Sergeant Joe Cross of O Company Special Brigade, Royal Engineers died aged 28 on 24 October 1918. He is buried at Etpales Military Cemetery.

43. Sergeant Don Britton of O Company Special Brigade, Royal Engineers died on 18 January 1920. He is buried Birmingham Warstone Lane Cemetery.

44. J. B. Platnauer, quoted by D. Richter, *Chemical Soldiers, British Gas Warfare in World War One* (Barnsley, Pen & Sword, 2014), pp. 210–11.

45. http://www.iwm.org.uk/collections/item/object/205387203

46. H. Samuelson, quoted by C. A. Cuthbert Keeson, *The History and Records of Queen Victoria's Rifles, 1792–1922* (London: Constable & Company, 1923), p. 448.

47. J. S. Garrett, quoted by C. A. Cuthbert Keeson, *The History and Records of Queen Victoria's Rifles, 1792–1922* (London: Constable & Company, 1923), pp. 449–50.

48. IWM SOUND: AC 10173, L. Fox, Reel 3.

49. IWM SOUND: AC 10173, L. Fox, Reel 3.

50. Lance Corporal Robert Cawley, 1/6th Cheshire Regiment, died aged 25 on 25 October 1918. He is buried at Harlebeke New British Cemetery.

51. W. Williamson, edited by D. Priddey, *A Tommy at Ypres: Walter's War* (Stroud: Amberley Publishing, 2011), pp. 305–6.

52. IWM SOUND: AC 9343, L. Gordon-Davies, Reel 9.

5. Battle of St Quentin Canal and Beaurevoir

1. Charles Repington (1858–1925) was a former British officer who gained notoriety as an influential military correspondent, best known for exposing the 'Shell Scandal' in 1915.

2. D. Haig, quoted by G. Sheffield and J. Bourne, *Douglas Haig: War Diaries and Letters, 1914–1918* (London: Weidenfeld & Nicolson, 2005), p. 462.

3. IWM DOCS: F. J. Rice, Typescript Memoir, 1918.

4. Sergeant Francis Sykes of C Battery, 82 Brigade, Royal Field Artillery, was killed on 18 September 1918. His grave was moved from the Moislains Cemetery to the Peronne Community Extension Cemetery.

5. Second Lieutenant Archibald Irving of C Battery, 82 Brigade, Royal Field Artillery, died 16 September 1918. He is now buried in the Peronne Communal Cemetery Extension.

6. E. J. Rule, *Jacka's Mob: A Narrative of the Great War by Edgar John Rule* (Melbourne: Military Melbourne, 1999), p. 143.

7. E. J. Rule, *Jacka's Mob: A Narrative of the Great War by Edgar John Rule* (Melbourne: Military Melbourne, 1999), p. 143.

8. E. J. Rule, *Jacka's Mob: A Narrative of the Great War by Edgar John Rule* (Melbourne: Military Melbourne, 1999), p. 145.

9. Sergeant Loftus Bauchop of the 14th Battalion, AIF was killed the next day, aged 24, on 20 September 1918. He is buried at Bellicourt British Cemetery.

10. E. J. Rule, *Jacka's Mob: A Narrative of the Great War by Edgar John Rule* (Melbourne: Military Melbourne, 1999), p. 143.

11. E. J. Rule, *Jacka's Mob: A Narrative of the Great War by Edgar John Rule* (Melbourne: Military Melbourne, 1999), p. 145.

12. J. Monash, editor F. M. Cutlack, *War Letters of General Monash* (Sydney: Angus & Robertson, 1934), p. 268.

13. Lieutenant Jack Wright, 7th Royal Sussex Regiment, was killed aged 24 on 18 September 1918. He is buried at Epéhy Wood Farm Cemetery.

14. S. A. Andrews, quoted by Owen Rutter, *The History of the Seventh (Service) Battalion The Royal Sussex Regiment, 1914–1919* (London: Time Publishing Company Ltd, 1934), p. 243.

15. H. J. R. Farrow, quoted by Owen Rutter, *The History of the Seventh (Service) Battalion The Royal Sussex Regiment, 1914–1919* (London: Time Publishing Company Ltd, 1934), pp. 245–6.

16. Second Lieutenant Sydney Huggett was killed aged 31 on 18 September 1918. He is buried at Epéhy Wood Farm Cemetery.

17. S. A. Andrews, quoted by Owen Rutter, *The History of the Seventh (Service) Battalion The Royal Sussex Regiment, 1914–1919* (London: Time Publishing Company Ltd, 1934), pp. 244–5.

18. A. L. Thomson, quoted by Owen Rutter, *The History of the Seventh (Service) Battalion The Royal Sussex Regiment, 1914–1919* (London: Time Publishing Company Ltd, 1934), p. 247.

19. W. C. Belford, *'Legs Eleven': Being the Story of the 11th Battalion, AIF in the Great War* (London: Naval & Military Press, 201), p. 644. In the original Belford refers to himself in the third person.

20. Captain Walter R. Hallahan was killed aged 29 on 18 September 1918. He is buried in Tincourt New British Cemetery.

21. Second Lieutenant Dudley Elliott was killed on 18 September 1918. He is buried in Tincourt New British Cemetery.

22. Lieutenant John Archibald was killed aged 28 on 24 September 1918. He is buried in Tincourt New British Cemetery.

23. Major Aubrey Darnell was killed aged 32 on 24 September 1918. He is buried in Tincourt New British Cemetery.

24. W. C. Belford, *'Legs Eleven': Being the Story of the 11th Battalion, AIF in the Great War* (London: Naval & Military Press, 201), pp. 645–7. In the original Belford refers to himself in the third person.

25. A. Montgomery, *The Story of the Fourth Army: In the Battles of the Hundred Days, August 8th to November 11th, 1918* (London: Hodder & Stoughton,1920), p. 151.

26. H. S. Rawlinson, quoted by F. Maurice, *The Life of General Lord Rawlinson of Trent* (London: Cassell & Co Ltd, 1928), p. 238.

27. H. S. Rawlinson, quoted by F. Maurice, *The Life of General Lord Rawlinson of Trent* (London: Cassell & Co Ltd, 1928), pp. 238–9.

28. H. Maslin, quoted by R. S. Sutcliffe, *Seventy First New York in the World War* (New York, J. J. Little & Ives Co, 1922), pp. 85–6.

29. Private Henry Reed

30. INTERNET SOURCE: F. E. Pierce, letter from 6 October 1918, provided by D. Pierce for site run by M. H. Feldbin: http://www.oryansroughnecks.org/buell.html (edited).

31. INTERNET SOURCE: After action report by R. P. Buell provided by C. Doane for site run by M. H. Feldbin: http://www.oryansroughnecks.org/buell.html

32. INTERNET SOURCE: After action report by R. P. Buell provided by C. Doane for site run by M. H. Feldbin: http://www.oryansroughnecks.org/buell.html

33. Leutnant Stoffel, quoted by R. Dahlmann, translated by J. Sheldon, *Reserve-Infanterie-Rgt. Nr. 27 im Weltkriege 1914–1918* (Berlin: Bernard & Graese), 1934), p. 533.

34. Hauptman Jahns, quoted by R. Dahlmann, translated by J. Sheldon, *Reserve-Infanterie-Rgt. Nr. 27 im Weltkriege 1914–1918* (Berlin: Bernard & Graese), 1934), p. 533.

35. Leutnant Steiner, quoted by R. Dahlmann, translated by J. Sheldon, *Reserve-Infanterie-Rgt. Nr. 27 im Weltkriege 1914–1918* (Berlin: Bernard & Graese), 1934), pp. 534–5.

36. H. Maslin, quoted by R. S. Sutcliffe, *Seventy First New York in the World War* (New York: J. J. Little & Ives Co, 1922), p. 89.

37. Captain Stanley Bulkley, commanding officer of 3rd Battalion, 105th Regiment.

38. H. Maslin, quoted by R. S. Sutcliffe, *Seventy First New York in the World War* (New York: J. J. Little & Ives Co, 1922), pp. 88–90.

39. H. Maslin, quoted by R. S. Sutcliffe, *Seventy First New York in the World War* (New York: J. J. Little & Ives Co, 1922), pp. 88–90.

40. Leutnant Nowakowski, quoted by R. Dahlmann, translated by J. Sheldon, *Reserve-Infanterie-Rgt. Nr. 27 im Weltkriege 1914–1918* (Berlin: Bernard & Graese, 1934), p. 537.

41. W. H. Downing, *To the Last Ridge: The Word War One Experiences of W. H. Downing* (London: Grub Street, 2005), pp. 178–9.

42. A. Jenkin, quoted by G. Chapman, *Vain Glory* (London: Cassel & Company Ltd, 1937), p. 671.

43. Arthur Jenkin may well be a pseudonym as I cannot trace him or his Tank Corps Battalion. Nevertheless, I am convinced of its authenticity – as indeed were reviewers and readers when his book, *A Tank Driver's Experiences or Incidents in a Soldiers Life*, was published by Elliot Stock in 1922.

44. A. Jenkin, quoted by G. Chapman, *Vain Glory* (London: Cassel & Company Ltd, 1937), pp. 671–2.

45. A. Jenkin, quoted by G. Chapman, *Vain Glory* (London: Cassel & Company Ltd, 1937), p. 672.

46. A. Jenkin, quoted by G. Chapman, *Vain Glory* (London: Cassel & Company Ltd, 1937), p. 673.

47. A. Jenkin, quoted by G. Chapman, *Vain Glory* (London: Cassel & Company Ltd, 1937), pp. 673–4.

48. A. Jenkin, quoted by G. Chapman, *Vain Glory* (London: Cassel & Company Ltd, 1937), pp. 674–5.

49. A. Jenkin, quoted by G. Chapman, *Vain Glory* (London: Cassel & Company Ltd, 1937), p. 675.

50. IWM DOCS: O. H. Woodward, Typescript Account, pp. 127–8.

51. E. Kabisch, quoted by R. Dahlmann, translated by J. Sheldon, *Reserve-Infanterie-Rgt. Nr. 27 im Weltkriege 1914–1918* (Berlin: Bernard & Graese), 1934), p. 538.

52. T. R. Evans, Letter, 25 September 1918. Thanks to A. Thornton.

53. IWM DOCS: G. Havard Thomas, Letter, 27 September 1918.

54. IWM DOCS: R. W. Brierley, Typescript account, p. 85.

55. IWM DOCS: G. K. Parker, Typescript Account, p. 29.

56. IWM DOCS: A. G. Shennan, Letter, *c.* February 1978.

57. IWM DOCS: H. J. C. Marshall, Transcript account, p. 12.

58. H. E. Boucher, quoted by J. E. Blore and J. R. Sherratt, *Over There: A Commemorative History of the Old Leek Battery, 1908–1919* (Staffordshire: Martin Publicity, 1991), pp. 130–31.

59. IWM DOCS: R. W. Brierley, Typescript account, pp. 85–6.

60. C. Hufton, quoted by C. Beresford, *The Christian Soldier: The life of Lieutenant Colonel the Rev Bernard William Vann* (Solihull, Helion & Company Ltd, 2017), p. 235.

61. J. D. Hills. *The Fifth Leicestershire: A record of the 1/5th Battalion, the Leicestershire Regiment, T. F. during the War, 1914–1919* (Loughborough: Echo Press, 1919), p. 307.

62. C. L. Hufton, quoted by Charles Beresford, *The Christian Soldier: The life of Lieutenant Colonel the Rev Bernard William Vann* (Solihull: Helion & Company Ltd, 2017), p. 235.

63. Padre Cyril Buck of the Army Chaplains Department attached to 1/5th Leicestershire Regiment, died aged 38 on 29 September 1918. He is buried in Busigny Communal Cemetery Extension.

64. J. D. Hills. *The Fifth Leicestershire: A record of the 1/5th Battalion, the Leicestershire Regiment, T.F. during the War, 1914–1919* (Loughborough: Echo Press, 1919), p. 310.

65. C. L. Hufton, quoted by C. Beresford, *The Christian Soldier: The life of Lieutenant Colonel the Rev Bernard William Vann* (Solihull: Helion & Company Ltd, 2017), pp. 238–23.

66. C. L. Hufton, quoted by C. Beresford, *The Christian Soldier: The life of Lieutenant Colonel the Rev Bernard William Vann* (Solihull: Helion & Company Ltd, 2017), p. 239.

67. Lieutenant Colonel Bernard Vann VC of the 1/5th Sherwood Foresters was killed aged 31 on 3 October 1918. He is buried at the Bellicourt Military Cemetery.

68. IWM DOCS: G. Havard Thomas, Letter, 6 October 1918.

69. F. V. Schürhoff, edited by J. Beach, *The Diary of Corporal Vince Schürhoff, 1914–1918* (Stroud: History Army Records Society, 2015), pp. 287–8.

70. P. W. Gleason, quoted by J. L. McWilliams and R. James Steel, *The Suicide Battalion* (Stevenage: Spa Books, 1990), p. 185.

71. P. W. Gleason, quoted by J. L. McWilliams and R. James Steel, *The Suicide Battalion* (Stevenage: Spa Books, 1990), pp. 185–6.

72. IWM DOCS: C. H. Dudley Ward, Manuscript diary, 3 October 1918.

73. J. B. Bickersteth, quoted by J. Bickersteth, *The Bickersteth Diaries* (Barnsley: Leo Cooper, 1998), p. 282.

74. C. E. Wurtzburg, *The History of the 2/6th (Rifle) Battalion, The King's Liverpool Regiment, 1914–1919* (Aldershot: Gale & Polden Ltd, 1920), p. 228.

75. Major G. Campbell, C Battery, 231st Brigade, RFA.

76. J. Robey, quoted by J. E. Blore and J. R. Sherratt, *Over There: A Commemorative History of the Old Leek Battery, 1908–1919* (Staffordshire: Martin Publicity, 1991), p. 130.

77. J. Robey, quoted by J. E. Blore and J. R. Sherratt, *Over There: A Commemorative History of the Old Leek Battery, 1908–1919* (Staffordshire: Martin Publicity, 1991), pp. 130–31.

78. L. W. Attwell, edited by W. A. Attwell, *Lawrence Attwell's Letters from the Front* (Barnsley: Pen & Sword, 2005), p. 203.

79. IWM DOCS: J. A. Whitehead, Manuscript account, Four Years' Memories, pp. 143–4.

80. IWM SOUND: AC 9483, C. G. Templar, Reel 9–10 (edited).

81. IWM SOUND: AC 9483, C. G. Templar, Reel 10.

6. Advance to the Selle

1. IWM SOUND: L. J. Hewitt, AC 00041, Reel 4.

2. C. M. Headlam, edited by J. Beach, *The Military Papers of Lieutenant Colonel Sir Cuthbert Headlam, 1910–1942* (Stroud: Military Press/Army Records Society, 2010), pp. 215–16.

3. C. E. Hudson, quoted by H. C. Wylly, *The 1st and 2nd Battalions The Sherwood Foresters in the Great War*, Aldershot: Gale & Polden Ltd, 1924), p. 178.

4. Second Lieutenant William Ware, 2nd Royal Welsh Fusiliers.

5. J. E. Nickson, quoted by J. C. Dunn *The War the Infantry Knew, 1914–1919* (London: Sphere Books, 1989), pp. 551–2.

6. Reverend William Evans-Jones, Army Chaplains' Department attached to the 2nd Royal Welsh Fusiliers was killed aged 24 on 8 October 1918. He is buried at Prospect Hill Cemetery, Gouy.

7. Frank Richards, *Old Soldiers Never Die* (London: Anthony Mott Ltd, 1983), p. 302.

8. J. C. Dunn *The War the Infantry Knew, 1914–1919* (London: Sphere Books, 1989), p. 556.

9. J. E. Nickson, quoted by J. C. Dunn, *The War The Infantry Knew, 1914–1919* (London: Sphere Books, 1989), pp. 552–3.

10. IWM DOCS: F. J. Rice, Typescript Memoir, 1918.

11. IWM DOCS: F. J. Rice, Typescript Memoir, 1918.

12. IWM DOCS: F. Meisel, Transcript account, p. 66.

13. IWM DOCS: F. J. Rice, Typescript Memoir, 1918.

14. H. E. Hart, edited by J. Crawford, *The Devil's Own War: The Diary of Hubert Hart* (Auckland: Exile Publishing Ltd, 2009), p. 260.

15. H. E. Hart, edited by J. Crawford, *The Devil's Own War: The Diary of Hubert Hart* (Auckland: Exile Publishing Ltd, 2009), p. 260.

16. J. Maclean, quoted by J. Baynes and H. Maclean, *A Tale of Two Captains* (Edinburgh: Pentland Press, 1990), p. 158.

17. A. Y. McPeake, quoted by H. F. N. Jourdain and E. Fraser, *The Connaught Rangers, Vol. III* (County Cork: Schull Books, 1999), p. 192.

18. Second Lieutenant Horace Ellis of 6th Squadron, Cavalry Machine Gun Corps, killed aged 29 on 9 October 1918. He is buried in the Highland Cemetery, Le Cateau.

19. Probably Lance Corporal Albert Brierley of 6th Squadron, Cavalry Machine Gun Corps, killed on 9 October 1918. He is buried in the Highland Cemetery, Le Cateau. The three men lie buried in adjoining graves.

20. Private John Harris of 6th Squadron, Cavalry Machine Gun Corps, killed on 9 October 1918. He is buried in the Highland Cemetery, Le Cateau.

21. J. B. Bickersteth, quoted by J. Bickersteth, *The Bickersteth Diaries* (Barnsley: Leo Cooper, 1998), p. 285.

22. W. S. Douglas, *Years of Combat* (London: Collins, 1963), p. 334.

23. IWM DOCS: C. A. Brett, Typescript account, p. 39.

24. A. Y. McPeake, quoted by H. F. N. Jourdain and E. Fraser, *The Connaught Rangers, Vol. III* (County Cork: Schull Books, 1999), p. 193.

25. IWM DOCS: C. A. Brett, Typescript account, p. 41.

26. IWM DOCS: C. A Brett, Typescript account, p. 42.

7. Battle of Selle

1. D. Haig, quoted by G. Sheffield and J. Bourne, *Douglas Haig: War Diaries and Letters, 1914–1918* (London: Weidenfeld & Nicolson, 2005), p. 472.

2. IWM DOCS: G. K. Parker, Typescript Account, p. 31.

3. IWM DOCS: G. K. Parker, Typescript Account, p. 31.

4. IWM DOCS: C. Carter, transcript account

5. Gunner Frank Gibson of C Battery, 231st Brigade, Royal Field Artillery died aged 32 on 19 October 1918. He is buried at Fresnoy le Grand Communal Cemetery Extension.

6. Sergeant Robert Lawrence of C Battery, 231st Brigade, Royal Field Artillery died aged 29 on 19 October 1918. He is buried at Vadencourt British Cemetery, Maissemy.

7. IWM DOCS: R. W. Brierley, Typescript account, p. 93.

8. IWM DOCS: C. H. Dudley Ward, Manuscript diary, 18 October 1918.

9. IWM SOUND: A. B. G. Stanier, AC 7175, Reel 4.

10. IWM SOUND: A. B. G. Stanier, AC 7175, Reel 4.

11. IWM SOUND: A. B. G. Stanier, AC 7175, Reel 4.

12. IWM SOUND: A. B. G. Stanier, AC 7175, Reel 4.

13. W. H. Lakin, quoted by C. H. Dudley Ward, *The Welsh Regiment of Foot Guards, 1915–1918* (London: John Murray, 1936), pp. 144–5.

14. C. H. Dudley Ward, *The Welsh Regiment of Foot Guards, 1915–1918* (London: John Murray, 1936), pp. 85–6.

15. IWM SOUND: AC 9955, H. Calvert, Reel 17.

16. IWM DOCS: F. J. Rice, Typescript Memoir, 1918.

17. IWM DOCS: F. J. Rice, Typescript Memoir, 1918.

18. IWM DOCS: F. J. Rice, Typescript Memoir, 1918.
19. IWM DOCS: F. J. Rice, Typescript Memoir, 1918.
20. IWM DOCS: F. J. Rice, Typescript Memoir, 1918.
21. H. Greenwood, quoted by D. Clayton, *From Pontefract to Picardy: The 9th King's Own Yorkshire Light Infantry in the First World War* (Stroud: Tempus Publishing Ltd, 2004), p. 21.
22. IWM SOUND: AC 7309, W. R. Chapman, Reel 9.
23. IWM SOUND: AC 7309, W. R. Chapman, Reel 11.
24. IWM SOUND: AC 7309, W. R. Chapman, Reel 9.
25. IWM SOUND: AC 7309, W. R. Chapman, Reel 9.
26. IWM SOUND: AC 004233, Reel 1.
27. Second Lieutenant Ralph Cresswell died aged 20 on 23 October 1918. He has no known grave and is commemorated on the Arras Flying Services Memorial.
28. C. E. Pereira, quoted by E. Wyrall, *The History of the Second Division, 1914–1918* (London: Thomas Nelson & Sons Ltd, 1921), p. 687.
29. IWM SOUND: AC 9415, G. Kidson, Reel 3.
30. IWM DOCS: R. J. Richards, Transcript account, 'My Own Last Phase'.
31. IWM DOCS: R. J. Richards, Transcript account, 'My Own Last Phase'.
32. IWM DOCS: R. J. Richards, Transcript account, 'My Own Last Phase'.
33. IWM DOCS: R. J. Richards, Transcript account, 'My Own Last Phase'.
34. IWM DOCS: F. J. Rice, Typescript Memoir, 1918.
35. Lieutenant Colonel Hugh Burnyeat of 65th Brigade, Royal Field Artillery was killed aged 37 on 30 October 1918. He is buried in Bousies Communal Cemetery.
36. Lieutenant Colonel Austin Thorp of 80th Brigade, Royal Field Artillery was killed aged 35 on 30 October 1918. He is buried in Le Cateau Military Cemetery.
37. IWM DOCS: F. J. Rice, Typescript Memoir, 1918.

8. Catching Up

1. H. Spieb, quoted by B. Ulrich and B. Ziemann and translated by C. Brocks, *German Soldiers in the Great War* (Barnsley: Pen & Sword, 2010), p. 165.
2. Hans Spieb was killed the day after he wrote this letter to his parents on 21 October 1918.

3. P. von Hindenburg, edited by C. Messenger, *The Great War* (Barnsley: Frontline Books, 2013), p. 217.

4. P. von Hindenburg, edited by C. Messenger, The Great War (Barnsley: Frontline Books, 2013), p. 218.

5. E. Ludendorff, *Ludendorff's Own Story: August 1914 – November 1918: Vol II* (New York and London: Harper & Bros, 1919), p. 376.

6. P. von Hindenburg, quoted by J. Lee, *The Warlords* (London: Weidenfeld & Nicolson, 1919), pp. 375–6.

7. E. Ludendorff, *Ludendorff's Own Story: August 1914–November 1918: Vol II* (New York and London: Harper & Bros, 1919), pp. 375–6.

8. P. von Hintze, quoted by J. E. Edmonds, *Military Operations France and Belgium, 1918, Volume V* (Nashville: The Battery Press, 1993), p. 111.

9. J. E. Edmonds, *Military Operations France and Belgium, 1918, Volume V* (Nashville: The Battery Press, 1993), p. 112.

10. P. von Hindenburg, quoted by J. E. Edmonds, *Military Operations France and Belgium, 1918, Volume V* (Nashville: The Battery Press, 1993), p. 144.

11. M. von Baden, quoted by J. E. Edmonds, *Military Operations France and Belgium, 1918, Volume V* (Nashville: The Battery Press, 1993), p. 144.

12. J. E. Edmonds, *Military Operations France and Belgium, 1918, Volume V* (Nashville: The Battery Press, 1993), pp. 144–5.

13. H. Horne, quoted by S. Robbins, *The First World War Letters of General Lord Horne* (Stroud, History Press/Army Records Society 2009), p. 264.

14. D. Haig, quoted, by G. Sheffield and J. Bourne, *Douglas Haig: War Diaries and Letters, 1914–1918* (London: Weidenfeld & Nicolson, 2005), p. 472.

15. H. S. Rawlinson, quoted by F. Maurice, *The Life of General Lord Rawlinson of Trent* (London: Cassell & Co Ltd, 1928), pp. 241–2.

16. T. G. Matheson, quoted by C. Headlam, *The Guards Division in the Great War, 1915–1918* (London: John Murray, 1924), Vol. II, p. 185 fn.

17. E. Ludendorff, *Ludendorff's Own Story: August 1914 – November 1918: Vol II* (New York and London: Harper & Bros, 1919), p. 394.

18. P. von Hindenburg, translated by J. Sheldon, quoted by M. von Gallwitz, *Erleben im Westen, 1916–1918* (Berlin: E.S. Mittler & Sohn, 1932), p. 398.

19. M. von Baden, quoted by R. B. Asprey, *The German High Command at War* (New York: William Morrow and Company Inc, 1991), p. 473.

20. E. Ludendorff, quoted by J. E. Edmonds, *Military Operations France and Belgium, 1918, Volume V* (Nashville: The Battery Press, 1993), p. 327.

21. E. Ludendorff, quoted by J. E. Edmonds, *Military Operations France and Belgium, 1918, Volume* V (Nashville: The Battery Press, 1993), p. 327.

22. Crown Prince Rupprecht letter, 18 October 1918, quoted by J. E. Edmonds, *Military Operations France and Belgium, 1918, Volume* V (Nashville: The Battery Press, 1993), pp. 327–8.

23. D. Haig, quoted, by G. Sheffield and J. Bourne, *Douglas Haig: War Diaries and Letters, 1914–1918* (London: Weidenfeld & Nicolson, 2005), pp. 475–6.

24. H. S. Rawlinson, quoted by F. Maurice, *The Life of General Lord Rawlinson of Trent* (London: Cassell & Co Ltd, 1928), pp. 244–5.

25. Quoted by J. E. Edmonds, *Military Operations France and Belgium, 1918, Volume* V (Nashville: The Battery Press, 1993), p. 401.

26. P. von Hindenburg, edited by C. Messenger, The Great War (Barnsley: Frontline Books, 2013), p. 221.

27. P. von Hindenburg, edited by C. Messenger, The Great War (Barnsley: Frontline Books, 2013), p. 221.

28. H. Sulzbach, *With the German Guns: Four Years on the Western Front, 1914–1918* (London: Leo Cooper, 1973), pp. 235.

29. IWM DOCS: E. Kent, Typescript account, pp. 118– 20.

30. L. Barthas, translated by E. M Struass, *Poilu: The World War I Notebooks of Corporal Louis Barthas, Barrelmaker, 1914–1918* (New Haven: Yale University Press, 2014), p. 381.

9. Americans on the Meuse, November 1918

1. E. E. Macklin, quoted by G. B. Clark, *Devil Dogs Chronicle: Voices of the 4th Marine Brigade in World War 1* (Lawrence, Kansas: University Press of Kansas, 2013), pp. 342–3.

2. J. Pershing, quoted by J. S. D. Eisenhower, *Yanks: The Epic Story of the American Army in World War I* (New York: Simon & Shuster, 2001), p. 263.

3. W. M. Wright, quoted by G. H. English, *History of the 89th Division, USA* (Denver, Smith-Brooks, 1920, p. 169.

4. Private Albert A. Banholzer was killed on 10 November 1918.

5. H. L. Baker, edited by R. H. Ferrell, *Argonne Days in World War I* (Columbia: University of Missouri, 2007), p. 95.

6. W. M. Wright, edited by R. H. Ferrell, *Meuse-Argonne Diary: A Division Commander in World War 1* (Columbia: University of Missouri Press, 2004), p. 130.

7. E. W. Sherwood, edited by R. H. Ferrell, *A Soldier in World War I: The Diary of Elmer W. Sherwood* (Indianapolis: Indiana Historical Association Press, 2004), p. 96.

8. C. S. Babcock, edited by R. H. Ferrell, *Reminiscences of Conrad S. Babcock* (Columbia: University of Missouri Press, 2012), p. 134.

9. R. J. Casey, *The Cannoneers Have Hairy Ears: A Diary of the Front lines* (New York, J. H. Sears & Co, 1927), p. 276.

10. R. J. Casey, *The Cannoneers Have Hairy Ears: A Diary of the Front lines* (New York, J. H. Sears & Co, 1927), p. 294.

11. R. J. Casey, *The Cannoneers Have Hairy Ears: A Diary of the Front lines* (New York, J. H. Sears & Co, 1927), p. 299.

12. R. J. Casey, *The Cannoneers Have Hairy Ears: A Diary of the Front lines* (New York, J. H. Sears & Co, 1927), p. 300.

13. R. J. Casey, *The Cannoneers Have Hairy Ears: A Diary of the Front lines* (New York, J. H. Sears & Co, 1927), pp. 301–2.

14. O. Lais, quoted by J. K. Reith, *Imperial Germany's 'Iron Regiment' of the First World War* (Winchester: Badgley Publishing Company, 2014), p. 272.

15. W. M. Wright, edited by R. H. Ferrell, *Meuse-Argonne Diary: A Division Commander in World War 1* (Columbia: University of Missouri Press, 2004), p. 140.

16. Second Lieutenant Jess Stribling, 305th Field Artillery.

17. L. G. Downs, quoted by C. W. Camp, *History of the 305th Field Artillery* (New York: Country Life Press, 1919), p. 303.

18. W. K. Rainsford, *From Upton to the Meuse with the Three Hundred and Seventh* (New York: Appleton & Company, 1920), pp. 252–3.

19. Captain Arthur Wear died aged 38 on 5 November 1918. He is buried in the Meuse-Argonne American Cemetery, Romagne.

20. J. J. Hook, quoted by J. H. Hallas, *Doughboy War: The American Expeditionary Force in WWI* (Mechanicsburg: Stackpole Books, 2009), p. 303.

21. W. M. Wright, edited by R. H. Ferrell, *Meuse-Argonne Diary: A Division Commander in World War 1* (Columbia: University of Missouri Press, 2004), p. 153.

22. H. L. Baker, edited by R. H. Ferrell, *Argonne Days in World War I* (Columbia: University of Missouri, 2007), pp. 109–10.

10. Battle of the Sambre

1. C. C. Carstairs, *A Generation Missing* (Stevenage: Strong Oak Press, 1989), pp. 193–19.

2. M. von Gallwitz, translated by J. Sheldon, *Erleben im Westen, 1916–1918* (Berlin: E.S. Mittler & Sohn, 1932), p. 442 .

3. H. R. Cumming, *A Brigadier in France, 1917–1918* (London: Jonathan Cape Ltd, 1922), pp. 265–6.

4. IWM SOUND: AC 7363, G. B. Jameson, Reel 17.

5. H. R. Cumming, *A Brigadier in France, 1917–1918* (London: Jonathan Cape Ltd, 1922), p. 266.

6. H. Hart, edited by J. Crawford, *The Devil's Own War: The Diary of Hubert Hart* (Auckland: Exisle Publishing Ltd, 2009), p. 263.

7. A. Bullock, quoted by J. Miller, *The Life and Letters of 2nd Lieut Alan Bullock, A Conscript of the Great War* (Broad Street Publishing, 2008), p. 55.

8. A. Bullock, quoted by J. Miller, *The Life and Letters of 2nd Lieut Alan Bullock, A Conscript of the Great War* (Broad Street Publishing, 2008), p. 56.

9. IWM SOUND: J. Gascoyne, AC 00016, Reel 3.

10. IWM SOUND: H. J. Andrews, AC 00984, Reel 2.

11. Eric Goodwill died aged 23 on 3 November 1918. He is buried in Ascq Communal Cemetery.

12. IWM DOCS: J. W. Stephenson, Typescript Account, p. 55.

13. R. S. B. Sinclair, quoted by A. F. Barnes, *The Story of the 2/5th Battalion, Gloucestershire Regiment, 1914–1918* (Gloucester: The Crypt House Press Ltd, 1930), pp. 141–2.

14. IWM SOUND: AC 9546, J. Fox, Reel 5.

15. IWM SOUND: AC 9456, J. Fox, Reel 5.

16. IWM SOUND: D. Price, AC 10168, Reel 14.

17. IWM SOUND: AC 9876C, G. Dennys, Reel 12.

18. IWM SOUND: AC 9339, William Holbrook, Reel 18.

19. Statistics from J. Boff, *Winning and Losing on the Western Front: The British Third Army and the Defeat of Germany in 1918* (Cambridge: Cambridge University Press, 2014), p. 33.

20. Statistics from J. Boff, *Winning and Losing on the Western Front: The British Third Army and the Defeat of Germany in 1918* (Cambridge: Cambridge University Press, 2014), p. 80.

21. D. Haig, quoted by J. E. Edmonds, *Military Operations France and Belgium, 1918, Volume V* (Nashville: The Battery Press, 1993), p. 463.

22. C. C. Carstairs, *A Generation Missing* (Stevenage: Strong Oak Press, 1989), pp. 196–8.

23. C.C. Carstairs, *A Generation Missing* (Stevenage: Strong Oak Press, 1989), p. 200.

24. Second Lieutenant Geoffrey Gunther died aged 20 on 4 November 1918. He is buried at Villers-Pol Communal Cemetery Extension.

25. H. Hart, edited by J. Crawford, *The Devil's Own War: The Diary of Hubert Hart* (Auckland: Exile Publishing Ltd, 2009), pp. 264–5.

26. H. Hart, edited by J. Crawford, *The Devil's Own War: The Diary of Hubert Hart* (Auckland: Exile Publishing Ltd, 2009), pp. 264–5.

27. INTERNET SOURCE: *Battle accounts, Lieutenant Averill*, URL: http:// www.nzhistory.net.nz/war/le-quesnoy/battle-accounts-lt-averill, (Ministry for Culture and Heritage).

28. H. Hart, edited by J. Crawford, *The Devil's Own War: The Diary of Hubert Hart* (Auckland: Exile Publishing Ltd, 2009), pp. 264–5.

29. Major Hugh McKinnon died aged 30 on 4 November 1918. He is buried in the Le Quesnoy Communal Cemetery Extension.

30. N. Ingram, quoted by N. Boyack, *Behind the Lines: The Lives of New Zealand Soldiers in the First World War* (Wellington: Allen & Unwin 1989), pp. 86–7.

31. R. N. R. Blaker, quoted by T. Donovan, *The Hazy Red Hell: Fighting Experiences on the Western Front, 1914–18* (Staplehurst: Spellmount, 1999), p. 209.

32. R. N. R. Blaker, quoted by T. Donovan, *The Hazy Red Hell: Fighting Experiences on the Western Front, 1914–18* (Staplehurst: Spellmount, 1999), pp. 209–10.

33. R. N. R. Blaker, quoted by T. Donovan, *The Hazy Red Hell: Fighting Experiences on the Western Front, 1914–18* (Staplehurst: Spellmount, 1999), p. 210.

34. R. N. R. Blaker, quoted by T. Donovan, *The Hazy Red Hell: Fighting Experiences on the Western Front, 1914–18* (Staplehurst: Spellmount, 1999), pp. 211–12.

35. H. Bashford, *A War Remembered* (The New Chequers: The Journal of the Friends of Lochnagar, No. 4, 1996), p. 42.

36. IWM SOUND: W AC 10441, E. Grover, Reel 5.

37. IWM DOCS: G. S. Potts, Typed letter and short memoir.

38. IWM DOCS: G. S. Potts, Typed letter and short memoir, January 1971.

39. IWM DOCS: G. S. Potts, Typed letter and short memoir, January 1971.

40. IWM DOCS: S. Hudson, Manuscript letter, January 1971 within G. S. Potts Collection

41. Lieutenant Colonel James Neville Marshall of the 16th Lancashire Fusiliers was killed aged 31 on 4 November 1918. He is buried in Ors Communal Cemetery.

42. IWM DOCS: G. S. Potts, Typed letter and short memoir, January 1971.

43. Lieutenant Wilfred Owen, 2nd Manchester Regiment was killed aged 25 on 4 November 1918. He is buried in Ors Communal Cemetery.

44. 2nd Lieutenant Alan Bullock, 1/4th (Royal Fusiliers), London Regiment, was 20 when he died on 4 November 1918. He is buried in St Roche Cemetery, Valenciennes.

45. A. Bullock, quoted by J. Miller, *The Life and Letters of 2nd Lieut Alan Bullock, A Conscript of the Great War* (Broad Street Publishing, 2008), p. 56.

46. J. Boff, *Winning and Losing on the Western Front* (Cambridge: Cambridge University Press, 2014), pp. 34–5.

47. J. Maclean, quoted by J. Baynes and H. Maclean, *A Tale of Two Captains* (Edinburgh: Pentland Press, 1990), pp. 163 and 164.

48. J. Maclean, quoted by J. Baynes and H. Maclean, *A Tale of Two Captains* (Edinburgh: Pentland Press, 1990), pp. 163–4.

49. IWM DOCS: W. A. C. Wilkinson, Letter, 6 November 1918.

50. IWM DOCS: C. P. Blacker Letter, 18 May 1970.

51. E. Jackson, quoted by C. Corns and J. Hughes-Wilson, *Blindfold and Alone: British Military Executions in the Great War* (London: Cassell & Co., 2001), p. 397.

52. Private Ernest Jackson was executed aged 32 on 7 November 1918. He is buried in Romeries Communal Cemetery Extension.

53. Private Louis Harris was executed aged 23 on 7 November 1918. He is buried in Ghissignies British Cemetery.

54. C. Corns and J. Hughes-Wilson, *Blindfold and Alone: British Military Executions in the Great War* (London: Cassell & Co., 2001), p. 401.

55. W. Gröner, quoted by R. B. Asprey, *The German High Command at War* (New York: William Morrow and Company Inc, 1991), pp. 485–6.

56. IWM SOUND: AC 9891, E. Cranmer, Reel 2.

57. J. de Pierrefeu, *French Headquarters, 1915–1918* (London: Geoffrey Bles, 1924), p. 303.

58. F. Foch, quoted by J. E. Edmonds, *Military Operations France and Belgium, 1918*, Volume V (Nashville: The Battery Press, 1993), p. 567.

59. F. C. Hitchcock, *Stand To: A Diary of the Trenches, 1915–1918* (Norwich: Gliddon Books, 1988), p. 312.

60. IWM DOCS: C. H. Bennett, letter, 6 November 1918.

61. R. D. Furse, quoted by Marquess of Anglesey, *A History of British Cavalry, 1816–1919: Volume VIII* (Barnsley: Pen & Sword, 2012), p. 274.

62. IWM SOUND: J. Gascoyne, AC 00016, Reel 4.

63. C. E. Wurtzburg, *The History of the 2/6th (Rifle) Battalion, The King's Liverpool Regiment, 1914–1919* (Aldershot: Gale & Polden Ltd, 1920), p. 250.

64. IWM SOUND: AC 12414, W. Rappolt, Reel 11.

65. IWM DOCS: E. Kent, Typescript account, pp. 120–21.

66. Captain Benjamin Croft of the 1/28th London Regiment (Artists' Rifles) was killed on 10 November 1918. He is buried in Harveng Churchyard.

67. Second Lieutenant Hubert King of the 1/28th London Regiment (Artists' Rifles) was killed aged 21 on 10 November 1918. He is buried in Harveng Churchyard.

68. Sergeant Joseph Garbutt of the 1/28th London Regiment (Artists' Rifles) was killed aged 22 on 10 November 1918. He is buried in Harveng Churchyard.

69. R. H. Goldthorp, quoted in *The Regimental Roll of Honour and War Record of the Artists' Rifles* (London: Howler & Son, 1922), p. xxxvii.

70. IWM DOCS: P. E. Williamson, Typescript account, p. 51.

11. Day of Days, 11 November 1918

1. IWM SOUND: AC 10441, W. E. Grover, Reel 6.

2. Statistics from R. A. Doughty, *Pyrrhic Victory: French Strategy and Operations in the Great War* (Cambridge: The Belknap Press, 2005), p. 505.

3. H. S. Rawlinson, quoted by F. Maurice, *The Life of General Lord Rawlinson of Trent* (London: Cassell & Co Ltd, 1928), pp. 249–50.

4. W. M. Wright, edited by R. H. Ferrell, *Meuse-Argonne Diary: A Division Commander in World War 1* (Columbia: University of Missouri Press, 2004), p. 163.

5. W. M. Wright, edited by R. H. Ferrell, *Meuse-Argonne Diary: A Division Commander in World War 1* (Columbia: University of Missouri Press, 2004), p. 164.

6. F. Jordan, quoted by G. Mead, *The Doughboys: America and the First World War* (London: Penguin Books Ltd, 2001), pp. 336–8.

7. W. M. Wright, edited by R. H. Ferrell, *Meuse-Argonne Diary: A Division Commander in World War 1* (Columbia: University of Missouri Press, 2004), p. 165.

8. M. L. Krulewitch, quoted by P. F. Owen, *A Battalion of Marines in the Great War* (College Station: Texas A&M University Press, 2007), pp. 198–9.

9. J. H. Strickler, quoted by G. B. Clark, *Devil Dogs Chronicle: Voices of the 4th Marine Brigade in World War 1* (Lawrence, Kansas: University Press of Kansas, 2013), p. 336.

10. W. G. Haan, quoted by C. Hanton, The 32nd Division in the World War, 1917–1919 (Wisconsin, Joint War History Commission, 1920), p. 210.

11. T. C. Thayer, *History of the 305th Field Artillery* (New York: Country Life Press, 1919), pp. 323–4.

12. R. J. Casey, *The Cannoneers Have Hairy Ears: A Diary of the Front lines* (New York, J. H. Sears & Co, 1927), p. 323.

13. R. J. Casey, *The Cannoneers Have Hairy Ears: A Diary of the Front lines* (New York, J. H. Sears & Co, 1927), p. 323.

14. H. L. Baker, edited by R. H. Ferrell, *Argonne Days in World War I* (Columbia: University of Missouri, 2007), pp. 135–6.

15. Private Henry Gunther was killed aged 23 on 11 November 1918. In 1923 his remains were repatriated and he is buried in Most Holy Redeemer Cemetery, Baltimore.

16. R. J. Casey, *The Cannoneers Have Hairy Ears: A Diary of the Front lines* (New York, J. H. Sears & Co, 1927), p. 323.

17. C. Struber, quoted by J. B. Nolan, *The Reading Militia in the Great War* (Reading: Historical Society of Berks County, 1921), pp. 173–4.

18. W. G. Haan, quoted in C. Hanton, *The 32nd Division in the World War, 1917–1919* (Wisconsin, Joint War History Commission, 1920), p. 210.

19. A. E. Yansen, quoted by G. Mead, by G. Mead, *The Doughboys: America and the First World War* (London: Penguin Books Ltd, 2001), pp. 344–5.

20. M. Laurentin, quoted by I. Sumner, *They Shall Not Pass: The French Army on the Western Front, 1914–1918* (Barnsley: Pen & Sword, 2012), p. 210.

21. H. Desagneux, edited by J. Desagneaux and translated by G. Adams, *A French Soldier's War Diary* (Morley: The Elmfield Press, 1975), pp. 103–4.

22. E. Brec, quoted by I. Sumner, *They Shall Not Pass: The French Army on the Western Front, 1914–1918* (Barnsley: Pen & Sword, 2012), p. 211.

23. L. Barthas, translated by E. M. Struass, *Poilu: The World War I Notebooks of Corporal Louis Barthas, Barrelmaker, 1914–1918* (New Haven: Yale University Press, 2014), p. 382.

24. H. Horne, quoted by S. Robbins, *The First World War Letters of General Lord Horne* (Stroud, History Press/Army Records Society 2009), p. 274.

25. IWM DOC: G. F. Tizard, Letter, 23 November 1918.

26. IWM DOC: G. F. Tizard, Letter, 23 November 1918.

27. IWM DOC: G. F. Tizard, Letter, 23 November 1918.

28. IWM SOUND: H. E. Hopthrow, AC 00034, Reel 5.

29. G. V. Wellesley, quoted by A. Keith-Falconer, *The Oxfordshire Hussars in the Great War, 1914–1918* (London: John Murray, 1927), pp. 338–9.

30. G. V. Wellesley, quoted by A. Keith-Falconer, *The Oxfordshire Hussars in the Great War, 1914–1918* (London: John Murray, 1927), pp. 339–40.

31. IWM SOUND: AC 9132, M. Walkington, Reel 6 and 7 (edited).

32. IWM SOUND: K. F. Officer, AC 004191, Reel 1.

33. IWM DOCS: W. House, Typescript account, '1914–1918 War Memoirs' p. 36.

34. IWM SOUND: C. G. Dennys, Reel 12.

35. IWM DOCS: C. R. Hennessey, Typescript Account, pp. 282–3.

36. IWM DOCS: R. Foot, Typescript account, 'Once a Gunner' p. 107.

37. IWM SOUND: AC 15347, D. Hodges, Reel 9.

38. IWM SOUND: AC 7363, G. B. Jameson, Reel 16 and 17 (edited).

39. R. H. Goldthorp, quoted in *The Regimental Roll of Honour and War Record of the Artists' Rifles* (London: Howler & Son, 1922), p. xxxix.

40. IWM SOUND: AC 7257, C. Lane, Reel 11.

41. N. D. Cliff, *To Hell and Back with the Guards* (Braunton: Merlin Books Ltd, 1988), pp. 100–101.

42. D. Haig, quoted by G. Sheffield and J. Bourne, *Douglas Haig: War Diaries and Letters, 1914–1918* (London: Weidenfeld & Nicolson, 2005), p. 487.

43. F. Noakes, *The Distant Drum: A Memoir of a Guardsman in the Great War* (London: Frontline Books, 2010), p. 194.

44. F. Noakes, *The Distant Drum: A Memoir of a Guardsman in the Great War* (London: Frontline Books, 2010), p. 194.

45. J. L. Jack, *General Jack's Diary: War on the Western Front, 1914–1918* (London: Cassell & Co, 2000), p. 297.

46. E. L. Bird, edited by S. Sturley, *Machine Gunner on the Somme* (Brighton: Reveille Press, 2012), pp. 157–8.

12. Aftermath

1. D. Haig, quoted by G. Sheffield and J. Bourne, *Douglas Haig: War Diaries and Letters, 1914–1918* (London: Weidenfeld & Nicolson, 2005), pp. 489–90.

2. D. Haig, quoted by G. Sheffield and J. Bourne, *Douglas Haig: War Diaries and Letters, 1914–1918* (London: Weidenfeld & Nicolson, 2005), p. 492.

3. G. Dodgson, quoted by R. H. Fair and C. S. Fair, *Marjorie's War: Four Families in the Great War, 1914–1918* (Brighton: Menin House Publishers, 2012), p. 395.

4. H. W. Dakeyne, quoted by R. H. Fair and C. S. Fair, *Marjorie's War: Four Families in the Great War, 1914–1918* (Brighton: Menin House Publishers, 2012), p. 397.

5. Lieutenant Guy Dodgson of the 1/1st Hertfordshire Regiment died aged 23 on 14 November 1918. He is buried at Caudry British Cemetery.

6. H. W. Dakeyne, quoted by R. H. Fair and C. S. Fair, *Marjorie's War: Four Families in the Great War, 1914–1918* (Brighton: Menin House Publishers, 2012), pp. 399–400.

7. P. Dodgson, quoted by R. H. Fair and C. S. Fair, *Marjorie's War: Four Families in the Great War, 1914–1918* (Brighton: Menin House Publishers, 2012), p. 398.

8. IWM DOCS: E. Kent, Typescript account, p. 122.

9. IWM DOCS: E. Kent, Typescript account, pp. 122–3.

10. IWM DOCS: E. Kent, Typescript account, pp. 123–4.

11. IWM DOCS: E. Kent, Typescript account, p. 125.

12. IWM DOCS: C. Dudley Ward, Manuscript diary, 15 November 1918.

13. K. Swallow, quoted by S. Gillon, *The Story of the 29th Division: A Record of Gallant Deeds* (London: Thomas Nelson & Sons Ltd, 1925), pp. 220–21.

14. IWM SOUND: AC 13717, C. Gee, Reel 10.

15. IWM DOCS: F. Meisel, Transcript account, pp. 78–9.

16. IWM DOCS: E. Kent, Typescript account, p. 142.

17. K. Swallow, quoted by S. Gillon, *The Story of the 29th Division: A Record of Gallant Deeds* (London: Thomas Nelson & Sons Ltd, 1925), pp. 223–4.

18. S. Graham, *A Private in the Guards* (London: Macmillan and Co, Ltd, 1919), p. 324.

19. IWM SOUND: AC 13717, C. H. R. Gee, Reel 10.

20. S. Graham, *A Private in the Guards* (London: Macmillan and Co, Ltd, 1919), pp. 325–6.

21. IWM SOUND: AC 9434, W. J. Collins, Reel 16.

22. N. D. Cliff, *To Hell and Back with the Guards* (Braunton: Merlin Books Ltd, 1988), p. 103.

23. F. Noakes, *The Distant Drum: A Memoir of a Guardsman in the Great War* (London: Frontline Books, 2010), p. 205.

24. IWM SOUND: AC 9955, H. Calvert, Reel 17.

25. Lieutenant Colonel Richard Luxmoore Ball, 1st Welsh Guards.

26. Captain Jack Stirling, 1st Welsh Guards.

27. Captain P. L. M. Battye, 1st Welsh Guards.

28. Captain F. A. V Copland-Griffiths, 1st Welsh Guards.

29. Second Lieutenant P. A. L. Evans, 1st Welsh Guards.

30. Colonel Charles Vickery of 74th Brigade, Royal Field Artillery.

31. IWM DOCS: C. Dudley Ward, Manuscript diary, 25 December 1918.

32. C. H. Dudley Ward, *History of the Welsh Guards* (London: London Stamp Exchange, 1988), pp. 292–3.

33. IWM DOCS: J. S. Blanford, Typescript manuscript, *Sans Escort*, Appendix D, pp. 40A–40B.

34. N. D. Cliff, *To Hell and Back with the Guards* (Braunton: Merlin Books Ltd, 1988), p. 103.

35. IWM SOUND: AC 9434, W. J. Collins, Reel 16.

36. IWM SOUND: AC 10699, R. Murray-Jones, Reel 11.

37. IWM SOUND: AC 13717, C. H. R. Gee, Reel 10.

38. IWM SOUND: AC 9955, H. Calvert, Reel 17.

39. IWM SOUND: AC 9424, H. Cooper, Reel 12.

40. IWM SOUND: AC 12414, W. Rappolt, Reel 11–12.

41. D. Haig, quoted by G. Sheffield and J. Bourne, *Douglas Haig: War Diaries and Letters, 1914–1918* (London: Weidenfeld & Nicolson, 2005), p. 487.

42. C. Headlam, edited by J. Beach, *The Military Papers of Lieutenant Colonel Sir Cuthbert Headlam, 1910–1942* (Stroud: Military Press/Army Records Society, 2010), pp. 217–21.

43. IWM DOCS: C. R. Hennessey, Typescript Account, pp. 283–4.

44. T. M Banks and R. A. Chell, *With the 10th Essex in France* (London: 10th Essex Old Comrades Association, 1921), p. 289.

45. IWM SOUND: AC 7257, C. Lane, Reel 11.

46. R. Feilding, *War Letters to a Wife: France and Flanders, 1915–1919* (London: The Medici Society, 1929), p. 367.

47. R. Feilding, *War Letters to a Wife: France and Flanders, 1915–1919* (London: The Medici Society, 1929), p. 368.

48. T. M. Banks and R. A. Chell, *With the 10th Essex in France* (London: 1011 Essex Old Comrades Association, 1921), p. 290.

49. C. E. Wurtzburg, *The History of the 2/6th (Rifle) Battalion, The King's Liverpool Regiment, 1914–1919* (Aldershot: Gale & Polden Ltd, 1920), pp. 257–8.

50. T. M. Banks and R. A. Chell, *With the 10th Essex in France* (London: 10th Essex Old Comrades Association, 1921), pp. 289–90.

51. N. D. Cliff, *To Hell and Back with the Guards* (Braunton: Merlin Books Ltd, 1988), pp. 103–4.

52. E. De Stein, *The Poets in Picardy* (London, John Murray Ltd, 1919), p. 89.

53. IWM SOUND: AC 9955, H. Calvert, Reel 17, 18 and 19 (edited).

54. IWM SOUND: AC 10434, A. Jamieson, Reel 3–4.

55. W. Williamson, edited by D. Priddey, *A Tommy at Ypres: Walter's War* (Stroud: Amberley Publishing, 2011), p. 318.

56. W. Williamson, edited by D. Priddey, *A Tommy at Ypres: Walter's War* (Stroud: Amberley Publishing, 2011), p. 32.

57. W. Williamson, edited by D. Priddey, *A Tommy at Ypres: Walter's War* (Stroud: Amberley Publishing, 2011), pp. 344–5.

58. IWM DOCS: C. R. Hennessey, Typescript Account, pp. 296–7.

59. IWM DOCS: C. R. Hennessey, Typescript Account, pp. 297–8.

60. IWM DOCS: C. R. Hennessey, Typescript Account, p. 298.

61. IWM DOCS: C. R. Hennessey, Typescript Account, pp. 298–9.

62. IWM DOCS: C. R. Hennessey, Typescript Account, pp. 301–2.

63. IWM DOCS: C. R. Hennessey, Typescript Account, p. 302.

64. IWM DOCS: C. R. Hennessey, Typescript Account, p. 299.

65. R. Feilding, *War Letters to a Wife: France and Flanders, 1915–1919* (London: The Medici Society, 1929), p. 373.

66. H. Hart, edited by J. Crawford, *The Devil's Own War: The Diary of Hubert Hart* (Auckland: Exisle Publishing Ltd, 2009), p. 286.

67. B. Williamson, *Happy Days in France and Flanders with the 47th and 49th Divisions* (London: Harding & More Ltd, 1921), p. 191.

LIST OF ILLUSTRATIONS

33 A British Army band parades in Cologne. (Historic Military Press)

34 A farmer works around the remains of a British tank, numbered C-31, which awaits removal, Frezenberg. (Historic Military Press)

35 US soldiers of the 803rd Pioneer Infantry Battalion pictured on the deck of the USS *Philippine*, for demobilisation, 18 July 1919. (Library of Congress, LOT 14024, No.39)

36 British troops work to remove a knocked-out tank from the battlefield after the end of the end of the fighting in 1918. (Historic Military Press)

While every effort has been made to contact copyright-holders of illustrations, the author and publishers would be grateful for information about any illustrations where they have been unable to trace them, and would be glad to make amendments in further editions.

INDEX

Page references for maps are in *italics*